The Romans and Their World

The
Romans and
Their World

BRIAN CAMPBELL

YALE UNIVERSITY PRESS
NEW HAVEN AND LONDON

For information about this and other Yale University Press publications, please contact:
U.S. Office: sales.press@yale.edu   www.yalebooks.com
Europe Office: sales @yaleup.co.uk   www.yalebooks.co.uk

Set in Fournier by IDSUK (DataConnection) Ltd
Printed in Great Britain by TJ International Ltd, Padstow, Cornwall

Library of Congress Cataloging-in-Publication Data

Campbell, J. B.
   The Romans and their world: 753 BC to AD 476 / Brian Campbell.
      p. cm.
   Includes bibliographical references.
   ISBN 978–0–300–11795–0 (cloth: alk. paper)
   1. Rome—History—Kings, 753–510 B.C. 2. Rome—History—Republic, 510–30
B.C. 3. Rome—History—Empire, 30 B.C.–476 A.D. 4. Rome—Politics and
government. 5. National characteristics, Roman. I. Title.
   DG209.C28 2011
   937—dc22
                                                                      2011006435

A catalogue record for this book is available from the British Library.
10 9 8 7 6 5 4 3 2 1

For Karen

Contents

Illustrations

Maps

Plans

Preface

WHEN FIRST APPROACHED BY YALE UNIVERSITY PRESS, I THOUGHT THAT IT would be a useful experience to write a book about ancient Rome without the tyranny of footnotes, and indeed be rather enjoyable, but it turned out to be much more challenging than I had imagined. The sheer amount of material and the number of scholarly contending views make it difficult to provide an account that is simultaneously readable, reasonably complete though concise, lively, but not so simplified as to mislead on the complexity of the subject matter. However, I have attempted to provide a straightforward guide to the world of the Romans for an interested general audience and students, using a chronological narrative that also embraces thematic treatment. I have frequently quoted directly from ancient writers in order to give a flavour of their interpretation of their world. The book begins with the earliest settlements at Rome and ends with the removal of Romulus Augustulus, the last 'Roman' emperor in the west, in AD 476.

In completing the text I am once again greatly in the debt of Professor David Buck and Dr John Curran, who read the whole typescript in a sympathetic and constructively critical way. Through many years I have been sustained by the erudition, humour and friendship of these two scholars. They are of course not responsible for the errors and misjudgements that remain. I especially thank Heather McCallum of Yale University Press, London for her patience, confidence, and support for a rather wayward author, and Richard Mason, my copy-editor, for his thorough work.

Finally, the love and calm common sense of my wife have over many years helped me to survive modern academic life.

CHAPTER ONE

Becoming Master of Italy

The Setting

With hindsight and patriotic fervour the historian Livy reflected on the advantages of the site of Rome with its hills and the river Tiber:

> With good reason did gods and men choose this site for founding a city; the hills promote health, the river (Tiber) is advantageous since along it are brought foodstuffs from inland areas and along it seaborne produce is received (in the city); it is convenient to the advantage of the sea but is not exposed to the dangers of enemy fleets by being too close; it is in the centre of the districts of Italy and is a site uniquely suitable for the development of the city. (5.54)

Livy ignores the serious flooding that the Tiber frequently inflicted on the low-lying areas of the city, but emphasizes the river as a route of communications and transport, that is, both down the Tiber valley from the north, and south of the city providing a way for the import of goods. Furthermore, a road (*via Salaria*) along the left bank of the Tiber carried the salt trade from the river mouth along the valley. The Tiber Island was the last major ford on the river and the adjacent readily defensible hills allowed the local population to control it.

On the site of the future city of Rome traces of permanent occupation in the area of the *forum Boarium* (cattle market) date from *c.*1000 BC, and the settlers lived by subsistence agriculture on cereals and legumes and by stock-raising. Around 830–770 small village communities started to come together; in this period reed and clay huts on the Palatine hill constituted the main form of dwelling. Around the early sixth century these huts were replaced with more elaborate, permanent structures, and archaeological evidence suggests that there was a wall around the early settlement on the Palatine. It is quite possible that various hills in the locality may have been occupied by different groups.

When Romans came later to discuss the foundation of their city (traditionally 754 or 753 BC), they naturally developed stories that established Roman identity and character as they hoped that other peoples would see them. Romantic stories of foundation by Romulus, who then became the first king, are probably fiction. According to one account, Amulius, king of Alba Longa, having deposed his elder brother Numitor, ordered the twin babies of Numitor's daughter Rhea Silvia to be drowned in the Tiber. But the river was in flood and as the waters subsided the basket containing the twins finally drifted ashore where a she-wolf found and suckled them, until they were discovered by the royal shepherd Faustulus who took them back to his wife. She named them Romulus and Remus, and Remus was eventually murdered by Romulus because he mockingly jumped over the wall as his brother started to build fortifications. Despite the traditional elements in the story, which by the way recognized the troublesome nature of the Tiber, it was almost certainly an indigenous legend, as we see from the splendid bronze statue of a she-wolf probably dating from the sixth century BC, indicating that the gist of the legend had been accepted early in Rome.

Another strand of the foundation legend put forward Aeneas as the founder of Rome; as the story goes, after the sack of Troy by the Greeks he fled into exile carrying his father Anchises on his shoulders. This legend was established by the sixth century BC and was subsequently to be bound up with the developing complex cultural interaction between the Romans and the Greeks. In the first significant urban development the nature of Roman society and government is shadowy, although there may have been a joint community of Romans and Sabines (with a functional interpretation of the traditional story of the rape of the Sabine women). Around 625 come the first signs of permanent buildings in Rome, and the earliest public building was probably the Regia, a residence for the rulers, which later served as a senate house. Certainly an urban community was developing, and the appearance of religious buildings and sanctuaries suggests a degree of organization of public cults and communal religious activity.

Early Roman society was probably divided into clans (in common with many other Italic communities), in which all members had a personal name and a clan name. In the mid-Republic Roman males had two names: a first name (*praenomen*), and a family name (*nomen*); aristocrats often had a third name (*cognomen*) to identify a particular branch of the family, and sometimes a fourth (*agnomen*) to mark a special characteristic or achievement, for example, L(ucius) Caecilius Metellus Delmaticus. Women normally took the female form of the family name, for example, Marcus Tullius Cicero's daughter was Tullia. Early society would have been dominated by small groups of wealthy nobles who expressed their superiority by fighting in war and by imposing public display on funeral tombs, partly influenced by the aristocratic societies in Greek colonies in southern Italy. Around 700 BC came the development of writing in Italy with an alphabetic script taken from the Greeks. Increasing literacy in Italic society assisted future developments by facilitating the recording and keeping of information that could then be used to advance state administration; government could now try to manage its population by organizing a census and establishing who was available for military service. The act of writing down the calendar showed a potential ability to organize state business and perhaps move to devise policy centrally.

No one could have predicted that the small city state of Rome would rise to dominate the Mediterranean world. In the early period it shared the Italian peninsula with other widely differing groups who all had their own cultural and social traditions. There existed about forty separate Italic languages or dialects before the success of Rome made Latin (spoken in Latium) the common language. In the central Italian highlands lived native peoples who were ethnically related to the Romans and spoke various forms of Italic languages related to Latin. Rome's persistent opponents, the Samnites, lived in the high Apennines, tending farms but also keeping pigs, flocks of sheep and herds of goats; they and others in southern Italy and Campania spoke Oscan. North of Rome the Volscians pursued the same lifestyle. Both groups periodically coveted the more fertile land on the plains of Campania and Latium. Other languages were Venetic (north-east Italy), Umbrian (central and eastern Italy), and Celtic spoken by the Gauls in the Po valley. In southern Italy many Greek communities had been established from the eighth century BC onwards; they were independent but normally copied the institutions, traditions and language of their mother-city. Indeed leading cities such as Cumae and Neapolis (Naples) were more sophisticated and culturally advanced than their Italic neighbours and retained a specifically Greek environment.

The Etruscans, whose origins remain obscure, spoke a non-Indo-European language and operated as a federation of city states with a distinct social system in which the ruling group was completely dominant over the mass of the people, who were virtual serfs. The religious practice of Etruscans was distinctive, using a number of sacred books and including ritualistic divination to discover divine intentions. They lived north of the Tiber in what is now Tuscany, and from the ninth century BC represented the important Villanovan iron-age culture, which stretched north and south of the Apennines down the peninsula beyond Rome. It was characterized by cremation of the dead (other iron-age cultures in Italy practised inhumation) and burial of the ashes in an urn in a deep shaft covered with a block of stone. Etruscan civilization was technically well advanced with sophisticated drainage and irrigation systems. They worked bronze and iron and produced fine-quality pottery, architecture, sculpture and painting, in which they borrowed much from the Greeks with whom they interacted and had good trading relations. It is interesting that the thirteen altars discovered at Lavinium (Pratica di Mare), which allegedly had been founded by Aeneas, show a markedly Greek influence in design and religious thought. The Etruscans were well established by the eighth century, and the sixth and fifth centuries saw them develop an empire in the valley of the Po and in Campania in southern Italy. Etruscan influence was widespread, though this need not have meant an occupation or complete control of Rome. It would be better to speak of interaction rather than domination either culturally or territorially. Probably some Etruscans settled in Rome, but this was a two-way process since the Romans made up a vibrant independent community that was part of developments affecting the entire Mediterranean area. Indeed Roman borrowings are hard to trace, though the bundle of rods and an axe (*fasces*), that famous Roman symbol of magisterial authority, probably derived from Etruria; a miniature set has been found in a tomb at Vetulonia, one of the Etruscan cities. The rods, about 1.5 metres long and bound together by red thongs, enclosed a single-headed axe and were carried in front of a magistrate by his attendants (*lictores*), making his authority visible to all. Eventually the Etruscan Empire crumbled under pressure from the Gauls in the north and the Samnites in Campania, and the Romans overcame the heartland, partly by absorbing the ruling elites, which they supported against the lower orders.

From Kings to Consuls

What were the early institutions of the Roman state? There were originally three tribes subdivided into *curiae* (each apparently a local division into which citizens were born), and this was a crucial part of political and military organization. The traditional story is that Rome was ruled by kings, the seventh and last of whom, Tarquinius Superbus, was tyrannical and was overthrown by internal rebellion. This sounds like a traditional historical ploy to account for a change of government, and many and perhaps all of the details of these kings as individual characters are probably fictional. On the other hand, it is likely that Rome (as other Italian communities) was indeed ruled by kings. If the regal period was very roughly 625–500 BC, it probably created or consolidated social and political institutions, and advanced religious worship and the role of priests. If there is any truth to the idea that some kings were aggressive warriors, then there may have been a period of substantial conquest, which means in turn some attempt to organize an army and a move to establish and protect state boundaries by forcing other peoples to recognize them. The senate perhaps originally served as an informal advisory council chosen by the kings.

In the traditional account Servius Tullius was the sixth king (conventionally dated 578–535 BC). Whether he existed with that name does not matter, although it is possible that Tullius was identified with the Etruscan hero Mastarna, or Macstrna (as the emperor Claudius, c.AD 41–54, was to mention in a speech to the senate), who also appears in the famous wall paintings from a fourth-century BC tomb at Vulci illustrating mythological scenes and events from Etruscan history. In any case Servius Tullius had a significant impact, and important reforms are associated with him. He allegedly organized the Roman people according to a new tribal system and conducted the first census, on the basis of which the citizens were divided into units called 'centuries' according to wealth and property. The exact number of tribes is not known, but there were twenty-one in 495 and the increase to thirty-five was gradual (this total remained into the imperial period). The crucial consequence of these moves was a change in the basis of political power from birth to wealth and in what it meant to be a Roman citizen; this redefined the relationship between the individual and what he owed to the community. One objective was certainly to establish clearly the military obligations of citizens by identifying how many were physically capable of bearing arms and what kind of equipment they could afford. It is possible that the reform was connected with the adoption by Rome from Greece of the phalanx method of fighting. However, this had probably taken place sometime earlier, though it is plausible that since the phalanx required a substantial number of soldiers operating as a solid unit standing shoulder to shoulder, the more men available the better, and also that uniformity of armour and weaponry would help.

Another view is that the change was significant as a new way of organizing the army, with each unit (century) as a cross-section of the whole citizen body drawn from the new local tribes. This would blot out any previous regional loyalties or obedience to aristocratic clan-bosses, enhancing the power at the centre, whatever precise form that took. Therefore the reform of Servius Tullius probably had a political purpose too; the male citizens under arms divided into their units met as an assembly (*comitia centuriata*), which could vote against the interests of the narrow aristocratic clique who expected to control things, and perhaps for the leader who had given them a chance to make their feelings known. It is true that the system ascribed by our sources to Servius Tullius is overly complicated in respect of the management of wealth groups and is unlikely to fit an early date. But it may be that towards the end of the fifth century BC this early census arrangement was modified in line with the prevailing political, military and social situation.

As noted, the seventh and last king of Rome, Tarquinius Superbus, was reportedly aggressive, building up Rome's relationship with the Latins, but also cruel, provoking internal rebellion. It is difficult to recover exactly what happened at the transition from monarchy to the Republic at the traditional date of 509 BC. It is possible that Tarquinius was regarded by aristocrats as a usurper and tyrant, who stirred up or relied on popular support against their interests. Archaeological evidence of burning and destruction in Rome suggests that there was a violent revolution, and the semi-mythical story of an intervention by Lars Porsenna, king of Clusium, adds another dimension. If it is true that he imposed a humiliating peace treaty on Rome, it is possible that Lars expelled Tarquinius before setting out to make war on the Latins. But Lars's defeat at Aricia in 504 undermined his influence, and in the aftermath of the removal of Tarquinius a group of aristocratic families combined to oust Lars and established a Republic with two chief magistrates (the consuls) in the hope of managing the state in their interests, though with concessions to the people and the army who made up the *comitia centuriata*. The senate remained as an advisory council for the chief magistrates.

Political divisions emerged as the young Republic developed, most noticeably between patricians and plebeians, a division often described as the 'Conflict of the Orders'. Later Romans thought that this division went back to early times, but it is more likely that it was the gradual result of new political struggles. In the later Republic the patricians were clearly demarcated within the nobility by dress and the ability to hold certain offices; the status was hereditary, being confined to the legitimate sons of patrician fathers. In the seventh century BC, patricians will have been rich landowners who under the kings had gradually acquired certain political and religious privileges that marked them out socially. Later, they held a large proportion of important offices and set out to exclude non-patricians from the consulship and from social integration. A law in the earliest Roman law code, the Twelve Tables (see p. 7), forbade intermarriage with non-patricians. During this period the plebeians emerged as a distinct group, possibly originally as a way of protecting themselves against the seemingly dominant patricians. Most, though not all, plebeians will have come from the poorest and most disadvantaged members of society, who perhaps served as light-armed troops. Better-off citizens served as heavily armed infantry and the richest as cavalry.

Under the pressure of debt and abusive treatment by their social superiors the plebeians apparently staged a kind of strike in 494 BC, withdrawing outside the city to the Sacred Mount. They must have had competent leaders of some wealth and education, since at least by the mid-fifth century they had succeeded in setting up their own organization with an assembly consisting entirely of plebeians (*concilium plebis*), and officials consisting of two tribunes and two aediles. By 449 there were ten tribunes of the plebs and they were held to be sacrosanct, so that any person who harmed them was reserved for divine vengeance; their role was to defend the person and property of plebeians. Plebeians steadily took increasing responsibility for their own organization and protection; although the decisions of the *concilium plebis* were in a sense unilateral, they were backed up by solemn oaths, the tribunes of the plebs, and the threat of another walkout. Nevertheless in the early Republic the plebeians faced a serious problem; since they often farmed small plots perhaps consisting of only two acres that could not sustain a family, they expected to use the common land (*ager publicus*) acquired by the Roman state in warfare. Unfortunately, the rich citizens used their influence to occupy parts of this land for their own purposes, making life particularly difficult for the poor. It is easy to see how they could get into debt, fail to pay off a loan (either for corn or agricultural implements) and end up in debt bondage (*nexum*) under the harsh law. Popular agitation demanded that public land should be distributed in allotments that could be privately owned.

Against this background there was some kind of serious political disturbance in 451–449 BC, arising partly from demands by the plebeians that the laws of Rome be set out clearly and published. First a body of ten men (*decemviri*) was appointed (supplanting other magistrates) to run the state and draft laws. Then a second group of ten was appointed, though this descended into tyranny and they refused to demit office. The arch-villain was Appius Claudius, who notoriously attempted to rape the virtuous Verginia, whose father killed her rather than allow her to be dishonoured: 'Appius was demented with love for this exceptionally beautiful young virgin and after he had tried to entice her with money and promises and discovered that she was entirely fenced in by her virtue, he decided on a brutal and arrogant use of force' (Livy 3.44.4). This provoked another withdrawal by the plebeians, this time to the Aventine hill and the overthrow of the tyrants. It is not clear how much of this uplifting tale is true, but out of the turmoil the consuls of 449, L. Valerius Potitus and M. Horatius Barbatus, made new proposals that probably recognized plebeian institutions, particularly the tribunate and the aediles, and the legal validity of the plebiscites (decisions of the *concilium plebis*); citizens may also have been granted the right of appeal (against the actions of magistrates).

The other great consequence of the Decemvirate interlude was the issuing of the Twelve Tables, which are of enormous significance even though we do not have the original text. The Tables consist of a series of limited instructions and prohibitions that help to illustrate legal practice in archaic Roman society. The text published now is a modern reconstruction, but despite difficulties of interpretation the original archaic language and format suggest a genuinely ancient tradition. Examples of provisions for settling disputes are:

If he (anyone) summons to a pre-trial, he (the defendant) is to go; if he does not go, he (the plaintiff) is to call to witness; then he is to take him.

If he has brought a false claim, he (the magistrate) is to appoint three arbiters of the case; by their arbitration he (the defendant) is to settle for a penalty at double.

If he has maimed a limb, unless he agrees with him there is to be retaliation. (Crawford, 1996, vol. 2, no. 40, 579ff)

As far as can be recovered, the main areas of interest in the Tables were family, marriage, inheritance, ownership and transfer of property, assault, debt and debt bondage, and legal procedures. The last two items will have been a concern to ordinary people; the existence of a recognized legal procedure might deter arbitrary actions where the rich and powerful would generally win. Topics such as marriage and property (the private ownership of property in early Roman law is significant) were principally of concern to the aristocrats. In the Roman family the position of the *paterfamilias*, that is, the oldest living direct male ascendant, was of crucial importance. He had to be a Roman citizen and not under the power of another. He had complete control over the family as long as he lived and was master of the house. His power, theoretically of life or death, was limited only by his own discretion, customary practice and social pressure from his peers. Ownership of all family property resided in him with the result that his sons had no independent property or wealth. When a man married, he assumed authority over his wife (marriage in *manus*). Marriages without *manus* were recognized (when the wife remained under the power of her father) and these became the norm in the later Republic, perhaps to protect the estates of individual aristocrats.

The Twelve Tables also marked out certain social distinctions, such as patron-client (see p. 48), and mention a division of the citizen body into *assidui* (men of landed wealth who were required to serve in the army and who could equip themselves with armour) and *proletarii* (poorer citizens without land, who had no armour and who were normally not expected to serve as soldiers), which must go back to the census arrangements introduced by Servius Tullius. The Twelve Tables make no mention of other issues such as slavery; but the laws were not intended to be comprehensive and although slavery is mentioned incidentally, therefore showing the presence of the institution, the position of slaves was common knowledge in archaic Rome and there was no need to set out owners' rights in detail.

At some time probably before 447 BC another assembly (*comitia populi tributa*) was established, containing the whole people, patricians and plebeians (*populus*); it operated like the *concilium plebis*, electing junior magistrates and passing laws. However, further political developments largely concerned the emancipation of the plebs. The context was continuing agitation about debt and the political rights of plebeians, who were still oppressed by large landholders extending their control of public land. Many plebeians found it impossible to rise above subsistence-level agriculture. Grants of land to individuals would alleviate this, and a second line of approach was legislation in 367 that placed restrictions on the occupation of public land. Meanwhile more peasants had been reduced to being debt bondsmen who had to work the fields of the rich. A series of measures was introduced to relieve debt and prevent interest charges, and the *Lex Poetelia* of 326 abolished debt-bondage. Plebeians now were experiencing more freely the benefits of Rome's success through land allocations and opportunities for colonization in newly conquered territories. Military victories brought more slaves who could be deployed to the land, perhaps creating the opportunity for more military service by Roman citizens.

Inevitably the wealthy and experienced leaders of the plebeians would want rather more, especially the right to hold the consulship and participate fully in political leadership of the Roman state. The pressures of these events saw the appearance in certain years from 445 to 367 BC of the mysterious military trib-unes with consular power (varying from three to six in number) who replaced the normal consuls; plebeians held this office, though irregularly, and it remains obscure why it was set up. More dramatic changes followed with the admission of the first plebeians to the consulship; then the praetorship (second magistracy after consul) was created and also the *curule aediles* (originally restricted to patricians, but later open to plebeians). By 342 one consular place *had* to be occupied by a plebeian. In 300 the *Lex Ogulnia* provided for the admission of plebeians to two major colleges of priests. The state was gradually moving towards a textured oligarchy with popular input, and competition among leading figures in a patrician-plebeian ruling group depended on distinction acquired through office holding and birth, which meant descent from former office holders. Once in office a man could gain influence by his achievements (particularly military), and a limited number of such men could direct public policy. But they were always competing against one another for political supremacy within the elite. Nevertheless the governing group in Rome was both flexible and innovative, and the nobility consisting of patricians and plebeians demonstrated its right to leadership by successfully extending the conquest of Italy. This brought booty and land, some of which was distributed to poorer people who could also look towards settlement in new colonies. This mutually beneficial process might make them more inclined to accept the domination of government by the elite.

As Rome became more militarily successful another significant political devel-opment took place through which the power and status of the senate were increased. The *Lex Ovinia* (between 339 and 318 BC) had provided for the censors to enrol senators according to certain rules. They were then senators for life and so were not subject to popular pressure or the compulsion of magistrates. Thus the position of assemblies and magistrates in political life became subordinate to the senate. The practice of holding repeated consulships was replaced by the idea that a man might expect to hold the consulship once in his life. Therefore honours were more evenly spread and the senate was not threatened by powerful individuals repeatedly elected with popular support. In this context, the senate came eventually to control important aspects of government such as finance, foreign policy and treaties. The Roman concept of political freedom (*libertas*) embraced the concept of contending with peers for political honours and enjoying the benefits of success by sitting in the senate. Around 287 the *Lex Hortensia* was passed, apparently the result of another withdrawal by the plebeians because of debt. The law removed restrictions on legislation by the *concilium plebis*, and now its enactments were legally binding on the whole people. This effectively meant the end of the Conflict of the Orders, though the assembly had by no means a free hand (see chapter 3).

Warfare in Italy

Rome's political development took place against a background of external contacts that were increasingly aggressive as she began to assert her power. The Greek historian Polybius describes an extraordinary treaty with the city of Carthage in north Africa, which he dates to 507 BC on his chronology (traditionally 509), and which he tells us was written in archaic language that even later Roman experts could not fully interpret. Most scholars now accept the treaty and its date, and it is true that the Carthaginians were actively trading along the Italian coast, as was recently confirmed by the discovery of bilingual inscriptions in Etruscan and Phoenician at Pyrgi (a port in the territory of Caere). According to the treaty of 509, Romans and Carthaginians agreed to be friends and not act against one another's trading interests. Another clause reads:

> As regards those Latin peoples who are not subject to the Romans, the Carthaginians shall not interfere with any of these cities, and if they take any one of them, they shall deliver it up undamaged. They shall build no fort in Latin territory. If they enter the region carrying arms, they shall not spend a night there. (3.22)

This shows that under the kings some kind of Roman hegemony had been established over the Latin peoples who identified with religious festivals held in common as well as certain social and legal traditions, especially relating to marriage and property-owning. However, following the battle of Aricia (*c*.504 BC), there was a revolt and the Latins broke away from Rome. What followed was a long struggle by the Romans to reassert control. The Latins responded by associating in a kind of League to oppose Rome with a chief official called the 'Dictator'. In 499 or 496 BC the Romans won a famous victory at the battle of Lake Regillus (probably just north of the modern town of Frascati), and this was followed in 493 by the treaty of Spurius Cassius, which established peace and provided for a defensive military alliance whereby the Romans and Latins undertook to share the spoils of war equally. The commander of joint operations seems usually to have been Roman. The Hernici (an Italic people in the valley of the river Sacco) joined this alliance in 486. Military operations were usually marked by the foundation of colonies, which were in fact independent sovereign states with their own citizenship and territory. These Latin colonies were placed on conquered land and Roman influence was strong since usually over 50 per cent of the colonists were Romans. The colonies also had a defensive role in protecting Latium against invasion, which was a real and continuous threat since there were substantial movements of people in the fifth century through the Italian peninsula that led, for example, to the invasion of Latium by hill tribes, particularly the Volscii. Rome also faced threats from the Sabines and Aequi to the north and east of the city.

There are fascinating stories told by later writers, such as that of the Volscian attack on Rome in 490–488 BC led by the Roman exile Coriolanus, who was persuaded to turn back only by the appeals of his wife and mother. This presumably reflects a tradition of panic and foreign invasion. The splendid story of L. Quinctius Cincinnatus tells how in 458 BC he was called from ploughing his fields to take the position of Dictator; this was an emergency magistrate appointed with senatorial approval to deal with a particular crisis (often military) and holding office for no more than six months. Assembling an army, Cincinnatus led it to rescue another force besieged by the Aequi at Algidus, and after his victory and triumph he surrendered the dictatorship and quietly returned to his farm, all within fifteen days. This certainly tells us how later Romans wanted their early history to be remembered, embodying noble, unselfish self-sacrifice, courage and quiet determination; in reality it probably preserves a memory of continuing difficult struggles and intense fighting against aggressive invaders. However, the situation had improved by 431 with a notable Roman military success again at Algidus. Livy describes the brutal battle in which the Roman commanders fought and bled:

> Only Postumius Albus left the battle line after his head had been fractured by a stone; neither the Dictator wounded in the shoulder, nor Fabius with his thigh pinned to his horse's flank by a spear, nor the consul with his arm slashed off could leave a battle poised on the knife edge. (4.28–9)

Indeed most of the fifth century BC was a hard time for Rome when ambition to expand had to take second place to battles to repel the irregular incursions of mountain peoples. There were annual military campaigns, generally from spring to autumn, which apart from occasional spectacular encounters usually resulted in desultory tit-for-tat raids where both sides looked for booty and revenge.

As Rome weathered this storm, attention moved to the Etruscan city of Veii about fifteen kilometres north of the city. The character of this conflict was different since Veii was a city state like Rome and had a large, fertile territory. The first war started in 483 BC over control of routes of communication running along the Tiber valley into the interior and also access to the mouth of the Tiber, vital for both communities. Fidenae at a crossing point on the Tiber was crucial and changed hands several times. Between 406 and 396 the third and final war centred on Veii with a ten-year siege, which ended with the fall of the city under the command of the Dictator M. Furius Camillus. The recorded details of the war are suspect but the outcome is not, and Veii ceased to have an independent existence, its lands being absorbed into Roman territory.

This vigorous transformation of the Roman state was interrupted in 390 BC when a band of Celts from the Po valley sacked Rome after previously defeating her troops at the river Allia. The Celtic leader Brennus forced the Romans to pay a ransom in gold and the traditional story has it that when the Romans quibbled over the weight of gold he flung his sword on the scales shouting 'woe to the conquered' ('*vae victis*'). In political and military terms the impact of the sack of Rome may have been limited, and at any rate it was followed by a resumption of Roman operations against the Volscii, with the foundation of more colonies. By the early fourth century Roman territory amounted to roughly 1,582 square kilometres and the city's status was confirmed by the building of a new wall with huge blocks of ashlar masonry quarried in the territory of defeated Veii. In territory and urban area Rome was now leaving behind other Italian communities and in the years between 361 and 354 her relentless expansion brought the city into conflict with Latin communities who had made alliances with the Volscians. The pattern of warfare is partly indicated by the holding of triumphs by Roman commanders who paraded in Rome with their soldiers and captives and booty to mark successful campaigns. Winners of this supreme honour had their names recorded on a public inscription. From 361 to 354 we find:

361 C. Sulpicius, son of Marcus, grandson of Quintus, Peticus, consul for the second time, triumphed over the Hernici, on ... March

360 C. Poetelius, son of Caius, grandson of Quintus, Libo Visolus, consul, triumphed over the Gauls and the Tiburti, on 29th July

360 M. Fabius, son of Numerius, grandson of Marcus, Ambustus consul, held an ovation over Hernici, on 5th September

358 C. Sulpicius, son of Marcus, grandson of Quintus, Peticus, consul twice, dictator, triumphed over the Gauls, on 7th May

358 C. Plautius, son of Publius, grandson of Publius, Proculus, consul, triumphed over the Hernici, on 15th May

357 C. Marcius, son of Lucius, grandson of Gaius, Rutilus, consul, triumphed over the people of Privernum, on 1st June

356 C. Marcius, son of Lucius, grandson of Gaius, Rutilus, dictator, triumphed over the Tuscans, on 6th May

354 M. Fabius, son of Numerius, grandson of Marcus, Ambustus, consul twice, consul for the third time, triumphed over the Tiburti, on 5th June. (Degrassi, 1954, 94)

These records show enormous pride in military achievement and honour, careful propagation of family names, and a pattern of extensive Roman warfare against, among others, Privernum Tibur and the Hernici, some of whom had allied with the Gauls to attack Rome. These campaigns were still concentrated around Latium, but Rome was certainly looking further afield and the outward signs of her increasing power are treaties with the Samnites in central-southern Italy (354) and another treaty with the Carthaginians (348).

It was indeed the Samnites who were the next target of Roman warfare; they lived in four tribal groups spread throughout small villages and made up a society that combined farming, pastoralism and the traditional raiding. In southern Italy they interacted with the Campanians and the long-established Greek cities. But when they attacked Capua the Capuans appealed to the Romans, who responded favourably despite a previous agreement with the Samnites and fought a successful campaign in the first Samnite war (343–341 BC). After peace had been established some disgruntled Campanians sided with the Latins in a revolt against Rome, but by 338 Rome was completely victorious and significantly dealt with the defeated communities individually in a series of formal agreements setting out both obligations and rights that established their relationship with Rome.

This was part of the long and extremely important process by which the Romans turned their conquests into a stable empire. Therefore the Latin League was broken up and each individual community was incorporated into the Roman state as a self-governing *municipium* with Roman citizenship; in some cases leading citizens were banished and their land was distributed to Roman settlers;

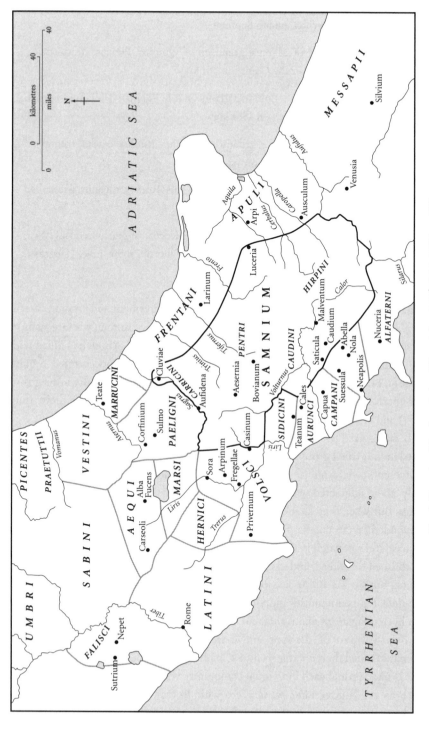

Map 1. Central and Southern Italy c.350 BC (after *CAH²* VII.2 (1989), p. 352).

other communities were granted the status of *civitas sine suffragio* (a community whose inhabitants were liable to the obligations of citizenship but who had no political rights, notably the vote in elections or the right to hold office in Rome). The largest group was that of defeated peoples now registered as allies of Rome who were obliged to levy troops for Rome. The formula, as reconstructed from a later law read: '[Whichever] Roman [citizen] or ally or member of the Latin name, from whom [they are accustomed to demand troops in the land of Italy] according to the list of those who wear the toga. . . .' (Crawford, 1996, vol. 1, no. 2, lines 21 and 50).

These arrangements were crucial because they increased Roman manpower without altering the political set-up and became the basis of Roman expansion and empire-building. The Romans also returned to the use of the Latin colony, which had this title only because of its specific relationship with Rome and that now could be placed anywhere, that is, outside territory directly controlled by or accessible from Rome. Each colony (often sited for strategic purposes) would be a reflection of the Roman state and Roman practices, and provided the framework for bringing every area of Italy under Roman control; the first was at Cales in the valley of the river Liris in Campania in 334 BC. In 328 the foundation of Fregellae, also in the Liris valley, led to another war with the Samnites who regarded this as their fiefdom. Things did not go entirely Rome's way and in 321 a Roman army suffered the humiliation of surrendering at the Caudine Forks, and a sign of military pressure was the increase in 311 of the army from two to four legions. In 304 peace was concluded with the Samnites, though this left Rome with the upper hand and in a dominant strategic position.

However, attention had already shifted to the Tiber valley after an attack on the colony of Sutrium by the Etruscans. The Romans advanced into central Italy and more colonies were founded. The Aequi can serve as an example of the fate of a people who resisted; other communities learnt the lesson, as succinctly described by Livy:

After the plans of the enemy had been discovered by scouts, by concentrating the war on individual towns they stormed and captured thirty-one settlements in fifty days; most of these were destroyed and burnt and the name of the Aequi was virtually totally exterminated. A triumph was held over the Aequi and their example was such a disaster that the Marrucini, Marsi, Paeligni and Frentani sent ambassadors to Rome to seek peace and friendship. (9.45.17–18)

The Roman advance through Italy seemed inexorable and the subjugation of communities one by one must have sent out some warning signals. By *c*.300 BC communities threatened by Roman encroachment on their liberty at last put

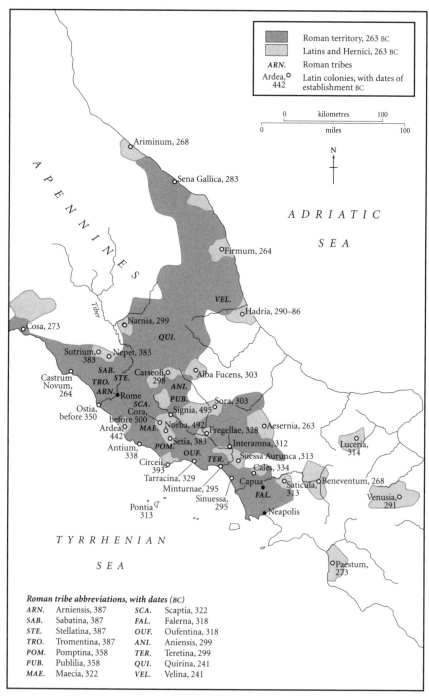

	Roman territory, 263 BC
	Latins and Hernici, 263 BC
ARN.	Roman tribes
Ardea,○ 442	Latin colonies, with dates of establishment BC

0   kilometres   100

0   miles   100

N

Ariminum, 268

Sena Gallica, 283

A D R I A T I C

S E A

○Firmum, 264

VEL.

○Hadria, 290–86

Narnia, 299

QUI.

○Cosa, 273

Sutrium,○ ○Nepet, 383
383

SAB. STE. Carseoli,○ ○Alba Fucens, 303
Castrum *TRO.* 298
Novum, *ARN.* *ANI.*
264 Rome *PUB.*
Ostia, *SCA.* ○Sora, 303
before 350 Cora, Signia, 495○
Ardea○ before 500
442 *MAE.*○Norba, 492 ○Fregellae, 328 ○Aesernia, 263
Antium, ○Setia, 383 Interamna, 312 Luceria,
338 *POM.* 314
Circeii,○ *OUF.* *TER.* Suessa Aurunca ,313
393 Cales, 334
Tarracina, 329 Capua ○Saticula,○Beneventum, 268
Minturnae, 295 313
Sinuessa, *FAL.* Venusia,○
Pontia○ 295 291
313 ○ ●Neapolis

T Y R R H E N I A N

S E A

○Paestum,
273

Roman tribe abbreviations, with dates (BC)

ARN.	Arniensis, 387		*SCA.*	Scaptia, 322
SAB.	Sabatina, 387		*FAL.*	Falerna, 318
STE.	Stellatina, 387		*OUF.*	Oufentina, 318
TRO.	Tromentina, 387		*ANI.*	Aniensis, 299
POM.	Pomptina, 358		*TER.*	Teretina, 299
PUB.	Publilia, 358		*QUI.*	Quirina, 241
MAE.	Maecia, 322		*VEL.*	Velina, 241

Map 2. Roman Colonies and Tribes, Italy in Mid-third Century BC (after Cornell, *The Beginnings of Rome* (1995), p. 382).

together a concerted effort, and Rome found herself fighting in Etruria, Umbria and Samnium. In 295 at Sentinum the Romans concentrated an army of four legions and allied troops against a joint force of Gauls and Samnites. This was certainly the largest battle in Italy up to this time and perhaps as many as 25,000 of Rome's enemies perished in the hard fighting. Rome followed up this victory enthusiastically and smashed the Samnites at Aquilonia in 293. There was now no hope that Italian communities could preserve a measure of independence, and there were further Roman advances to the Adriatic and in Samnium, though the details are hard to recover. The foundation of Hadria (290–286) on the Adriatic coast was followed by the takeover of Picenum in the 260s. After the battle of Sentinum in 295 no more major wars were fought in Italy until the Social War in the 90s, except against the foreign invaders Pyrrhus, king of Epirus in Greece, and the Carthaginian Hannibal.

By the 280s BC the Greek cities in southern Italy saw the way the wind was blowing and began to put themselves under Roman protection. This was opposed by Tarentum, the most influential of these cities, and after some violent incidents involving a Roman fleet the Romans sent an embassy, which led to a notorious confrontation in the assembly at Tarentum:

> The people of Tarentum mocked the ambassadors whenever they made a mistake in their Greek and laughed at their togas with their purple stripe. Then one Philonides, a man who enjoyed jokes and vulgar abuse, going up to Postumius the leader of the embassy, turned his back on him and bending over pulled up his clothes and covered him in excrement. (Appian, *Samnite History* 7.2)

This story vividly illustrates some features of the time, particularly Roman confidence and their ability to work outside the Italic context and speak Greek (even if badly) in a public gathering, but also the flavour of Greek politics where concepts of freedom were not yet dead. The Romans tended to find their support among the ruling group, and facing a popular assembly was a different matter. Defiantly, Postumius promised to clean his toga in Tarentine blood. When war broke out Tarentum called in Pyrrhus, king of Epirus, an enthusiastic if erratic military leader. He won two victories at great cost against dogged Roman resistance, apparently commenting 'another victory like that will finish us off', and was then defeated at Beneventum in 275 BC. This was followed by the fall of Tarentum in 272, and with the defeat of Samnium and Lucania, which had risen in revolt, Rome effectively controlled all of Italy up to the Po valley.

This means that within a period of about seventy years after 338 BC the Romans had brought about an astonishing transformation in Italy and assumed a domination that could not be reversed. They did indeed have strong military customs, incorporated to some extent in national practices such as the triumph, the commander's right to extend the official boundary of the city (*pomerium*) if he had annexed new territory, and the official prayer at the end of a censor's term of office that the Roman state might have greater wealth and extent. However, this warlike ethos, which was anyway shared by many other Italic peoples, cannot alone explain Rome's rapid success in Italy. There was no coherent plan of imperialist aggression; initially the Romans vied with other peoples in raiding but proved to be more persistent, resilient and innovative. Crucially, in the aftermath of the settlement of 338 the Romans developed a constructive and flexible approach in dealing with defeated communities which, by combining toughness and generosity, converted them into allies in carefully calibrated relationships, sometimes including Roman citizenship; it is another indication of innovative Roman leadership to have added new members to the citizen body in this way. By the 260s Rome may have made as many as 150 separate agreements – an amazing figure that raises interesting if unanswerable questions about who negotiated them and how records were kept.

The vital aspect of these agreements was that those in alliance with Rome had to provide soldiers for joint military operations; the allies served alongside Roman troops, sometimes making up more than half the army. This gave the Romans a huge reserve of manpower and meant that they could sustain large battlefield losses but continue campaigning. In the early years it could be argued that levying extra manpower was necessary for protection, but later that was less and less true and Rome had to give all these soldiers something to do. This produced a momentum for war because for the Romans to get the benefit of the diplomatic agreements they had to keep fighting. The allies also tended to remain loyal, partly because Rome usually had the support of the propertied classes who would have dominated the government and looked to Rome to support their position. Also those Italians who served in the army and survived would have enjoyed the booty from successful battles and probably also had access to the distribution of conquered land. There was therefore a community of interest in making war and being part of successful war-making. For many Italian communities the Roman presence was not particularly intrusive and the various conditions of alliance offered a kind of ladder that perhaps encouraged people to aspire to improving their lot; for example, *civitas sine suffragio* could be seen as a kind of halfway stage on the road to full Roman citizenship.

It is not surprising therefore that many communities in Italy increasingly identified themselves with Roman practices and customs. Colonies to some extent were a replica of the city of Rome even in their buildings; for example, at Cosa (founded in 273 BC) on the coast of Etruria the senate house was linked directly to a circular assembly building just as in Rome. Furthermore, one visible expression

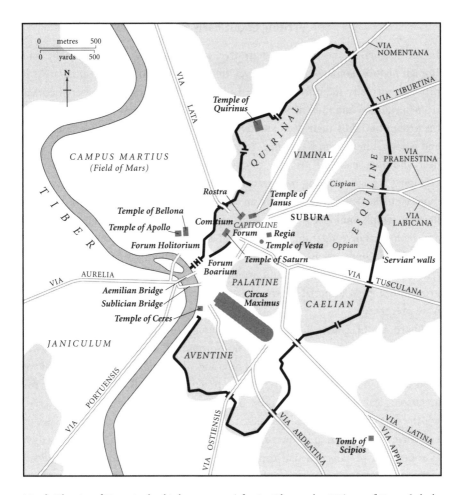

Map 3. The city of Rome in the third century BC (after Le Glay, et al., *A History of Rome*, 3rd edn (2005) figure 4.1).

of Rome's dominance in Italy was the construction of roads; as early as 312 the via Appia was built along the west coast linking Rome and Campania; others followed converting the paths taken by marching armies into permanent roads, and a planned network eventually connected Rome with outlying colonies, demonstrating the power of the conquerors and their determination to overcome natural obstacles.

Internally Rome had of course effectively organized her citizens for military service and had achieved relative political stability, as the upper classes worked together for their own benefit and the plebeians were brought into the political structure. The increasingly strong social fabric and political coherence allowed the Romans to turn their attention to external matters. It was the combination of these factors that contributed at different times to Rome's success in these years.

Writing about Early Rome

In reconstructing the historical narrative of the earliest period of Italic and Roman history, archaeology has a very important role to play; in some areas it provides virtually the only evidence. In particular, much useful material comes from burial sites and their deposits, since ancient societies were enthusiastic about the proper burial of their dead and tended to place in tombs valuable household and personal items and weaponry. So items were buried at the same time as the dead and then sealed off. If they can be related to other tomb finds in the same cemetery, a relative dating pattern can be worked out, which is potentially even more valuable if it can be linked to an independently verified date. The development of temple-building and the nature of sanctuaries can also be observed from archaeological investigation. An important aspect here is the layout of the city of Rome itself. Since the Romans valued highly the buildings of old Rome, they tended to preserve them or build around them, and therefore even as the city grew into a great imperial centre, the shape and facilities of the ancient layout were preserved.

There are of course limitations, since archaeologists can be overconfident in identifying from scanty remains the purpose of buildings. Archaeological remains on their own often cannot tell how and why things happened; for that we need other evidence. Therefore the best practice (Cornell, 1995, 26–30) is for archaeological evidence to be used in conjunction with the literary material, which often produces difficulties because these are significantly different types of evidence, each requiring its own approach. Archaeology cannot stand on its own as some kind of talisman that can verify or contradict ancient writers. Indeed archaeological evidence itself requires a context through interpretation based on literary texts. Therefore, for the historian the relationship is complex and archaeological indications can often offer only vague guidance.

In fact, historians usually turn first to the literary evidence where possible. The problem is that for the early history of Rome established Greek historians took little interest in a remote Italian city state that seemed of no account. The beginning of the Roman historical tradition came around 200 BC when Fabius Pictor, a Roman senator, wrote a history of Rome in Greek. But only fragments survive of his writings and of the work of those who followed him and wrote in Latin. Similarly, little remains from later Greek historians, such as Timaeus of Sicily, who offered an outsider's view of Rome, which had come to seem more important and to be more relevant to the Greek world. The most notable surviving Greek historians of Rome are Polybius and Posidonius. Polybius (c.200–118 BC) was unique in being an active politician in his community of Achaea, who became an object of suspicion to Rome and was deported to

Italy. But he was eventually welcomed by the upper class and became friends with leading Romans. He therefore was able to view Rome simultaneously as an outsider and also as one intimate with the governing class. His theme is the emergence of Rome as a Mediterranean power, defeating Carthage and the hitherto powerful Hellenistic monarchies. But he also took time to examine how Roman government and politics worked. Polybius's history of Rome was carried on by Posidonius (c.135–51 BC) from Apamea in Syria, who wrote on a wide range of subjects from history to philosophy. However, his text is fragmentary and because so much historical work has been lost we often have to fall back on general histories of Rome written in the early first century AD, especially those of Livy and the Greek, Dionysius of Halicarnassus. Of later writers on aspects of the early Republic the three most important are Greek: Plutarch, Appian and Cassius Dio. Plutarch (c.AD 50–120) wrote a series of biographies comparing famous figures in the Greek and Roman world. His work can be only as good as his sources, and he was principally a moral philosopher interested in the character of his subjects and why they did things rather than in offering a continuous historical narrative with clear chronology. Appian (born c.AD 100) from Alexandria in Egypt held minor office under the emperor Antoninus Pius and wrote a Roman history based on the wars Rome fought to subdue individual peoples. In a way this shows us something of Roman ideology and Appian illuminates many topics, especially Roman landholding and the civil wars. Cassius Dio, a high-ranking senator from Nicaea in Bithynia, wrote in the third century AD and his narrative history of Rome is a fundamental source of information, although for the middle Republic it survives only in a series of excerpts made in the Byzantine period. These writers are of limited value for the early Republic.

Other works potentially of great value have survived only in fragmentary form. Ennius, from Messapia in southern Italy, came to Rome in 204 BC. His poem, the *Annales* (using the title of the records of the *pontifex maximus*), was a narrative of the history of the Roman people from the fall of Troy to his own day. Only about six hundred lines remain, but this great patriotic poem certainly influenced the way in which Romans thought about their early history. M. Porcius Cato (234–149 BC), who brought Ennius to Rome, was an important political and cultural figure. Among his literary efforts, 'The Origins' (*Origines*) was the first historical work in Latin; the first book dealt with the foundation of Rome and the kings, while the next two covered the origins and customs of towns in Italy.

An important strand of the historical record is found in the work of antiquarians; they were not concerned like historians to write the account of men and events, but delved into institutions, customs and practices of the ancient Roman state. Arguably, they were less subject to deliberate distortion or partisan rivalry, but just as liable to simple errors. Varro, writing towards the end of the Republic, was enormously prolific and established among other things the chronology of early Rome that came to be widely accepted, namely 753 BC for the foundation date (Livy favoured 754), 509 for the first year of the consuls, 390 for the sack of Rome by the Gauls. This tradition was taken up by Verrius Flaccus (died *c.*AD 20), who produced a study of antiquities and the Latin language, quoting many early authors. The work of established historians and antiquarians can be supplemented by what we can call accidental literary evidence, namely the work of poets and commentators who in passing describe or comment on contemporary society and figures. For example, the twenty-one surviving plays of Plautus (*c.*200 BC) are the earliest Latin works to have come down to us intact, and in some cases like 'The Boastful Soldier' (*Miles Gloriosus*) might be seen as an ironic comment on some Roman values.

Reliable sources of documentary evidence did exist, though it is not clear how much use literary sources made of them. The Romans recorded laws, treaties and agreements, and also made lists of officials, notably inscribing the consuls year by year from 509 BC. This list, known as the *Fasti*, was used as a form of dating, for example 'in the consulship of Spurius Larcius Rufus and Titus Herminius Aquilinus' (506 BC). The senior priest (*pontifex maximus*) of the college of priests published a list of events in Rome that he presumably thought prodigious or significant, day by day for each year. These *Annales Maximi* go back to the fifth century at least, and entries become more detailed later. Inscriptions recording events on stone for public display either relating to private individuals or state decisions are a very useful source of reliable information, but are few and far between for the early and middle Republic. The erection of inscriptions was in the main the work of the better-off and thus they tend to reflect the elite's view of how government should work and the best way to present it.

Traditional practices and ancient terminology preserved in later activities can be useful evidence. For example, Romans were very conservative about religious practice, and while being amenable to accepting new deities, tended to keep old cult activities, which duly became fossilized and can show at least the outline of the society of old Rome. Nevertheless, many later writers undoubtedly had to rely on what they could glean from the stories and oral family histories transmitted by aristocratic houses. The fact that much of the literary tradition is probably dependent on an oral tradition is not necessarily a bad thing, since this can preserve valuable stories. However, such stories can also distort genuine historical information in the interests of later family groups, tending to exaggerate the role of certain individuals, fabricating where facts failed, and also possibly denigrating the role of other political figures. Sometimes an apparently ancient tradition may have been invented in later times for some political or family reason. Therefore the oral tradition is uncertain evidence, but it remains possible that some was based on authentic material, which also could be preserved in song and by dramatic performances at public games from the third century BC onwards.

Overall there was little chance that our ancient writers would find a clear-cut, coherent history of the early period, and a consequent danger that they simply invented material to fill the gaps. All modern historians of ancient Rome struggling to construct a reliable narrative have to bear in mind two general problems. First, one period of republican history may seem distinct or different just because we happen to be better informed about it. For example, the early history of the Republic is poorly documented, whereas the period from the mid-fourth century BC onwards is well served by Greek historians and the earliest Roman historians who could have used oral records. On the other hand, for the period from 293 to 264 the valuable history of Livy is missing and there is no convincing narrative. Second, our whole outlook is conditioned by the fact that because of the loss of much of the non-Roman historical tradition (since Rome's opponents lost), we are left with an entirely Romano-centric view.

Furthermore, ancient historians who wrote the year-by-year history (annalistic) of the early and mid-Republic betray certain characteristics that complicate their use. They produced not just analysis of data that they had researched, but also tried to recreate what they thought was in the minds and hearts of the main characters. Speeches put in the mouths of central figures were, by universal convention, written to convey what historians thought were crucial issues at the time. Furthermore, it is likely that some battle descriptions contained at least some elements thought to be typical of all battles. This is not necessarily a drawback, since the historian's judgement may be sound and the story appropriately enlivened. On the other hand, we have to remember the rhetorical context of ancient historical writing. Tacitus, one of the greatest of the ancient historians of the imperial period, was a distinguished orator. Those writing about the early Republic, when confronted with the difficulty of a less clearly established historical record, will have made additions, embellishments and, at worst, inventions. Great set-piece speeches could be self-consciously moral essays. That can tell us a lot about Roman ideology and how Romans wanted others to see them, but makes it harder for the modern historian to uncover the facts.

CHAPTER TWO

Conquering the Mediterranean

Carthage and Illyria

Rome's dealings with Carthage mark her first military intervention outside Italy. In 264 BC the Mamertini (renegade Roman mercenaries who had seized Messina in Sicily) appealed to Rome against Syracuse, though some had wanted to appeal to Carthage. Although the Romans were becoming suspicious of the Carthaginians, they had negotiated previous pacts with them in 507, 348 and 278, and although some senators were reluctant to get involved in such a disreputable case, the people voted for war against Carthage nevertheless. To some extent the popular view was probably influenced by hopes of booty. According to Polybius, the Romans were worried by Carthaginian control of Africa and much of Spain. He probably exaggerated this view, which was particularly attractive to upper-class generals. On the other hand, it was plausible that Carthaginian control of Sicily might be a threat to Rome, and if they captured Messina the way would be open to attack Syracuse and secure a dominant position on the island.

The First Punic War (264–241 BC) reached stalemate since the Romans lagged behind the Carthaginians in naval warfare. Eventually, however, they built a fleet using a captured Carthaginian ship as a model and went on to invent the grapnel (*corvus*), which was hooked onto enemy ships, locking them together so that it became a battle of footsoldiers at sea. The rapid development of a shipbuilding capacity and a willingness to absorb huge losses of men and material at sea show the determination and increasing strength of Rome. Her first naval victory was won by C. Duilius in 260, but a land campaign in Africa in 255 saw the defeat and capture of M. Atilius Regulus. Although he died in captivity, probably of natural causes, a legend later grew up that the Carthaginians had released him on his word that he would persuade the Romans to negotiate peace terms; once back in Rome, Regulus advised against peace but returned to Carthage to face torture and execution. Horace eloquently wrote up the story: 'And yet he knew what the barbarous torturer had waiting for him; but he moved aside the relatives who stood in his path and the people who would delay his return . . .' (*Odes* 3.5.49–52; translation by Williams, 1969, p. 57).

This tale of Roman honour may have a more disreputable origin, aiming to mask the fact that Regulus's widow had avenged her husband by torturing two Punic prisoners. In any case, in a war lasting twenty-three years the Romans persevered despite numerous setbacks, while the Carthaginians were ground down by the strategic problem of simultaneously defending the homeland and prosecuting a war abroad. In 241 BC after a Roman naval victory at the Aegates Islands off the west coast of Sicily, Carthage made peace, agreeing to withdraw from Sicily and pay an indemnity, and soon after Rome got control of Corsica and Sardinia while Carthage was distracted by internal disturbances. This victory in the First Punic War dramatically illustrates Roman ingenuity, adaptability, and economic and technical resilience in repeatedly building fleets.

Roman confidence was therefore at a high point, and they were not minded to tolerate increasing incidents of Illyrian piracy. Under Queen Teuta, the Illyrians became bolder and seized Phoenice opposite the island of Corcyra, and in controversial circumstances a Roman envoy was murdered and so war was declared in 229 BC. Although the Romans had immediate motives, it is also true that Illyria and the principal town of Rhizon in its bay (modern Kotor) were potentially well placed for raids on Italy. During the war, Corcyra defected to the Romans and, along with some other communities, was accepted into Roman friendship (*amicitia*). Teuta was defeated by 228 and her territory restricted; tribute was also imposed and Rome made a formal announcement of the victory to Aetolia and Achaea, Athens and Corinth, where they were significantly admitted to the Isthmian games. This may be seen as a clever ploy or a conciliatory gesture by the Romans towards Greek communities. At this stage, however, it seems unlikely that they were already planning further moves on the Greek mainland. Demetrius of Pharos, who had assisted them in the war, was allowed to remain as a powerful figure in Illyria, perhaps in the hope that he would preserve the status quo.

Meanwhile Carthaginian power continued to grow in Spain, where Hannibal of the aristocratic Barcine family had come to exercise supreme command on the death of his father. There was certainly a feeling among some military leaders in Carthage that they had been betrayed into surrendering at the end of the First Punic War, and resentment was one motive for renewed hostilities. The previous agreement had marked the Ebro river as the limit of Carthaginian expansion in Spain, and therefore when the city of Saguntum well to the south of this line appealed to Rome for help in 219 BC it should have been none of Rome's business, but the senate, concerned that the Carthaginians should not use Spanish resources to finance expansion elsewhere, sent an embassy to warn Hannibal off. However, Rome did nothing when he besieged the city and captured it in 218. Then the Romans sent an embassy to Carthage demanding the surrender of Hannibal, which merely infuriated the Carthaginians. When the Roman ambassador theatrically displayed the folds of his toga, saying that one contained peace, the other war, they replied that he could give them whichever he chose.

The Second Punic War (218–201 BC) began with Hannibal's strategic decision to march from Spain across the Alps and into Italy. He led about 50,000 infantry, 9,000 cavalry and thirty-seven elephants. This turned out to be a deadly threat to Rome's primacy in Italy, and indeed her survival. Hannibal established himself in Italy by several victories in the Po valley at the rivers Ticinus and Trebia in 218, and won over many of the Gauls in Cisalpine Italy. He then moved southwards towards Arretium and on 21 June 217 encountered C. Flaminius, who had been swept into the consulship for 217 and the command against Hannibal by enthusiastic popular support. The consul was lured into an ambush on the northern shore of Lake Trasimene, where, trapped by the Carthaginians, he fell with about 15,000 of his soldiers; many more were captured. Flaminius was criticized for not waiting for reinforcements, but he probably expected that Roman arms would win the day.

Hannibal had turned out to be a skilful and resourceful general, and for a time under the leadership of the Dictator Q. Fabius Maximus Verrucosus the Romans followed a policy of attrition, avoiding pitched battles, dogging Hannibal's footsteps and denying him supplies. Fabius acquired the nickname 'Cunctator' (the Delayer) and a long-lived reputation as a clever general. Frontinus, writing in the first century AD, said of him: 'Fabius Maximus, when fighting against Hannibal, who was arrogant because of his successful battles, decided to avoid any dangerous risks and to concentrate on protecting Italy' (*Stratagems* 1.3.3). However, many senators were impatient with this policy and urged a more aggressive approach. In 216 BC C. Terentius Varro was elected consul partly because of popular dissatisfaction with the prolongation of the war by the cat-and-mouse tactics of Fabius Maximus. So, when Hannibal marched into southeast Italy in 216 he met at Cannae in Apulia a large Roman army (perhaps up to 80,000) under the command of Varro and his fellow consul, L. Aemilius Paullus. Hannibal out-manoeuvred the Romans by reinforcing his wings, allowing the centre to give way slightly and then encircling the Roman infantry as it plunged forward. Meanwhile his cavalry dispersed their opponents and attacked the rear of the infantry. As many as 50,000 Romans and their allies perished in a single day's fighting and Aemilius Paullus was killed, but Roman spirit and determination shine through in the response of the senate after Varro had limped back into

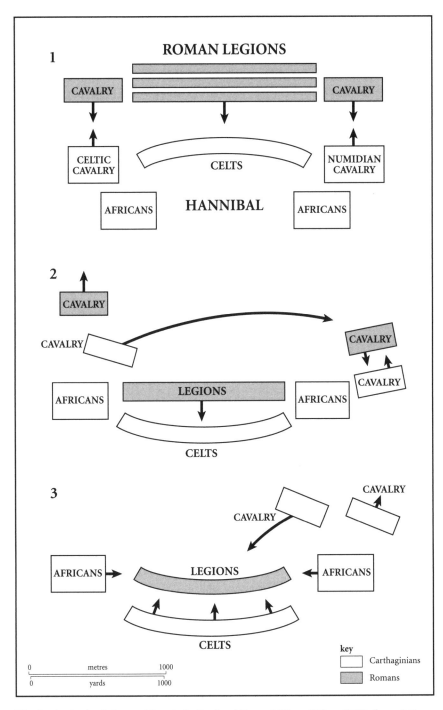

Plan 1. The Battle of Cannae (Campbell, *Greek and Roman Military Writers* (2004), figure 3.1).

Rome with a few survivors; he was publicly thanked for not despairing of the Republic.

Despite these spectacular military successes Hannibal could not hope to persevere with his campaign in Italy unless he found reinforcements. He did not attack the city of Rome directly (perhaps hoping that Rome could be forced into territorial concessions outside Italy acceptable to Carthage). Naturally he tried to win over Rome's Italian allies, and there were revolts, some people willingly joining Hannibal's side, others being forced by military circumstances. He concentrated his efforts on the rich land of Campania and his most notable success was the revolt of Capua. However, the majority stayed loyal to Rome partly no doubt from a sense of shared interests but also because Hannibal had to live off the land and his troops caused much devastation. The loyalty of her allies was a big factor in Rome's eventual victory. It helped the Romans to manage a long campaign and confirmed their determination not to surrender. Eventually Roman successes outside Italy turned the pressure on Hannibal. In Sicily, Syracuse was recovered in 211 BC after a three-year siege. (In the storming of the city the great Greek mathematician and inventor, Archimedes, was killed.) In Spain, Roman operations were under the command of the brothers Cnaeus and Publius Cornelius Scipio, who aimed to prevent Carthaginian supplies and troops from getting to Italy. Although the brothers were eventually defeated and killed in 211, Publius's son (also Publius Cornelius Scipio) was given the command in Spain in 210 by the people (even though he had not yet been consul). In the following year he captured the major Carthaginian base in Spain, Nova Carthago, and with innovative tactics won a series of victories that threatened to wipe out Carthaginian control in the area. Scipio had already made a name for himself by saving his father's life at the battle of the river Ticinus and as a military tribune rallying the survivors after Cannae. He was an adept self-publicist and pushed the idea of divine assistance, telling the troops in Spain that Neptune had promised his help.

Hannibal was now running out of options and asked his brother Hasdrubal to march the remaining Carthaginian forces from Spain. Hasdrubal managed to evade Scipio but was caught in northern Italy at the river Metaurus and his army destroyed. Hasdrubal's head was tossed into Hannibal's camp as an act of revenge and a sign that the war would be fought to the bitter end. Hannibal was forced to withdraw from Italy through lack of reinforcements and supplies and the steady encroachment by Rome on those communities he had previously won over. After his return to Africa he organized another army. Opinion was divided in Rome about whether to carry the war into Africa, but P. Cornelius Scipio (elected consul in 205 BC) was assigned the province of Sicily with the understanding that he could cross to Africa if he wished. Initially using only volunteers, he established

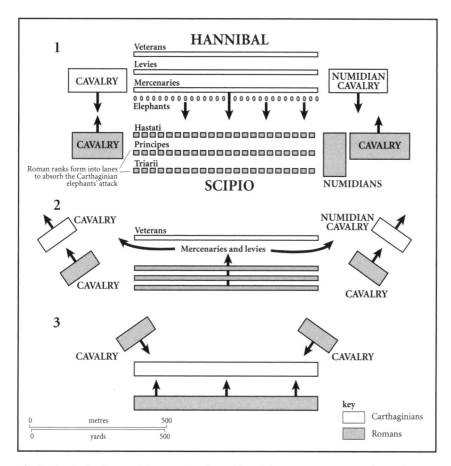

Plan 2. The Battle of Zama (after Keppie, *The Making of the Roman Army* (1984), figure 6b).

a strong Roman position in Africa and formed an alliance with Masinissa, king of Numidia. After a successful operation against Hannibal and abortive peace negotiations, Scipio decisively defeated him at the battle of Zama in 202, earning the name 'Africanus'. Next year Rome imposed tough peace terms by which Carthage, although keeping its possessions in Africa, had to pay a huge indemnity of 10,000 talents over fifty years, hand over its fleet, war elephants and prisoners, and swear not to rearm or make war without Rome's permission. Hannibal remained in civilian life, was elected to the chief magistracy and in 196 reformed Carthaginian finances. But he had enemies who stirred up Roman suspicions and he fled to the east and the court of king Antiochus III.

The defeat of Carthage was a dazzling success for Rome and Scipio won outstanding prestige from his military career and especially the final defeat of Hannibal. But this was not welcomed by all his peers, who perhaps unreasonably suspected the political ambitions of a great, charismatic military leader with

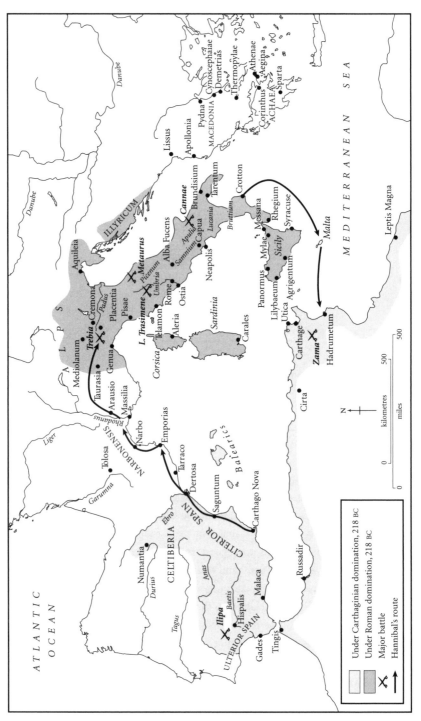

Map 4. Rome and Carthage: The Second Punic War (after Le Glay et al., *A History of Rome*, 3rd edn (2005), figure 4.2).

popular support. Scipio was to continue to serve the state loyally, but in the future the role of warlords backed up by enthusiastic and personally loyal armies was to destroy the Republic. The war years had highlighted political tensions and unresolved issues.

The Greek East

In the east, after Alexander the Great had died in 323 BC without naming an heir, his generals had carved up his empire, claiming the name and status of king and establishing dynasties. The descendants of Alexander's general Antigonus controlled Macedon itself, most of mainland Greece and parts of Asia; the Seleucids (after the first king, Seleucus I Nicator) controlled most of Asia and Syria and regions stretching to the Far East; the Ptolemaic dynasty (founded by Ptolemy) controlled Egypt. Eventually, out of the Seleucid territory around Pergamum, a new kingdom was created ruled by descendants of Attalus I (269–197 BC). These Hellenistic kings were absolute rulers who depended on their advisers, military commanders and mercenary armies, and came to claim a divine status for themselves; they frequently fought against one another, seeking territorial gains. The traditionally independent Greek city states came under the control directly or indirectly of one of these contending monarchies. One way of preserving some independence was to combine in leagues or confederations like the Achaean or Aetolian Leagues, which could assemble stronger military resources. By relying on its strong fleet and astute diplomacy, the island of Rhodes managed to retain a degree of independent action. Politically and socially this was an unstable time and there was no central power-bloc that could command obedience and organize resistance against the Romans. Furthermore, despite the overwhelming power of the kings, their relationship with the Greek cities in their domains was delicate, since traditionally these cities were free and democratic or liked to think that they were. Even in an age of power politics the niceties were important, and kings found it politically expedient to honour at least nominally the concept of freedom and autonomy of the Greek cities. Many Greek city states were therefore susceptible to those claiming to be their protector. This is the situation the Romans found when they came on the scene at the end of the third century BC.

Polybius, trying to analyse the collision of Rome and the Greek east, put forward his idea of the interconnectedness of events: 'This time and this conference (217 BC) first intertwined the affairs of Greece, Italy and Africa. For Philip (of Macedon) and the leading politicians of the Greeks no longer made wars, truces and treaties with each other in relation only to events in Greece, but all looked to what was happening in Italy' (5.105.5). Roman military intervention,

increasingly violent, was the crucial element in the fundamental changes that took
place in the Hellenistic world during this period. After the Romans had withdrawn
their troops from Illyria, leaving Demetrius of Pharos as an influential figure, he
became too ambitious, powerful and potentially disruptive, especially as
Rome and Carthage were manoeuvring and moving towards war. Demetrius
eventually fled to Philip V, king of Macedon, who aspired to leadership of all
Greek cities and saw Rome as a potential rival for Greek affections or protection.
Therefore, he took the gamble of making an alliance with Hannibal in 216 BC
in the hope of prising Greek communities like Corcyra and Apollonia from
Roman control. In 214 when Philip V attacked Apollonia, Rome reacted by
sending a Roman fleet against him and then making an alliance with the Aetolians
in 212:

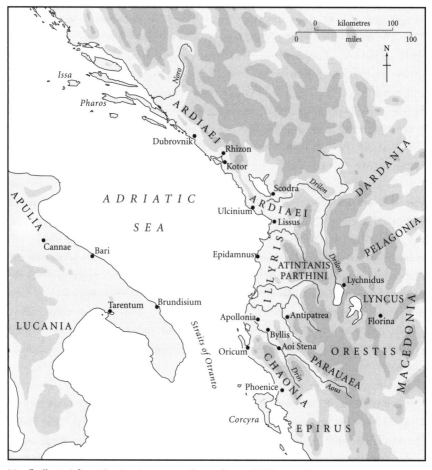

Map 5. Illyria (after Eckstein, *Rome enters the Greek East* (2008), map 1).

If the Romans take by force any cities belonging to these people, the cities and their territories shall, as far as the Roman people is concerned, belong to the Aetolian people; anything the Romans get hold of apart from the cities and their territories shall belong to them. If the Romans and Aetolians operating together get control of cities, they also belong to the Aetolians, other spoils jointly. (*Inscriptiones Graecae* IX, I², 2, 241)

The Romans wanted to keep Philip occupied and also help themselves to movable plunder, but beyond this seem not to have had a clear policy for further intervention in Greece. However, they were starting to look dangerous and so Aetolia decided to make peace with Philip in 206 BC. Then Rome also concluded peace with Philip, both sides probably wanting time to assess their objectives and means. But by 200 Rome had declared war on Philip and this time there was to be no compromise. What were the motives of the Romans? They could claim that complaints from her allies Rhodes and Pergamum required intervention and that Philip must at least be warned about his conduct. Rhodes had a significant role in Greek politics, and it was important that both Attalus of Pergamum (an old ally of Rome) and Rhodes had sent envoys to Rome complaining about the aggressive behaviour of Philip. Rome sent an embassy and warned off Philip's general Nicanor from Athens; the message to the king was unambiguous: not to make war on any of the Greeks, and to face judgement for wrongs done to Attalus. If he did this he could have peace with Rome – if not, the opposite (Polybius 16.27).

Possibly Roman policy was influenced by an alleged pact between Philip and the Seleucid king Antiochus III to cut up the failing Ptolemaic kingdom of Egypt, which might decisively have changed the balance of power in the east. But the significance and even the fact of this agreement are disputed, and in any case it seems unlikely that the senate, being generally well informed about circumstances in the east, was stampeded by news of such a pact. Arguably it had always intended to pursue revenge against Philip, since he had sided with Rome's bitter enemy Hannibal and had stirred them into thinking that the Hellenistic monarchies needed to be weakened. The senators probably wanted to demolish the Macedonian hegemony and work out the consequences afterwards. Furthermore, the glittering career of the great military leader Scipio Africanus had set a powerful example of political success that could come with military victories. And a war in the east offered hopes of great booty. The rather murky context of this conflict is perhaps one reason why the assembly first declined to vote for war, a decision that was reversed at a second meeting some time later.

By 200 BC, once the Romans were determined on war against Philip, they skilfully set out to win over Greek public opinion to their side. By their intervention to protect Athens they stepped directly into the role of the Greek kings as protectors of the freedom and autonomy of the Greeks. They could therefore not neglect the diplomatic route through which Greeks could be persuaded of the benefits of Roman guidance and goodwill. As the Romans wrestled with the complexity of inter-state relations in the east, the problem was how to manipulate the Greeks for their own interests, while being sympathetic to Greek expectations and opening up effective channels of communication. From the Greek point of view, as old power structures collapsed it was not easy for the city states to find ways of making their concerns known to Rome, since even powerful Roman commanders did not have the status or influence of a king. Roman senators and commanders, despite their claims of being liberators and protectors, did not think of the Greeks as being on equal terms, and all expected obedience of a kind. Out of this in the end emerged directly administered Roman provinces.

From 199 to 198 BC fighting spread through Macedonia and Thessaly, and in 197 at the battle of Cynoscephalae the Roman commander Quinctius Flamininus decisively defeated the army of Philip V and ended the war. The sequel was in line with Roman diplomatic thinking, as Flamininus continued to emphasize the idea that Rome was protecting vulnerable Greek communities. He was present in Greece from 197 to 194, and at the Isthmian Games at Corinth in 196 he dramatically proclaimed the freedom of the Greeks:

> The senate of Rome and Titus Quinctius Flamininus, proconsul, having defeated king Philip and the Macedonians in battle, leave the following states free, without garrisons, subject to no tribute and in full enjoyment of their ancestral laws: the peoples of Corinth, Phocis, Locri, Euboea, Phthiotic Achaea, Magnesia, Thessaly and Perrhaebia. (Polybius 18.46.5)

This was greeted with tremendous excitement, and Flamininus received 114 gold wreaths. On more sober reflection, however, the Greeks will have realized that this freedom was relative and would be limited by what suited the Romans now and in the future. The Romans wanted to win Greek support against the suspected ambitions of the Seleucid king Antiochus III 'the Great'. The reality was that representatives were sent to the senate, which then decided on what was to happen next in Greek affairs. And everyone now knew what a Roman legion could do:

> But now they (the Macedonians) saw bodies cut in pieces by the Spanish sword, arms hacked off along with the shoulder, or heads severed from the body with the neck entirely sliced through, or entrails hanging out, or other appalling

wounds, and there was a total panic when they found out what kind of weapons and what kind of men they had to fight against. (Livy 31.34)

When Roman troops were withdrawn from Greece in 194 BC, even though Antiochus III was potentially a threat to developing Roman interests in the east, it was a symbolic though important gesture. In 192 Antiochus provoked matters by crossing over to Greece, but he failed to win over most of the Greeks. The Achaean League then declared war on him and was rewarded by the senate with an alliance. As Rome responded to the continuing manoeuvres of Antiochus, once again the freedom card could be played, and Antiochus was ordered to leave Greek communities in Asia free and evacuate mainland Greece. The king was incensed: 'Regarding the autonomous cities of Asia, it was not right for them to receive their freedom by order of the Romans; rather, they should receive it by his own generosity' (Polybius 18.51.9). This of course was an illogical sham. Freedom should be freedom no matter who guaranteed it. From the Roman point of view, although they were in complete control when they declared all Greek cities to be free and autonomous, it would be naïve to think that the senate intended real freedom for Greeks. This was a carrot to get the goodwill of the Greeks against Antiochus, especially after the Roman withdrawal of troops from Greece. It was part of the game of power-politics and Antiochus saw clearly what was going on — it was his game too, after all.

Antiochus was defeated at Thermopylae in 191 BC by an army under the command of the consul Manius Acilius Glabrio. Along with the king the Aetolians were crushed (they had made the wrong decision and sided with Antiochus). They had to pay a fine of 500 talents and agree to have the same friends and enemies as the Romans, and there was a further clause in the treaty that shows increasing Roman consciousness of their power; the Aetolians had to 'respect the empire and sovereignty (*maiestas*) of the Roman people without fraud'.

The fate of the Aetolians shows what it meant to incur Roman displeasure, and they soon found themselves in difficulties; they had previously dominated Delphi and seem to have occupied lands there improperly. Glabrio wrote to Delphi in 190 BC and his letter was inscribed on the base of his equestrian statue set up there ordering the recovery of land that had been in the hands of Aetolians: 'And if any persons cause opposition about the estate or the fruits from them or the buildings or the possessions, saying that they are theirs, concerning these matters whatever decisions have been made during our presence, let these be legally binding' (Sherk, 1984, no. 12).

After Antiochus had been pushed out of Greece the war moved to Asia. There was no escape for the king since no one could hope to be Rome's equal once it had demonstrated a territorial or any other kind of interest. What is more, Antiochus had caused further offence by giving sanctuary to Hannibal. In 190 BC a Roman army arrived in Asia under L. Cornelius Scipio (with his more famous brother Africanus as an adviser). He won a devastating victory at Magnesia and Antiochus was compelled to evacuate Asia Minor north and west of the Tauros mountains, pay 15,000 talents of silver over twelve years (about 400 metric tons), and his fleet was destroyed except for twelve ships.

During this period the Romans still tried to get on the right side of the Greeks by emphasizing the ideal of freedom of the city states. Furthermore, individual Romans in their dealings with the Greeks tended to harp on certain virtues that might win respect and acceptance. For example, an inscription from the city of Teos contains a letter from the praetor, M. Valerius Messalla, to the city in 193 BC concerning its traditional inviolability:

> Of the Romans. Marcus Valerius, (son) of Marcus, praetor, and the tribunes and the senate to the Council and People of Teos, greetings. . . . That we wholly and constantly have attached the highest importance to reverence of the gods one can estimate from the goodwill we have experienced on this account from the supreme deity. . . . Therefore, because of these things and because of our good-will towards you and the one who made the request, the envoy, we judge your city and its territory to be holy, as it is now, and inviolable and immune from taxation by the people of the Romans, and as for the honours to the god and privileges to you, we will try to help increase them, while you carefully maintain, for the future, your goodwill towards us. Farewell. (Sherk, 1984, no. 8, adapted)

This cleverly combines the god-fearing decency of the Romans and their willingness to preserve Greek prerogatives and privileges with a burden of return, in that they expect Teos to remain loyal to Rome (with just a hint of a threat). They appear to be moderate and to be using their force wisely. This can hardly be an accident but must have been part of a diplomatic initiative. The advantages of supporting Rome were apparent in the case of her principal allies, Pergamum and Rhodes, who had a dominant position in Asia Minor, though only with Rome's approval. Hannibal now sought refuge with king Prusias I of Bithynia, who found his advice useful in his war with Eumenes II of Pergamum. But, under pressure from Flamininus, Prusias prepared to surrender Hannibal, who, with nowhere safe left to hide, committed suicide.

The year 171 BC marked the start of the final war against Macedon and its new king Perseus; his sister was married to Prusias II of Bithynia and Perseus himself married a daughter of Seleucus IV. Eumenes of Pergamum began to worry about a Macedonian resurgence and went to Rome to complain about Perseus, although he had done nothing against Rome directly. But he was cutting quite a figure in

Greece and could be seen as an alternative focus of loyalty to Rome. Polybius thought that he wanted to reinforce Macedonian prestige and dissuade Rome from 'giving harsh and unjust orders to the Macedonians' (27.8.3). The Romans duly became suspicious (the senate now expected Greeks to toe the line), and other wars in Liguria and Spain had quietened down, allowing an opportunity. Perseus briefly got the upper hand with a cavalry victory at Calinicum in 171, but Roman superiority in material and manpower was overwhelming. Perseus's attempts at negotiation were brushed aside and in 168 a new commander, L. Aemilus Paullus, was sent to Macedonia with a consular army. Perseus tried to negotiate but got nowhere and eventually in 168 at Pydna for the last time the Macedonian phalanx faced the Roman legions and suffered a catastrophic defeat, with nearly 20,000 dead. The result was the end of the Macedonian monarchy. Perseus appeared in the triumphal procession of Paullus and died soon afterwards in captivity in Italy. The whole aspect of the Greek world was changed and Rome inevitably had a much greater presence. Macedonia was initially divided up into four regions and by 148 had become Rome's fifth overseas province. For Macedon's erstwhile allies, the Molossians of Epirus, retribution was savage; their land was sacked and 150,000 were deported.

The Romans were not finished with the Seleucid monarchy, which in the early 180s BC was still pursuing its ambitions in Egypt against the Ptolemaic dynasty. In 168 Roman envoys came to Egypt where Antiochus IV was besieging Alexandria and warned him to stop the war and withdraw. When Antiochus asked for time to consider, Popillius Laenas famously drew a circle around the king in the sand and told him to decide before he left the circle. The king accepted the inevitable and withdrew his troops, a vivid illustration of the by now virtually irresistible authority of Rome. The continuing problems of Eumenes of Pergamum are a case in point. After 168 he was certainly less popular in Rome, which began to favour his brother Attalus. The Romans seem to have been trying to limit the power of Pergamum in Asia, and their dominating influence is apparent in a letter written c.159 by Attalus (who had now become king as Attalus II) to the priest of the Great Mother at Pessinus about some kind of cooperative military action. The advice the king had received from his council was that to launch an expedition without consulting Rome would 'hold great danger'. It would always be better to consult Roman officials, since:

To us if successful would accrue envy, a taking away (of success), and hateful suspicion such as they conceived about my brother, and if unsuccessful, ruin in plain sight. . . . But as things are at present, if – may it never happen – we were unsuccessful in anything, after having with their approval done each and everything, we would receive their help and might retrieve a defeat, with the goodwill of the gods. Therefore I decided in each case to send to Rome men who would immediately report (to the Romans) those things about which we are in doubt. (Sherk, 1984, no. 29)

This is an excellent example of attitudes to Roman power. When Prusias II of Bithynia, who was not so wise, attacked Pergamum, he was forced by Roman diplomatic intervention to accept a settlement in 154 and pay reparations. Later Attalus III was to bequeath his kingdom to the Roman people.

In Egypt, the weak and incompetent Ptolemaic dynasty struggled along and, as we have seen, was rescued by the dramatic intervention of Laenas. Though an independent kingdom, it was effectively under the protection of Rome, and when a senior Egyptian official came to Rome to express gratitude the senate proclaimed that they would continue to operate in such a way that the Egyptian monarchs 'would reckon the faith (*fides*) of the Roman people as being the most powerful support for their kingdom' (Livy 45.13.4–8). An example of the thinking of the Ptolemaic ruling hierarchy comes across in the will of Ptolemy VIII Euergetes II, who was joint ruler of Egypt with his elder brother. A serious dispute between the brothers had led to Roman intervention and the division of the kingdom so that the younger brother Ptolemy VIII ruled Cyrenaica. In his will inscribed at Cyrene in 155 BC he planned to leave his part of the kingdom to Rome if he had no heirs: 'And to the same Romans I entrust my possessions for them to protect, appealing to them by all the gods and by their own good reputation that, if any persons attack either my cities or my territory, they may help, in accordance with the friendship and alliance which towards each other we now have and (in accordance with) justice, with all their power' (Sherk, 1984, no. 31). The story here is one of the inescapable power and influence of the Romans in Greece and Asia.

The final eclipse of Macedon demonstrates the limits of any notional Greek independence. In 148 BC the four Macedonian republics rebelled under one Andriscus, who claimed to be a son of Perseus and promised to revive the monarchy. He managed to raise some troops and invade Macedon but was soon crushed and Rome rapidly annexed Macedonia. The Achaean League did not learn from Roman ruthlessness and carelessly came into altercations with Rome after a series of internal disputes over the jurisdiction of the League, particularly involving Sparta, which wished to secede and was an ally of Rome; after an internal war the senate sent Lucius Mummius with two legions to sort matters out. He defeated the League's forces and completely destroyed Corinth in 146, selling the surviving population into slavery and taking a huge quantity of loot. Polybius was appalled by the destruction: 'I was there; I saw paintings trampled underfoot; soldiers sat down on them to play dice!' (Polybius 39.2). Mummius, who sought the advice of Polybius, dissolved the Achaean League and so any semblance of Greek independence was ended, the southern Greek states being put under the supervision of the governor of Macedonia, whose organization as a province Mummius also completed. The name Achaia (or Achaea) was later to emerge as the designation for the province of Greece.

During these wars the Romans were slowly changing their methods for dealing with non-Romans. Whereas previously they had entered into separate agreements with individual communities, now a treaty of alliance was rarely granted and those states that were considered friendly were entered on the 'list of friends' (*formula amicorum*). Roman control became more direct with the appointment of a leading senator to govern each province and the gradual establishment of an army of occupation in certain areas. Many delegations were sent in a two-way process by which the Greeks learnt more about how to do business with Rome while the Romans learnt more about Greek culture and practices. The Romans now mediated Greek inter-community strife, just as the Hellenistic kings had done, and it is striking how they became involved in the detail of community affairs, balancing the demands of city states that considered themselves allies. For example, in the mid-second century BC, envoys from Magnesia and Priene approached the praetor Marcus Aemilius, who granted them an audience with the senate:

> In respect of the matters about which the Magnesian envoys Pythodorus, Heracl[itus. . .], fine and honourable men from a fine and honourable people who are our friends and allies, spoke in person, and in respect of the matters about which the envoys from Priene [. . . .], fine and honourable men from a fine and [honourable] people who are our friends and allies, spoke in person, concerning the land that the Magnesians had evacuated and of which land they had granted possession to the people of Priene in accordance with the decree of the senate, that a special court should be set up for them. The senate decreed as follows in relation to this matter:
>
> The praetor Marcus Aemilius, son of Marcus, is to appoint as arbitrator a free people that is agreeable to both parties. If a mutually acceptable state is not found, the praetor Marcus Aemilius, son of Marcus, shall appoint as arbitrator for this matter such a free people as in his view seems to be in line with the public interest and his own good faith.
>
> It was so decreed. (Sherk, 1984, no. 34)

The senate's view was that the remit for the arbitrator should be to support the cause of the party that held the disputed territory when the litigants had entered into the alliance with Rome. The adjudicators were from Mylasa and they ruled in favour of the Magnesians, who inscribed all the documents 'because with the just judgement of the praetor the gods put an end to the dispute and our people defeated the people of Priene for the second time'. This strikingly assigns the success to the gods but mediated through the Roman praetor. Few people escaped the Romans' scrutiny, even in one case their ally Athens, on the island of Delos. Athens had been given right to administer Delos, but Demetrios, priest of Sarapis on the island, complained to Rome that the cult had been suppressed by the Athenian rulers. The senate decided that the cult should continue as usual: 'About this matter it was as follows decreed: just as formerly he used to administer it, as far as we are concerned he is to be permitted to administer it, so that nothing contrary to the decree of the senate is to be done' (Sherk, 1984, no. 28).

Gradually, however, the Romans adopted a more aggressive and demanding approach; they imposed institutions and practices that suited their interests first and foremost. Rome looked favourably on those people in the Greek states who had demonstrated themselves as reliable supporters, but by contrast life became difficult for others. With striking arrogance, the senate declined to meet any reigning king, and for example sent a junior magistrate to meet Eumenes of Pergamum, who had come to Italy to exculpate himself for his apparent lack of enthusiasm for Rome's interests during the final war against the Macedonians. Those deemed hostile to Rome were rounded up, and one thousand leading citizens of Achaea (including Polybius) were transported to Italy to act as hostages for the good (i.e. pro-Roman) behaviour of the remaining members of their families. It was a short step from arbitrating Greek affairs to interfering at will.

Spain and Africa

Events in the west proved troublesome and the Romans did not have things all their own way as they pursued an increasingly interventionist policy. In Spain, after the expulsion of the Carthaginians they did not necessarily have plans for permanent occupation, but gradually came to accept that troops would remain there. Two provinces were established, Nearer and Hither Spain, and seemingly random and inconclusive campaigns followed as Spain became a venue for a search for booty and military renown. The Spanish peoples refused to recognize Roman control while the Romans obdurately made war. The struggle came to centre on the town of Numantia in the upper valley of the river Durius (Douro), which was the focal point of the resistance of the Celtiberians and came under siege frequently from 195 BC onwards. In fifteen years of warfare various Roman commanders failed to capture the town. The peace agreement negotiated in 179–178 by Ti. Sempronius Gracchus was not conclusive and by the mid-150s serious war had been resumed, which culminated in 137 when Hostilius Mancinus was defeated and trapped with his army. Tiberius Gracchus (son of the commander in 179) negotiated a compromise deal, but the senate rejected this and handed over Mancinus to the Numantines. Rome's military capability was faltering in this long campaign, but war was resumed and Numantia eventually capitulated in 133, though only after an eight-month siege by P. Cornelius Scipio Aemilianus Africanus, an event that exemplified Roman determination to brook no opposition despite the casualties and political consequences. The city was destroyed and the survivors sold into slavery. A commission was sent out to establish peace and order for the places that had been subdued. Previously, Sempronius Gracchus had apparently negotiated treaties with local peoples and a form of taxation had been established. Furthermore, from 206 with the foundation of Italica by Scipio for his wounded soldiers, settlements of Romans had been set up, including Corduba (Córdoba) and Valentia (Valencia), consolidating a permanent Roman presence. Nevertheless, the Spanish were less receptive to diplomacy than the Greeks, and a legacy of military power and brutality remained.

The Third Punic War in 149–146 BC also revealed a tendency to aggression and brutality. Carthage had been quietly rebuilding its position in Africa but in 149 revolted against persistent Roman arbitration in favour of Rome's old ally Masinissa in border disputes with the Carthaginians. Already M. Porcius Cato, who had visited Carthage on an embassy in 153 and was impressed by the revival in the city's fortunes, had been keeping up alarmist rhetoric in Rome warning against increasing Carthaginian militarism with his stock phrase: 'Carthage must be destroyed.' War was declared and the Romans sent a large expedition, at which point Carthage tried to back down, offering unconditional surrender and the handing over of hostages and all weapons. But they furiously rejected a provocative demand to abandon the city and resettle at least ten miles from the coast. The Romans were not interested in a negotiated settlement, but there followed a story of military failure and incompetence until P. Cornelius Scipio Aemilianus, the future victor of Numantia, blockaded the city and harbour with a rampart and stormed it in 146. The population was sold into slavery, the city wiped out and its site declared *sacer*, or pledged to the gods for extirpation. Carthage's territory became another Roman province, Africa, with Utica as its capital.

Rome in Control

During his account of the Second Punic War, Polybius offers a digression on the Roman army (6.19.1), which probably describes the military set-up after the defeat of Hannibal. From the early Republic, ability to serve in the army had depended on having sufficient property, meaning that service was not only a duty and responsibility as a citizen, but also a kind of privilege. The levy (*legio* = legion) of Roman citizens consisted of 4,200–5,000 men, and recruits were normally selected from those aged 17–46 who were then expected to be available for up to sixteen seasons of service; legionaries received a daily allowance during service. Those eligible were required to present themselves in Rome and the best were selected (the *dilectus*). Originally, the legion fought as a phalanx in the Greek style with heavily armed infantry moving in formation. Before the Punic wars this had been modified and each legion was deployed in three lines – the *hastati*, *principes* and *triarii*, with the most experienced troops in the third line. Each battle line was subdivided into smaller units or maniples, producing a flexible but strong structure. The legionaries were equipped with oval shields, body armour, and the first two lines had a throwing spear (*pilum*), while the last had a thrusting spear (*hasta*). All troops also carried the short Spanish sword (*gladius*). Troops supplied by the Italian allies fought under their own commanders, and it was the Italians who usually provided cavalry. Light-armed troops (*velites*) advanced in front of the legions to skirmish.

Polybius clearly admired the Roman military structure, which carried into action a developing imperialist instinct in the Roman government that also connects with the social and cultural context and Roman ideology. There is no doubt that the Romans were notorious for making war. Polybius said of them that: 'They rely on force in all their undertakings, and consider that having set themselves a task they are bound to carry it through, and that nothing is impossible once they have decided on it' (1.37.7). Doubtless his study of the history of Rome and the sheer scale of military activity seemed to bear this out, involving a long story of conquest and aggrandizement apparently unrelieved by reflection or compassion. Polybius was indeed perplexed by the extent of Roman success:

> For who is there so worthless or lazy that he would not wish to know how and under what kind of government the Romans have brought under their sole rule almost the whole of the inhabited world in less than fifty-three years; for nothing like this has ever happened before. Or who can be so devoted to any other subject of study that he would regard it as more important than the acquisition of this knowledge? (1.1.5–6)

An important factor must be the Roman ideology of warfare, in particular the significance of military prowess. Traditionally, the Roman upper classes had a tremendous respect for the glory (*gloria*) that came from success in battle, since this brought praise (*laus*) and established renown based on valour (*virtus*). Therefore, one important route to social and political advancement lay in acquiring military commands, winning battles and obtaining wealth and booty; the supreme military honour of the triumph was the zenith of senatorial accomplishment. Roman politics were highly competitive and in the struggle for advancement those taking major decisions might well be loath to see an end to wars. In other words, the prevailing social ethos could influence the senate, under pressure from prominent individuals or groups, to allow disputes to grow into war, or even to provoke war. Of course the Roman people had the final say in voting for war, but without leadership they would find it very hard to resist senatorial advice and pressure.

The prospect of new lands and booty was doubtless attractive to all; enrichment from military campaigns benefited commanders, especially the less scrupulous, but also individual soldiers, who got a proportion of the spoils; successful wars could bring generous benefits to the plebs. Consequently, the *concilium plebis*, where some of the voters would have to do the fighting, might go along with senatorial opinion. Few Romans would have questioned the concept of ruling others; in a sense it was their duty, and subject peoples would benefit from Roman control and benevolence, and the peace and order that Rome brought, unless they were irredeemably savage, in which case they deserved retribution. It was accepted at all levels that the Roman state should profit from its acquisitions, and of course distinguished military leaders convinced the people of the benefits of conquest and produced a kind of momentum for military action. Furthermore, there was also the availability of a large reserve of manpower and an army that was coming closer to being a permanent force.

On the other hand, although the expansion of Roman territorial control was a legitimate war aim among the upper classes, in the context of intense political rivalry it will also have been true that some senators, having achieved military excellence, might jealously attempt to restrict the opportunities of others to command armies by refusing to vote for expansive military campaigns. Furthermore, senators had to consider that the emergence of the quasi-professional army had encouraged a style of dashing personal leadership, and that special commands, though profitable to the state, might also be politically dangerous.

Given that decisions on war and peace had complex motivations, it is very difficult to believe that the Romans were concerned with precise definitions (whether imperialist or not) that would fit their activities with foreign peoples. Although they were capable of carefully modulated policy and at times considerable restraint, as in their dealings with the Greek states, they clearly set no limits to what could be achieved by force of arms, even if their realization of this was inconsistent. Although it is unlikely that sophisticated economic motives other than the windfalls associated with the aftermath of conquest influenced the Roman government in its acquisition of new territory, Rome probably did begin to recognize the economic benefits of occupation in that businessmen and traders followed military conquest. For example, the island of Delos was made a free port with no harbour dues, many Italians settled there, and it became a centre of trade connecting Italy and the west with the Greek east.

With hindsight Roman expansion looks inevitable, but that is misleading and the reality is more complex. There was no coherent plan for conquest of the Mediterranean section by section. Early Roman advances east of the Adriatic were very hesitant and exploited immediate benefits without a long-term plan of occupation. Annexations of territory and the creation of provinces were inconsistent. In fact, in Spain and Africa and in Greece the Romans were slow to occupy large areas of land. However, by 150 BC the momentum of conquest was such that no opposition was tolerated by Rome to her policy, arbitration or decisions, even though enforcing them was becoming more difficult and expensive. As enthusiastic commanders looked for an area in which to display their prowess, the confident ruling oligarchy was less responsive to local conditions and the niceties of diplomatic contact. Furthermore, the Romans also had good luck in that many of the Hellenistic kingdoms proved to be paper tigers. They inherited the kingdom of Pergamum, and Egypt almost fell into their hands. Despite making grandiose threats, the Seleucids and Macedonian kings could not resist Roman military skill, manpower resources, financial strength and political determination. The way was open for further conquest.

CHAPTER THREE

The Transformation of Rome

The Political Scene

'The power that each part (of the political system) has in blocking the others or co-operating with them is such that their working together is sufficient to meet all emergencies, with the result that it is impossible to discover a better form of constitution than this' (6.18). In this famous summary of the working of Roman government Polybius noted elements of monarchy, aristocracy and democracy, and in his view the result was a successful union. Certainly in the early third century BC there was a period of comparative stability when the upper classes worked largely in harmony and the mass of ordinary plebeians went along with their leadership. After all, they were citizens of a state that had become wealthy and most of Italy up to the Po was under their control.

The two chief magistrates (consuls), who had effectively replaced the king as head of state, were enormously powerful. Livy commented:

> We should consider that the origins of freedom lay more in the fact that the power of the consul was made annual than that there was any reduction in the royal power. The first to hold the position of consul had all the royal rights and symbols. The only safeguard taken was to prevent both from holding the *fasces* simultaneously, so that the terror they brought should not be doubled. (2.1.7–8)

Polybius too had no doubts about the power of the consuls: 'They exercise supreme authority in Rome over all public affairs. All other magistrates with the exception of the tribunes are subordinate to them and are bound to obey them, and it is the consuls who introduce embassies to the senate' (6.12). The consul-ship was at the pinnacle of achievement dreamed of by patricians and well-off plebeians, with a role in politics, military command and state ceremonial that kept men in the public eye. Up to 153 BC they began their year of office on 15 March, thereafter on 1 January. At least to the end of the second century the consul was expected to conduct military campaigns where necessary during his year in office, and might be in Rome only at the beginning and end of the political year. Despite the aura of power surrounding the consuls, they had only limited time to make a name for themselves, and an ambitious man might find it difficult to get round the opposition of his colleague.

The senate as a powerful body of ex-magistrates offered guidance to the consuls and other magistrates. In Rome anyone in a position of authority or responsibility would informally ask senior figures whom he trusted for advice. At one level, the head of a family consulted a gathering of family members, while a magistrate outside Rome consulted his officers and friends (*amici*) who had accompanied him. When magistrates were elected by the people they had a free hand to operate as they thought best, and if they needed advice or help they inevitably turned to the senate; when magistrates consulted the senate they initiated a free debate, which often led to an expression of the majority view in a decree (*senatus consultum*). Consuls and others would find it difficult to ignore the concerted opinion of senators, given the accumulated prestige, status and unrivalled experience of the body. Effectively therefore the senate was able to influence much of the state's business, resolve disputes between magistrates and adjudicate their role and responsibilities; as a result, it came to control the assignment of military command, financial matters, the management of Rome's relations with Italian communities and foreign states, and also proposals for legislation. Consequently, the fact that the senate could not legislate was not necessarily a great restriction on its power. So it was much more than a passive *concilium*, and its decisions often established norms over a long period.

Legislation was the responsibility of other assemblies, which in a sense gave representation to all male Roman citizens. However, the sovereignty of the Roman people was severely limited. The *comitia centuriata* consisted of all citizens divided into five groups according to wealth and then subdivided into 170 'centuries', with an additional twenty-three centuries including eighteen of *equites* (cavalry). It was probably at the end of the fifth century BC, when pay was introduced for the legions and a tax (*tributum*) imposed on Roman citizens, that the system traditionally ascribed to Servius Tullius was altered. The highest census groups, which had fewest citizens, made up the largest number of centuries; for example, the first group, comprising the wealthiest citizens (with property valued at 100,000 *asses*; an *as* = one pound of bronze), made up eighty centuries. Each group was further subdivided according to age into equal numbers of centuries of *seniores* (46–60) and *iuniores* (17–45); since younger citizens will have been more numerous, it must be that there were fewer people in the centuries of the *seniores*. Therefore, in political terms the *comitia centuriata* was slanted in favour of the well-off and the older, presumably more conservative elements, since it did not vote by a simple head count but by centuries, of which the wealthy had dispropor- tionately large numbers. The proletarians (*proletarii*), who fell outside the minimum property qualification, were put into a single century. This assembly elected magistrates (especially consuls and praetors) and could also pass laws, declare war and make peace.

In the *comitia plebis tributa* (or *concilium plebis*) consisting of plebeians only, and the *comitia populi tributa* consisting of the whole people (see chapter 1), the voting units were the territorial tribes (eventually thirty-five), but the represen- tation was unfair since the poor living in the countryside would have found it difficult to walk to Rome to vote, meaning that voting in the rural tribes was likely to be dominated by the better-off. The large urban population of Rome was contained within four tribes; nevertheless these tribes probably had a dispro- portionate impact on voting since they could be influenced or intimidated by the great noble families. Both these assemblies could elect magistrates only from the candidates presented to them, and had no control over proposals for legislation; they could merely accept or reject and not amend. Those who wanted to speak had to be invited by the presiding magistrate (who would often be aristocratic). Nevertheless, the *concilium plebis* in particular was the focus for political agita- tion, especially in the election of tribunes of the plebs and the passing of laws (*plebiscita*), which, after the *Lex Hortensia* in 287 BC, were binding on the whole people.

As Rome grew more ambitious and acquired more responsibilities, govern- ment required more magistrates. The praetor held *imperium* (power to give orders and demand obedience), and in the absence of the consuls he was the senior magistrate in Rome and came to have a significant role in hearing legal cases; probably after 244 BC a second praetorship was established. Two quaestors (usually at age 27–30) served as financial officials of the consuls, but more were created to administer the state treasury and for other functions; by the late Republic there were twenty. An ex-quaestor normally expected to be enrolled in the senate. The aediles, who began as virtual secretaries to the tribunes of the plebs, came to supervise the buildings and amenities of the city of Rome, including the water supply and market. The ten tribunes of the plebs elected annually by the *concilium plebis*, as well as protecting the life and possessions of plebeians against the exercise of a magistrate's power (*ius auxilii*), were sacro- sanct (protected from attack by religious sanction), could summon meetings of the *concilium plebis* and propose resolutions. Most importantly, they had the right of veto against any action of another magistrate in relation to state business.

Therefore, potentially they were powerful protectors of popular rights and the sovereignty of the people, as Polybius emphasized: 'They are bound to do what the people decide and pay particular attention to their wishes' (6.16.5). Polybius thought that this was one factor in persuading the senate to have regard for the will of the people. Indeed, the office of tribune was to become crucial and potentially disruptive in the late Republic as political consensus declined. Sometimes sons of senators held the position of *tribunus militum* (six in each legion) normally occupied by men of equestrian rank, as a start to their service of the state. The principal non-military position of a senator who had held the consulship was the censorship, established in 443; two were elected every four or five years to serve for eighteen months and had enormous prestige, since they were empowered to conduct a census of the Roman population and scrutinize the suitability of members of the senate; they also organized lucrative public contracts.

As the Romans established a permanent presence in lands outside Italy, they decided that a senior magistrate at the end of his year of office could have his *imperium* prorogued (normally for one year, though often for longer), which enabled him to take a military command or govern Rome's subject areas. The magistrate then exercised *imperium* in a *provincia* (his sphere of operations), a word that later came to describe a territorial area, or province, and he had the title of proconsul or propraetor depending on his status, since ex-praetors were also employed in this way.

The influence of the upper classes in government and society and religious organization remained all-pervasive. This was accentuated by the practice of *clientela*, by which individuals deemed of inferior status (clients) were personally dependent on a more socially distinguished person (patron), offering him political support by voting for him or attending him in public at political gatherings or even by abusing his opponents; in return the great man offered benefits in kind, such as loans, or protection, for example by using his influence in law courts. In this way the aristocratic houses could keep the plebs in Rome obedient to their wishes and manipulate political office, since a prominent man could extend his influence among other senators by manoeuvring his clients in support of his friends. The *clientela* obligation could extend to *equites*, who originally served as cavalry and subsequently formed a rich and well-connected group outside the senate, and others who were reasonably well-off, which was acceptable as long as there was a consensus on the proper government of the state. However, if this broke down resentment was never far beneath the surface.

To sum up, the Roman people were technically sovereign and their approval was needed for legislation and for declaring war (this was useful for the upper classes in order to drum up popular support for military campaigns since the people had to fight in them). The senators expected to decide who would command the legions, though that might be frustrated by popular vote. Although the constitution was not truly democratic, those who chose to emphasize the popular element for personal ends or who wanted the people's vote might at least be expected to offer some benefit in return. Polybius also shrewdly observed that the possibility of using one institution of the state to frustrate another would lead to compromises.

The Breakdown of Consensus

The government of the Roman Republic worked through cooperation between consuls, other magistrates, senate and assemblies. Within the senate, age, merit, reputation and standing (*dignitas*) allowed a few men to have a particularly influential voice, but most would have agreed on the importance of the status quo and the right of free competition for office and honour between men of settled respectability. And of course the great senatorial families never presented a static picture since some died out while others were admitted to the senate and gained distinction by holding office. At the start of the third century BC there were few rules for office-holding, though some military service was expected before the consulship. The elite needed to ensure that there were enough benefits of office to go round, and the senate had long struggled to protect its position against men who became overly powerful or influential by holding repeated consulships, and felt able to ignore senatorial opinion. In 342 a ten-year interval between tenures of magistracies had been required, and around 197 it was decided that all candidates for the consulship must have previously held the praetorship. The *Lex Villia annalis* of 180 laid down minimum age limits for holding office (forty-two for the consulship). The ruling group tried to regulate access to the rewards of political and military success and promote a clear-cut framework of office-holding (*cursus honorum*). Indeed the checks and balances that Polybius had noted in the Roman constitution could be used to block innovative measures, and many among the elite had an underlying and not entirely cynical concern for traditional practices.

Nevertheless, there were increasing signs of the breakdown in the natural authority of the senate and the established political norms. For example, T. Quinctius Flamininus was elected consul in 198 BC, although he seems to have held only junior offices previously; but he exploited the favour he had won in 201 by organizing a distribution of land for the veteran soldiers from Scipio Africanus's campaigns. Then in 152 M. Claudius Marcellus, who had held a second consulship in 155, was elected to a third in defiance of the law requiring a ten-year interval. This prompted a law to prevent a second tenure of the consulship. P. Scipio Aemilianus was elected consul for 147, though he was five or six years younger than the minimum age and had not even held the praetorship; his election was against the will of the senate, but in the face of strong popular support the tribunes passed a bill temporarily suspending the relevant legislation. The plebs voted him the command in the Third Punic War against Carthage; Scipio was subsequently elected consul for 134 despite the recent law prohibiting second tenures; and another popular vote gave him the command in the stubborn war against Numantia in Spain. Of course he had aristocratic backers, but a hostile senate refused him funds and permission to hold a levy of recruits.

Respect for the integrity of the office of tribune of the plebs and the veto was essential, not least because a tribune could bring public business to a halt. But gradually this too was eroded. In 143 BC Appius Claudius Pulcher celebrated a triumph without senatorial approval, and when a tribune tried to interpose his veto Claudius took his daughter, a Vestal Virgin, with him in the triumphal chariot and prevented its enforcement, since out of respect for the Vestal no one would dare to intervene. Three years later, when a tribune tried to use his veto to prevent Caepio, consul in 140, from taking up his command in Spain, Caepio threatened to use force. A climate was being created in which lack of respect for established institutions and practices was tolerated as senators manoeuvred increasingly unscrupulously for political power. Therefore, there were disturbing signs that men of the upper classes could build up personal political standing and a revolutionary career on the twin pillars of the support of the people and the senator's traditional prerogative to command an army. Lurking behind this was the threat of violence. The role of the people was unpredictable; they might expect that those who courted their support would carry out their promises and deal with their discontent, and violently turn against those who betrayed them.

Optimates and Populares

In the Roman Republic political parties did not exist in the modern sense with fixed membership, clearly articulated policies and organized majority voting in assemblies. Instead, much depended on individuals in the aristocracy to give a lead by gathering around them all those who were of a similar view or whom they could persuade or cajole to support them. This produced groups loosely based on friendship or community of interest as well as the support of clients. In this way political groupings emerged, but they were fluid and unstable in that supporters could come and go and members of the group might not agree on every issue. In the second century BC as competition became more intense and personal ambition eclipsed concern for the state, two political groups emerged: the *optimates* and *populares*.

The *optimates*, the self-styled people of quality, made up of aristocrats and other wealthy men with property to protect, aimed fundamentally to preserve the status quo as the best way to guarantee their own standing and influence and access to the riches generated by conquest. They pursued the traditional operation of the political structures and the unimpeded right to compete with their peers. Although they tended to oppose the excessive influence of the people, they sometimes sought popular support in a cynical or manipulative way, and got compliant tribunes to use their veto. They also tried to block special military commands that seemed likely to offer outstanding influence to one individual.

The *populares* were generally of the same social rank as the *optimates* and also sought political advancement for themselves, but were prepared to overturn traditional political practices and alliances, particularly by seeking popular support and implementing measures that benefited the people, such as land distribution to the poorer citizens, colonial foundations, subsidized corn and mitigation of debts. Such measures could often be introduced by tribunes of the plebs and passed in the *concilium plebis* despite the opposition of the senate. The tribunes might promote the interests of a leading senator by supporting his candidacy for a military command, hoping for reciprocal benefits from his success. There was absolutely no coherent policy here and many who used *popularis* methods had selfish motives of self-aggrandizement, while some genuinely believed in the need for reform. Both political groups used the courts in a bid to ruin an opponent's reputation by prosecution, and neither was averse to exploiting the state religion to block unwelcome developments. But both groups operated inconsistently and with differing levels of intensity. The contention between *optimates* and *populares*, while often about personal advancement, did reflect a serious underlying political question: how far did popular sovereignty extend and in what sense and how far were the tribunes the people's genuine representatives? Cicero in his political speech on behalf of Sestius summed up the contending groups:

> Politicians in Rome who are eager to get to the top have always fallen into two broadly defined categories, the *populares* and the *optimates*, the men of the people and the men of quality, and their choice of name is a good guide to their policies. Those who wish to commend themselves to the masses both in word and deed are described as *populares*, those who seek to commend their policies to all the best elements in our society as *optimates*. (*For Sestius* 96)

Cicero, who of course was strongly on the side of the *optimates*, goes on to define the best elements as leaders of opinion in the senate and those who followed their guide, including *equites*, the rural population of Italy and their leaders and even freedmen. Their objective was peace and order and honour for those who deserved it.

Economic Life

The Twelve Tables suggest a largely agricultural way of life in Rome (as in most other Italic societies) in the fifth century BC. Agriculture was to remain the essential basis of Roman economic activity, generally through smallholders working their land, and arable farming and viticulture were more common than stock-raising. The basis of the wealth of the better-off was also land, and this emphasis on agriculture as an indicator of wealth remained the case throughout most of Roman history. Although a monetary system was in operation, transactions were in bronze, measured by weight. Coins were probably not issued until about 300 BC, but as Professor Michael Crawford has pointed out, the most important stage in the development of money is the designation by the state of a fixed metallic unit, and this happened early in Rome. It is possible that Servius Tullius set the *as* (pound of bronze) as the accepted unit. Outside agriculture, trade was initially limited to essential items or a few luxury goods for the well-off, and the men who traded were not held in great respect, though in time many acquired wealth by this route. Manufacture was on a small scale, conducted usually by individuals or small groups making items for everyday use like bricks, tiles and pots, or working in leather or clothing.

Economic development was constrained by a lack of large-scale borrowing facilities, and the profitability of large estates, which were often devoted largely to cereal crops, was limited. Slaves were a feature in this society and there were perhaps as many as two million in Italy by the end of the Republic. Roman warfare outside Italy in the second and first centuries BC made the largest contribution to the supply of slaves, though banditry and piracy were also important sources, and the marketing of slaves was facilitated by the entrepreneurial activities of slave traders. Numbers were swelled by children born from unions of slaves, which were sometimes encouraged by slave-owners. Slaves were increasingly used to work the land of the wealthy in large estates (*latifundia*), though the impact of this on restricting development of new farming methods (because slave-owners did not need to invent labour-saving devices) has probably been exaggerated.

The problem of land transport was a more serious constraint. Main roads were relatively few and were initially for military use, and even along a paved route movement by cart was slow and the carrying power of animals limited. Based on a calculation for moving wheat, the cost of land transport by wagon would be between 36.7 and 73.4 per cent of the value of the wheat for every one hundred Roman miles. The effort involved will have made it expensive. Particularly heavy loads could most effectively be carried on wagons pulled by oxen, but in hilly environments they might travel only five to six miles a day. The carrying power of pack animals was limited, though donkeys, which were sure-footed and relatively inexpensive to maintain, could carry up to 150 kilograms.

On the other hand, transport by ship in the Mediterranean was much cheaper but required considerable initial investment. At sea, merchant ships under sail might average two knots with a following wind on the trip from Rome to Alexandria. A smaller, fast sailing ship could manage four and a half to five knots. A small merchantman had about 150 tonnes of cargo capacity; many could carry about 400–500 tonnes and a few over 1,000 tonnes. Moving goods by navigable rivers was important, though often on a small scale; on inland waterways it is very difficult to calculate the speed achieved by ships sailing or being rowed or towed upstream. Perhaps a riverboat of an average size of six tonnes might average nine to ten kilometres upstream every day, while two men on a tow rope could pull 80–100 tonnes fourteen kilometres in a day. On a reasonable calculation the cost ratios for various modes of transport are roughly: sea – 1; inland waterway – 4.9; road – 28–56. Within Italy the Tiber was very important, especially as a route for goods being imported via Ostia or Puteoli to Rome. In northern Italy the Po (Padus) and its tributaries stand out as routes of communication both along the navigable rivers and through their valleys. They were valuable within the self-contained area of Cisalpine Gaul, though the estuary of the Po was far distant from Rome, making the onward movement of goods expensive.

The wealth and status of Rome had been sustained and enhanced by her conquests and the taking-over of fertile land from defeated peoples and the foundation of colonies. With more land for Romans there came other developments in farming. Although cereal production in Italy continued to be important and was necessary for subsistence, more cash crops like olives and vines were planted, though these tended to benefit the rich since they take years to produce fruit. Stockbreeding became more important, and as the Romans came to control more and more land in southern Italy transhumance was more profitable. This practice involved moving animals to graze in high pastures in the summer and moving them back to lowland pasture in the winter; the wider the area controlled, the more effectively this worked. Ownership of land remained as the main measure of wealth, and while many rich men acquired large estates, some owned a number of smaller properties in different areas of Italy. Arguably it was good insurance against bad weather and crop failure in one location. The importance of landed wealth was symbolically confirmed by a law of 218 BC restricting the size of seagoing ships that a senator might own; this was obviously something that a gentleman should not publicly do (senators could of course hire others to operate ships on their behalf).

Poorer people of necessity worked small areas of land. The traditional distribution to colonists often amounted to no more than ten *iugera* (1 *iugerum* = 0.252

hectares), and a family will have found it difficult to make ends meet. However, poor farmers hoped to exploit public land and pasture their animals there, and looked for occasional seasonal work at harvest time on the great estates. In that respect they will not have been in direct competition with slaves since it was not economical to buy slaves for short-term work.

Those involved in manufacturing now had more opportunities; there was a healthy market for everyday objects since the rich kept large, ostentatious establishments to demonstrate their place in society, which required keeping up by the acquisition of pots, household implements, clothes and shoes; luxury items could be imported but were made very expensive by the cost of transport. The manufacture of weapons was obviously a business in constant demand as annual warfare continued. In the First Punic War the Romans discovered that they needed to fight at sea and so men had to be found to build and maintain the ships. The growing city of Rome reflected the presence of its manufacturers in the names of quarters or streets, preserved in the later city – for example, the street of the scythe-makers, potters, silversmiths, sandal-makers, even makers of perfume. Although much work was done by slaves and freedmen, short-term work for the freeborn was available for labourers loading and unloading ships in the docks. The first and earliest port was the *Portus Tiberinus* near the Pons Aemilius, south of Tiber Island, exploiting the loop in the river. Later, as this proved increasingly inadequate, the main port facility developed in the late third and early second centuries BC south of the Sublician bridge and consisted of a large roofed construction for the checking and storage of goods; these were unloaded at stone wharves, which were built *c*.174 BC and extended over one kilometre.

The government of the Republic did not obtain enormous revenues from taxation; there was a levy of 0.1 per cent on those whose wealth qualified them for military service (*assidui*) until the levy was abolished in 167 BC, though extra levies were imposed in times of crisis such as the war with Hannibal. Customs taxes and a charge on sales by auction were also collected; rents on public land could provide some revenue, but as Rome's overseas empire grew the main source of wealth was the tax imposed on subject peoples. By the early first century BC this can be calculated roughly at 50 million *denarii* a year. New business opportunities were offered and tax-farming companies (*societates*) grew up; the shareholders (usually *equites*) bid for a contract to collect the taxes in a province; this meant that the government got an assured sum of money immediately and did not have to deploy its own officials; the company then had to collect this sum plus whatever profit it could manage.

Booty from successful military campaigns will have boosted the state's resources, though much of it went straight into the pockets of the ordinary soldiers, and a much greater proportion to their generals. On the other hand, the state's expenditure was rising all the time, particularly the need to fund overseas warfare, supply the army and pay the soldiers. Rome was becoming a major urban centre and that required suitably elaborate public buildings and a sound infrastructure, in which an ample water supply was crucial. As early as the fourth century BC the ambition and engineering skill of the precocious government appear in the construction of the *aqua Appia* in 312 to bring water into the city, mainly by underground tunnels. In 272 the *aqua Anio Vetus* tapped into the river Anio and brought fresh water to Rome over a long distance. The *aqua Marcia* in 144 was the first aqueduct in Rome to carry the water in a channel (90 centimetres wide by 2.4 metres high) supported on arches; it was approximately 91 kilometres long and was enormously expensive to construct (about 45 million *denarii*). The population also expected the proper celebration of games and festivals, and the poorer element came to expect various handouts including corn, which became an object of political argument in the first century.

The developing economic sophistication of Rome contributed to a more elaborate system of coinage. Military victories in Italy had brought in supplies of precious metals – gold, silver and bronze – and the opportunity for minting coins. The Greek cities in southern Italy had a developed system, so the Romans did not have far to go to find an example. The earliest known Roman coin was minted in 326 BC with the legend 'of the Romans'. By the 270s a regular coinage had appeared bearing the name 'Roma', and around 211 Rome was minting bronze coins (the *as*, weighing about two ounces) and silver coins (the *denarius*, which was worth ten *asses* and approximated to one Greek drachma). Minting was limited until 157 when a much larger issue of silver coinage appeared, derived from booty and the produce of the silver mines in Macedonia. Roman coins, which had become the accepted medium of exchange in Italy, now spread to Rome's overseas possessions. There coins no longer carried the name of Rome since it was now obvious which state minted them. Large numbers of them would be required as a convenient way of funding large capital projects like aqueducts, paying the army and collecting taxes. The actual production of coins was organized by young men of the upper classes who were starting to make their way in political life, and they chose types that made a statement about the status of their families. In time the coinage came to convey a message throughout Rome's empire from those in power.

Soldiers and Farmers

The census figures (including all adult male citizens) compiled by the Roman state are preserved from the third to the second century BC, and although they are doubtless inaccurate and reflect under-registration by the very poor who did not pay tax, nevertheless they show us how the state was developing. In 233 BC there were registered 270,713 citizens; from 189 BC when 258,318 were registered there is an uneven rise until 164 BC (337,452), and then some decline to 136 BC (317,933). It is possible that in this context of a general increase in population, the group of the *assidui*, that is, the citizens who had sufficient property qualification to serve in the legions, was declining significantly. Some support for this occurs in the gradual reduction in that qualification (from 11,000 *asses* originally to 1,500 before 141 BC). Furthermore, in this period the proportion of Italians serving with Roman armies increased, and in the second century they equalled the number of Romans in service. More compelling evidence is found in the persistent disturbances that accompanied the levy, as recruits were reluctant to serve, or to continue serving, or to be called up again. Commanders naturally preferred experienced troops. In some cases the consuls conducting the levy were consigned to prison by tribunes protecting the interests of protesting recruits. Part of this may be due to the particular problems of the long and unrewarding campaigns in Spain.

The process of recruitment is linked to economic developments in Italy and the exploitation of the profits of empire by the elite. Poorer farmers were losing their plots of land necessary to support the qualification for military service and to sustain family life. The rich sought to increase the size of their estates, which they achieved by absorbing the land of poorer farmers and also by occupying areas of public land (*ager publicus*), which was an essential resource for the poor. Long-distance transhumance between winter and summer pastures required extensive pasture land for larger flocks. Doubtless some small farmers willingly sold up in the hope of finding wealth in Rome or Italian towns, or rich pickings in the developing empire in the east. However, scholars have long argued that military service contributed to the decline of small farmers in Italy and that this led to a shortage of recruits with the necessary wealth qualification. This process had become so severe by the later part of the second century BC that it influenced Tiberius Gracchus in his determination to reform the system (see chapter 4). When a man served in the army for long periods without returning home it was easier for greedy, powerful neighbours to get hold of his land. An absent soldier's wife and the rest of the family might be unequal to the struggle to maintain the property and so be prepared to sell up. Once forced off the land, the dispossessed had few opportunities. Previously they could have escaped to a colony; the provision of colonies and individual land grants for settlers had been substantial from the early second century, but tailed off as there was less strategic need for them in Italy. The senate was not disposed to help, as we can see from the furious opposition to a law proposed by the tribune C. Flaminius in 232 to distribute some public land in individual allotments; this of course would have brought him enthusiastic popular support. The idea was resurrected nearly one hundred years later when C. Laelius (consul in 140) proposed the distribution of land to the poor so that they had sufficient property to be registered for service in the army (Plutarch, *Tiberius Gracchus* 8). Prudently, he withdrew in the face of strong senatorial opposition. From now on support for new colonies became part of a way of rousing popular support by the *populares*.

Plutarch and Appian certainly indicate that the number of smallholders was declining and that there were serious military consequences. Appian sums up the situation: 'Therefore, powerful men became very rich and slavery multiplied all over the country while the Italians faced decline and shortage of manpower since they were worn down by poverty, taxes and military service' (*Civil Wars* 1.7). But both Appian and Plutarch were Greek, writing in the second century AD long after the event, and through the sources they used were subject to the kind of political propaganda that emerged among the contending factions after the traumatic tribunates of the Gracchi. However, Plutarch does report a speech made by Tiberius Gracchus (*Tiberius Gracchus* 9.5), who said that men who fought for Rome wandered homeless with their wives and children. Although he may be exaggerating, Gracchus certainly believed that service in the army had reduced men to this pass: 'These (Romans) fight and die for the luxury and wealth of others; they are said to be the masters of the world but they have not one clod of earth to call their own.'

It is, however, doubtful to what extent year-round military service and subsistence agriculture were in conflict in the mid-Republic. First, in maintaining the farm and producing enough food for the family, typical subsistence farmers may have been able to spare the labour of one son or even two sons (for military service). Second, the age of marriage for men in Rome (supposed normally to be around thirty) was well beyond the age of eligibility for the draft (seventeen), and so perhaps the conscription of breadwinners with young children would have been rare. Third, most conscripts were probably unmarried young men not required to labour on the family farm and not yet expected to support a family of their own. By contrast, older soldiers, who were more likely to be married, served in the third rank (*triarii*), in the legions, and being generally held in reserve had a lower death rate. So, even if there was a very high mortality rate in the mid-republican army (and one calculation puts it at about 40 per cent), those being killed off were not the fathers producing children, and to some extent family structures could remain intact, and there may not have been an unsustainable drain on smallholders.

It would of course be foolish to deny that tough annual campaigns had a serious impact on the rural peasantry and that the unscrupulous rich could not find ways of edging out poor farmers whose lives had been disrupted and their wealth diminished by military service. But the point is that the agrarian crisis that provoked Tiberius Gracchus to take action in 133 BC had complex origins. The census figures do show an increasing population, and if the bulk of this increase was among the class of rural smallholders, this will have put more pressure on available land; the practice of subdividing inheritance between all eligible children will have made the situation worse. Too many people were attempting to start out in life with too little land; smallholders were unable to maintain an economically successful development. Throughout this period access to land, and the prevalence of debt, remained the main concerns of the lower classes.

The Transformation of Rome

Rome had been a parochial city state but was changing rapidly into an outward-looking power closely connected to the Mediterranean world. This process was helped by a ruling elite that was innovative and willing to adapt. Years of steady military advance by the legions brought changes in the traditional Roman way of life through an influx of astonishing wealth, booty and artefacts; there were also huge war indemnities like that paid by the defeated Carthage. The rewards of office-holding and military command were now greater and provided a strong incentive to stand for election. But with success came significant problems. Some senators became so successful and charismatic that they garnered unstoppable popular support, overshadowing the oligarchy and the common good. Many became excessively rich and demonstrated this by embarrassingly ostentatious display. For example, L. Aemilius Paullus, who defeated the Macedonians in 168 BC, had an estate worth 360,000 *denarii*, but was not considered exceptionally rich. Peculation of state funds was rife and bribery became the solution to many political problems. Within the upper classes a series of laws against private expenditure tried to curb display and protected those who would not or could not keep up with the extravagance of the super-rich. For example, laws limited the number of guests at dinner parties and regulated the kind of food that could be served as well as the amount that could be spent on a dinner.

Senators did at least recognize the major problems. A law was passed in 159 BC against bribery and later a secret ballot for elections was introduced. Cato noted the importance of (his) personal example, and regretted the loss of traditional 'small town' morality, yet it is interesting that he felt the need to say this:

> I have never divided booty nor anything captured from the enemy nor spoils between a few of my friends and therefore deprived those who captured them of their reward. . . . I have never distributed the allowance for the soldiers' wine among my staff and friends and I have not made them rich at the state's expense. (Malcovati, 1953, p. 70, 44.173)

The senate also regulated office-holding by increasing the number of praetors; by 197 BC six were elected annually. Although this provided more opportunity for the ambitious, it also placed more pressure on the consular elections, since there were still only two annual vacancies. In this context we can understand attempts to restrict the holding of repeated consulships. The senate's good intentions towards the governed appear in a law of 149 (*Lex Calpurnia*), which tried to deal with provincial misgovernment by setting up a senatorial court with rules of procedure. This was a start, but its impact was limited since plaintiffs could seek only repayment of damages; there was no formal penalty. Furthermore, governors tended to extend the traditional Roman social practice of patron and client to the provinces, building up networks of dependants, which sometimes made prosecutions difficult.

After the defeat of Hannibal in 202 BC, most of Rome's attention had been focused on the east, which helped to create the background for the engagement of the Roman aristocracy with the cosmopolitan world of Greek political ideology, literature and philosophy — 'that most learned of all peoples', as Livy described the Greeks (39.8). This was partly a matter of individual choice and taste, but it was a tribute to the awareness and intelligence of the upper classes in Rome that in political terms they quickly worked out the best diplomatic approach for dealing with Greek communities and their response to the Roman presence. Romans had plenty of Greeks to consult, since according to Polybius many were living in Rome. Polybius himself, having been kept under house arrest in Italy as a potential opponent of Rome, and then befriended by P. Cornelius Scipio Aemilianus and brought to Rome, was well placed to explain 'Greekness' to the ruling power.

This had two aspects: custom and literature. There was an increasing interest in Greek games, and in 186 BC M. Fulvius Nobilior brought Greek actors to Rome as well as Greek-style athletic contests. The upper classes, either to show off or from genuine interest, were keen to demonstrate that they understood Greek culture and literature by employing Greek teachers or, even better, by speaking and writing Greek. These developments were to be the basis of Graeco-Roman culture for the rest of Rome's history and beyond, and the beginning of a bilingual approach that was eventually to characterize Roman administration in the east. For example, T. Quinctius Flamininus, who had a crucial role in executing Roman policy in Greece, spoke excellent Greek, and we have seen how as early as the 280s a Roman ambassador had addressed the assembly at Tarentum in Greek (chapter 1). Aemilius Paullus chose as his portion of booty the library of the Macedonian king after the battle of Pydna in 168 BC. This kind of interest was an effective way of engaging with opponents or subjects and recognizing their potential contribution. Cato represents a reasonably balanced view of the contemporary fascination with Greek intellectual achievement. On the one hand, he delivered a scathing judgement on doctors from Greece, who in his view were likely to destroy Rome, and he had little time for philosophers. However, he was also familiar with Greek literature and in his famous work written in Latin, the *Origines*, expressed Rome's individuality and achievement but in a Greek context.

By the second century BC Rome was a self-confident, powerful community and certainly not culturally backward, but as Romans moved increasingly among civilized Hellenistic city states and absorbed the influences that came from them, contemporary literature began to move in new directions. Livius Andronicus, a Greek captured at Tarentum in 272 BC, translated Homer into Latin. This shows something of current interests among the Roman literate audience. In drama, Naevius and Pacuvius were heavily influenced by Attic comedy and tragedy, although Naevius went on to write an epic on the First Punic War, in which he had served as a soldier. Plautus and Terence exploited Greek New Comedy for plots and presentation, although Plautus in particular often has references to Roman social customs and practices. Terence notably developed a naturalistic Latin style, but the atmosphere for performance in Rome was boisterous rather than intellectual, and there were many competing attractions, as he makes clear in the prologue to the *Hecyra*:

> I have never been permitted to put this play on in silence. Disasters have dogged its appearance, but you (the audience) can rectify this by your under-standing. At the first performance the popularity of some boxers and the report that a tightrope walker was going to appear, the crowd of their supporters, the uproar and the screams of women forced me to abandon the performance before the end. (lines 29–36)

Terence enjoyed the support of upper-class patrons, and P. Cornelius Scipio Aemilianus and his brother commissioned a play for the funeral games of their father. Aemilianus was also a friend of Lucilius, a rich landowner of equestrian status who developed the new genre in Latin of verse satire. Ennius (see chapter 1) had the support of eminent men, particularly Cato, and taught Greek and Latin grammar to the children of the well-off; he also translated Greek works into Latin. His most famous work, the *Annales*, a genuine Roman epic celebrating the rise of Rome from earliest times, was distinctly patriotic, containing the famous line: 'The Roman commonwealth stands upon ancient traditions and strengths.' Among writers of prose, Fabius Pictor's history of early Rome, although written in Greek, used a distinctly Roman methodology by presenting the facts year by year.

Religious Practices

In this exciting period of Roman military victory and expansion and cultural experimentation, Roman religious practice, at least in the opinion of Polybius, helped to preserve the order of society: 'The quality in which the Roman state in my view is most clearly superior lies in its attitude towards the gods. I think that something that is held as a criticism among other peoples, namely religious feeling, binds together the Roman state' (6.56.6–7). He goes on to suggest that the Roman leaders used religion to keep the people under control. It might be more accurate to say that religious observance combined with social conservatism and the checks and balances in the Roman constitution helped to preserve a relatively stable political framework. The Romans tried to regulate divine law (*fas*) and human law (*ius*), with one-third of the days in the calendar marked as *dies nefasti* (reserved to gods) and the rest *dies fasti* (reserved to humans). This meant that the occasions on which public business could be conducted were conveniently limited. Furthermore, military operations had to be conducted properly, could begin only on certain days, and priestly brotherhoods supervised the details, including the formal declaration of war (*fetiales*); the Romans liked to believe that they always waged just war, on the argument that their enemies had committed an offence and failed to atone for it. The Arvals formed a brotherhood originally responsible for purifying the boundaries of the Roman land. Signs and portents were respected and special colleges of priests had the job of interpreting them. The Augurs were principally responsible for maintaining augural lore and replying to questions from officials; they could also take the auspices before major undertakings and had the right of making a binding pronouncement of adverse omens that had appeared unsought; this had the effect of ending any assembly in progress. There was scope for using the alleged appearance of omens to prevent unwelcome political developments. Nevertheless, that should not detract from the fact that many took seriously the possibility that the gods might intervene in human affairs and make their intentions known. Attempts were made in the mid-second century BC to establish the grounds on which assemblies could be prevented on religious grounds or decisions of previous assemblies annulled.

The most important of the priestly colleges was that of the *pontifices* ('bridge-makers'), who originated in the regal period and had a very influential role in managing religious practice and advising on sacred law. The senior priest (*pontifex maximus*) was originally co-opted by the college but from the mid-third century BC was elected. All the *pontifices* were from the upper classes and were not professional priests, being embroiled in the cut-and-thrust of political life. Priests called *flamines* were associated with individual gods, the three major being Jupiter, Mars and Quirinus. The *flamen Dialis*, the priest of Jupiter, was the most senior and was obliged to live according to a restrictive archaic ritual aimed at avoiding pollution.

State worship in Rome was built around certain traditional deities and changed little. Jupiter was traditionally king of the gods; well known throughout Italy, he was later identified with the Greek Zeus. He held a sceptre to symbolize his sovereignty, and lightning was the sign of his overwhelming strength and power to intervene. As Jupiter Optimus Maximus (Jupiter the Best and Greatest) he was central to the political and military achievements of the Roman state. Jupiter's queen was Juno, a leading Italian deity whose worship was very important in Rome. She was associated with women and in the form Juno Lucina presided over childbirth. Mars was an old Italian god associated with war and the campaigning season. Before going to war a commander shook the sacred spears of Mars and intoned 'Awake, Mars'. Quirinus was also an ancient deity, seemingly important but rather obscure; he was often associated with Mars though not exclusively warlike. Ceres was important to the poor because she was the goddess of growth, particularly of crops and corn, and came to be identified with the Greek Demeter. Minerva was an Italian goddess who presided over handicrafts and artistic activity and was associated with Jupiter and Juno in worship in Rome. She came to be identified at some stage with her Greek equivalent, Athena. Vesta was the goddess of the hearth fire and had no image but only the sacred fire in her temple; she was served by six Vestal Virgins who ceremonially prepared the grain mixed with salt used in public festivals. In addition, numerous other deities existed all around in daily life, for example in rivers (Tiberinus in the Tiber), woodland (Silvanus), hills (Quirinus on the Quirinal) and gates (Janus). As Janus represented doorways, he pointed in two directions and is depicted as double-headed; he also presided over beginnings, as in the start of the year. Traditionally, the doors of his temple were ceremonially closed in times of total peace (unusually this happened three times during the reign of Augustus). Other important manifestations of belief appear in the *penates*, spirits of the innermost part of the household, which received worship both in private and public, and the *manes*, spirits of the dead, which had special festivals but also private ceremonies on the birthday of a dead ancestor. The *lares* were guardians of crossroads and travellers, and by extension, of the state.

Since the Romans expected deities to be present in all kinds of human activities, there was virtually no limit to the existence of divine spirits, including Cloacina (goddess of the main Sewer, the Cloaca Maxima) and Sterculinus (god of manure). Religious ritual was aimed at persuading deities to assist in the working of natural processes and human activities for the benefit of individuals and the state. Performance of the proper ceremonies and sacrifices would help to ensure divine favour. The formal vow (*votum*) encapsulated the idea of a deal between worshipper and deity. If the prayer was answered certain actions would follow; hence on inscriptions phrases like *VLMS (votum libens merito solvit)*, frequently abbreviated because they were so commonplace, mean 'he/she willingly and deservedly paid their vow'. At the national level, the relationship between Rome and the gods was summed up by the praetor, M. Valerius Messalla, writing rather self-righteously to the city of Teos: 'That we entirely and constantly have attached the highest importance to reverence of the gods one can estimate from the goodwill we have experienced for this reason from the supreme deity' (Sherk, 1984, no. 8).

The Romans had no religious books, but from time to time on the decision of the senate they consulted the Sibylline books, a collection of prophecies said originally to have been bought by Tarquinius Priscus from the Sibyl at Cumae in southern Italy and subsequently entrusted to a college of fifteen priests, to be consulted on the decision of the senate. Despite the intellectually conservative and formulaic nature of Roman religious practice, innovation did occur, and it is interesting how the festival of the rather mysterious Italic god Saturn turned into a period of merrymaking with seven days of celebration in December, present-giving, and inversion of normal roles so that slaves got to take the place of masters. In 205 BC Cybele, a nature goddess from Asia also known as the Great Mother, was brought to Rome in the form of a black stone and worshipped with un-Roman orgiastic ritual. On the other hand, any form of worship that threatened social cohesion or the mastery of the ruling elite was dismantled, as in 186 in the case of Bacchus (the Greek Dionysus, god of wine and ecstasy), whose small cells of worshippers had proved disorderly and a rival source of influence to government authority. The senate treated this as a conspiracy against the state (though not excluding individual worship) and imposed its will throughout Italy, emphatically showing how Rome was the master of the peninsula: 'In the matter of the Bacchic orgies they passed a decree that the following proclamation should be issued to those who are allied by treaty with the Romans: Let none of them be minded to maintain a place of Bacchic worship' (*Corpus Inscriptionum Latinarum* I^2.581).

At all times the oligarchy that monopolized the major priesthoods and controlled access to archaic religious lore and records could dictate the rhythms of religious observance, the admittance of new forms of worship and the interpretation of signs. The secular priesthood was never far removed from politics, but their actions could always be presented as being for the benefit of the state and permitting the expression of the divine will. Cicero, himself an augur, had no qualms in asserting: 'Taking the auspices is intended to facilitate plausible excuses for delay in order to postpone unproductive meetings of the assembly. For the immortal gods have through the auspices often blocked improper declarations of the people's will' (*On the Laws*, 3.27).

CHAPTER FOUR

The Sewer of Romulus

Upper-Class Reformers

According to the historian Sallust the most important reason for the decline and fall of the traditional form of government in Rome was the grasping greed and personal ambition of members of the ruling class, who selfishly kept the fruits of empire for themselves regardless of the misery of the plebs, and in their ambition to advance personal careers by whatever means were indifferent to the public good. As a partisan of Julius Caesar and failed politician of dubious morality who had been expelled from the senate and was later accused of corruption, Sallust had a realistic insight into the seamier side of Roman politics, and his opinion is plausible no matter how sceptically we take his tone of moral uprightness and glorification of the old Republic. He also thought that the political revolution began with men from the upper classes. Therefore, it is no surprise that a great part of the story of the fall of the Republic is concentrated on the breakdown of consensus among the wealthy and the role of individuals who became predominant often by holding military commands or exploiting popular support. And people tended to support a personality rather than policies or programmes.

Tiberius Gracchus was elected tribune of the plebs for 133 BC. He came from the highest social class; his mother was the daughter of Scipio Africanus and his father had been censor in 169. He also had support from other aristocrats, including Appius Claudius Pulcher, consul in 143 and *princeps senatus* (leader of the senate) from 136, and P. Mucius Scaevola, consul in 133. Tiberius's proposals may have been an attempt by one group of political allies to gain an advantage by exploiting popular discontent. However, some later writers claimed that he was motivated by personal pique because the senate had rejected the treaty he negotiated with the Spanish at Numantia in 137. On the other hand, Sallust believed that Tiberius and his brother Gaius had honest intentions to reform persistent social problems. Such is the turmoil of conflicting emotions and opinions generated by the brothers. It is likely that both did genuinely want to help the poorer citizens, without being blind to the opportunities or aware of all the consequences.

Tiberius proposed an agrarian law aimed at preventing any individual from holding more than 500 *iugera* (126 hectares) of public land, with an additional allowance for his sons. A three-man commission was charged with overseeing this process and distributing the recovered land to landless citizens. Tiberius was not the first to address the landholding question, but unlike others he was not about to back down. The poor flocked to Rome from the countryside to support the bill, which Tiberius took straight to the *concilium plebis* without asking the senate's opinion. Conservatives in the senate hated any interference with land ownership and arranged for a tribune, Octavius, to veto the bill. Tiberius then persuaded the *concilium plebis* to depose Octavian from his tribunate. This caused furious controversy, not because it was illegal but because it raised crucial questions about the rights of the people to control the magistrates they had elected. The senate retaliated by refusing to vote sufficient funds for the expenses of the commissioners. Tiberius's response was characteristically direct. When the will of Attalus III of Pergamum, who had just died, was announced in Rome, bequeathing his kingdom to the Roman people, Tiberius introduced a bill to use the royal assets to assist citizens receiving redistributed land to stock their new farms. The senate felt that its traditional prerogative to manage the monies of the state had been challenged. Opposition to Tiberius's methods intensified and partly to protect himself against reprisals he stood for a second tribunate. Many must have wondered what would happen if he was successful. Was he setting himself up for personal domination (*regnum*) so hated by the Romans? However, Tiberius was vulnerable since many of his poorer supporters had drifted back to the countryside, and a group of senators and their attendants led by Tiberius's cousin, the *pontifex maximus* P. Cornelius Scipio Nasica Serapio (consul in 138), attacked Tiberius and beat him to death along with many of his supporters.

Despite this shocking violence the work of the land commission continued. But a new problem was steadily taking shape, namely the position of Rome's Italian allies. Roman colonies and individual Roman settlers lived side by side with Italian communities throughout Italy. This assisted Roman control and the gradual assimilation of the local population, but Italians came to expect some form of recognition, especially given their contribution to military campaigns. Feelings were running high and in 125 BC M. Fulvius Flaccus made a limited offer of citizenship to the Italians. When this was brushed aside by the senate, the Latin colony of Fregellae revolted and was ruthlessly obliterated by the Romans.

Tiberius's brother Gaius was elected to the tribunate of 123 BC on a programme of reform, and was successful in being elected to a second tribunate in 122.

Because of the inadequacy of our sources, it is not clear exactly what measures he introduced or in what order. It is also difficult to judge whether Gaius had a clear policy intended to create a coalition of vested interests to facilitate reforms or whether he proposed a series of individual measures aimed at important issues but also likely to boost his own popularity. He could not avoid the issue of Italian citizenship, but his ambitions were wide and the scope of his interventions is striking. A series of humane measures assisted the urban and rural poor; land distribution in Italy was continued; there was also to be a new colonial foundation overseas at Carthage, which was controversial since the site had been pledged to the gods for destruction; free clothing was to be provided for soldiers, and young men under eighteen were not to be enlisted in the army; Gaius provided for a supply of grain in Rome at a fixed price probably subsidized by the state and built granaries to store an adequate supply; an increased road-building programme will have provided work for the poor as well as assisting communications and commerce. Gaius won over the *equites* by his arrangement of a profitable tax-collecting contract in the new province of Asia. Furthermore, a law effectively gave control of the juries in extortion trials to *equites*, though this was not necessarily a happy outcome for the provincials since it opened up the possibility of collusion between the jurors and equestrian tax-collectors. Gaius struck at the senators who had persecuted his brother's supporters, through a law requiring that courts using capital sentences be empowered only by the people.

Against this backdrop Gaius brought forward a dramatic measure proposing to grant citizenship to Italians. But his opponents played on the selfishness of the plebs, arguing that they might find themselves pushed out of their usual benefits and privileges by a group of new citizens. A tribune, Livius Drusus, tried to outbid him and entice his support away by proposing new colonies and offering himself as the people's champion. Gaius was not elected for a third term and resorted to violence to oppose any attempt to block the colony at Carthage. The senate passed the final decree (*senatus consultum ultimum*), which gave moral authority to the magistrates to take suitable action to protect the state in an emergency, and the consul Opimius had Gaius and three thousand of his supporters killed.

The careers of the Gracchi brothers had a tremendous impact in Rome. First, the people through their tribune had been empowered to take control of the financial windfall from king Attalus. The benefits of empire were for the whole people and there was an incentive and precedent here for *popularis* leaders to win the support of the people by proposing to spend public funds on measures to benefit them. Second, the Gracchi had exploited the potential political power of the tribunate and raised questions about concepts of popular sovereignty, such as the right of the people to depose or elect tribunes as they wished, in defiance of what the senate considered traditional and proper; some senators would see this as virtual dictatorship. Third, the upper-class consensus had been undermined by members of the ruling oligarchy. Finally, the use of extreme violence was a strong indication of the increasing disorder of public life, and a consequence of the use of non-traditional methods; a tribune in office had been murdered and the tribunician inviolability had been transgressed in disorder inspired by senators; violence as a political weapon set a very dangerous precedent. The murder of the Gracchi was seen as a great watershed and the start of a decline in political and moral integrity that eventually led to civil war, and in the political struggles of the years to come their fate was used by conservatives and revolutionaries to justify their case. The historian Velleius Paterculus writing in the early first century AD sums this up:

> This was the first occasion in the city of Rome when the blood of Roman citizens was shed and recourse was had to the sword, in both cases without fear of punishment. After this, law was overwhelmed by force and greater respect was accorded to greater power, and civil disagreement which in the past had been resolved by agreement was settled by the sword. (2.3.3)

The Charismatic General: Gaius Marius

For the moment the senate had won, but in the following years it proved impossible to contain the pressures that had been created. Powerful individuals came to exploit popular support, disdaining to abide by normal conventions or being forced to circumvent them by the obduracy of traditionalists in the senate. The career of Gaius Marius added a further dimension, that of the military leader who simultaneously enlisted popular support and exploited military success to win further office. Marius came from a fairly humble equestrian background in the small town of Arpinum but was able to make his way into the senate through distinguished military service and support from some leading senators. In 109 BC he served in Africa under Q. Caecilius Metellus Numidicus as his senior officer in the war against Jugurtha, who had seized power in Numidia, upsetting Roman arrangements and killing some Italian businessmen. But Marius fell out with his commander, who declined to endorse his candidature for the consulship, and went his own way, winning election for 107 partly by criticizing the aristocrats' conduct of the war; it was known that Jugurtha had many friends in Rome, where in his view everything had its price. Marius intrigued to build a block of support based on the plebs, *equites* and some aristocrats, and was elected consul again for 104 (this required a special derogation), and then he was re-elected year after year on the argument of military emergencies. After senatorial commanders had suffered a disastrous defeat at Arausio (Orange) in 105 against invading German tribes (Teutones and Cimbri), Marius confirmed his military reputation by comprehensive victories in 102 at Aquae Sextiae and at Vercellae in 101. His sixth consulship in 100 was the peak of his popularity. He made an important change to military equipment by modifying the design of the legionary's throwing spear (a new fitment of the metal head and the shaft caused it to bend on impact and become unusable by the enemy), but his crucial change was to accept volunteers for the army without the usual property qualification. He did not recognize or exploit the potential political and social significance of this. However, in the future an ambitious military commander could turn his army into a personal following that would owe allegiance to him rather than the state and look to him for rewards and the distribution of plots of land, with the implication of the veterans' support in future political struggles in order to ensure that their benefits were maintained.

A sign of the times was the career of L. Appuleius Saturninus, characterized by violence and populist measures; tribune in 103 and 100 BC (when he murdered a rival for office), he passed laws to grant land in Africa to Marius's veterans, established other colonies and introduced a grain law to ensure a low price. The last straw was his murder of one of the candidates for the consulship of 99. For the moment the senate's authority prevailed and Marius connived with the aristocracy to arrest Saturninus, who was subsequently murdered. The major issue of the rights of the Italian allies who aspired to Roman citizenship had been left unresolved. It would upset traditional politics to bring in a large influx of new voters outside the usual range of the influence of the *optimates*. This became a major source of dispute because other politicians, particularly the *populares*, welcomed anything that was likely to disrupt the established pattern of political alliances. M. Livius Drusus, elected tribune for 91 BC, proposed an eclectic collection of measures including a cheap corn distribution, reform of the law courts and citizenship for the Italians. He had the support of some leading senators and possibly aimed at genuine reform, but the consul Marcius Philippus stirred up opposition, there was little support among the plebs for an extension of citizenship, and Drusus became another victim of the increasing political violence. He was murdered in his home by an unidentified attacker.

The Unlikely Revolutionary: Cornelius Sulla

In the midst of this turmoil the Italians resorted to war in 91 BC, exasperated by the attitude of the Romans, who seemed to regard people of the same race as foreigners. Italian businessmen provided the wealth to fund the war, the same wealth that had for example financed the building of a stone theatre in the late second century at the small Samnite town of Pompeii. The Italians were self-confident and experienced in warfare and were formidable opponents, issuing a coinage and establishing a senate. Rome eventually won the Social War (from *socii* – allies) but only after several military defeats and heavy losses (more than 250,000 men were under arms), and was soon forced to concede citizenship to all those Italian communities that had not revolted; fighting in Samnium dragged on to 87 and there was a lingering cause of resentment in that the new citizens were placed in only a small number of the voting tribes, effectively restricting their political influence.

The war had an unforeseen consequence in the military success of L. Cornelius Sulla, who came from an old patrician family; he had previously served under Marius in Africa and against the Germans, was elected consul for 88 BC and at the age of fifty embarked on his fourth marriage, to the daughter of the *pontifex maximus*, L. Caecilius Metellus Delmaticus. Sulla was firmly bound into the *optimates* and the senate voted him the governorship of Asia and the command against king Mithridates VI of Pontus, who had become a most dangerous enemy of Rome. Having annexed Bithynia and Cappadocia, he brought most of Greece over to his side and invaded Asia, calling for the massacre of all resident Roman citizens and Italians. The first war against Mithridates was to last from 89 to 85 BC. At this point there was a startling intervention by the tribune Sulpicius Rufus, who among other things proposed to expel from the senate those with debts over a set limit, to distribute the Italians fairly over the thirty-five tribes, and to transfer the command against Mithridates from Sulla to Marius. Sulla refused to accept this quietly, and going to his army that was assembling at Nola in Campania, he appealed directly for their support. Although only one officer was won over, the soldiers supported Sulla and marched on Rome. This was the most important event in Sulla's career and had momentous consequences. For the first time the army had been introduced into politics to achieve personal ends; the precedent could not be erased and would be followed by other military commanders. The immediate outcome was that Sulpicius was hunted out and murdered (although Marius escaped) and his laws were repealed. Sulla tried to ensure that his enemies did not take advantage of his absence in the east to reverse the situation. But L. Cinna, one of the consuls elected for 87, remained hostile. The traditional consensus that had underpinned the operation of senatorial politics had been shattered.

After Cinna had been forced out of Rome, he raised a small force in Italy mainly from a legion left behind by Sulla, and, accompanied by Marius, captured Rome. Within a year, therefore, Sulla's example had been followed. Marius allowed the soldiers to loot and murder at will, and took vengeance on his enemies, but he died a few days after entering his seventh consulship. Cinna was left in charge from 86 to 84 BC, and this period was depicted by Sulla as an unconstitutional interlude. Yet it seems unlikely that senators were simply waiting for

Sulla to restore legitimate government (subsequently this became the official version). Some accepted office from Cinna, who carried useful measures such as a remission of some debts. However, his biggest problem was what to do with Sulla, who consolidated his position and made a treaty with Mithridates before his power had been fully eliminated. Meanwhile Cinna was murdered by mutinous troops as he tried to organize an army. In 83 Sulla landed in Italy and, marching on Rome for the second time, dispersed Cinna's supporters at the battle of the Colline Gate on the outskirts of the city; people started to change sides as they saw that Sulla was likely to win.

Sulla took practical measures to safeguard his own security. In a reign of terror individuals and whole communities who had supported the wrong side were butchered and their property confiscated; lists of victims were published (proscriptions), with a reward for those who killed anyone on the list. Among the Italians the Samnites were particularly harshly treated:

> The remainder, three or four thousand men, who had thrown down their weapons (after the battle of the Colline Gate) he brought to the Villa Publica in the Campus Martius and imprisoned there. But three days later he sent in soldiers and massacred them all . . . and to those who complained that he had been brought to this pitch of rage he replied that he had learnt from experience that the Romans could never live at peace while the Samnites existed. (Strabo 5.4.11)

At least 40 senators and 160 *equites* were murdered. Sulla kept a strong link with his troops on whose support he initially depended, and he provided land (often taken from his political opponents) for over 120,000 veterans. These soldiers were now in Sulla's debt and it was in their interests not to let him be defeated politically. He also kept an unofficial bodyguard of 10,000 freed slaves.

Sulla then set about establishing a secure political base. In 81 BC he was appointed Dictator 'with the purpose of making laws and setting the state in order'. There was no time limit on this office (normally a Dictatorship lasted for six months) or any veto on his decisions. He created new senators by promoting his own supporters who would presumably be loyal to his policy, which was to smother the tribunate; tribunes lost the power of initiating laws and the ability to prosecute before the tribal assembly; restrictions were placed on their veto and they were debarred from holding any other public office after the tribunate. These measures cleverly reduced the importance of the tribunes as a political weapon of the *popu-lares*, and Sulla made the office a kind of dead-end since no one of ability and ambition would stand for election to a position that would rule him out of any further office. Sulla was aware of the threat from higher office-holders and reaffirmed the law on the minimum age for holding office as well as that barring any man from holding the same office twice within ten years. He had observed the power to be gained from repeated tenure of the consulship, as Marius and Cinna had done.

However, the main danger was of course the example Sulla had set. How could he prevent provincial governors and army commanders from using their armies against the government? He tried to ensure that the senate directly controlled who governed each province and introduced a treason law (*lex de maiestate*), which meant that a governor could not start a war on his own initiative, lead his troops outside his province, or leave his province for any reason. Therefore, theoretically a commander could not lead his troops back to Rome. This was an attempt to legislate against revolution, and was probably futile since it is unlikely that a man prepared to overthrow the government by armed force would be put off by the fact that there was a law against it. But it does show the consequences of what had been done in 88 BC. Finally, Sulla established new lawcourts to try major crimes such as murder, forgery, treason and extortion, and gave control of the juries to the senate, an indication of the fact that political prosecutions were an important part of life in Rome.

Sulla was consul in 80 BC and resigned the Dictatorship in that year, retiring to the country where he married his fifth wife. He died in 78. Julius Caesar said that Sulla's retirement showed that he did not know his political ABC. Sulla by instinct was on the side of the *optimates* and tried to prop up the authority of the senate, but there was little reason why he should have had any great respect for his fellow aristocrats who seemed to have acquiesced in the rule of Cinna and supported Sulla only when things were going his way. Perhaps he thought that he had done enough to secure his version of ordered government. If so, he seriously miscalculated. Although Sulla tried to block the route of popular support as a means of changing the constitution, he had not dealt with the fundamental problems inspiring disruption, namely popular misery and discontent at the unequal distribution of the profits of empire, and the absence of a framework for the orderly distribution of rewards to discharged soldiers, who would make up the personal armies of the future. Sulla was murderous and cruel and in the end achieved little, except the memory of his marching on Rome and his ruthlessly successful methods.

War and Politics: Pompey

The aftermath of Sulla's dictatorship saw the senatorial oligarchy under attack from various directions: the ambition of prominent senators, who for personal advancement could not let the status quo endure; persistent popular agitation among the poor and those dispossessed by Sulla, and also the problem of debt; in order to preserve and develop the popular policy of conquest and exploitation, special commands were voted, which again demonstrated how important popular support was and how valuable the prestige of successful campaigning to achieve political power. Large military forces provided the means for powerful individuals to undermine the senate's position and facilitated the rise of the military dynasts. Wars were fought and territory organized without systematic consultation of the senate. In these years important figures such as Lucullus, Pompey and Catiline had all been officers of Sulla, an indirect but pernicious legacy of his career.

Sulla had not finally defeated Mithridates, who evacuated Asia, paid an indemnity, and surrendered seventy ships. Hostilities were briefly resumed in 83–82 BC, but in 74 Mithridates invaded Bithynia whose king had bequeathed the land to Rome. Lucullus, one of the consuls of 74, had the right to act against Mithridates and routed the king at the battle of Cabira in Pontus. Mithridates fled to his son-in-law Tigranes in Armenia while Lucullus systematically captured the remaining fortresses. He also addressed the problems of the cities in Asia who had borrowed money from Roman moneylenders to pay fines imposed by Sulla. Lucullus scaled down the interest owed and worked out payment by instalments, which earned him the goodwill of the cities but the hatred of the *equites* who made the loans.

Lucullus went into Armenia after Mithridates, rightly judging that the war would not be ended until he was captured or killed. Although he had no authority from the senate for extending the war and only about 16,000 men, Lucullus attacked the main fortress of Trigranocerta. Tigranes, on seeing the Roman army approaching, remarked that they were too few for an army and too many for an embassy. Lucullus won a brilliant victory and pursued the retreating kings, but a mutiny among his own troops forced him to retreat. His main problem was the political situation in Rome, where opponents prevented the voting of supplies and reinforcements. Many supported the law of the tribune, Aulus Gabinius, to remove from Lucullus the right of commanding in Bithynia; although often tactically brilliant, Lucullus was a tough disciplinarian and seems to have lost the goodwill of his men. Political rivalries in Rome finished him off.

Meanwhile, control of Spain had effectively been lost to the senate because of the extraordinary career of Quintus Sertorius. From an equestrian background, he had performed distinguished military service and eventually participated with Cinna in the capture of Rome in 87 BC. In 83–82 Sertorius took command in Spain, was briefly expelled but then returned at the invitation of the anti-Sullan faction in 80 and succeeded in winning the respect of much of the native population. He was brave and resourceful and a skilful commander who developed hit-and-run tactics to combat the Roman army sent against him. By 77 most of Roman Spain was in his hands. Whether genuinely or not, Sertorius put himself forward as a reformer, reduced taxation and the abuses of Roman rule, and tried to win over the local nobility. Though popular, he took care to arm the Romans in the province and put in their hands the manufacture of military equipment.

The Romans could not concentrate their forces in Spain since other major operations were needed against the pirates and in Italy itself in 73 BC when Spartacus led a revolt of gladiators and slaves, a nightmare in a slave-owning society. He showed up the incompetence of several commanders before Licinius Crassus finally defeated him in Lucania in southern Italy. These campaigns were costly in men and resources, and dangerous in that Sertorius opened contact with the pirates and also formed an alliance with Mithridates. Even more significant were the political repercussions in Rome. The senate found itself in a position partly of its own making (it stubbornly refused to reach an accommodation with Sertorius) where it needed the help of the ambitious Pompey (Gaius Pompeius). He came from a family outside the traditional aristocracy and had on his own initiative raised troops in his native district of Picenum in support of Sulla. Violent and devious from the start, Pompey had pursued an extraordinary career combining military success and illegality, holding commands under Sulla and celebrating a triumph though still an *eques*. In 77 the senate unwisely made a grant of proconsular power to Pompey (even though he had held no office) and sent him to bring reinforcements to Metellus Pius in Spain.

The senate may have hoped to bring Pompey over to their side by freely offering what he could take anyway by simply refusing to disband his army. Instead, it simply created more unconstitutional precedents. The atmosphere can be judged by a letter sent by Pompey to the senate in which he demanded more supplies with the threat that he could not prevent his army from returning to Italy if the supplies were not sent. Pompey did not find it easy to campaign against Sertorius, and at the river Sucro it was only the timely intervention of Metellus Pius that saved him from disaster, provoking Sertorius to say: 'If that old woman had not come up I would have given this boy a good hiding and packed him off to Rome' (Plutarch, *Life of Sertorius*, 19). Eventually, Pompey succeeded in wearing down Sertorius and brought about his murder by one of his officers, Perperna. Sertorius had not been a threat to the Roman Empire. Although his tactics were well suited to Spain, it is unlikely that his followers would have marched with him far from their homeland. However, the war in Spain had political significance in Rome by furthering Pompey's unconstitutional career. His appointment to the consulship of 70 BC (with Licinius Crassus as colleague), which was Pompey's first formal magistracy, set the worst possible example, was a massive break with tradition, further undermined Sulla's provisions, and emphasized once again the importance of army command in Roman politics. Furthermore, Pompey was awarded a triumph (his second).

While Pompey had been in Spain, political agitation allegedly in his name pursued the restoration of the powers of the tribunes. The senate was distracted by the problem of a corn shortage, some embarrassing trials of corrupt governors and crooked judgements by juries composed of senators. Pompey and Crassus were very popular with the people because of their victories over Sertorius and Spartacus, and they used this support to arrange the political situation to suit their interests. Pompey in particular needed to deal with the question of his future career, which so far had been based on commanding soldiers. His first step, with the support of Crassus, was to restore the former powers of the tribunate. In his self-interested view of things, a tribune might be valuable in acquiring another command. He also reformed the lawcourts through a law that established that juries were to be chosen from senators, *equites* and *tribuni aerarii* (army paymasters whose sympathies were equestrian rather than senatorial); in future, senators might be at the mercy of adverse political judgements. Most importantly, Pompey provided land for his veterans, who as usual had a vested interest in keeping their benefactor in political power.

In the first instance Pompey wanted to remove the restraining influence of Sulla's measures and open the way to his personal advancement. Part of his political stature now depended on his ability to protect not only his veteran soldiers but all those who looked to him as a friend or patron. Hence it was crucial that he help his many clients in Sicily since the island had been oppressed by the notoriously brutal and corrupt governor, Verres. Marcus Tullius Cicero, then a young advocate on the way up, undertook for Pompey the task of prosecuting Verres and presented the evidence so effectively (this was before the jury composition was changed) that his opponent abandoned the case and Verres went into exile. The publication of Cicero's speeches provided a damning indictment of the worst aspects of senatorial administration and stirred up support for Pompey's subsequent changes.

Neither Pompey nor Crassus took a provincial command for 69 BC, but Pompey was certainly involved in the manoeuvres that undermined Lucullus's campaign against Mithridates. Pompey realized that he needed to keep himself in the public eye by military exploits and in 67, on the initiative of a tribune, a command against the pirates was proposed, involving unlimited power (*imperium infinitum*) extending fifty miles inland from the Mediterranean coast, 500 ships and 120,000 soldiers; four years previously Pompey had not even been senator. This was so worrying to the senate that they put another tribune up to veto his command, but there was popular support for the measure since the people feared corn shortages. The price of corn fell as soon as the command was voted to Pompey. Once again, the enormous political importance of popular support and army command had been conclusively demonstrated.

After Pompey had confirmed his reputation as Rome's greatest general by rapidly destroying the pirate threat, another tribunician law in 66 BC brought him

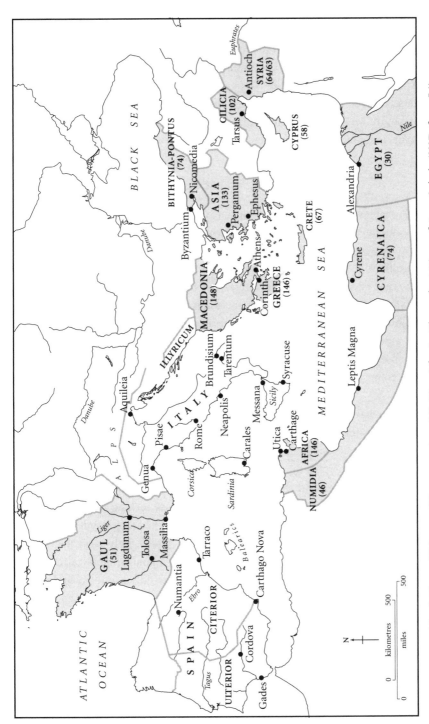

Map 6. The establishment of Roman provinces 148–30 BC (after Le Glay et al., *A History of Rome* 3rd edn (2005), figure 5.1).

the provinces of Cilicia, Bithynia and Pontus, and command of the war against Mithridates. Pompey, who now had unrivalled prestige, was invested with a general authority to deal with Rome's enemies in the east and effect a settlement. He enormously enhanced his status and wealth; Mithridates was speedily defeated and committed suicide, Syria was annexed as a province and administrative structures were established, and the territory of Judaea was rearranged. Pompey, however, stopped short of making war on Parthia despite his cognomen 'Great' in imitation of Alexander.

Revolution and Reaction

In Rome individual ambition and intrigue combined to disrupt the settled pattern of government. In this context of suspicion and political manoeuvring the conspiracy of Catiline took place in 63 BC. L. Sergius Catilina had been defeated in elections for the consulship that year and lost again in the election for 62. Genuinely or not, he backed the interests of the indebted, poor and dispossessed, everyone who had lost out in the preceding violent land settlement. His cause had little future without the use of violence, and Cicero, watchful consul in 63, used a brilliant speech to force Catiline to leave Rome. When Cicero finally got written evidence, the conspirators in Rome were arrested and Catiline, who had taken command of a force of disgruntled veterans in Etruria, was defeated and killed.

Cicero, having gained the consulship as a *novus homo* ('new man' – the first of his family to hold major public office), was now at the peak of his influence, though the execution of the Catilinarian conspirators without trial cast a shadow and left him vulnerable to recriminations. At least Cicero made some effort at a constructive response to the threats facing the traditional government of the Republic, both from the political agitation of those seeking to redress popular grievances, and from army commanders who exploited their armies to promote their careers unconstitutionally. Cicero's idea was loosely described as the 'concord of the orders', in which he hoped for a kind of political concordat involving senators and *equites*, that is, all men of property and settled respectability, in defence of the established order of society. If they could cooperate in the courts and at elections they could defeat the reformers and agitators. Cicero hoped that this alliance could be guided by an influential and respected man. Finding one was the problem. Whereas the upper classes had come together to defeat revolution, it would be much harder to keep them together in normal conditions. And powerful individuals had their own agenda. Crassus and Julius Caesar, who also knew the value of the support of the *equites*, would be working to obtain it; Pompey, whose previous career was marked by violence and unconstitutional office-holding, was hardly a suitable man to support the status quo. In fact, in the aftermath of 63 BC the *optimates* behaved irresponsibly by continuing to neglect the interests of the people. They remained exclusive and unimaginative and did not grasp that only by curing these ills could they remove the weapons from the hands of their political enemies. The behaviour of the *optimates* succeeded in alienating not only the *equites* but the three most powerful men in Rome – Pompey, Crassus and Caesar.

When Pompey returned to Rome in 62 BC to celebrate his third triumph, he surprised everyone by disbanding his army and entering the city as a private citizen. Presumably even he could find no justification to use his army against the government, but he needed to get his settlement of the east ratified and to acquire land for his veterans. Cicero seems to have thought that he was a reformed character and less likely to court mass popularity (*Letters to Atticus* 2.1.6). Pompey certainly made moves towards the *optimates*, divorcing his wife and seeking to marry the niece of Marcus Porcius Cato, who had enormous influence among the senatorial nobility. He also claimed in a speech that the authority of the senate had always carried most weight with him. Pompey's efforts (even if insincere) to operate through constitutional methods were rebuffed by the nobility. Cato refused the marriage of his niece and prevented efforts in the senate to find land for Pompey's veterans, while Lucullus led the opposition to the ratification of the eastern settlement. Cato then annoyed the *equites* by blocking their request for a readjustment of a tax-collecting contract for Asia. Cicero, though recognizing the justice of this, criticized the disastrous political timing:

> We live in a state that is weak, wretched and unstable. I expect that you have heard that our friends the *equites* have almost split from the senate. . . . The demand (for the tax-collecting contract to be rescinded) is scandalous and simply reveals their recklessness. But if they do not get what they want, they really will be at odds with the senate; that is the real danger. (*Letters to Atticus* 1.17.8, 61 BC)

Through Cicero's speeches, letters and philosophical writings we are exceptionally well informed about this period, and of course Cicero was a major player from the 60s BC. He is enormously important precisely because he is a contemporary witness and knew and corresponded with many of the crucial decision-makers in Rome; he knew why decisions were taken and how they played out. But he had strongly conservative political views and wrote from that angle. For example, he was hostile to the Gracchi brothers whom he saw as destructive revolutionaries. He spoke of his natural allies as those 'whose fortunes have been increased and acquired by the support of heaven' (*Catiline* 4.19), while he despised the plebs, 'the wretched half-starved common people, who attend mass meetings and suck the blood from the treasury' (*Letters to Atticus* 1.16.11). However, his prejudice can be useful for showing how one group of senators thought. Although he did not write a continuous history, Cicero's personal letters reveal the passion of Roman politics in these years.

These problems were compounded by the return of Julius Caesar to Rome from Spain. Caesar belonged to the socially pre-eminent Julian family, which had been in recent political eclipse. Winning a reputation as an orator and displaying courage in his early military service in the east, he proved to be both unscrupulous and resourceful. He beat off senior consulars to be elected *pontifex maximus* in 63 BC, allegedly by extravagant bribery. His governorship of Spain (62–60) was in his terms successful, including substantial military action and booty. He requested a triumph and permission to stand in absence for the consulship of 59, since to triumph he would have to retain the command of his army and therefore could not enter the city to take part in the elections. Cato, by speaking all day in the senate, blocked the proposal to grant a dispensation. Typically, Caesar did not hesitate; he disbanded his army, entered the city and was duly elected consul for 59, though by extensive bribery the *optimates* succeeded in getting Cato's son-in-law, Bibulus, elected as his colleague.

Meanwhile Pompey had resorted to a tribune, Flavius, to get his settlement of the east ratified and land for his veterans. But the consul Metellus Celer put every obstacle in the tribune's way, even calling a meeting of the senate in his jail cell after Flavius had had him imprisoned. Eventually Pompey had to back down, but the senate was unrealistically making enemies of important men, and the pragmatic Cicero expressed his frustration with the upright but inflexible Cato: 'He delivers opinions that would be more at home in the pages of Plato's Republic than in the sewer of Romulus here' (*Letters to Atticus* 2.1.8, 60 BC). Pompey, Crassus and Caesar reached an informal accommodation to cooperate as far as possible to protect their individual interests in the face of the *optimates*' influence in the senate. The essentially negative aim according to Suetonius was 'that no action should be taken that did not suit any one of the three'. Florus's description of the three men is perceptive:

> They readily agreed to make an assault on the constitution because each had similar desires for power, although Caesar was anxious to achieve status, Crassus to increase his, and Pompey to retain his. (2.13)

Caesar was still some distance behind Pompey and Crassus in dignity and achievement, and he needed them on his side. Crassus was immensely rich and influential but had been left behind by Pompey's success in the east. Pompey had suffered political embarrassment in the senate and could not find an excuse to use open violence; Caesar's executive power as consul offered the best route to organize land for his veterans and to protect his dignity. This loose political arrangement was sealed by the marriage of the much older Pompey to Julia, Caesar's daughter.

Caesar as Consul

Caesar brought a proposal before the senate that provided for the distribution of public land in Italy (except in Campania) to a large number of needy citizens, including Pompey's old soldiers. Despite Caesar's efforts to win support, Cato spoke until sunset hoping to force an adjournment without a decision. When Caesar had him led off to prison, many senators followed him. M. Petreius said: 'I would rather be in prison with Cato than stay here with you.'

The bill was now brought before the *concilium plebis*, but Caesar's fellow consul, Bibulus, shouted: 'You are not going to get the bill this year, not even if you all want it' (Dio 38.3–4). Caesar exploited the stubborn selfishness of his opponent and received the public support of Pompey, who promised to be ready with his shield if anyone took up a sword. Bibulus used sympathetic tribunes to obstruct the bill and finally resorted to extreme tactics, claiming to be watching the heavens for omens (no public business could be conducted) and declaring all remaining days on which the assembly could meet as public holidays. Finally, when Caesar ignored all this, Bibulus tried to veto the bill; he was showered with filth and attacked by thugs while many of his followers were beaten up. The bill was passed and another agrarian bill specifically provided some of the public land in Campania for Pompey's veterans; the new colonists would be important political supporters of Pompey and Caesar. Only Cato spoke against the bill and he continued to speak as he was dragged away on Caesar's orders, a violation of civic freedom that created a very painful impression among senators. It was a sign of determination to stifle opposition and debate. Other measures ratified Pompey's arrangements in the east and sorted out the equestrian tax contract.

Caesar also introduced a statesmanlike law to deal with the maladministration of Roman governors in the provinces. The *Lex Julia* revised all previous legislation on bribery and extortion in the provinces by defining offences and the classes of people within its scope, laying down a new procedure for the conduct of trials, and setting out many new regulations for provincial administration. However, political expediency came first in the restoration to his throne of the incompetent king, Ptolemy Auletes of Egypt; the senate and people made an alliance with him, and it was said that Pompey and Caesar had received huge bribes from the king – both men had other ideas for future military activity and wanted to maintain the status quo in Egypt for the moment.

Recent events had demonstrated that the political future rested increasingly with military commands, the consulship and the tribunes of the plebs, and not with the senate. Caesar turned his attention to the year after his consulship. He needed to secure a military command, since otherwise it was likely that his opponents would try to prosecute him for his actions as consul. A supportive tribune, Vatinius, had the plebs vote on the proposal that Caesar should receive as his provincial command Cisalpine Gaul (on the Italian side of the Alps) and Illyricum, with three legions, and that no further arrangements should be permitted for this until 1 March in 54 BC. Then Pompey proposed that Caesar should receive responsibility for Transalpine Gaul (beyond the Alps) and another legion. Once again Cato unsuccessfully opposed the idea, saying that the senate was placing the tyrant in the citadel. Caesar was now unassailable for the next four years with a strong military base close to Italy. It was also an important part of Pompey's domination that he keep political allies in important positions.

Superficially, political life in Rome continued as usual but there was now a looming atmosphere of threats and violence, as Cicero discovered when he rebuffed Caesar's attempts to lure him to join his staff and made some critical comments about the prevailing political situation. Within hours, Cicero's deadly enemy Publius Clodius, who was a patrician, changed his status by being adopted into a plebeian family – as a plebeian he could stand for the tribunate and move against Cicero. Caesar as consul and chief priest waived most of the restrictions that normally surrounded adoptions of this type. This was probably meant as a warning to Cicero, who wrote in June 59 BC: 'We are boxed in on all sides; we do not mind this slavery as much as the fear of death and eviction even though they are really lesser evils. But no one lifts a hand or voice against this state of affairs, even though the dissatisfaction is universal' (*Letters to Atticus* 2.18). Cicero may have exaggerated the extent of the dissatisfaction, but there was continuing opposition to the domination of powerful individuals, and amid great excitement the consular elections for 58 were postponed. Later in 58, Clodius attacked Cicero by bringing a bill directed at those who had executed a Roman citizen without trial, harking back to the Catilinarian conspiracy. Cicero fled the country and his house in Rome was destroyed by Clodius's thugs; a shrine to liberty was built in part of the site. Cicero was declared an exile. More generally, the endemic violence in Italy in the 60s was such that men of substance did not travel outside Rome without the services of an armed escort.

The political situation was very unstable, and therefore when Caesar took up his provincial command he could not afford to mark time; he needed to distinguish himself as a general, enrich himself and his supporters, and return much stronger in order to preserve his standing. Earlier in his career, in 61 BC, passing through a poor Alpine village on the way to Spain and being asked jokingly what kind of political life that country had, Caesar had commented tellingly: 'I would rather be first among these people than second at Rome' (Plutarch, *Caesar* 11.3). As well as fighting a war, Caesar had to keep an eye on events in Rome. Once Pompey had got what he wanted, he might begin to resent Caesar's success and respond to the *optimates'* attempts to win him over. The programme of 59 had been carried through partly by illegality and violence and what the *optimates* needed to do was acquire sufficient force to back up their arguments. Pompey could provide that force. On the other hand, his marriage to Caesar's daughter Julia remained a strong bond.

In the fever of political excitement during the years after Sulla the story inevitably revolves round dominating personalities and the pursuit of power and wealth. However, not everyone, even among the upper classes, was fascinated by politics, and two of the most famous poets of the age offer a timely antidote by expressing contempt for political ambition. Lucretius (*c.*100–55 BC) wrote an epic on the nature of the universe, expounding the teaching of Epicurus based on atomistic physics. He wanted to dispel superstitions by a scientific approach, but also reminded people of the futility of seeking political distinction – those men you could see 'contending for precedence struggling night and day with unending effort to scale the pinnacles of wealth and power' (*De Rerum Natura* 2.13). Catullus (*c.*84–54 BC) from Verona in Transalpine Gaul wrote lyric poetry with themes based on the high society of the late Republic. With his original and passionate voice he found time to be rude to Caesar and his chief of engineers, Mamurra, both dismissed as a 'Peerless pair of brazen buggers' (Poem 57). And Catullus was apparently confident enough to reject an overture from Caesar: 'Utter indifference to your welfare, Caesar, is matched only by ignorance of who you are' (Poem 93; translation by Whigham, 1966).

The Political Cauldron: Rome, 58–55 BC

Pompey, manoeuvring to win some friends and perhaps build bridges with the *optimates*, pursued the idea of bringing Cicero back from exile. Tribunes friendly to Cicero, particularly Annius Milo, organized their own gangs and beat Clodius at his own game. A bill for the recall of Cicero passed, and he returned in 57 BC to widespread approval. Just three days after his return, Cicero proposed that Pompey be given a special corn commission for five years, though Pompey may have expected even more. The problem of Egypt had also resurfaced; King Ptolemy Auletes, driven out by a popular revolt, had fled to his benefactor

Pompey. Political infighting followed, which strained relations between Pompey and Crassus. Pompey told Cicero that there was a plan to murder him and that Crassus was financing Clodius, but there was little sympathy for Pompey as people could not really trust him, since he often said one thing while thinking another. Cicero said of him that it was difficult to know what he wanted and what he did not want. Pompey never asked for anything openly, and in that way would not lose face if he did not get his wish.

Meanwhile Caesar had won conspicuous military success in Gaul. A move by the Helvetii tribe, which could be represented as threatening the province, allowed Caesar to start a major campaign that led to the conquest of all of Gaul after ten years' fighting, the death of perhaps up to one million Gauls and the plundering of the country. Caesar fought the war largely without reference to the senate and made war on the German king Ariovistus, who had been recognized as a friend of the Roman people, as well as invading Britain and Germany. Although war booty gave Caesar the wealth needed to bribe important figures in Rome, he needed to shore up his political arrangements; in April 56 BC he came to meet Crassus at Ravenna and they then moved south to meet Pompey at Luca. Much of the negotiation and diplomatic tact needed to bring Pompey and Crassus together was probably down to Caesar. Some of the decisions taken were of unambiguous clarity. With the help of the votes of Caesar's soldiers home on leave, Pompey and Crassus were to be elected consuls for 55 and substantial commands were likely to follow the consulship. Caesar's governorship of Gaul was to be prolonged for another five years, and he would hope to stay with his army until safely elected to the consulship of 48. He would therefore be immune from prosecution. The plans were radical and, as Plutarch put it, 'the three men decided to tighten their hold on public business and to assume complete control of the state' (Life of Crassus 14).

Pompey went to Sicily to deal with the corn commission while Caesar returned to his province. Senatorial decrees that voted funds to support four new legions raised by Caesar and to appoint ten officers (*legati*) had the effect of giving validity to his actions in Gaul since 58 BC. Cicero spoke in support of Caesar at this point; he found it hard to resist the powerful influence of the three men, even though he did not like his role as an apologist for them. Amid much violence Pompey and Crassus were elected consuls for 55; the only candidate to remain in the field was Domitius Ahenobarbus, supported by his brother-in-law, Cato; in the disorder, Domitius's torch-bearer was killed and Cato wounded. Cato was indomitable, saying that the fight was not for office but for freedom in the face of tyranny.

Gradually the three men, relying on lucrative commissions and military commands and confident of the support of the people, were subverting normal political activities. It is no surprise, therefore, that they had a tribune bring forward a bill granting the province of Spain to Pompey and Syria to Crassus for five years with unlimited powers to raise troops, declare war and make peace. Cato and two tribunes fought bravely against this bill; having been excluded from the assembly, Cato stood on the shoulders of a man to shout an adverse omen, but the bill was passed amid violence in which four people were killed. Chicanery, illegality and violence were now routine in political life. Crassus left Rome for his province in November 55 BC, pursued to the gates by a tribune who tried to arrest him and pronounced curses on him. Pompey stayed in Rome for the moment, apparently to keep order; he still had his corn commission, which would give him a legal pretext for remaining near the city. Nevertheless, the *optimates* still had influence in the electoral assemblies and the will to fight on; Domitius Ahenobarbus was elected consul for 54 and Cato praetor.

Civil War

Pompey's wife Julia died in August 54 BC. Both her father Caesar and her husband had been devoted to her and she had been an important element in keeping the two men together. Then in 53 Crassus was defeated and killed at Carrhae by the Parthians and his army wiped out. In the Parthian campaign state policy, military command and strategy were subordinated to personal ambition. Apart from the loss of life and the threat to Roman interests in the east so carefully arranged by Pompey, this was very significant since it made the political scene look more like a direct confrontation between Pompey and Caesar. In Rome there was a serious breakdown of law and order. By the end of 54 no consuls or praetors had been elected for the following year and the followers of Milo and Clodius fought it out in the streets. At the start of 52 again no consuls had been elected and in January in a pitched battle on the Appian Way, Clodius and many of his followers were killed by Milo's gang. In their grief the mob in Rome set fire to the senate house. The plebs demanded that Pompey be made dictator, and perhaps to counter this Cato engineered a proposal in the senate that Pompey be elected sole consul. This position was unconstitutional; what is more, Pompey had been consul in 55 and was ineligible to stand again at this time, and he simultaneously held proconsular power since he was governor of Spain. This was the most extraordinary office of Pompey's unconstitutional career, and Cato and the *optimates* had endorsed it.

Pompey now seemed to turn away from Caesar, rejecting another marriage alliance and instead marrying a daughter of Metellus Scipio, an ardent anti-Caesarian whom in August 52 BC Pompey had had elected to share his consulship. However, Pompey had by no means committed himself to the *optimates*; he knew that he could not trust them. Caesar had defeated a serious revolt in Gaul in 53 and may have been distracted from events in Rome. But his principal concern remained his ability to stand in his absence for the consulship of 48. According to Cicero, Pompey was not unwilling to support this move, although his behaviour was ambiguous. In any case, Caesar from 52 to 51 had a serious war on his hands against the Gallic leader Vercingetorix. It now seemed likely that sooner or later the contest for political power and prestige would be settled by force of arms. Caesar's position, based on his enormous wealth and his powerful, battle-trained army schooled in personal loyalty, was virtually beyond the reach of political counter-measures taken in Rome. He was now the leader of a strong political faction.

Although Cato was defeated for the consulship of 51 BC, Claudius Marcellus was elected and he had a programme of relieving Caesar of his command and impeaching him as a private citizen. Many of his initiatives were vetoed by tribunes and the situation worsened when Marcellus beat with rods a citizen of Novum Comum (a settlement whose colonists had been given Roman citizenship by Caesar). This was a blatant challenge to the authority of Caesar and he responded by sending a legion to northern Italy to protect the communities. He also published his war commentaries, which lucidly described his success in Gaul, his courage and sense of duty to the empire, and his heroic legions. At the end of September the senate met to discuss Caesar's Gallic command and Pompey at last made his views clear: Caesar could not be disturbed before 1 March 50; at that point the issue was often discussed in the senate.

Ties between Caesar and Pompey were by now severely compromised and Caesar reinforced his position by doubling military pay and continuing to recruit. Significantly, he did not neglect his standing with the people and invested in building activities in Rome. Many senators in Rome wished to keep the peace and did not follow the more extreme elements among the *optimates*. Caesar also used bribery astutely; the tribune Curio, whose debts Caesar had settled, repeatedly used his veto to block attempts to replace Caesar, who stood on a principle of equality, namely, that Pompey should give up his province at the same time as he gave up Gaul. Then, in December 50 the consul Marcellus tried to persuade the senate to relieve Caesar of his command while Pompey retained his. But when Curio proposed that both men should give up their commands, this was accepted by 370 votes to 22 as the best way to avoid civil war. Marcellus and his supporters took matters into their own hands and went to Pompey offering him authority to defend the state. Caesar, sincerely or not, continued with negotiations, finally on 1 January 49 sending a letter to the senate listing his achievements and asking that he keep his provinces until the consular election was over or that he and Pompey should lay down their commands together. A motion that Caesar should dismiss his army or be regarded as a public enemy was vetoed by the tribune, Marcus

1. These holes dug on the summit of the Palatine Hill were intended to support the wooden framework of primitive huts and are the earliest evidence for settlement of the site in the Iron Age, ninth–eighth centuries BC.

2. The Capitoline Wolf. This bronze statue of a she-wolf probably dating from the sixth century BC suggests that the foundation story of Romulus and Remus was of an early date. During the Renaissance the figures of the boys were added.

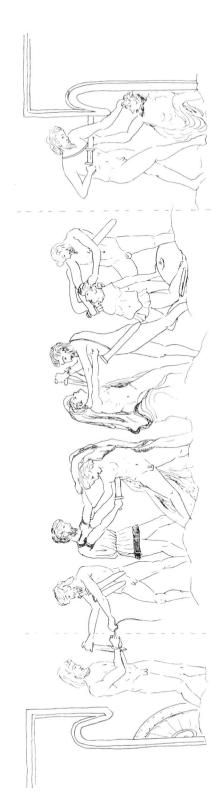

3. François Tomb at Vulci. Wall paintings from this fourth-century BC tomb depict events from Greek mythology and Etruscan history, perhaps an incident in a war waged by Vulci against outsiders. On the left the Etruscan hero Macstrna frees a captive while his comrades kill enemy soldiers whom they have apparently taken by surprise. On the extreme right the victim about to be killed is Cneve Tarchunies Rumach, Gnaeus Tarquinius from Rome (Cornell (1995), p. 138).

4. This statue probably dating from the time of Augustus shows a Roman nobleman carrying images of his ancestors. It was the practice to bring ancestral death masks to a funeral to demonstrate the importance of the family.

5. This denarius minted in Rome in 113 or 112 BC celebrates the voting process. Obverse: Helmeted head of goddess Roma with legend ROMA. Reverse: on the left a man receives from the figure standing below a ballot on which he can record his choice. The figure on the right has crossed the gangway and is placing his ballot in the voting urn. The purpose of the gangway was to prevent interference with or intimidation of the voters. The sign above carries the first letter of the voting tribe represented. P. Nerva is the name of the moneyer responsible for minting the coin (M.H. Crawford, *Roman Republican Coinage* (1974), no. 292).

6. Triumphal Monument of Cornelius Sulla depicting a suit of armour, two trophies with armour, and a shield with the helmeted head of Rome, suggesting that Sulla's victory was that of the state.

7. Portrait of Pompey. His unconstitutional career was instrumental in the fall of the Republic, although he ended his life as its defender.

8. Portrait of Cicero. Orator, constitutional theorist, philosopher and assiduous correspondent, Cicero was one of the leading players in the last generation of the Republic and helped to make it one of the best-known periods of Roman history.

9. Portrait of Caesar. Ruthless in achievement of what he considered to be his proper place in Roman society, he combined the skills of a decisive and aggressive general with the abilities of an orator and writer. His political skills, however, failed to find an accommodation between his dominant position and the framework of the Republic.

10. Denarius minted in Rome, 44 BC. Obverse: wreathed head of Caesar; legend: CAESAR DICT PERPETVO (Dictator in perpetuity). Reverse: Venus, holding Victory in her right hand and a sceptre in her left; at the bottom of the sceptre is a shield; legend: P. SERVILIUS MACER (the moneyer). The Julian family claimed descent from Venus and Aeneas (M.H. Crawford, *Roman Republican Coinage* (1974), no. 480 (6)).

11. Denarius 43–42 BC, from mint moving with Brutus. Obverse: head of Brutus; legend: BRUTUS IMP (Brutus Imperator), L. Plaet(orius) Cest(ianus) (the moneyer). Reverse: slave's cap of liberty, two daggers with the legend: Ides of March; the cap of liberty was traditionally worn by slaves when they received their freedom. Brutus followed Caesar by having his image on the coinage, often seen as a mark of kingship (M.H. Crawford, *Roman Republican Coinage* (1974), no. 508).

12. Denarius 36 BC and after, from mint moving with Octavian. Obverse: head of Octavian with legend: IMP CAESAR DIVI F II VIR ITER RPC (Imperator Caesar, son of a god, triumvir for the second time for setting the state in order). Reverse: temple with four columns and a star in pediment; veiled figure inside holding a lituus (staff carried by priests); lighted altar; the inscription on architrave of temple reads DIVO IUL (In honour of the Divine Julius); legend COS ITER ET TER DESIG (consul for the second time and designated for a third). This coin celebrates Octavian's relationship with Julius Caesar, now a god with his own temple; the star represents his ascent to heaven (M.H. Crawford, *Roman Republican Coinage* (1974), no. 540).

13. This statue of Augustus was found during the excavation at Prima Porta of a villa that probably belonged to Augustus's wife Livia, and represents Augustus in the dress of a Roman general. The central scene depicted on his armour shows a Parthian returning a Roman military standard, either to Augustus's stepson Tiberius, or possibly to Mars, the god of war. This celebrates Augustus's recovery of military standards (in reality as the result of a diplomatic deal) lost by Crassus and Antony.

14. Denarius 28 BC, eastern mint (?). Obverse: head of Octavian with legend: CAESAR COS VI (Caesar, consul for the sixth time). Reverse: crocodile with legend: AEGYPTO CAPTA (the capture of Egypt). This celebrates Octavian's defeat of Antony and Cleopatra and the addition of Egypt to the Roman Empire (*The Roman Imperial Coinage* I², no. 275a).

15. Ara Pacis. The Altar of Peace was voted in honour of Augustus by the senate in 13 BC. The enclosing wall depicts the arrival of the priestly orders and imperial family at the altar. Various scenes emphasize the blessings of peace established by Augustus.

16. Portrait of Agrippina the Elder (14 BC–AD 33). Agrippina was the daughter of Marcus Agrippa and Augustus's daughter Julia, and was married to Germanicus, who was subsequently adopted by Tiberius. Germanicus died in AD 19 after which relations between Tiberius and Agrippina declined since she may have suspected the emperor of plotting against her husband and then against her family. Eventually banished from Rome she was starved to death in exile.

17. Tombstone of Marcus Caelius, a centurion who was killed in the military disaster in Germany in AD 9 under the command of Quinctilius Varus; see p. 106.

18. This statue found at Lanuvium shows the emperor Claudius in the guise of Jupiter, supreme god of the Roman state, whose bird was the eagle. The emperor wears an oak wreath and holds a sacrificial offering bowl in his right hand, emphasizing his role in the life of the Roman state. The statue illustrates the tradition of idealized portraiture of imperial figures. Claudius suffered from various physical and mental problems and was not naturally a charismatic figure.

19. Brass sestertius, AD 71, mint of Rome and Lugdunum. Obverse: Vespasian; legend: IMP CAESAR VESPASIANUS AUGUSTUS PM TP PP COS III (Imperator Caesar Vespasian Augustus, pontifex maximus, holding tribunician power, father of the fatherland, consul for the third time). Reverse: wreath with legend inside: The Senate and people of Rome: In Honour of the Restorer of the State's Liberty. Vespasian celebrates the liberty of Roman people achieved under his rule, in contrast to the tyranny of Nero (*The Roman Imperial Coinage* II, no. 456).

20. Bronze military diploma of AD 103 showing holes for binding wire. This folding tablet was carried by a soldier to prove his entitlement to the benefits and status of a veteran; a copy was kept in Rome.

21. This gilded silver helmet, dating from the third–early fourth centuries AD, was found at Deurne in Holland and belonged to a cavalryman; it has a ridge and nasal-piece, and is divided into six segments with an embossed anchor on each.

Antonius. On 7 January the senate issued a final decree granting to the magistrates authority to protect the state; the tribunes fled to Caesar. Caesar will have heard the news by 10 January. Now that the majority (either through conviction or intimidation) was against him and placing the greatest possible legal power in the hands of his enemies, he had to act decisively. Caesar, declaring 'the die is cast', crossed the river Rubicon (the boundary between his province and Italy itself), and on the morning of 11 January 49 his troops entered the town of Ariminum. The civil war had begun.

This prolonged civil war was fought by Roman citizen soldiers from the rural areas of Italy, but commanded by members of the upper classes many of whom had held the highest offices in the state and had enjoyed the riches and honours conferred by conquest. But they wanted more, aiming to secure their personal standing (*dignitas*) and a leading place in the state, and were prepared to accept the consequences, even though the majority of upper-class Romans did not want civil war. The *optimates* in the end went to war to preserve the status quo and their particular view of freedom, which was a narrow one for their benefit and ignored the interests of the people. Their indifference to popular concerns and their unwillingness to compromise brought them into conflict with ambitious individuals from their own class. Since the Roman constitution offered much scope for interference with the popular will, the scene was set for violent confrontation. The ideal of collective rule of the Republic by senators competing fairly for office had been overcome first by the selfish use of *clientela* and then by appeal to the people or soldiers through military command and tribunes of the plebs. Caesar could claim to be protecting the tribunes and the rights of the people, but in reality his personal standing was at issue. And, in the words of Tacitus, reflecting on the decline of the Republic and the role of the dynasts, 'Pompey was more stealthy but no better' (*Histories*, 2.38).

During the war Caesar once again demonstrated tactical brilliance, decisiveness and speed. Rapidly overrunning Italy, he defeated Pompey's officers in Spain and captured Massilia (Marseilles), ensuring that Italy could not be encircled. In 48 BC he crossed to Greece and after suffering a defeat at Dyrrhachium (Pompey privately was astonished at the meagre rations that Caesar's troops had survived on), brought his opponents to battle at Pharsalus where he won a comprehensive victory. Surveying the fallen on the field of battle, Caesar commented, 'They wanted it this way', and then made a striking personal justification: 'I, Caius Caesar, would have been condemned despite my great achievements if I had not looked for the protection of my army' (Suetonius, *Divus Julius* 30).

Pompey fled to Egypt where, in 48 BC, as he stepped ashore he was treacherously stabbed to death by agents of the young king Ptolemy (the son of Ptolemy Auletes whom Pompey had helped). His head was cut off for display to Caesar.

But Caesar was angry at the manner of his opponent's death though it is difficult to see what he could have done with Pompey had he lived. Cicero said: 'I cannot but grieve for his fate. I knew him for a man of good character, clean life and serious principle' (*Letters to Atticus* 11.6.5). Caesar settled affairs in Alexandria and took up with Cleopatra VII, whom he made queen of Egypt, before organizing Syria and the eastern provinces and defeating the rebellious Pharnaces II of the Bosporus at Zela in a lightning campaign ('I came, I saw, I conquered'). Back in Rome in September 47 BC he soon set out to deal with the last stand of the republican forces in Africa. The battle of Thapsus sealed his victory, soon followed by the suicide of Cato at Utica. He celebrated four triumphs in 46, but two of Pompey's sons raised substantial forces in Spain, which required Caesar's personal presence. At Munda (near Urso) the civil war was finally brought to an end with the death of 30,000 soldiers, and by March 45 Caesar was the undisputed master of the Roman world.

Caesar in Power

Caesar had little opportunity to enjoy his success. The civil war had seen parts of Italy and the provinces devastated; many of Italy's best fighting men had been killed and many of the leading citizens were in exile or dead. Thousands of veteran soldiers were expecting rewards and settlement on farms. Furthermore, Caesar inherited serious, long-standing social and economic problems because of the failure of the ruling oligarchy to deal with the problems of the empire they had conquered. He went out of his way to show that he was not going to repeat Sulla's methods, and he avoided confiscating land to satisfy his troops. The defeated troops of his opponents were either enlisted in his legions or pensioned off. In 49 BC Caesar had attempted to reduce the burden of debt by arranging an agreement between creditors and debtors. In a series of measures between 49 and 44 he reformed the administration of Italy and the provinces. There were new measures for the municipal government of Italy and in certain provinces taxes were reduced (direct collection of taxes in Asia reduced the amount by a third), perhaps as a temporary measure for those who had suffered badly in the civil war; and about twenty new colonies were established, for example in Spain, at Urso and in Gaul at Lugdunum.

Caesar dealt with the situation in Rome by cutting the recipients of free corn from 320,000 to 150,000, partly by settling large numbers in the new colonies overseas. Furthermore, public security in Rome was improved by a measure to ban all private clubs (*collegia*) except religious associations; the *collegia* had been a great source of political disorder and had been used by Clodius and others as a focus for political agitation. A double law reorganized the system for dealing with criminal and civil trials, and increased penalties; juries were to consist of senators and *equites*. Among miscellaneous measures Caesar obliged owners of estates to recruit one-third of their labour force from free men, and the calendar was reformed on the basis of the solar year, which was to prove his longest-lasting change. He tried to distract the poor by games, shows and the corn dole, although the quality of life in Rome probably remained appalling for the lower classes.

Caesar did not set out from the start to create a monarchy; he had competed with his peers for political supremacy, but after the civil war he had no peers and he had to decide whether to prop up the old constitution, supervise it and then retire like Sulla. Arguably that had been disastrous and Caesar had been critical of Sulla. But if Caesar remained in active politics his position was in some way bound to be virtually autocratic; he could guide the state so that constitutional government could return when he died, or he might try to pass on his power to a successor. It looks as though he had not made up his mind on this point. His intended military expedition against the Parthians would have diverted him to the more congenial task of military command and postponed the time for awkward decisions.

Sallust, who was a political partisan of Caesar as well as a historian, in several open letters advised him to stand above factions, restore the Republic to working order and maintain the policy of reconciliation. Cicero, who certainly was no partisan, was nevertheless deeply impressed by Caesar's practice of clemency towards defeated enemies. In his speech for M. Marcellus, consul for 51 BC, one of Caesar's bitterest enemies, delivered after Caesar had pardoned him, Cicero defined it as Caesar's task to establish the Republic on firm principles and again make it workable: 'Our whole way of life was destroyed, and, as you are well aware, Caesar, it is in ruins. It could not be helped, but you are the only person who can restore it' (*On Behalf of Marcellus* 23). Caesar's general objective was to win the nobility over to his side by conspicuous displays of clemency. He declared that despotism was alien to his character and even granted offices to his erstwhile opponents, for example the praetorship to M. Junius Brutus who had fought for Pompey at Pharsalus and begged Caesar for pardon, and C. Cassius Longinus who as tribune in 49 had also supported Pompey and then obtained a pardon. Caesar also showed respect for the senate and republican practice by submitting his measures for its approval; but he did not invite the senate to join him in formulating policy.

Furthermore, Caesar's constitutional position became steadily more remote from the norms of republican practice. From October 48 BC he was Dictator 'Rei Publicae Constituendae causa' ('Dictator to set the state in order'), and in 46 this office was voted to him for ten years. As Dictator he was immune to the veto of tribunes. It could be argued that this position was legitimate while Caesar tried to reform the constitution. However, he accumulated other powers; he was consul in 48 and 46–44 and had censorial powers from 46 to 44, which allowed him to control the lists of the senators. At meetings of the senate he had the right to sit between the consuls and to speak first. A law passed by a tribune gave Caesar a binding right of recommendation for half the candidates in the elections for magistrates, except the consuls; but he also effectively controlled access to the consulship. Caesar preserved the fiction of genuine elections by sending round a note to the tribes in the electoral assembly setting out the candidates whom he wished to be elected 'according to their vote'. His birthday was declared a public holiday and the month Quinctilis was named Julius (July) after him. He received the inviolability of a tribune, and most ominously, in 44 he became Dictator *perpetuus* (for life). In February 44 he appeared in the ceremonial dress of the ancient Roman kings, although he refused a crown offered to him by Marcus Antonius, his *Magister Equitum* (Master of Horse, the Dictator's second-in-command). He acquired extraordinary honours including his portrait on the coinage and was offered a quasi-divine position with Antony as his priest. Here he was building on the steady cheapening of honours; Pompey after all had received a cult at Delos, Athens and Philadelphia.

By becoming Dictator for life Caesar had prepared the way for his own downfall. The nobles whose support was essential were alienated by the permanent dictatorship since it seemed to end their custom of striving for political supremacy with their equals. With Caesar's planned expedition to Parthia they were faced with a virtual absentee king. The Roman aristocracy thought that effectively they had been deprived of country, rank and honour. In March 45 Servius Sulpicius Rufus wrote to Cicero to commiserate with him on the death of his daughter, Tullia, and commented vividly on political life in Rome:

> Or can it be for her sake that you are mourning? So that she might have children, and the joy of seeing their success? Children who would be able to maintain freely the inheritance their father left them, and to stand in due course for each office, with freedom of action in public life and in promoting the interests of their friends? There is not one of these promises that has not been snatched away before it was fulfilled. To lose one's child, you will say, is a calamity. I agree; but to have to endure all this may well be worse. (*Letters to his Friends* 4.5)

This sums up the depth of feeling among senators and their irreconcilable differences with Caesar. In addition, Caesar at times was intolerably autocratic in manner. When an *eques*, Laberius, wrote a mime containing satiric references to Caesar, he was forced to act one of his own parts – a great insult for a Roman *eques*. Senators were infuriated when, on the death of a consul on the last day of his year of office in 45 BC, Caesar had a new consul (Rebilus) elected to hold the consulship for the remaining hours of the day. Cicero said that one who had experienced these events could not hold back his tears (either of fury or dismay). Cicero was also bitter about the fact that resolutions of the senate appeared with his name appended among those supporting, even though he had not even attended the relevant meeting.

Caesar was a thoughtful administrator and was entirely disillusioned with the old system of government. He had little time for the practices of the old Republic, which he described as a mere name without form or substance. As early as January 49 BC he had bluntly told a meeting of the senate that henceforth he would run the state on his own. He tended to think that he knew best and to brush aside attempts to block his acts, though he had no clear plans for wide-ranging social regeneration and constitutional reform. He may have hoped to unite all those who were amenable behind him as a kind of super-patron and put an end to traditional party politics. In the end his pre-eminent position was unbearable for some and a conspiracy was hatched among leading senators, including men like Brutus and Cassius whom he had pardoned. On the Ides of March (15 March) 44, in the theatre built by Pompey, Caesar was assassinated at a meeting of the senate. He had been unwell but attended the meeting despite his wife Calpurnia's warnings. While Mark Antony was manoeuvred out of the way Caesar was surrounded by the conspirators pretending to make personal petitions and fell under twenty-three knife wounds as he wrapped himself in his toga.

The End of the Republic

Antony (Marcus Antonius) had served under Caesar in Gaul, and as tribune in 49 BC had defended his interests. He was trusted enough to command the left wing at Pharsalus and was later Caesar's *Magister Equitum* (Master of Horse), and then consul in 44. He was a good soldier and a talented politician with a disorderly private life. His attitude was crucial for the murderers of Caesar (the self-styled 'Liberators'), who found that there was no upsurge of popular support in their favour. Antony conciliated them but also did not neglect his own military and popular credentials. He first got hold of Caesar's papers and will, consulted prominent Caesarians, and then as consul called a meeting of the senate on 17 March. Here he took control of the meeting and brought about a statesman-like compromise, avoiding reprisals against the Liberators but ensuring that Caesar's measures were confirmed and that there should be a public funeral. The position of Dictator was abolished for ever, which sounded good but was largely meaningless. Caesar had been popular with the plebs, and after a short speech by

Antony at the funeral they burned Caesar's body in the forum. The Liberators had not planned ahead and found themselves increasingly isolated, not least because most of the army was controlled by Caesar's appointees. Antony did not intend to set himself up in Caesar's place, but he needed to maintain his position within the group of Caesar's supporters. He showed skill and restraint and in no way resembles the hopeless drunk portrayed by his opponents, especially Cicero.

The unexpected element was Gaius Octavius, Caesar's seventeen-year-old great nephew, whom he had adopted in 45 BC. Octavius took up his inheritance energetically (becoming Gaius Julius Caesar Octavianus, or Octavian) and worked to acquire money, allies and Caesar's old soldiers in a bid for leadership of all those who had stood to gain from Caesar's victory. Antony may initially have underestimated Octavian, saying that he owed everything to his name. But Octavian arrived in Rome in May and managed to put together a coalition including the consuls of 43, Hirtius and Pansa (old supporters of Caesar). Antony came to an agreement with Octavian partly through pressure from the veterans, and this made it difficult for him to continue to conciliate the Liberators, particularly Brutus and Cassius. Antony now had the Gallic provinces assigned to him. Octavian had little to gain from settled government, but Cicero thought that he could be used as a way of outmanoeuvring Antony and worked energetically to preserve the Republic. The governor of Cisalpine Gaul, D. Junius Brutus Albinus, refused to vacate his command and was besieged by Antony at Mutina. Here Antony, having been defeated by an army led by the consuls Hirtius and Pansa and Octavian, was forced to withdraw to Narbonese Gaul, where he consolidated his forces with the support of the governors of the western provinces, especially M. Aemilius Lepidus.

Cicero optimistically thought that Octavian would be a mere cipher, allegedly saying that he was to be 'praised, lifted up and taken off' (*Letters to his Friends* 11.20.1). But events were moving against him, especially since Hirtius fell in the battle of Mutina and Pansa later died of his wounds. Octavian was now in sole control of the army and with remarkable poise, displaying intelligence, ambition and cruelty in equal measure, marched on Rome in July 43 BC to seize the consulship at the age of nineteen. He ended the amnesty for the murderers of Caesar, and at the conference of Bononia (Bologna) was reconciled with Antony and Lepidus; the three men were appointed Triumvirs (group of three men) 'for restoring the state'. The proscriptions of their enemies followed, among whom Cicero in December 43 was a leading victim. He had sealed his fate with a series of vitriolic speeches against Antony, whom he had persuaded the senate to declare a public enemy. He was murdered and his head and hands (which had written the speeches abusing Antony) were displayed on the speaker's platform (*rostra*) in Rome.

In 42 BC the republican forces that Brutus and Cassius had gathered in the east were defeated at Philippi and the leaders killed. This victory confirmed Antony's status as a competent general, and the Triumvirs then set out to control the state in their interests by controlling magistracies and appointments and dividing up provinces and responsibilities. Antony predominantly controlled the eastern provinces and Gaul, Octavian the west, and Lepidus Africa. In Egypt Antony met Cleopatra VII, by whom he was to have three children, and the eastern regions occupied much of his attention. However, the situation in Italy was unstable, with much resentment at Octavian's settlement of veteran soldiers, and trouble was stirred up by L. Antonius (consul in 41), Antony's brother, and the Triumvir's wife Fulvia, who were eventually besieged in Perusia by Octavian. The bitterness of the conflict can be judged from the large quantity of lead sling-bullets from both sides found on the site inscribed with a variety of insulting messages for the leaders. After the surrender of Perusia, Antony came to Brundisium in 40 and a new agreement was negotiated, sealed with the marriage of Octavian's sister, Octavia, to Antony. Now the empire was effectively divided between Octavian in the west and Antony in the east, with Lepidus in Africa. In 37 another meeting in Italy at Tarentum renewed the triumvirate for five years, although Antony left Octavia behind when he returned to the east. He now became fully occupied with his invasion of Parthia in 36 (the Parthians had invaded Roman territory in 40) and his continuing liaison with Cleopatra. The failure of the Parthian campaign was a serious setback for Antony, while Octavian, helped by competent military commanders, particularly Marcus Agrippa and Salvidienus Rufus, improved his position with the defeat in 36 of Pompey's younger son, Sextus Pompey, who had used his fleet to control Sicily. At the same time Lepidus was disgraced and deprived of his army, although he was allowed to live in Italy.

There was now a straight confrontation between Octavian and Antony in which Octavian cleverly manipulated public opinion against his rival by presenting him as the un-Roman ally of a degenerate eastern queen, who gave away Roman possessions while he posed as the defender of traditional Italian values and the *imperium* of the Roman state. The propaganda of the victor usually holds sway, and in fact Antony seems to have been a competent and dutiful administrator. Nevertheless his allies were intimidated out of Rome and his divorce of Octavia seemed to confirm his removal from the Roman scene. Military operations took place in western Greece and skilful naval manoeuvring by Agrippa gave the advantage to Octavian; when the fleets met near Actium in 31 BC, Antony's force was defeated though he and Cleopatra managed to break away and escape; his army melted away and other supporters defected to the winner. Antony and his lover committed suicide and Octavian's entry into Alexandria in August of 30 BC marked the end of long years of civil war. The battle throughout the last thirteen years had been for supreme power, whatever the propaganda of the protagonists alleged. Brutus had issued coins before Philippi celebrating the murder of Caesar by depicting on one side daggers and the cap of liberty (traditionally given to a slave when he was set free) with the legend 'Ides of March', and on the other his own portrait, the usual symbol of a monarch. Gaius Julius Caesar Octavianus now had that supreme power. He knew exactly what he wanted to do with it.

CHAPTER FIVE

Augustus and the New Order

Writing Imperial History

The battle of Actium ushered in a new era of historical writing, or so it seemed to later writers trying to piece together a credible history of the rule of the early emperors. On the one hand there was much useful information, many contemporary writers, and unusually the words of the main protagonist. Augustus left to posterity a brief autobiographical memoir, 'The Achievements of the Divine Augustus' (*Res Gestae Divi Augusti*), to be inscribed outside his mausoleum in Rome and at various centres in the empire. Addressing Roman citizens, he justified his career through a statement of what he had done for Rome in politics, military affairs and public service. This is how Augustus wanted to be remembered and of course he omits or doctors anything inconsistent with the picture of a benevolent benefactor of the Roman world. The *Res Gestae* are no more reliable than most modern political memoirs; like Augustus himself, they are duplicitous and self-serving, but also fascinating.

Velleius Paterculus from the Italian municipal aristocracy in Campania was the principal contemporary witness whose history survives; as a military officer he was actually part of the events he describes. A friend of Augustus and Tiberius and promoted by them, he exemplifies the social progress of the *equites* under Augustus, and his history may well be derided as sycophantic and misleading. Nevertheless, as well as his eyewitness accounts, his work is valuable precisely because we can observe its bias and recognize the official version of events, and because Velleius highlights contemporary attitudes of a group who supported everything Augustus represented. Quite different was Livy, the great historian of Rome, who was from Patavium (Padua) and also a friend of Augustus. He ended his history in 9 BC and his account of the civil wars and the victory of Augustus is unfortunately lost (though later summaries of these books exist). Livy

remained aloof from public life but his commentary on public figures would have
been invaluable. He was apparently so generous in praise of Pompey in his
history that Augustus jokingly called him a 'Pompeian'. And Livy's rather
gloomy preface suggests that he offered a more penetrating account of the political revolution inspired by Augustus than we might expect. He notes the qualities
of early Rome and then goes on:

> He (the reader) should consider carefully how bit by bit discipline gave way
> and then how morality first declined and then slipped ever more rapidly before
> eventually crashing headlong and coming to the present situation when we can
> endure neither our vices nor their cure. (1, Preface 9)

Other contemporaries of Augustus were close to the regime in different ways
and are valuable for what they tell us, often accidentally, about life during his
reign. For example, the architect Vitruvius helped design public buildings and
also military engines for Augustus and enjoyed his patronage: 'Since therefore I
was in your debt for benefactions that meant that to the end of my life I had no
fear of poverty . . .' (*On Architecture*, Preface 3). He is refreshingly direct in his
statement of his patron's dominant position in the Roman state (p. 100). Strabo
from Amaseia in Pontus (born *c*.64 BC) wrote a *Geographia* in seventeen books;
he was well connected, and understanding the direction of Roman government,
he interpreted the Augustan revolution and the developing territorial empire in
terms of the organization and management of space and exploitation of the
natural environment; he also praised Augustus for his beautiful and practical
buildings in Rome. All this evidence is Rome-centred since even a non-Italian
like Strabo was a man whom the Romans had won over to their way of thinking.

Poets like Horace, Virgil, Ovid and Propertius had contact, good and bad,
with Augustus or his entourage and in various ways help to illuminate contemporary events. They highlight a particular problem for the historian in that it is
debatable how far those who accepted imperial patronage directly voiced the
policies of the regime.

The official version of administrative decisions or their reception by the
provincials is reinforced by formal inscriptions, which also show some of the
diplomatic avenues for approaching Augustus in the new order. Coins minted by
the Roman government took the image of the emperor to all parts of the empire
and commented on policy in words and pictures. It is unclear what impact they
had or were intended to have on the recipients, but they remain another useful
guide to ideas that emperors and their advisers thought worth propagating.

The official version receives a useful dose of scepticism from later historians,
who tried to analyse the difficulties of writing imperial history. Cornelius

Tacitus, a senator from Narbonese or Cisalpine Gaul and author of the *Histories* and *Annals*, which centred on events in Rome in the first century AD, examines the eternal problem of historians working in an autocracy, namely that those writing long after the event might be excessively hostile to an emperor and his advisers, while contemporary historians might be reduced to subservient flattery (*Annals* 1.1). The other major historian to wrestle with the problems of the history of Augustus's regime was Cassius Dio, a senator from Bithynia in the Greek eastern part of the empire, writing in the early third century AD. He complains about how difficult it was to get accurate information in contrast to the more open society of the Republic: 'After this time (27 BC) most things began to be done secretly and kept hidden, and even if some events are made public they are distrusted because they cannot be checked; for people suspect that everything is said or done according to the wishes of the people in power and their allies' (53.19). Yet for us he is the main narrative source for Augustus's regime, even though for events after 10 BC only substantial excerpts of his original text remain. Suetonius (second century AD) makes little effort at analysis but offers a biography of Augustus containing a wealth of detail, not all of which is reliable or checkable; but by virtue of his access to imperial archives as Hadrian's correspondence secretary, he does preserve verbatim some fascinating personal letters of Augustus that seem genuine. Suetonius at least casts some light on the enigma of Augustus's personality.

The Political Leader

After Actium in 31 BC Octavian was master of the Roman world. In theory he could have wiped out the senate and ruled with a few personal advisers. But the majority of his most persistent upper-class opponents were dead and the senate now contained many of his supporters. He needed senators as his senior administrators, his governors, and his army commanders, and the senate came with them. What is more, he needed the old aristocracy to add lustre and respectability to his regime. He had after all proclaimed himself as the selfless liberator of the state from 'the tyranny of a faction'. Yet Octavian clearly intended to be in charge, and consequently an autocracy emerged with a façade of republican institutions, in which his own powers were voted by the senate and people and carefully articulated. Therefore, the senate continued to conduct business, and the *comitia centuriata* continued to elect consuls and praetors. Measures were proposed in the senate and the *concilium plebis* passed the legislation; this formal framework of law-making was maintained, although gradually the *concilium plebis* became more of a rubber stamp and the Senate's decree came to have the force of law. Traditional magistrates were elected according to established

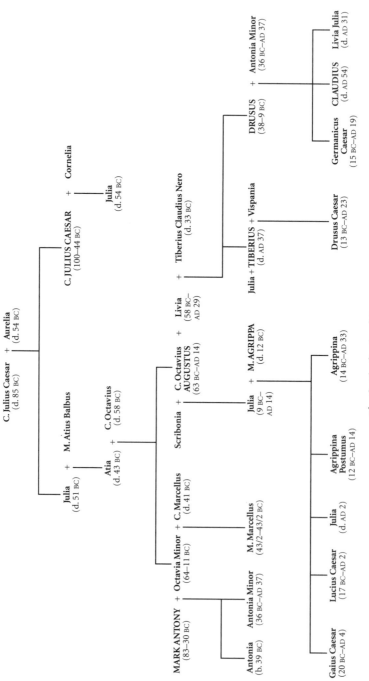

Plan 3. The family of Augustus.

procedures, and the lawcourts still functioned. A returning Cicero might have agreed at first sight with the enthusiastic judgement of Velleius: 'The old traditional format of the state was restored' (2.89).

Behind the façade, Octavian insinuated himself surreptitiously into the traditional mechanism of government. From 31 to 23 BC he held the consulship every year. But gradually from 28 onwards he gave up the dictatorial powers associated with the triumvirate. He shared the fasces (the consul's symbol of office) with Agrippa, his chief henchman and colleague as consul in 28, and took the traditional oath on leaving office that he had done nothing contrary to the laws. A coin minted in 28 shows Octavian sitting on a magistrate's chair holding a scroll, with the slogan 'he restored to the Roman people their laws and rights'. He approached the senate formally in 27 and in a piece of well-rehearsed political theatre apparently offered to give up his powers, returning the state (*res publica*) to the decision of the senate and people (*Res Gestae* 34). In reality there was no question of 'restoring the republic'. The senate wisely returned the responsibility to him, and while retaining the consulship Octavian accepted a large sphere of operations (*provincia*), voted to him initially for ten years, consisting of most of the provinces with legionary troops whose governors he appointed directly as his deputies (*legati Augusti*). The senate had the right to appoint governors (proconsuls) to the remaining provinces. Both Cassius Dio and Tacitus firmly believed that Octavian's position was in essence monarchical and that he had tightened his control – 'from then on the chains were tighter' (*Annals* 3.28). Dio observed sarcastically that Augustus had apprised his supporters in the senate about his intentions in advance, and at the end of the process established his personal bodyguard, the Praetorians, at a premium rate of pay. This was a symbol of virtual monarchy, and behind all the political niceties the army expressed the realities of power. Nevertheless, the grateful senate bestowed upon Octavian the name Augustus, which, with its quasi-religious overtones, celebrated his pre-eminent role as saviour of the state.

In 23 BC Augustus surrendered his consulship, holding it on only two more occasions, in 5 and 2 BC; he therefore avoided the stigma of the untraditional permanent occupation of a magistracy and gave senators extra opportunity to hold this prestigious office. However, he assumed the power of a tribune and 'greater proconsular power' (*proconsulare imperium maius*); the former was vaguely defined but impressive, associated with protecting the people and giving him the permanent sacrosanctity of a tribune and the right to introduce legislation or veto business, without the trouble of seeking election. By having the power of an office without actually holding it, Augustus was liberated from its constitutional constraints. It was so important to him that he numbered the years of his rule by it. With the latter he controlled his *provincia*, and he could also give instructions to the proconsuls in those provinces outside his *provincia* for whose appointment the senate was responsible. We see this in the series of edicts published in the marketplace at Cyrene in the public province of Crete and Cyrene, by which Augustus settled outstanding problems. For example, the third Cyrene edict of 7–6 BC reads:

> Imperator Caesar Augustus, *pontifex maximus*, holding the tribunician power for the seventeenth time declares: If any people from the Cyrenaican province have been honoured with Roman citizenship, I order them to perform the personal (?) public services. . . . (Sherk, 1984, no. 102, edict III)

Both these powers could be voted by the senate to another person of Augustus's choice, and therefore secured the way for him to designate a successor, which he had always intended.

In 19 BC Augustus was granted further powers, which may have amounted to the right to sit between the consuls, have the insignia of a consul and effectively to exercise consular power without holding the consulship. Ostensibly, he worked within legal forms and republican precedent with a hint of popular appeal, but in reality he was a revolutionary who made a travesty of traditional titles. In the same way he preserved those parts of traditional electoral practice that suited him while ensuring that he got the right people elected. Dio summed up the position neatly: 'Nothing was done that did not please him' (53.21.6), and this is endorsed by Tacitus: 'Up to that time (AD 14) the most important elections were resolved by decision of the emperor' (*Annals* 1.15). Augustus canvassed in person in the forum and gave public support to his favoured candidates. This of course was traditional practice, but his own men were sure to be elected, as the grateful Velleius Paterculus, one of 'Caesar's candidates', points out proudly (2.124). The emperor's candidates were probably declared elected outside the normal electoral process. Since Augustus would not care or need to intervene in every election, it was possible to keep up the façade of free election, in which bribery and violence (traditional republican practices) sometimes occurred.

Affairs of state should run smoothly and without controversy, and to this end Augustus introduced a constitutional novelty, a senatorial committee to discuss business before meetings of the full senate. The senate, therefore, felt involved in government and Augustus, avoiding publicly embarrassing scenes, quietly and politely got what he wanted. The really important political decisions were taken by Augustus and his advisory council, consisting of members of his family and trusted *amici* (literally 'friends'), men whose advice was worth considering. This body met irregularly at Augustus's whim, generally behind closed doors, with the result that we have little reliable information about its deliberations.

Furthermore, Augustus intervened when it suited him to get the administration of Rome and Italy moving in the direction he wanted, by appointing officials outside the traditional magistracies who were often directly responsible to him.

Augustus was also active in areas of civil and criminal jurisdiction; he did not replace the courts and the responsible magistrates but offered another avenue of jurisdiction. With his advisers he acted as a court in the first instance in both civil and criminal jurisdiction and in time also received appeals. The story goes that one day Maecenas, one of Augustus's most trusted advisers, finding him delivering capital sentences in the middle of a throng of people, tossed a message to him to get up and stop. Gradually, Augustus came to be seen as a benevolent adjudicator and source of justice. We see him in action in a letter to the Greek city of Cnidos in 6 BC, where a lady named Tryphera and her husband (now deceased) had apparently been unjustly accused of murder. Augustus had arranged for an interrogation of the witnesses, noted that the attitude of the city had been unfairly harsh and unjust to the defendant, and concluded: 'But now you would seem to me to act correctly, if to my decision in this matter you paid attention and made the records in your public archives agree with it' (Sherk, 1984, no. 103).

Augustus was the paymaster of the Roman world, spending lavishly on the army, new buildings and the restoration of temples in Rome, and bringing help to provincial communities. He was proud of his generosity, boasting in the *Res Gestae* (15) of his distributions of money and corn to the Roman plebs: 'In my thirteenth consulship (2 BC) I gave sixty *denarii* each to the plebs who were then receiving public grain; they made up a few more than 200,000 people.' He also paid out huge sums for the purchase of lands in Italy and the provinces for veteran soldiers; the wealth of the empire was at his disposal, including the booty of conquest and the fabulously rich land of Egypt, which he made into a new province. From the start the personal wealth of Augustus merged almost imperceptibly with that of the state that he embodied: 'On four occasions I assisted the public treasury with my own money, with the result that I transferred one hundred and fifty million sesterces to the administrators of the treasury' (*Res Gestae* 17).

The emperor made decisions on taxes and tax collection and the organization of the census of the whole empire; he kept the financial resources under his control by appointing procurators of equestrian rank directly to supervise revenue, tax-collecting and resources in provinces to which he appointed a governor (also keeping administration and finance separate). We know, for example, that the procurator in Spain, and presumably in other provinces, was responsible for ensuring that monies were available to pay the soldiers stationed there. The public treasury (*aerarium Saturni*) was under the charge of two prefects of praetorian rank, ambitious senators who would want to please the emperor. It was Augustus who took the initiative in the creation of a new military treasury (*aerarium militare*) in AD 6, which typically he funded partly by his own money and also by taxes on inheritances and auctions imposed on Roman citizens in Italy (the first since 167 BC). No one would be permitted to interfere with the revenues, which Cicero had called the 'sinews of the state'.

The establishment of an orderly government without many of the usual threatening features of autocratic rule was an impressive achievement. Ideally, Augustus wished to appear as *princeps* (first citizen), giving advice and guidance. He himself chose to emphasize his informal influence (*auctoritas*) rather than his power, and was proud of the golden shield voted to him celebrating his noble qualities – courage, clemency, justice and piety (*Res Gestae* 34). He had lofty ambitions, talking of how he had established institutions of government that were to remain as a model for the future, and his boast about finding Rome built of brick and leaving it clothed in marble also had political overtones. He must have been well satisfied when in 2 BC the whole people conferred on him the title of 'Father of the Fatherland' (*Pater Patriae*).

However, Augustus was ruthless and relentless in the pursuit of power and opposition was crushed, sometimes brutally, as with the judicial murder of the alleged conspirators Primus and Murena in 22 BC. He never resolved the contradictions in his political position. On the one hand, in discussions with his eventual successor Tiberius, he advised him that it was desirable to permit free speech and not pay attention to critics, but he also extended the treason law to include not only actions but also slander and libel. Tacitus thought that this was one reason for the sinister development of this law. He barred the learned Greek writer Timagenes from his home because he had been critical of the imperial family, but refrained from any further action. Despite the republican framework of government and Augustus's consistently restrained demeanour and outward deference to tradition, he was an autocrat. Vitruvius, the architect and protégé of Augustus, in the preface of his book *On Architecture* tells us more about life in Rome and the position of its *princeps* than all the elaborate political manoeuvring:

> When your divinely-guided intelligence and holy spirit, *imperator* Caesar, gained mastery of the world, having destroyed all your enemies by your irresistible might, the citizens delighted in your triumph and victory, and the subdued peoples awaited your command, and the senate and Roman people, freed from fear, were guided by your profound thoughts and advice. . . . (1, *Preface* 1)

The Military Leader

No artifice could conceal Octavian's weak health and undistinguished military performance during the civil wars, which became the butt of Antony's jokes. Yet he owed his mastery of the Roman world to victory in battle and the elimination of his opponents by warfare. In 31 BC sixty legions looked to him as their leader and the army was to remain the cornerstone of his regime. Augustus inherited an army traditionally built around the strength of the heavy infantry organized in legions, which were subdivided into ten cohorts with 480 men in each, though the first cohort was probably larger and organized differently. A cohort had six centuries of eighty men commanded by a centurion. The legions were traditionally Roman citizens and in the early first century AD many were of Italian origin. After reorganization and pensioning off veterans at great expense, Augustus was satisfied for the moment with twenty-eight legions, about 150,000 men. But he shrewdly exploited the fact that Rome had always used non-Roman peoples as specialist fighters, particularly cavalry, and brought these auxiliary formations into the army at first under their own chieftains in ethnic groups. Later, they were assimilated more formally into the military structure under Roman officers. This was an enormous reservoir of manpower, and by AD 14 auxiliaries matched the legionaries in number, making an army of about 300,000 men. After the naval success at Actium, Augustus located strong fleets with 10,000 men in each at Ravenna on the east coast of Italy and Misenum on the west coast. Commanded by equestrian officers, the fleets routinely protected the corn ships and transported troops. Augustus's personal security was in the hands of the praetorian guard, consisting probably of 9,000 troops recruited exclusively from Italians and organized in nine cohorts, three of which were based in the heart of Rome. The security of the city was the responsibility of the 3,000 men of the urban cohorts and at least as many *Vigiles*, the freedmen fire-brigade.

This large army was an ornament to Augustus's rule, a confirmation of imperial dignity, a buttress against revolution and potentially a vehicle of conquest. Augustus decided not to return to the practice of recruiting troops to meet immediate needs and instead maintained a standing professional army that was to be permanently based in provinces where warfare was certain or imminent or the subject population restive. This meant that there were fewer disruptive levies and the army over time could be trained in personal loyalty to him. Augustus avoided conscription in Italy except in times of extreme crisis such as the defeat of Varus in Germany in AD 9. To maintain the army, however, was enormously expensive (more than 40 per cent of the state's annual income in Augustus's day) and remained a constant concern for his successors. In 13 BC Augustus set service conditions at sixteen years for legionaries (twelve for praetorians) at the existing rate of 2.5 *sesterces* a day (a labourer in Rome could earn about 3 *sesterces* a day), but subsequently increased this to twenty years, partly because of the difficulty of finding recruits and of paying discharge bonuses (*praemia*). On leaving the army, a legionary received a plot of land or a cash payment of 12,000 *sesterces*.

The ordinary soldier was not well-off and there were deductions from his pay for food and clothing and this was certainly one of the reasons for the mutiny of AD 14. Nevertheless, the soldiers were better off than others in the class from which they came, mainly the rural lower class. From time to time Augustus distributed money in the form of donations to the troops, and he was to leave them money in his will. No subsequent emperor could ignore the need to give the army suitable financial inducements.

Augustus went to great lengths to make sure that the soldiers were loyal to him as their sole paymaster and benefactor, and not to their individual commanders, which had been the old problem of the Republic. As noted, he avoided confiscations of land and spent huge sums on buying land in Italy and the provinces for distribution to soldiers in the substantial discharge of veterans in 30 and 14 BC – 600 million *sesterces* for land in Italy, 260 million for land in the provinces. He proudly boasted that he was 'the first and only one to have done this in the memory of my contemporaries' (*Res Gestae* 16). In AD 6, when Augustus persuaded the senate to establish the military treasury to pay *praemia*, he contributed 150 million *sesterces* of his own money, keeping up the idea of his personal role. It is a measure of the importance of the army in the new regime that in the long term the treasury was to be funded by direct taxes on legacies and auctions (see above, p. 100).

The loyalty of the army to Augustus was also sustained by the centurions (fifty-nine in each legion), who were much better paid and had reasonable opportunities for promotion. They had a major role in maintaining discipline, were often better educated than the rank-and-file, and are likely to have been a strong focus of support for Augustus. Furthermore, junior officers of equestrian rank in command of the auxiliary units had every reason to make sure that Augustus remained in power, since he offered an avenue for their advancement that would have been denied to them under the old senatorial oligarchy. Velleius Paterculus followed in the footsteps of his grandfather and father in holding equestrian military posts, including that of military tribune and cavalry commander, and from AD 4 to 12 was campaigning with Tiberius in Pannonia and Germany. He was deeply loyal to the imperial family and Augustus's regime and was eventually promoted to the rank of senator. At a somewhat lower social level, Marcus Vergilius Gallus Lusius, chief centurion of legion 11, prefect of engineers and commander of an infantry and cavalry unit, proudly records how he was: 'awarded two headless spears (military decorations) and gold crowns by the divine Augustus and Tiberius Caesar Augustus' (Braund, 1985, no. 478). This idea that the decorations came personally from Augustus and Tiberius emphasizes the personal connection between emperors and their officers.

There was now a new dynamic in Roman life, politics and military service. Augustus, who had adopted as his first name *imperator* (general; from the Latin comes the English 'emperor'), a word redolent of the ethos of military command, was effectively commander-in-chief. He was quite capable of referring to both 'the army of the Roman people' and to 'my army' (*Res Gestae* 30). He appointed most military commanders personally as his *legati* and issued instructions to them. In the early years he went personally to areas of military activity and made sure that members of his family were prominent in military command; his stepsons Drusus (up to his death in 9 BC), and Tiberius, his grandson Gaius Caesar, and finally Tiberius's adopted son Germanicus were all sent to trouble-spots to command armies. It marked them out as men of importance and also kept ambitious senators away from too much military glory. Augustus held three triumphs on 13–15 August, 29 BC, and gradually the imperial family came to monopolize major military honours. The last triumph by a senator was in 19 BC; they had to make do with triumphal ornaments. Augustus had been seriously embarrassed by the exploits of the senatorial proconsul of Macedonia, Marcus Crassus, in 29–27 BC; not only did he earn a triumph but he also slew the enemy leader in battle, earning the supreme honour of the *spolia opima*, which Augustus denied to him on a technicality. Indeed, he strove to distance himself from all others in military glory, receiving acclamations as *imperator* (associated with successful military command) on twenty-one occasions, often for the military exploits of others. His symbolic military prowess is powerfully demonstrated by the great statue found at *Prima Porta* in Rome; Augustus, barefoot in semi-heroic guise, clad in armour and wearing the commander's cloak, gestures imperiously. The people could have confidence in their great military leader. Augustus's sumptuous new forum also had a distinctly martial ambience. The setting was dominated by the temple of Mars the Avenger, which proclaimed the avenging not only of Julius Caesar but of previous Roman military defeats. Authority had been restored by new military victories, and on the dedication of the forum in 2 BC a statue of a four-horse chariot was erected with an inscription recounting all of Augustus's victories. Statues of great generals of the Republic stood along each side and Augustus decided that all commanders who won triumphal honours should have a bronze statue in the forum.

Throughout his long reign Augustus maintained a close personal association with his army despite attempts in public to distance himself; so when the civil wars were over he refused to address his men as 'fellow-soldiers' (Suetonius, *Augustus* 25), a term that did not fit in with the peaceful nature of his regime and his own dignity. Nevertheless, all soldiers swore an oath of loyalty (*sacramentum*) to Augustus personally, and in private Augustus looked after the interests of his men, even appearing in court in the interests of one of his bodyguards. Three legions, the II, III and VIII, were named *Augusta* to mark either reorganization or a victory under Augustus. The military calendar, which set out the festivals to be celebrated by soldiers, sums up his personal involvement with the army and attention to detail. A copy found at Dura-Europos on the Euphrates frontier dates to the third century AD, but the idea goes back to Augustus; and among the many celebrations linked to the reigning emperor appears: '23 September: For the birthday of the divine Augustus, to the divine Augustus an ox' (Campbell, 1994, no. 207). It was entirely fitting therefore that on the day of his funeral, after a procession by senators and *equites*, praetorian guardsmen ran around the pyre and threw into it their medals gained for valour, while the centurions applied torches.

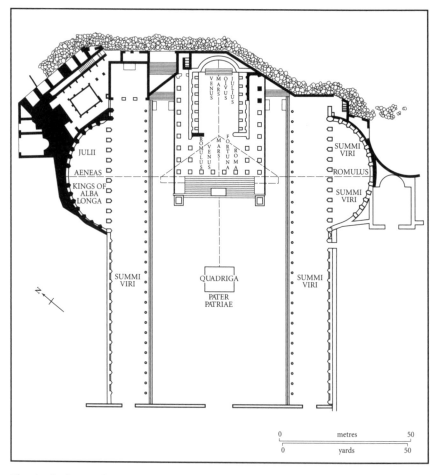

Plan 4. The forum of Augustus in Rome (Campbell, *War and Society in Imperial Rome* (2002), figure 6.1).

The Conqueror

The Greek geographer Strabo succinctly described Augustus in 27 BC as 'Lord of war and peace'. Declaring war, making peace and negotiating treaties had been the prerogative of the senate and people, but Augustus, as master of the Roman legions, was able to dictate policy, though in practice this was limited by the financial resources of the empire, the capacity of the Roman army and its commanders, and also by the traditional prejudices of the upper classes. We can see Augustus's mastery of foreign relations in the meeting of his advisory council in AD 6 when the emperor decided and promulgated by edict the future government of Judaea (p. 108). Indeed Augustus's rule saw a period of unprecedented conquest and expansion, with the creation of new provinces or extension of existing ones, and more rulers brought within Rome's orbit: 'I extended the territory of all those provinces of the Roman people on whose borders lay peoples not subject to our government' (*Res Gestae* 26.1).

The emperor's partisan memoir is of course not necessarily a good guide to imperial policy, and the enthusiastic celebrations by contemporary poets of Rome's impending world domination should not be taken entirely seriously. Horace, for example, vividly imagined Augustus's majestic progress throughout the world:

> He (Augustus) whether leading in entitled triumph
> the Parthians now darkening Rome's horizon,
> the Indian or Chinese peoples huddled
> close to the rising sun
> shall, as your right hand, deal the broad earth justice. (*Odes* 1.12.53–7)

Virgil, in his epic poem the *Aeneid* about the adventures of Aeneas as he founded Rome, presumably struck a responsive chord with his audience when he has Jupiter promise: 'To this people I assign no boundaries in space or time. I have granted them power without limit' (*Aeneid* 1.278–9). And his comment on Rome's imperial destiny – 'to spare the humble and war down the arrogant' (*Aeneid* 6.851–3) – made a typically Roman distinction between those who surrendered and those who chose to resist. However, Augustus did not have an empire-wide programme or policy of world conquest (even with the Romans' rather limited concept of the world), with clearly defined stages and outcome. On the other hand, he had no narrowly defensive view.

Certain areas more or less demanded action of some kind. Spain, long a Roman province, was still not secure, especially in the north, in the Cantabrian highlands. The Alps, dominating the approaches to Italy, had been strangely neglected in the past and had no provincial structure. Illyricum and the surrounding area raised the issue of the unity of the empire and the security of east–west communications. In this geographical and strategic context, Augustus could opportunistically indulge in annexation or further wars when local peoples fought back. Gradually, the Alpine provinces were established, Roman territorial control advanced right up to the banks of the Danube, and Spain was subdued in the presence of Augustus.

Elsewhere, the fabled wealth of Arabia attracted Roman attention, though the campaigns were short-lived and did not add new territory. But a major effort was expended on the Rhine. The conquest of Gaul had been achieved only seventeen years before the battle of Actium in 31 BC, and Julius Caesar had completed his campaigns against the Gallic tribes in just ten years; it may have seemed to Augustus that Germany was the continuation of this and an opportunity for glorious conquest by Caesar's heir. Augustus was in Gaul from 16 to 13 BC overseeing preparations, and from 12 to 9 Drusus commanded in a series of annual campaigns, finally reaching the Elbe in 9 BC. Soon after, however, he died after a riding accident. His elder brother Tiberius carried on the campaigns and it seems that Germany between the Rhine and Elbe was being prepared as a province. After Tiberius withdrew from public life in 6 BC, Lucius Domitius Ahenobarbus marched to the Elbe and crossed it. By AD 9 an altar and cult of Augustus had been established at Cologne as a focus of German adherence to Roman rule. P. Quinctilius Varus seemingly had the task of organizing a formal provincial structure, but according to the official version was careless and allowed himself to be deceived and ambushed by Arminius, chief of the Cherusci and a Roman citizen of equestrian rank who had served in the auxilia. Three legions and auxiliaries were destroyed (c.20,000 men) probably near Osnabrück. Augustus was distraught at the disruption of his plans, allegedly roaming the palace sleeplessly, and emergency recruitment was undertaken. Tiberius, now back in command, restored the situation, and in AD 15 Germanicus found the site of the battle and erected a burial mound. On a personal level individual victims of the disaster were remembered by their families. A monument to the centurion Caelius was set up at Vetera (Xanten) in Lower Germany by his brother, with a carving of Caelius in full uniform holding his centurion's staff and displaying his military decorations:

> Marcus Caelius, son of Titus of the tribe Lemonia, from Bononia, centurion of legion XVIII, fifty-three and a half years old, fell in the Varian war. Permission is granted to place his bones within (the monument). Publius Caelius, son of Titus, of the tribe Lemonia, his brother, set this up. (*Inscriptiones Latinae Selectae (ILS)* 2244)

Incidentally, this shows how in public opinion this was Varus's, not Augustus's, disaster. However, the crisis passed and the Germans drifted off to fight among themselves. Nevertheless, Roman territorial control was firmly anchored on the Rhine, though they operated freely beyond it, even imposing taxes on Frisii (in modern Holland). The conquest of Germany was postponed, not necessarily abandoned.

Tiberius had campaigned in Illyricum from 12 to 10 BC, eventually creating a series of provinces (Raetia, Noricum, Pannonia, Moesia) and advancing to the Danube. In AD 6, in an act of spectacular aggression beyond the river, the Romans planned war against king Maroboduus and the conquest of Bohemia. These plans were dashed by a major uprising in Illyricum, which was suppressed only after three years of fierce fighting and the concentration of huge numbers of troops under Tiberius. Roman victory confirmed that the Danubian area was to be under Roman control, but along with the defeat of Varus marked the low point of Augustus's military fortunes.

In the east, Parthia and Armenia stood on the periphery of Roman territory, and from the start Augustus followed a quite different policy, which indicates his flexible approach. He could not ignore the area because Roman military honour demanded that something be done to avenge the loss of Roman standards in the defeat of Marcus Crassus at Carrhae in 53 BC and in Antony's campaigns of 36. Furthermore, since the time of Pompey, Armenia was considered to be within the Roman orbit, even though strategically it was not essential to Roman control of Syria. Now, although public opinion may have expected that Augustus would make war on Parthia and indeed even invade Britain, all-out war in the east did not seem a rewarding option in view of the difficulty in dealing with Parthian tactics, and the possibility of a significant setback and loss of face, perhaps with serious political implications.

In no real sense at this time was Parthia a threat to the rich province of Syria. Therefore, even though there was a strong pretender to the Parthian throne seeking his assistance, Augustus moved circumspectly and exploited the fact that Parthia, being the only civilized state on the empire's boundaries with a relatively stable government structure, was susceptible to diplomacy. Augustus personally came to Syria in 20 BC and summoned Tiberius with an army to install a suitable king in Armenia. Eventually, with appropriate diplomatic fanfare, a deal was done with the Parthian king Phraates. The standards were returned, an episode which Augustus celebrated as a great victory, claiming that he had *compelled* the Parthians to surrender the standards and 'as suppliants seek the friendship of the Roman people' (*Res Gestae* 29.2). Coins were minted showing a kneeling Parthian returning a standard. Then in 1 BC a kind of treaty was agreed by which the Romans undertook not to go beyond the Euphrates or try to destabilize the

Parthian king, while the Parthians effectively accepted that the Romans could nominate and install the rulers of Armenia, as long as they did not establish a permanent military presence. The deal was sealed with a spectacular diplomatic jamboree (witnessed and vividly described by Velleius Paterculus as a young military officer) when the young king Phraataces met Gaius Caesar, Augustus's grandson, adopted son and intended successor and emissary: 'This spectacle of the Roman army drawn up on one side, the Parthian on the other, while the two outstanding leaders of their empires and the peoples of the world met together, was a striking and memorable sight' (2.101).

Throughout his long reign Augustus was the nucleus for all kinds of diplomatic activity. Numerous potentates came to seek his support and he received embassies from many foreign peoples even from as far afield as India: 'Embassies from kings in India were frequently sent to me; never before had they been seen with any Roman commander' (*Res Gestae* 31–2). One embassy came with a gift of tigers, a novel sight for Greeks and Romans. In dealing with foreign affairs Augustus did not have an overall policy; he was guided sometimes by strategic necessity, but more often by expediency, profit, self-interest and the promotion of his own image, not to mention the need to keep a large army occupied. Decisions were taken on an ad hoc basis, sometimes by trial and error, and exploited the emperor's significant friendships with friendly local dynasts, notably Herod of Judaea. However, after Herod's death when Augustus felt that he could no longer trust that family, he reluctantly decided to annex Judaea as a province, under a governor of equestrian rank.

Augustus's decisions established the essential layout of Roman territory (he advised his successor not to extend the empire 'beyond its present limits'), the disposition of the provinces and legions, and indeed the shape of future European geography. He also established the pattern of provincial governorships and army command, by which the governors he appointed operated entirely at his pleasure and directly under his auspices, and any military success accrued to him. By AD 14 Africa was the only province containing legionary soldiers under the command of a governor appointed by the senate, and it was relatively unimportant in military terms with its single legion. Finally, through unrelenting military activity Augustus left for his successors the paradigm of the conquering emperor, and reinforced the Roman ideology of military *virtus* and aggressive self-confidence that recognized no formal limits to their power. This helps us to understand the Roman concept of peace, as Augustus put it himself: 'When victories had secured peace by land and sea throughout the whole empire of the Roman people' (*Res Gestae* 13). There was no inconsistency in formally closing the doors of the temple of Janus to indicate peace throughout the empire during the rule of one of Rome's most militarily active emperors.

The Administrator

City administration was less spectacular than military conquest but was nevertheless important for Augustus's relationship with the Roman people and also demonstrated his willingness to deal with areas of government and public amenities
neglected during the late Republic. The poorer citizens in Rome needed corn, not
just the free distribution, which was provided on a limited scale to a defined
number of recipients, but more importantly a consistent supply of cheap corn; the
onus was upon Augustus to provide it. Improved and newly constructed aqueducts brought running water to the city for drinking, washing and also putting out
fires; the fire brigade (*Vigiles*) had outposts throughout the city. Augustus also
tried to reduce the danger of fire and the collapse of buildings, especially tenement
blocks, by introducing regulations restricting height and ensuring proper repair.
He made a start on preventing the frequent, destructive flooding of the city by the
river Tiber. Rome, with a population perhaps close to one million, many of whom
lived in tenement flats, was doubtless not a pleasant place to live in, but the plebs
could at least believe that they had not been abandoned by the government, and
had a champion to whom they could look for protection.

To organize these services Augustus employed senators and *equites*, but in a
new way. So, for example, the water supply was supervised by curators of senatorial rank, who were chosen by the emperor and formally appointed by the
senate. Augustus continued to take a personal interest, as is celebrated on an
inscription from the Aqua Marcia aqueduct:

Imperator Caesar Augustus . . . repaired the conduits of all the aqueducts'.
(*ILS* 98)

Senators of praetorian rank also served as 'prefects for the distribution of corn'.
In AD 6 two senators of consular rank were in charge of the overall corn supply,
but eventually a man of equestrian rank was put in charge (*Praefectus Annonae*).
He was a personal appointee of Augustus, as was the Prefect of the *Vigiles*, first in
office in AD 6. These officials superseded the traditional magistrates in the
managing of the city's services, and reported directly to Augustus. Sometime after
11 BC two 'curators of the sacred buildings and the public works and places' were
appointed. Augustus cautiously and surreptitiously extended his control in this
piecemeal fashion: 'He moved forward gradually and absorbed into himself the
role of the senate, magistrates and laws' (Tacitus, *Annals* 1.2).

Although Augustus indulged the people of Rome, he would not tolerate
disruption of his regime, which after all was based on the premise of the return
of peace and ordered government. For security in the streets he had at his
disposal the 3,000 men of the paramilitary police force, the Urban Cohorts, and

of course the praetorians whenever needed. Supervision and management of the city were facilitated by its division in 7 BC into fourteen regions, subdivided into 256 wards (*vici*), each of which elected four local magistrates (*vicomagistri*), who among other things dealt with local religious cults. Over time many of these officials were freedmen, providing another role for this important group in Roman society. Legal jurisdiction for the city of Rome was eventually assigned to the Prefect of the City (*Praefectus Urbi*), which provided an important job for senators once they understood and accepted the prefect's role. The first incumbent, Messalla Corvinus, resigned after a few days, claiming that the position was *incivilis* (that is, tyrannical or against the laws).

The long arm of Augustus extended throughout Italy, which he divided into eleven districts; he established twenty-eight colonies of veteran soldiers, and arranged for the completion and publication of a survey of land allocation in the territories of Italian towns. He took a practical interest in the whole process of land survey and settlement, and the marking of holdings; indeed in the early empire boundary stones were known as 'Augustan'. His interest in detail appears in a letter he wrote to the veterans of the fourth legion established at Firmum in Picenum, in which he helpfully advised them to sell off the *subseciva* (unsurveyed land) around their settlement. He also undertook an extensive programme of road building and repair, using his own money and encouraging senators to take responsibility for individual roads. He took charge of the via Flaminia running from Rome to Ariminum on the Adriatic. Finally, in 20 BC a board of senatorial 'curators of the roads' was established. This facilitated the movement of troops throughout the country, but the improved communications also linked Italy more closely to the capital and offered scope for economic development and regeneration against a background of peace compared to the previous twenty years. It is not surprising that in 12 BC for Augustus's election as *Pontifex Maximus* people poured into the city from all over Italy in numbers the like of which Rome had never seen (*Res Gestae* 10.2).

Provincial communities also had reason to thank Augustus. He was a highly visible figure to whom complaints could be sent and who might offer help. Although governors appointed by the senate were chosen by lot to serve for one year, Augustus's hand-picked governors were often in office for a number of years and were directly responsible to him. It might be hoped (admittedly not always realized) that the emperor's appointees would be more efficient and honest. Furthermore, tax collection was now at least based on an empire-wide census of the available resources. Augustus apparently accepted that the provincials deserved responsible government, and expressed his ideal in an edict introducing a senatorial decree proposing new measures for the trial of Roman officials accused of misgovernment:

Imperator Caesar Augustus . . . since it pertains to the security of the allies of
the Roman people, in order that it might be known to all those under our care,
I have decided to send it to the provinces and to append to it this, my edict,
from which it will be clear to all inhabitants of the provinces how much
concern I and the senate have that no one of our subjects may suffer unduly any
harm or extortion. (Sherk, 1984, no. 102, p. 130)

Father of the Fatherland

Augustus as the benevolent patron of his subjects had a presence and influence far
beyond the formal impact of his constitutional arrangements. He was always an
intruder in upper-class social life, but having decided to work with the senate he set
out to enhance its status. As a body it represented continuity and traditional practice in Roman life. His revisions of the senatorial role, although doubtless painful
for senators, removed (so it could be argued) unworthy members, and he ensured
that meetings were conducted according to a proper format. By 11 BC membership
was about 600, and legislation in 9 BC ensured that meetings were held on fixed
days, established quorums for various kinds of business, and imposed fines for
absence without excuse. With the dignity of the senate preserved, Augustus could
also ensure the prerogatives and dignity of the upper classes. Further legislation
confirmed senatorial and equestrian status and prevented degrading activities like
appearing on the stage or appearing as a gladiator. But he also needed to remind the
upper classes of their duties, and here his actions were not popular. In 18 BC and in
AD 9 provisions encouraged marriage by offering privileges to married people,
especially those with children. Intermarriage by people of senatorial family with
ex-slaves, actors and their children was forbidden down to great-grandchildren in
the male line. Also, tougher penalties were laid down for adultery, which now
became a criminal offence for the first time; a woman convicted of adultery lost half
her dowry and one-third of her property. A man was guilty only if he had sexual
relations with a married woman. Augustus wanted a pure citizen body and placed
restrictions on the manumission of slaves, since freedmen normally became Roman
citizens, insisting that anyone freeing slaves had to be over twenty and that the slave
must be over thirty. The number of manumissions in a will had to be in proportion
to the number of slaves owned.

Augustus's personal demeanour was all-important; once he was securely in
control he was consistently moderate and affable in his personal behaviour. He
tolerated a degree of free speech and lived to a large extent without ostentation
or pomp. He liked jokes provided that they were not ribald and did not detract
from his dignity. He wanted respect and not sycophancy; when a man timidly
sidled up to him he said: 'You are like a man giving a coin to an elephant'. But

there were limits; when the writer Asinius Pollio was the object of some abusive comments by Augustus, he said: 'I'm saying nothing. It's not easy to inscribe lines against a man who can proscribe' (Macrobius, *Saturnalia* 2.4).

For the Roman people Augustus was always a great benefactor, generously distributing money and corn, providing popular entertainments, and funding the infrastructure. In 29, 23 and 11 BC he granted 400 *sesterces* per man to the Roman plebs, never fewer than 250,000; in 5 BC he granted 240 *sesterces* to 320,000 and in 2 BC 240 *sesterces* to 200,000 who were receiving public grain. Grain was distributed from his private granary, for example in 18 BC reaching more than 100,000 people. Augustus proudly records at least sixty-one games or shows in his name, or that of his children, or other magistrates (*Res Gestae* 22–3), as well as a huge naval battle in a specially constructed lake in which 3,000 gladiators fought. By appearing in person at these public spectacles Augustus associated himself with his people and their amusements.

The principal venue for Augustus's generosity was of course Rome, and he changed the physical landscape of the city. Political power was closely linked with architecture, in which it often found its clearest expression. His claim to have left Rome a city of marble, although the comment probably had a political implication, was to an extent literally true. Pride of place must go to the Forum of Augustus and the temple of Mars the Avenger, built from the proceeds of booty in a great space in the centre of Rome and expressing the emperor's grandeur (see above, p. 104). In building the senate house he associated himself with political continuity, and embraced religious tradition in constructing the temple of Apollo and repairing many other temples; he honoured the past by completing the forum and the basilica begun by Julius Caesar, and displayed self-effacing magnanimity by restoring the capitol and theatre of Pompey 'at great expense without inscribing my name on either'. He also built for entertainment, erecting a theatre on ground largely bought from private owners and simultaneously promoted his family by naming it after his son-in-law, Marcellus. The Altar of Peace (*Ara Pacis*), voted by the senate in 13 BC and dedicated in 9 BC, symbolized the imperial family as sponsors of the peaceful regeneration of Italy, now that all enemies had been eliminated.

Augustus was also generous to colonies and provincial communities which solicited assistance from the man they clearly saw as the source of goodwill and benefactions. This was at his discretion and he imposed his own rules, as we see from his response in turning down a request from the inhabitants of Samos for freedom and immunity from taxation, on the grounds that they had not directly helped him in the civil war: 'For it is not appropriate for the greatest privilege of all to be granted at random and without cause. I am well disposed towards you and would like to grant this favour to my wife, who is eager on your behalf, but not to the extent of breaking my established rule' (translation by Millar, 1977, 431–2). This nicely illustrates the process of diplomacy and the pressures (including domestic) on Augustus. Others had more success. In 26 BC, after a serious earthquake had devastated the Greek city of Tralles, an enterprising herdsman came to Rome and then all the way to Spain in search of Augustus to ask for help. Augustus was so moved by his story that he appointed a commission of senators who inspected the damage in person and provided money for rebuilding (Agathias, *Histories* 2.17). Other members of Augustus's family were also generous. We find the people of Mytilene dedicating a statue of Augustus's daughter Julia, wife of Agrippa: 'our benefactress, because of her excellence in every way and her goodwill towards our city' (*Inscriptiones Graecae* XII.2.204; translation in Sherk, 1984, no. 98). Local rich men could observe the signs of urban regeneration in Rome and the imperial example, and were encouraged to bestow largess on their native cities.

Augustus had a large pool of potential supporters among Italians living in the provinces and also wealthy people who coveted Roman citizenship, and he cemented the loyalty of the latter by extending citizenship to worthy locals. For example, C. Julius Vepo from Celeia in Noricum records on his tomb that: 'He had been granted Roman citizenship individually, and immunity, by the Divine Augustus' (*ILS* 1977). He then took the name 'Julius' to mark the benefaction. Of course, Augustus won over people most of all by ending civil war and bringing peace and order. The spirit of the times is superbly illustrated in a decree of the League of Asia in 9 BC bestowing honours on Augustus as their saviour and benefactor; gratitude is mingled with expectations of more benefactions: 'He who put an end to war and will order peace, Caesar, who by his epiphany exceeded the hopes of those who prophesied good tidings, not only outdoing benefactions of the past, but also not leaving any hope [of surpassing him] for those who are coming in the future' (Sherk, 1984, no. 101.VI). This shows a framework of sophisticated diplomatic contact, and the formal process of finding the emperor and approaching him in the proper way appears in a papyrus reporting his reception of an embassy from Alexandria in 10–9 BC:

Imperator Caesar Augustus . . . to the people of the Alexandrians, greetings.

The envoys whom you sent came to me in Gaul and made your representations and in particular informed me of what seems to have troubled you in past years. . . . (Braund, 1985, no. 555)

An inscription in Latin and Neo-Punic from Leptis Magna in north Africa reveals the kind of response that Augustus wanted from his careful cultivation of local goodwill: 'For Imperator Caesar Augustus, son of a god.... Father of the Fatherland, Annobal Rufus, adorner of his country, lover of concord, priest, suffete, prefect of sacred rites, son of Himilco Tapapius, had this made at his own expense and also dedicated it' (Braund, 1985, no. 660). Here we see a man of local culture with Roman connections contributing to his city's welfare and simultaneously honouring the emperor.

Augustus sealed his fatherly image and role of caring *princeps* by the performance of due religious observances. In the rebuilding of Rome's temples and the regeneration of appropriate rituals, he offered expiation for crimes of the past in the civil wars and the inauguration of an age of traditional religious practice and moral rectitude. Augustus had been *Pontifex Maximus* from 12 BC, scrupulously offering himself for election after the death of the incumbent, the disgraced triumvir Lepidus. He also held a large number of the other religious traditional priesthoods and took this role seriously; one statue type represents him performing religious observances as a priest with covered head. He set about reviving the practice of the state religion, and boasted of his restoration of eighty-two temples in the city and his beneficial impact: 'I restored many excellent practices that were disappearing in our time and I myself passed on to posterity many excellent practices for imitation' (*Res Gestae* 8.5).

Since Julius Caesar had been declared a god after his death, Augustus was officially son of a god (*divi filius*), which brought him prestige and a certain aura, and he exploited this by cautiously advancing the idea of his own supernatural being. Beginning in the eastern provinces, a cult to Augustus, initially linked to Roma, was established or fostered. Eventually temples and priests appeared, and worship emerged smoothly from Augustus's role in ending the civil wars and bringing peace, order, concord and prosperity. An inscription from Halicarnassus in Asia sets the tone:

> Since the eternal and immortal nature of everything has bestowed upon mankind the greatest good with extraordinary benefactions by bringing Caesar Augustus in our blessed time the father of his own country, divine Rome, and ancestral Zeus, saviour of the common race of men, whose providence has not only fulfilled but actually exceeded the prayers of all. (Braund, 1985, no. 123)

Doubtless this kind of expression reflects some genuine feeling. But there were other factors, since the mechanism for the worship of the emperor provided opportunities for the local elite in the cities to hold the important post of priest of Augustus and associate themselves with the regime, and also offered a useful channel of diplomatic communication between city and emperor. Augustus's attitude was pragmatic, best illustrated in his treatment of the Jews. He respected their religious traditions:

> Since the Jewish nation has proved itself to be well disposed to the Roman people, not only in the present time, but also in the past and especially in the time of my father, Imperator Caesar, and also their high-priest Hyrcanus, I and my council have decided under oath, with the agreement of the Roman people, that the Jews may follow their own customs in accordance with their ancestral law, just as they did under Hyrcanus, high-priest of the highest god. (Josephus, *Jewish Antiquities* 16.162–5; translation after Braund, 1985, no. 547)

Consequently, to avoid a clash between the monotheism of the Jews and his divinity, it was agreed that they should pray to their god for his welfare.

In the western provinces there were only altars and no temples to Augustus, and in Rome itself his inherent spirit (*genius* or *numen*) received offerings; this was originally linked to procreation and a man's ability to secure his family's continuity, but was easily associated with the powerful father of the fatherland who ensured the continuity of the empire. Augustus received many other acts of egregious respect; a month (August) was named after him; the sacred fire was carried before him in processions; there were sacrifices to his *genius* on two great state festivals, his birthday and the birthday of his power. Eventually subtle distinctions became blurred during Augustus's long and stable rule, and even in Italy, at Naples, he was worshipped as a god by AD 14. Augustus, with his military dominance, his enormous personal wealth, his accumulation of priesthoods, honours, titles and a quasi-divine mystique, was far above any other individual in status, prestige, honour and public recognition. Among potential rivals, who could possibly hope to match his position?

Augustus's Legacy

Augustus expressed the hope not only that his political arrangements were the best, but that the 'foundations I lay for the state will remain in their place' (Suetonius, *Divus Augustus* 28.2). His hope was to be fulfilled, and his successors by and large accepted his way of doing business. Luckily, he lived to be seventy-six, and when he died many had forgotten the Republic and its troubles. Unlike Julius Caesar, he had the time to see how his innovations worked, smooth out the rough edges, and make sure that a period of great political and social confusion had definitely been laid to rest. His legacy was complex and all-pervasive. The central element was personal autocratic control in a framework of powers voted individually within a quasi-constitutional context of senate, traditional magistracies and assemblies.

Roman practices were flexible and vague enough to accommodate this. Augustus managed the upper classes so that they had a privileged social status and a defined role that suited the emperor without excessively impairing their dignity. This involved a delicate relationship with senators, which others not so skilled or so lucky might find difficult to sustain. Augustus was subject at times to flattery and adulation, and this could turn to abject sycophancy of the type that annoyed Tiberius and could undermine the honour of the upper classes. What is more, since senators and *equites* served as Augustus's senior administrators and moved in the same circle as the imperial family, this opened the door to court intrigue.

Augustus employed many *equites* in his service to supplement the role of senators, in junior military commands, as financial officials (procurators), as governors of small provinces, and gradually in more high-profile roles including the governorship of Egypt. He showed the way in exploiting this large reservoir of talent of men who were likely to be loyal to him (potentially every Roman citizen with resources to the value of 400,000 *sesterces* and three generations of free birth), since they would not have had this role in the old Republic. So successful was Augustus's policy that by the late third century AD *equites* had replaced senators in most of the major offices of state.

Augustus assiduously courted popular support, and in many ways was an even greater showman than Nero claimed to be, providing corn, giving games at which he presided, appearing frequently in public as patron and benefactor of his people, putting up his statues, adorning Rome with magnificent buildings that changed the shape of the city and inspired artistic developments. His buildings combined grandeur and practical benefit, and Rome was more beautiful and safer thanks to him. He was also the benefactor of Italy and the provinces; the small-town elites of Italy and the wealthy provincial communities were among his most enthusiastic supporters. Augustus's generosity also touched individual writers who were patronized by his circle. His patronage was not exactly disinterested and views favourable to the regime could be discreetly disseminated, and sometimes more obviously, as in Horace's hymn for the Saecular Games in 17 BC; these were normally celebrated every 110 years, and on this occasion expressed expiation and hope for a new age and the continuity of Rome's destiny. Horace's hymn was sung by a choir of twenty-seven boys and twenty-seven girls.

Augustus supported men of talent, even listening patiently to poetry and history readings; he was particularly fond of uplifting precepts or maxims (Suetonius, *Augustus* 89.3). Augustus's henchman Maecenas also introduced young poets to the emperor, and mediated in their relationship with him, at least up to 11 BC. It is interesting that some of these writers were of fairly humble origin: Horace, the son of a freedman; Virgil, the son of a small farmer; Propertius, Cornelius Gallus and Ovid, all of equestrian rank. Augustus did not dictate topics or usually impose censorship, and indeed most poets, following Greek tradition, wrote love and personal poetry with only occasional references to Augustan topics. Even Virgil's great epic poem, the *Aeneid*, although it mentions Augustus and his family and praises Roman qualities and achievements, expresses the poet's interpretation of the epic tradition. It is true that some of Ovid's erotic verses may not have fitted with the moral tone of Augustus's legislation, but Ovid's exile to Tomis in Moesia seemingly had more to do with an obscure political misdemeanour associated with the emperor's wayward daughter Julia. In general, Augustus created a peaceful and stable environment, favourable to traditional cultural pursuits that could enhance his court.

The other side of Augustus's rule was a close personal association with the soldiers. His legacy here was a large professional standing army with enormous cost to the empire's taxpayers. Augustus with his personal bodyguard presented himself as the military leader with all the trappings and titles of the *imperator*; all victories were his, but he maintained a certain distance so that he could avoid responsibility for defeat. Augustus was effectively commander-in-chief, though much of the real commanding was left to others. He used the army to assert vigorously and aggressively Rome's power in foreign relations, and committed the empire to a provincial structure that was to remain for centuries, with troops permanently stationed in camps and frontier zones on the Rhine, Danube and Euphrates. His demeanour as *imperator* influenced all his successors, and his warlike foreign policy was an incentive to the ambitious.

Augustus was unshakeable in his belief that one of his own bloodline should succeed him. But since he was officially not a monarch, he had to enhance gradually the status of his intended successor with duly voted powers and military commands. There were likely to be setbacks, and as he had no son of his own there was enormous scope for manoeuvring among the imperial siblings. His family structure was complicated and irregular since in 39 BC he took as his wife Livia Drusilla, who was speedily divorced from her husband Tiberius Claudius Nero (a political opponent), by whom she was pregnant with her second son Drusus (the brother of Tiberius); these boys, Augustus's stepsons, were inevitably important figures. Julia, Augustus's only daughter from his earlier marriage to Scribonia, was first married to Marcellus (son of Augustus's sister Octavia), and on his death to Marcus Agrippa. Among her children from this marriage were three boys, Gaius and Lucius Caesar and Agrippa Postumus, born in the year of his father's death in 12 BC. Augustus came to adopt Gaius and Lucius as his own sons. Inevitably, Tiberius was seen as a rival to these boys and this was played out in public and caused considerable social disruption, with the embarrassing withdrawal of Tiberius from public life in 6 BC and the disgrace and exile of his wife Julia, whom he had married in 11 BC.

An oath of loyalty sworn to Augustus *c.*5–2 BC by the Conobarians in Spain shows the need to keep up with the changing political situation:

> I swear that I, on behalf of the salvation, honour and victory of Imperator Caesar Augustus, son of a god, his son the princeps of the youth, consul designate, priest (Gaius Caesar), and on behalf of Lucius Caesar, son of Augustus, and Marcus Agrippa, grandson of Augustus, shall assuredly take up arms . . .
> (*L'Année épigraphique* 1988.723)

At this stage Gaius and Lucius Caesar and their younger brother Marcus Agrippa (Postumus) seemed likely to be in favour to succeed Augustus, with Tiberius relegated to the shadows. But it was not to be, and with Lucius dead from natural causes and Gaius possibly as a result of a wound during his campaigning in the east, and Agrippa Postumus murdered probably on Augustus's orders at the end of his reign, Tiberius eventually emerged as the emperor's son and successor. This set the scene for the future, not only the disastrous relations within the Julio-Claudian family, but also the problem of the succession in years to come: personal choice or blood relation?

Augustus had edged towards divine worship, and after his death he was elevated to the ranks of the gods, becoming Divus Augustus. His mortal remains were deposited in the imposing Mausoleum he had built close to the Tiber. The practice of conferring this last mark of respect on an emperor who had been popular, or whose successor insisted on it, was to last until the empire became Christian in the fourth century AD.

Augustus had set out as a teenager on a career of violence, treachery and illegality. He ruthlessly exterminated his enemies and manipulated his own family to his wishes; in a sense he was murderous and controlling to the end, as the fate of Agrippa Postumus shows. Seneca, who as adviser to Nero knew something of the whims of autocrats, was sceptical of Augustus's reputation for mildness, restraint and mercy, calling it instead 'weariness of cruelty' (*On Clemency* 1.11). Like many revolutionaries, Augustus aimed to acquire respectability and leave behind his disreputable past, but he seems to have established a genuinely stable and calm atmosphere in which the new form of government could develop. Cassius Dio, who was well aware of Augustus's past and careful manipulation of Roman institutions, shrewdly and fairly sums up his rule:

> The Romans greatly missed Augustus because by combining monarchy and republican institutions he guaranteed their freedom and also established order

and stability; in this way they could live with restrained freedom in a monarchy that brought no terrors, and were free from the licence associated with popular government and from the abuses of a tyranny. (56.43.4)

Augustus would surely have been pleased with these comments, though in his last words to his friends he was rather more cynical about the façade he had constructed: 'Since well I've played my part, all clap your hands and from the stage dismiss me with applause' (Suetonius, *Divus Augustus* 99.1).

CHAPTER SIX

Running the Empire

Men and Dynasties, AD 14–235

Tiberius (r. AD 14–37) rapidly lost the trust that Augustus had built up with the upper classes. He had good intentions to start with, great respect for the law, and tried to encourage independent judgement in the senate. But he failed to preserve the consistency and demeanour that might have made this work. Dour and unpredictable, he overestimated the senate's ability to play the role he wanted. In military terms the reign got off to a bad start with serious mutinies, partly due to the soldiers' uncertainty after the death of Augustus. Then Germanicus, Tiberius's adopted son, conducted short campaigns in Germany, but Tiberius eschewed great ventures, although Cappadocia was turned into a province without fighting. There were fewer games and displays for the people. The sinister atmosphere was compounded by family troubles, with the death of Germanicus (of natural causes), and the emperor's own son Drusus, allegedly poisoned by his wife and her lover Sejanus, the praetorian prefect. The children of Germanicus and Agrippina, who never forgot that she was of the blood of Augustus, were involved in a family catastrophe as Tiberius turned against her and Nero and Drusus Caesar, who were imprisoned and soon killed. The emperor withdrew to Capri where Sejanus controlled access; he was very influential and possibly hoped for an imperial role. But Tiberius, becoming suspicious, had him executed in 31 and the reign drifted to its unhappy close with Tiberius probably murdered by the surviving son of Germanicus, Gaius (Caligula).

Caligula's short reign (AD 37–41) had no significant impact on the administrative structure. He was unstable and came to be hated by the senators; he disregarded the traditional protocols, and had grandiose plans for the worship of himself and farcical military pretensions. But his rule showed exactly how much power was inherent in Augustus's position.

After Caligula had been murdered by officers of his bodyguard there was a temporary vacuum, but while the senate dreamed of taking some kind of control the praetorians acted, and finding Claudius lurking in the palace effectively proclaimed him emperor. He was the brother of Germanicus but had been kept in the shadows because of physical and perhaps mental infirmities; he was not even a senator until the reign of his nephew Caligula. After some negotiation he was accepted by the senate. On his good days Claudius (r. AD 41–54) was fair-minded, concerned with justice and the proper administration of the provinces. He was intelligent, well educated, interested in history and liberal pursuits; quite possibly he had constructive ideas on developing a central executive machinery by organizing a secretariat staffed by freedmen. But his behaviour was inconsistent, and in the view of senators tended to be excessively under the influence of his various wives. His wife Valeria Messalina's arrogance and sexual desire led her to an ill-advised 'marriage' with Gaius Silius; both were executed. Claudius then married his niece Agrippina with a special dispensation from the senate. She pursued the interests of her son Nero, though Claudius had a son of his own, Britannicus. He was named in honour of his father's exploit in invading Britain in AD 43 under the command of Aulus Plautius and creating a new province. Claudius turned up in person for two weeks in order to shore up a weak political position by a display of military *virtus* and *gloria*. Claudius became more unpopular because the senate resented the leading role played by some of his freedmen secretaries, particularly Pallas and Narcissus. He was probably murdered by poisoned mushrooms in a family conspiracy involving Agrippina.

Agrippina pushed her son forward, the praetorians recognized him, and Britannicus was soon murdered. But Nero (r. AD 54–68) soon came to resent the influence of his mother, who had ambitions to interfere in government, and she was brutally murdered on the emperor's orders, the assassin told to strike her womb. For a time Nero abided by the advice of his praetorian prefect Burrus, and Seneca, a rich, influential senator, writer and Stoic philosopher. Eventually Burrus died or was murdered and Seneca was forced to commit suicide, leaving Nero free to indulge his passion for singing, chariot-racing and all kinds of curiosities and novelties. He used to roam the streets at night in disguise, drinking and joining in common pursuits. For senators, dignity and responsible behaviour were replaced by embarrassment and humiliation. The future emperor Vespasian was nearly killed for falling asleep at one of Nero's interminable performances. Nero loved all things Greek, which influenced many of his pursuits and may have contributed to his unpopularity with some senators. The great fire of Rome in AD 64 was not Nero's doing but he was widely blamed for it, which shows popular hostility, and he persecuted the Christians in the city to divert attention. In 68 several provincial governors rebelled, though in an uncoordinated way. In the end Nero was deserted by nearly everyone (though the praetorians maintained a loyalty to the imperial house) and killed himself with the famous last words: 'What a showman perishes in me!' This was the traumatic end of the Julio-Claudian dynasty.

The year AD 68–69 was one of turmoil as professional Roman armies fought each other, carried out massacres of civilians in Italy, and devastated property. As Tacitus put it, 'the secret of empire was out, an emperor could be created elsewhere than in Rome'. In quick succession Galba, Otho and Vitellius seized power, and then lost it. Galba (governor of Spain) was too much of a disciplinarian ('I don't buy my soldiers'); Otho was never in control, having no provincial army to back him, but when his cause was lost he at least committed suicide to avoid further slaughter; Vitellius lazily failed to secure his advantage of controlling Rome and being supported by the strong German armies. Vespasian (r. 69–79), fresh from his success in Judaea in quelling the rebellion of the Jews, arrived from the east and imposed order, stability and the Flavian dynasty. His stolid, measured approach was probably what Rome needed and he built up state finances. His son Titus (r. 79–81) succeeded him; he was popularly known as the 'darling of the human race' and his reign was too short to disprove it. His brother Domitian (r. 81–96) was an efficient administrator and seems to have ruled conscientiously. He was not without a sense of humour, once saying of a narcissistic man: 'I wish I was as handsome as Maecius thinks he is.' He conducted vigorous military campaigns of varied success on the Rhine and the Danube, the last being an area that was to be of great interest to the Romans in the future. But the real story of Domitian's reign is the breakdown of his relations with his senior senatorial administrators, who thought him cruel, capricious and hostile to talented individuals, especially army commanders. The truth is difficult to recover since our upper-class sources are hostile, and Tacitus was particularly irked by the removal of his father-in-law Agricola from the governorship of Britain before his war of conquest was complete (though he had been there for seven years). But a potentially serious revolt by Saturninus, governor of Upper Germany, was put down by the future emperor Trajan, and Domitian increased military pay by a third. Eventually he was murdered through a plot involving his entourage, including his wife, and his memory was condemned by the senate.

Nerva (r. AD 96–98) was a senator of blameless background and pleasant disposition; he was to be the last truly Italian emperor. He set out to be a contrast to the previous regime, issuing coins celebrating 'freedom'. Nerva, who had no children, struggled to preserve authority, especially after he had to surrender the murderers of Domitian to the resentful praetorians. In October 97, amid deepening crisis, he adopted as his son and successor Trajan, previously appointed as governor of Lower Germany, and inaugurated a period when emperors chose their successor.

On Nerva's death Trajan (r. AD 98–117), whose family came from Spain, took over smoothly and became popular with the senate since he ruled with equity, consistency and good humour, always keeping the soldiers in order. The notable features of his reign were stability at home and an expansive foreign policy. He initiated or carried on a programme to support poor children in Italy, and pursued many building projects in Rome; his sound principles of conduct in public business appear in his letters to Pliny the Younger, governor in Bithynia: 'Let us not forget that the chief reason for sending you to your province was the evident need for many reforms' (*Letters* 10.32). Two wars in Dacia (modern Romania) were followed in 106 by the creation of a new province. In the east, Arabia was annexed and in 114 Trajan invaded Parthia. The campaign was initially successful and the Parthian western capital Ctesiphon was captured. The emperor subsequently marched to the Persian Gulf. He intended to create new provinces, but a serious insurgency broke out in the occupied territory followed by an uprising of the Jews in the eastern provinces. Trajan tried to restore the situation but died suddenly at Selinus in Cilicia. His military exploits seem to have been the result of his desire for martial glory. He had no children but had shown special favour to Hadrian, who came from Italica in Spain and whose father was Trajan's cousin. Hadrian's adoption was announced the day after Trajan's death.

Hadrian (r. 117–38) pulled the troops out of Parthia and abandoned the new provinces. He fought no wars of aggression but travelled assiduously, visiting most provinces, inspecting military establishments and conducting exercises. His famous wall built in northern Britain was not necessarily intended merely as a defensive measure. He founded a Roman colony, Aelia Capitolina at Jerusalem, and forbade the practice of circumcision; this contributed to the outbreak of a serious rebellion in Judaea in 132–5, which was vigorously put down with great loss of life. Hadrian had uneasy relations with the senate, and the execution of four men of consul rank early in the reign, allegedly for treason, cast a long shadow. Hadrian was renowned for literary pursuits, an interest in things Greek and an infatuation with a young man from Bithynia, Antinous, who, when he drowned in the Nile, was declared a god. Hadrian eventually named Aurelius Antoninus Pius as his successor, requiring him to adopt his nephew Marcus (Aurelius) and the son of Aelius (a previous candidate for the succession), Lucius (Verus).

Antoninus Pius (r. 138–61) was popular with the senate, being polite, consistent and moderate. There was limited military activity, which led to the reconquest of southern Scotland and the building of the Antonine wall. In 148 he celebrated with games the 900th anniversary of Rome's foundation. Financial management was prudent. The orator and lawyer Cornelius Fronto was a friend of the imperial family and his letters are a valuable source.

Marcus Aurelius (r. 161–80) and Lucius Verus (r. 161–9), in Rome's first experience of joint rule, carried on good relations with the senate and the tradition of stable, well-managed government. Marcus was a thoughtful man and in his *Meditations* he expressed his eclectic philosophical ideas. But the empire was convulsed by a series of military crises in several frontier zones. First there was further war with the Parthians, who invaded Syria and took control of Armenia after the defeat and death of the governor of Cappadocia. Lucius Verus went in person to the east and took charge of the campaign, though victory was won by his generals. He held a triumph with Marcus in 166 and both took grandiose military titles. But plague broke out in the eastern army and spread to Rome, which delayed a response to a crisis on the Danube. In 168 both emperors set out for the front. Verus soon died of a stroke, and in 170 the Marcomanni and Quadi defeated Marcus and crossed the Julian Alps, invading Noricum, Pannonia and northern Italy. Long campaigns followed in 172–4 to clear them out. Then in 175 Avidius Cassius, governor of Syria, revolted in an obscure conspiracy. The revolt collapsed in three months, and in 178 warfare in the north resumed. Marcus died before realizing his intention of creating new provinces beyond the Danube. In contrast to emperors from Nerva onwards, he was succeeded by his son Commodus, who had been virtual co-ruler from 177.

Commodus (r. 180–92) made peace and returned immediately to Rome; there were to be no further wars in his reign except for limited operations in northern Britain. The process of government deteriorated and was run by the emperor's increasingly disreputable favourites while he devoted himself to his gladiatorial interests. His unpredictable behaviour alienated the senate. The contemporary senator and historian, Cassius Dio, vividly describes how the emperor one day cut off the head of an ostrich in the arena and waved it threateningly at the senators. Dio wanted to laugh, which would have been dangerous, and so chewed vigorously on a laurel leaf. In due course there was a palace plot and Commodus was strangled on the night of 31 December 192.

In this dangerous situation Pertinax (who may have been implicated in the plot) was declared emperor. He had been an efficient commander but was rapidly overthrown by the praetorians, having tried to 'reform too much too quickly too austerely', as Dio pointed out. Then the Praetorian Guard notoriously 'auctioned' the empire by offering their support for a price, and the successful bidder was Didius Julianus, a senator of some standing. He had little authority or respect and a climate had been created in which provincial governors could realistically consider seizing power. Septimius Severus (r. 193–211), governor of Upper Pannonia, marched on Rome and captured it. Pescennius Niger (Syria) and

Clodius Albinus (Britain) also tried to sieze power. Severus temporarily won over Albinus by making him Caesar; from 193 to 195 several bloody battles took place in the east, ending in the death of Niger. Then Severus made his elder son Caesar and turned on Albinus, finally defeating him in the battle of Lugdunum in 197 with up to 80,000 casualties. To overcome the odium of civil war Severus launched a campaign in Parthia, which produced a new province, Mesopotamia; towards the end of his reign he led a major expedition into northern Scotland, which proved abortive, and he died at York. Away from the battlefield, Severus sought respectability by claiming descent from Marcus Aurelius and adopting the family name (Antoninus). He maintained a stable administration, and eventually won grudging respect from senators despite reinstating the memory of Commodus and executing supporters of Albinus. But his rule saw the advancement of significant trends resulting from his seizure of power by military force and his march on Rome, the first example for 124 years. The military aspects of the emperor's position were enhanced. Severus came from Africa (of a senatorial family) and his wife (Julia Domna) was Syrian, adding further diversity to the empire's cultural mix. He was succeeded by his two sons Caracalla and Geta.

Caracalla (r. 211–17) soon murdered his brother and became obsessed with the army; he admired Alexander the Great, proclaimed that he wanted to live with his soldiers, granted a large pay rise, and spent the days drinking with them while senators were treated with contempt, although he was capable of generous gestures, the most striking of which was the emperor's extension of citizenship to all inhabitants of the empire. He fought inconclusive military campaigns in Germany and Parthia and was murdered by his praetorian prefect, Macrinus, who replaced him as emperor.

Macrinus (r. 217–18) was the first equestrian to become emperor and he was undone by the cost of Caracalla's pay rise, which he attempted to reduce, and by the aftermath of the war in Parthia. Elagabalus, priest of the sun-god at Emesa in Syria and son of the niece of Septimius Severus's wife, was proclaimed as a son of Caracalla and used as the figurehead of a rebellion against Macrinus, who was defeated and murdered.

Elagabalus (r. 218–22) soon became unpopular in Rome with his plan to make the sun-god the supreme god of the Roman state instead of Jupiter Optimus Maximus; his outlandish behaviour, bizarre sexual promiscuity, and use of disreputable favourites in government alienated public support and caused discontent within the imperial family, which forced him to adopt his cousin, who was renamed Alexander in 221. Elagabalus tried to reverse the adoption and was murdered in 222, when he was replaced by Alexander, who ruled as M. Aurelius Severus Alexander.

Severus Alexander (r. 222–35) had the distinguished jurist Ulpian as his praetorian prefect and adviser until his murder in 223–4 by the praetorians. Alexander was dominated by his grandmother and by his mother (Julia Mamaea). The regime tried ostentatiously to be a contrast to the previous years and senators were regularly consulted on policy. But the emperor seemed weak and not in control of events. Cassius Dio held a second consulship with the emperor as colleague in 229 but had to spend the time outside Rome because the praetorians threatened to kill him. Dio complained about indiscipline in provincial armies and there was a two-day battle in Rome between the praetorians and the plebs. In the east the Parthian monarchy was replaced by the more aggressive Sasanid Persians, against whom Alexander fought an inconclusive war, though his conduct of the campaign was criticized, and he then had to go to the northern frontier zone to repel an incursion by the Alamanni. Maximinus, a tough junior officer, instigated a rebellion among the soldiers, claiming that Alexander was a 'sissy' and timid 'mother's boy' and ungenerous with money. He murdered both Alexander and his mother. Maximinus was the first genuine soldier-emperor who fought in person in the battle-line and was proud of it; the emperor now had to operate in a different context where he was routinely expected to take charge of military campaigns, and where capacity to rule was dangerously associated with personal military aptitude.

Administration

Roman administration was not like the modern world of management training, career patterns, and a bureaucracy with a hierarchy of responsibility. In fact, the process of government tended to be non-specialist. Until well into the third century AD senators held the major administrative posts and their advancement depended on a curious mixture of age, experience, honour and an upper-class ideology whereby men of senatorial family could perform without much preparation or training in any task that the state asked of them. Social status was very important; senators continued to be marked out by distinctive clothing, the title 'most distinguished man' (*vir clarissimus*), and the privilege of sitting in special seats at games and shows. Theoretically, there was a minimum age for holding the traditional magistracies (still of annual duration) such as the praetorship (thirty-nine) and the consulship (forty-two). This remnant of the old *cursus honorum* made it difficult for the emperor (who was himself usually a senator) to promote quickly the very talented or those from outside the senatorial class. A young man of senatorial family, after some minor administrative offices and a stint as one of the six military tribunes in a legion (the other five were *equites*), entered the senate on being elected *quaestor*, and was normally posted to a province to look after the financial accounts. The position of praetor (there were twelve each year), as well as offering the opportunity of an important role in civil jurisdiction, provided an avenue to a wider range of posts, including some provincial governorships and also the command of a legion as legionary legate (*legatus legionis*). The two annual consuls remained the chief magistrates of the Roman state, with a high profile and important ceremonial functions, and after the consulship a range of more senior positions was open to those with ambition. For example, it was virtually unheard of for the governor of an important province with legionary troops not to have held a consulship. Because emperors needed senior administrators, the number of consuls tended to increase; the so-called 'ordinary consuls' served for the first part of the year but were then replaced by 'suffect' or substitute consuls; on one occasion in the reign of Commodus more than twenty consuls served in one year.

Within Italy senators were kept busy in the range of posts largely devised by Augustus, generally operating in committees reporting to the senate and thence to the emperor, looking after the roads, the beds and banks of the Tiber and the sewers of the city, sacred buildings and public works, the state treasury (*aerarium Saturni*) and the military treasury (*aerarium militare*). At the top was the prestigious prefect of the city, whose jurisdiction by the late second century AD extended to the hundredth milestone from Rome. The post about which we know most is the curator of the aqueducts (*curator aquarum*), because Sextus Julius Frontinus, who was appointed to the position in AD 97, wrote a detailed account of his role and duties, partly in a process of self-education since he had had no professional preparation for the post. He gives a fine statement of the responsibilities of the conscientious administrator in all ages:

> There is nothing so shameful to a capable man as to conduct a task delegated to him through the advice of subordinates. Yet this is inevitable whenever someone inexperienced of the task before him turns to the advice of these people. Although they do have an essential role in giving assistance, nevertheless they are merely the hands and implements of the directing intelligence. (*On the Aqueducts, Preface* 2)

Equites in the Roman Empire were just as prickly as senators about their status and rights, having their own distinctive clothing and seats in the theatre. They saw more of junior army commands than senators, not only holding military tribunates, but also commanding auxiliary infantry and cavalry. Other positions were available that senators initially might have disdained, such as the procurators who managed financial affairs in the emperor's provinces, including taxation, estates and public operations such as mining; others held lesser governorships in districts or small provinces, not usually commanding legionary troops. But *equites* were more numerous than senators because from the early empire all those with Roman citizenship, a census valuation of 400,000 *sesterces* and three generations of free birth were regarded as *equites*. They came to make a substantial contribution to Roman government in army, finance and administration by supplementing the role of senators, sometimes holding top posts like the prefecture of Egypt (with its two legions) and the command of the emperor's bodyguard. An important role was filled by freedmen (ex-slaves) who, for example, worked with more senior personnel as secretaries or personal assistants. But the emperor also needed secretaries for his correspondence, petitions and accounts, and these jobs, initially seeming too subservient and beneath the dignity of a senator or *eques*, were given to freedmen. But a good secretary is often a useful confidant and source of advice, and Claudius made intelligent use of his freedmen secretaries. Narcissus (correspondence) and Pallas (finance), however, were detested by senators because they seemed to have exceeded their proper role, even advising the emperor on the succession and receiving excessive honours. One consequence was that the secretariat positions acquired greater significance and status and gradually *equites* came to hold them.

The administration of the provinces was in the hands of the same small group of senators and *equites*. There were two lines of responsibility – emperor and senate. The emperor continued to have charge of the militarily more important provinces containing legions. The most important of these were governed by *legati Augusti* directly appointed by the emperor and supported by legionary legates and military tribunes, and a small personal staff. The smaller provinces were governed by men of praetorian rank and might have just one legion or be without a garrison (like Lusitania). All held office for about three years, but there was no fixed period of tenure. Julius Agricola, Tacitus's father-in-law, governed Britain from AD 77 to 84. Since financial matters were in the hands of equestrian procurators, this meant that there was an effective separation of power between administration and money. In time a hierarchy of equestrian procuratorships developed, with a salary range from 60,000 to 200,000 *sesterces*. The senate appointed proconsuls by lot to serve for one year; some were of praetorian rank like the proconsul of Sicily, others were of consular rank, and the proconsulship of Asia was regarded as a plum job usually held late or last in a senatorial career. Proconsuls were supported by *quaestors* to deal with financial matters, a small personal staff, and a few soldiers to act as messengers and bodyguards. Of course, imperial decisions applied to all provinces equally.

The Roman governor of the imperial period was in some ways no less a king in his province than in the Republic; he was in complete control of the administration, was supreme in jurisdiction, and acted as commander of the troops in the province. Of course, he received instructions (*mandata*) from the emperor, dealing with general and specific areas of interest, but once in his province to a large extent he would be acting on his own initiative. In large, urbanized provinces like Syria or Asia, the governor will have spent much time in dealing with city governments and self-important Greek communities; a conscientious governor would also devote much effort to the judicial circuit (*conventus*), in that he travelled around the province from city to city receiving complaints and hearing cases. Furthermore, governors had to liaise with the provincial council (*koinon*) representing all communities. This body contained representatives from all the main cities in the province and discussed matters of common interest. There was considerable uniformity to the pattern of Roman provincial government, and only in Egypt do we find substantial differences, largely because the Romans took over the highly bureaucratic system of the previous rulers, the Ptolemies, and it was their policy to adapt rather than change structures wholesale. Here, the whole country was divided into three areas, each under the control of an *epistrategos* (senior administrative official); these areas were subdivided into *nomes* (regional administrative areas) each under the control of a *strategos* (local government official); the detailed administration of the *nomes* was carried out by local officials, and in Egypt the large cities (only four in number) were not important administratively. The *diocetes* (financial controller) supervised all regular financial arrangements, while the *idiologos* (keeper of the private account) administered the special account relating to fines and irregular exactions.

Part of a provincial governor's job was to mediate between the communities of his province and the emperor and to convey the emperor's wishes. We see this in an inscription from the reign of Claudius:

> Paullus Fabius Persicus . . . proconsul of Asia, proclaimed, at the instigation of Tiberius Claudius Caesar Augustus Germanicus himself, an edict beneficial to the city of the Ephesians and the whole province, which he published at Ephesus and ordered to be inscribed on a column before March 28th:

> While it is very much my own view, above all else, that magistrates in charge of the province must perform the office entrusted to them with all steadfastness and good faith, in such a way that they give thought to the long-term good of the individual, of the whole province, and of each city. . . . (Braund, 1985, no. 586)

Persicus goes on to deal with a matter of the corrupt selling of public priesthoods and other unsatisfactory practices concerning the famous temple of Artemis.

This was a two-way process and cities made their feelings known to the emperor, usually by sending an embassy, which was in fact part of a diplomatic process whereby the expression of a city's loyal devotion was also an opportunity to get attention and perhaps benefactions. This comes across clearly in the record of an embassy sent to Rome by Assos in the Troad in Asia to present good wishes to the new emperor, Gaius (Caligula); the flowery language and flattery are combined with self-interest:

> Since the rule of Gaius Caesar Germanicus Augustus, the hope of the prayers of all mankind, has been proclaimed, the joy of the world knows no bounds, and every city and every province has hastened to set eyes on the god, as the happiest of ages is now dawning for men: it was voted by the council and the Romans in business among us and the people of Assos to appoint an embassy of the foremost and best Romans and Greeks to address and congratulate him, and to beg him to remember and care for the city. . . . (translated by Millar, 1977, p. 412)

Exactly the kind of response that a city would want comes in a message of Gordian III in the third century AD to the population of Aphrodisias, recorded in another inscription:

> It was appropriate, Aphrodisians, to the antiquity of your city, to its goodwill and friendship towards the Romans, for you to be disposed towards my kingship as you have shown in the decree addressed to me. In return for which, and in response to your loyal disposition, I maintain securely the enjoyment of all your existing rights that have been preserved up to the time of my kingship. (Reynolds, *Aphrodisias and Rome*, 1982, no. 20)

Conscientious governors could facilitate this process and help a community to get the emperor interested in local projects. There is a large body of evidence in the correspondence between Pliny the Younger and Trajan. In AD 111 Pliny had been sent on a special appointment as Trajan's representative in the province of Bithynia and Pontus with the task of sorting out defective administration and dishonest accounting at a local level, which had led to bankruptcy in several communities and political disorder; the central government had not been blameless since two previous governors had been charged with corruption by the province. In a characteristic exchange, Pliny informed the emperor that the public bath at Prusa was old and dilapidated and that the people were keen to build a new one, for which he was confident that the money could be found: 'This is, moreover a scheme that is worthy of the city's prestige and the splendour of your reign'. Trajan replied: 'If building a new bath at Prusa will not strain the city's finances, there is no reason why we should not grant their petition, provided that no new tax is imposed and there is no further diversion of funds intended for essential services' (*Letters* 10.23–24; Penguin translation).

The small bureaucratic provision for Roman governors meant that they relied on local elites in the cities, who were responsible for running their territory. The rich relied on Rome for help and support to sustain their privileged position and in return they worked for Rome, for example, organizing the collection of taxes and carrying out important local services for their community. Against this background, cities in the provinces competed vigorously for honour and status with rival communities; for example, there was a strict order of precedence by which the proconsul of Asia when he first arrived in the province was expected to land at Ephesus because of its leading position; it was incumbent upon the new governor to listen with good humour to endless speeches of welcome, and he must be careful not to accept too many gifts or to appear ungrateful and indifferent by refusing them. Rivalry between cities and the example of the emperor's benefactions produced an incentive for private individuals to invest money in their communities to provide buildings and other facilities.

The administration of the provinces depended to a large extent on the consent of the governed since governors had only a small number of attendants and guards, and in many provinces no Roman troops were stationed; the resources available to local communities to keep law and order were limited. The Roman government certainly had a concept of good government, even though Tiberius referred to his subjects as sheep. Enforcing an acceptable standard of conduct was another matter. Governors were in theory strictly controlled by legislation introduced by Augustus in 4 BC, and he and his successor followed this up in their instructions to governors. The governor of Galatia, Sextus Sotidius Strabo Libuscidianus, reflects on his duties: 'It is the most unjust thing of all for me to tighten up by my own edict that which the emperors, one the greatest of gods (Augustus), the other the greatest of emperors (Tiberius), have taken the utmost care to prevent, namely that no-one should make use of carts without payment' (S. Mitchell, *Journal of Roman Studies* 66, 1976, 107).

Strict procedures were laid down for bringing charges against corrupt governors. But the onus was still on the provincial communities to make their complaints known, potentially an expensive business and daunting for a small village or individual, though a large city or the provincial *koinon* might have a better chance. The real problem lay in the behaviour of the government's agents, particularly soldiers, who were difficult to control despite repeated interventions by the government. We find Domitian issuing instructions to Claudius Athenordorus, his procurator in Syria, to prevent the commandeering of beasts of burden without authority, and noting that the provinces 'with difficulty have enough for the necessities of life'; the emperor adds a note to the procurator himself to observe the proper rules (Sherk, 1988, no. 95). Despite imperial intervention, abuse and corruption continued, as a second-century AD edict of the prefect of Egypt shows:

Marcus Petronius Mamertinus, prefect of Egypt, declares: I have been informed that many of the soldiers, while travelling through the country without a certificate, requisition boats, animals and persons beyond what is proper, on some occasions appropriating them by force, on others getting them from the *strategoi* (local government officials) by exercise of favour or deference. Because of this private persons are subjected to arrogance and abuse and the army has come to be censured for greed and injustice. (AD 133–7; Campbell, 1994, no. 293)

The government's battle to enforce its will often failed and the lot of many provincials, especially those who lived close to main roads or military camps, will often have been extremely unpleasant. The villagers of Scaptopara in Thrace suffered because their community not only had hot springs and was near the site of a famous festival, but was also situated between two military camps. They complained to the emperor that soldiers had repeatedly ignored the instructions of the governor of Thrace that they be left undisturbed, and had left their proper routes to come and demand hospitality for which they paid nothing: 'For we made clear that we could no longer put up with it but intended to leave our ancestral homes because of the violence of those who descend upon us . . .' (Campbell, 1994, no. 301). The villagers got their complaint to the emperor's attention because a local man served in the praetorian guard and presumably was able to use his position to present the petition.

Persistent misgovernment was certainly one factor in revolts from Rome and continuing banditry. Even in Italy under Septimius Severus, despite the presence of the praetorian guard, the notorious and romantic brigand Bulla roamed far and wide before he was betrayed by his mistress. A good indication of feeling among those who may be seen as outsiders, who had not been accommodated to Roman rule, is the appearance of a subversive form of literature predicting a reversal of fortune and the fall of Rome. Most dramatic is the book of Revelation, which belongs to a genre of Jewish and Christian apocalyptic literature, aiming to reveal the truth of God's purpose partly through prophecy. The author imagines the overthrow of the dominating economic and political power of Rome (Babylon). During the overturning of the existing world order seven angels appear with seven plagues: 'The third angel poured his bowl on rivers and springs, and they turned to blood'. The sixth angel caused the 'great river Euphrates' to dry up, and finally the book predicted an earthquake that would bring Babylon crashing down with the disappearance of islands and mountains (16.4; 12; 17–20). Certainly this vision of the reversal of the normal order vividly emphasizes the end of Rome's calm and uncontested control of her empire and the natural environment.

The problems of provincial administration bring us back to Rome. How was policy formulated and how were problems identified and solved? The social context was a small upper-class world that provided a narrow circle of advisers for the emperor. He could not master every field of government and in the Roman tradition called upon friends (that is, men whose advice was trusted) to advise him; they met in his council (*consilium principis*) when and if he wanted; it consisted of senators and leading *equites* but had no set list of members. The emperor was not obliged to take their advice and he could also ask anyone else he chose. In time, however, the council came to have a more fixed membership, with for example the praetorian prefects and the emperor's secretaries in regular attendance. Legal experts were called in when the need arose, for the council also heard legal cases and petitions; after the litigants withdrew the council members gave their opinion in order of precedence.

Legal matters potentially could take up much of an emperor's time if he had the will or inclination to deal with them. Following on from Augustus's interference with the judicial system, the emperor could act as a court of the first instance in criminal and civil cases. Here he operated side by side with the normal court and process of jurisdiction. Any Roman citizen could approach the emperor and frequently did, either with a petition on a point of law or by exercising his right as a Roman citizen (like St Paul) to appeal against trial by a magistrate on a capital charge. In response to petitions, a reply (rescript) was appended by the emperor at the bottom, though this may have been composed in the main by his legal advisers; eventually the rescripts became an important source of law. The emperor heard legal cases in person or with his *consilium* or delegated them to another official, such as the praetorian prefect. Imperial jurisdiction was in a sense a duty and often a chore. Pliny the Younger describes how he acted as legal assessor when Trajan held a judicial session at Centumcellae (Civitavecchia) north of Rome to deal with a variety of cases, including charges against a leading citizen of Ephesus, an accusation that a military tribune's wife had committed adultery with a centurion, and an inquiry into allegedly forged clauses in a will (*Letters* 6.31).

The Role of the Praetorian Prefect

Since there was no administrative hierarchy in Rome, many officials reported directly to the emperor. At the same time government was becoming more complicated as the empire expanded and more people gained Roman citizenship. Romans tended to find ad hoc solutions to this kind of management problem, and gradually more officials were brought into the system beyond the actual responsibilities of their office. The developing career of the prefect of the praetorian guard offers a vivid picture of the inner workings of government. He began life in 2 BC as mere deputy bodyguard commander under Augustus. Yet when the guard was abolished by Constantine in AD 312, the prefect remained because by then the

prefecture had become an indispensable office of state. The role and development
of the praetorian prefecture in administrative and military affairs, and also in jurisdiction, are an excellent guide to Roman thinking on administrative procedures.
Augustus, recognizing the potential of the position, first appointed two prefects,
both men of equestrian rank. The prefect was close to the emperor, accompanied
him everywhere, and was the only man permitted to wear a sword in his presence.
Trajan told one prefect to use his sword for him if he ruled well and against him if
he ruled badly. It was natural that the emperor would take the prefect into his confidence, since he was responsible for the only military force at the centre of power.
Therefore, emperors tended to choose men they believed to be trustworthy and
competent and to keep them fully informed. There developed a personal association between prefect and emperor, and consequently prefects became crucial
figures because it was known that they had the ear of the emperor. Several individual prefects made themselves far more important than the legal context of their
office strictly allowed by exploiting their relationship with the emperor. Sejanus in
the reign of Tiberius shows that the exploitation of the office had begun early. Not
only was he sole prefect (and there were to be numerous exceptions to the practice
of having two prefects), but he also persuaded Tiberius to concentrate all the
cohorts of the praetorians in a permanent barracks in Rome (previously there were
three in Rome, and six in neighbouring Italian towns); this made sense in terms of
efficient command, but it also concentrated a formidable body of troops under the
prefect's command at the centre of power.

When the emperor looked round for people to whom he could delegate
responsibility, the praetorian prefect was a natural choice because he was already
so closely associated and familiar with imperial business. So as the influence and
role of prefects increased, their prestige and status increased, as the outward
signs show. Most importantly, after AD 69 the praetorian prefecture was the top
post for an *eques*, even more important than the prefecture of Egypt. The prefect
received certain distinctive decorations, notably the title 'most eminent man' (*vir
eminentissimus*), a generation before other *equites*, and on retirement became a
senator, usually holding the consulship at once.

By the late first century AD, the prefect's role and duties more and more
matched his honours and prominence. He loomed large in imperial administration and we find him formally present at meetings of the emperor's advisory
council. On imperial military campaigns one prefect normally accompanied the
emperor, and again it would be reasonable for him to be closely consulted.
However, from time to time prefects were given command of large bodies of
troops well beyond their responsibilities with the praetorians, and for example in
178 Paternus, prefect of Marcus Aurelius, took command of an army. For a time,
probably in an emergency, Marcius Turbo, Hadrian's prefect, served as governor

of Dacia. In many cases prefects will have had superior military experience to the emperor's senatorial advisers.

In legal matters the prefect came to exercise original jurisdiction. This will have begun with minor cases where the prefect's troops had arrested someone in Italy. Other routine duties involved the supervision of executions and torture, and the reception of prisoners sent to Rome, like St Paul: 'And when we came to Rome the centurion delivered the prisoners to the captain of the guard; but Paul was allowed to dwell by himself with a soldier who kept him' (*Acts* 28.16). However, eventually the prefect's jurisdiction was extended to cases beyond those arising from arrests made by his troops, because the emperor, frequently being too busy, passed on a case to the nearest convenient official. This jurisdiction therefore developed in a haphazard way, though there are clear signs of the prefect's role. Hadrian replied to a petitioner about unfair moneylending: 'My praetorian prefect will judge this and report to me.' His prefect Marcius Turbo held regular judicial sessions in Rome even late at night, and famously replied to the emperor's warning to look after his health: 'A prefect should die on his feet.' In the reign of Marcus Aurelius his prefects are found adjudicating between local communities near Saepinum in Italy and the lessees of an imperial sheep ranch, who claimed that they had been abused: 'We warn you to refrain from abusing the lessees of the flocks of sheep to the serious detriment of the treasury, lest it be necessary to investigate the matter and punish the act, if the facts are as reported' (Lewis and Reinhold, 1990, vol. II, p. 100). By the late second century AD a formal demarcation line had been drawn between the jurisdiction of the prefect of the city and that of praetorian prefects, which was valid beyond the hundredth milestone from Rome. It is hardly surprising, therefore, that by the early third century we find leading jurists such Papinian and Ulpian holding the position of praetorian prefect, highlighting the change in role.

The praetorian prefect was now a senior administrative official intimately and indispensably involved in many aspects of government. The story of the development of the office shows how Roman government lacked a clearly defined administrative structure, was extremely flexible, and was willing to adopt new forms and employ different people. This involved the delegation of power, and the government that emerged tended to be non-specialist and haphazard, developing gradually and not according to any management plan, with ad hoc solutions to particular, immediate problems. In many ways it was never fully bureaucratic.

Taxation and Finance

Roman citizens in Italy from 167 BC had happily paid no direct taxes. It will have been an unpleasant shock when in AD 6–7 Augustus imposed new taxes to support the military treasury. Even so, the tax of 5 per cent on inheritances (excluding those from near relatives) and 1 per cent on auction sales were not excessive. In the provinces direct taxes consisted of land tax (*tributum soli*) or poll tax (*tributum capitis*), paid by everyone, including Roman citizens, but excepting citizens of colonies that had special rights, and other cities that had been granted immunity. The land tax could be a fixed sum or a tithe that was paid in kind. The poll tax is poorly documented, though we know that in Syria male inhabitants were liable from the age of fourteen, females from twelve, up to sixty-five. In the case of the land tax paid in kind, the system of the Republic persevered for a time and the contract for collection was leased to tax-collecting companies (*societates*) in Rome. Eventually the onus was placed on the cities, each of which was responsible for its territory and its own tax assessment; this was based on a regular census, which established the size of population and available resources, and the local magistrates had to ensure the collection of the tax. They dealt with the imperial procurator (or the quaestor), who supervised the whole process.

The Roman government also imposed a range of inventive indirect taxes. Among the most lucrative was a tax on the movement of goods primarily within the empire (*portorium*). The tax was a percentage (usually between 2 and 5 per cent) of the value of goods carried across circumscription boundaries by which the empire was divided. Circumscriptions might coincide with provincial boundaries, but not always; for example, the whole of Spain (comprising three provinces) constituted one circumscription. Many tax-collecting posts (*stationes*) were dotted around the empire and the *portorium* was initially collected by private enterprise; companies would bid for the contract in certain areas and pay the government a sum in advance. Searches by collectors could often be intrusive: 'Customs-officials . . . in search for concealed goods pry into baggage and merchandise that are another's property' (Plutarch, *On Curiosity* 7). Gradually, the government assumed more control over the process and by the late second century AD procurators collected the tax directly. Taxes were also levied on goods entering or leaving the empire. On the eastern frontier, at 25 per cent the rate was unusually high, probably because the Romans hoped to stop the drain on bullion exported to pay for luxury imports from India and Arabia.

Other taxes show the range of devices for raising money; at Chersonesus in the Crimea there was a tax on prostitutes, and the city of Aphrodisias managed to obtain from Hadrian exemption from a tax on nails:

Having been requested by an embassy concerning the exploitation of iron and the tax on nails, although the matter is disputable, since it is not now for the first time that the collectors have attempted to raise it from you, nevertheless knowing that the city both otherwise deserves honour and has been removed from the

framework of the province, I exempt it from the tax, and have written to my
procurator, Claudius Agrippinus, to instruct the man who has contracted for the
tax in Asia to exempt your city. (Reynolds, *Aphrodisias and Rome*, 1982, no. 15)

The government had at its disposal other significant sources of income such as
the produce from publicly owned mines and rent on public land leased out; it also
demanded supplies and accommodation for officials and soldiers on the move
around the empire, and transport animals and maintenance for the public post
(*vehiculatio*). Even if properly administered, this was burdensome for communities close to main roads. Labour could also be exacted for essential public works,
for example repairing the dykes in Egypt. Irregular exactions could be very
damaging, especially under corrupt officials. Increasingly, the system was kept
running in these cities where individuals had to perform a range of services in
their communities by taking on local offices at their expense and often subsidizing
local facilities. The state also imposed compulsory public services (liturgies),
which could be very demanding, especially responsibility for ensuring taxes were
collected. In Egypt this practice was to become particularly oppressive.

The imperial period brought vast increases in public revenues, not least when
Augustus added Egypt to the empire. In the early first century AD annual state
income may have been in the order of 1,000 million *sesterces* (rising steadily
thereafter), though there were also huge financial responsibilities in preserving
the infrastructure, particularly the upkeep of the elaborate road system and the
numerous aqueducts and bath buildings so essential to the Roman way of life; the
construction of public buildings that matched the grandeur of the imperial ideal,
though some were built out of the spoils of war (like the Colosseum after the
Jewish War, 66–70); the distribution of corn and gifts to the Roman people; and
the staging of games and spectacles. Political stability to some extent depended
on the maintenance of a large standing army. In the time of Domitian, the annual
cost of the army will have been in the order of 600 million *sesterces*, not counting
special donatives.

The management of these funds was overseen by the emperor and his
advisers, not by the senate or the people's assembly. Nevertheless, some traditional aspects remained, and the state's cash reserves were lodged in the treasury
of Saturn (*aerarium Saturni*), which was originally administered by two
quaestors, but from AD 56 by two prefects of praetorian rank, a position once
held by Pliny the Younger. The military treasury (*aerarium militare*) originally
dealt with payments of discharge benefits to soldiers, and was administered by
three prefects of praetorian rank. The appointment of prefects in both treasuries
will have been controlled by the emperor. In many cases tax revenues will not
have been physically brought to Rome, but retained in each province to meet

local expenses. Public accounts were published and the records were kept by a financial secretary (*a rationibus*) directly responsible to the emperor. This was one of the offices that became so important that it was often held by men of equestrian status.

The emperor himself was a major financial figure with a vast personal wealth built up from legacies, gifts and confiscations. Large imperial estates, like the *saltus Burunitanus* in Africa, were run by a procurator and leased out to farmers, who had to pay a proportion of their crops and also provide a fixed number of days' work on the estate. In the case of the imperial sheep ranch near Saepinum (see p. 135), the financial secretary was concerned in case the treasury suffered any loss of revenue. At some stage in the first century AD a special imperial treasury known as the *fiscus* (original meaning: strongbox) was created. The relationship of the *fiscus* to the state treasury is rather obscure, in that the *fiscus* represented both the emperor's personal fortune howsoever obtained, and more generally, the financial management system under his control. Imperial wealth was so great that it was difficult to distinguish it from state resources, and gradually emperors came to exercise greater control over state funds, which virtually merged with monies held in the *fiscus*; this institution, therefore, came to be a separate imperial treasury. Some of the emperor's property would be passed on to his successors (not necessarily heirs of his family) and held in the *fiscus*.

The basic coinage of the imperial period consisted of the gold *aurei* and silver *denarii* at a ratio of 25 *denarii* to 1 *aureus*. Fractions of this were made up by copper coins, notably the *as* and the *sestertius* (4 *sestertii* = 1 *denarius*). From the mid-first century AD, the minting of gold and silver coins tended to be concentrated in Rome. However, especially in the Greek cities in the eastern part of the empire, some local coinage continued. The silver content of the *denarius* declined slowly and Emperor Caracalla issued a coin weighing about one-and-a-half *denarii*, though with the face value of two. This coin (conventionally described by scholars as the *antoninianus*) eventually came to replace the *denarius*, and as political stability declined in the mid-third century and emperors were unable to enforce the central authority or protect the empire's territories from invasion, destruction and disruption, it became more difficult to collect taxes and raise revenue; consequently, the coinage was debased; by the 260s precious metal content of silver coinage was down to 5 per cent. In general, the Roman monetary system operated on very narrow margins; in normal times about 80 per cent of the imperial budget was covered by tax revenues, while the shortfall was made up by coins from newly mined metal.

Ancient writers were rarely interested in economic details, and the amount of data available for analysis of the Roman economy is inadequate in qualitative and quantitative terms. Archaeological evidence, although valuable, is subject to bias in that some areas have been more studied than others and some artefacts have a better chance of surviving. Recent approaches have placed the ancient evidence within a framework of theoretical analysis. One, the 'primitivist' theory, holds that the ancient economy was too primitive to be examined in terms of modern economic structures or practices, and that society was organized in independent, largely self-sufficient segments. Governments had no economic policies, the upper classes were hostile to commerce and manufacture; consciousness of status and class dominated the ancient mentality and consequently the economic relations of the Roman world. On this view the high level of urbanization in the Roman Empire is not necessarily an indication of economic development.

Some scholars have followed a more modernist approach, arguing that trade and commerce were not outside the ideology of the upper classes and the main social and political structures of the Roman state. There were centres of production and manufacturing both of luxury items for long-distance transport, but also of low-grade material such as clothes and pottery. Although the Roman economy was not modern, it was not crude or necessarily small scale. Trade was an important factor and we can use evidence of inscriptions for the prevalence of trade and manufacture, underwater investigation of shipwrecks, case studies, for example, of the wine trade or fish processing, and coin hoards. The volume and value of trade in the ancient world remain significant questions, as does the importance of a growing agricultural surplus, which could be traded, and an increase in the production of manufactured items. Roman taxation forced farmers to produce a bigger surplus, and since taxes were often spent in areas different from those where they were collected, this stimulated long-distance trade. Towns had an important role to play as the centres in which local craftsmen produced higher-value goods for sale in distant markets. Furthermore, the volume of coined money was increasing, suggesting increased trade with money as the medium of exchange.

There is also some suggestion of an integrated economy based on the long-distance exchange of goods supported by Roman imperial dominance, the uneven distribution of resources, and the needs of army supply. For example, by the late second century AD the army will have required huge amounts of wheat and animals every year (see p. 154). Many military camps will have needed goods such as wine and olive oil that had to come by long-distance trade. Large cities and the market economy were also important for trade. There was probably a degree of economic integration over a wide area in a fairly limited sense and urban demand sufficient to sustain production and distribution of a wide range of commodities in economically significant quantities. However, no emperor had an economic policy as such and none could have much direct impact on economic development.

Changing Relationships

When Septimius Severus set out from Upper Pannonia on the river Danube in 193 AD, it was the first time for 124 years that an army commander had marched on Rome and captured it. This traumatic event conditioned much of what happened subsequently, in that the new ruler had to make sure that he would not be overthrown in a similar fashion. It put a harsh light on the role of the army in politics, which Augustus (who also relied on the army) had been able to cover up to some extent. Severus openly relied on the military, granting a pay rise, allowing soldiers to marry legally, and disbanding the Italian praetorian guard, which he replaced with soldiers from the Danubian legions that had first supported him. The unreliable and corrupt guard probably deserved this fate, but the contemporary historians Dio and Herodian (a Greek from Syria) allege that Severus corrupted military discipline, though this has perhaps been exaggerated. The army fought tough campaigns between 193 and 211 and in a way established a militaristic ambience for his reign. On his deathbed Severus advised his sons to 'stick together, give the soldiers plenty of money and to hell with the rest'.

In other respects of his administration Severus tried to maintain traditional practices, diligently carrying out his responsibilities in legal jurisdiction. But his relationship with the senate was uneven; although he tried to be conciliatory there were executions and confiscations. Particularly embarrassing was the murder of Julius Solon, the senator who had helped to formulate the decree in which Severus promised not to execute any senators (Dio 75.2.2). He may have found it difficult to trust some senators, and indeed the role of the senate and senators was called into question as *equites* began to creep into more positions normally held by senators. We find them assuming command of the legion Severus stationed in Italy, and of the two in Mesopotamia, where the governor of this new province was of equestrian rank. This was not necessarily sinister or a matter of policy, since it may have been difficult to find a suitable senator to govern Mesopotamia, and once an *eques* was in place then the legionary commanders had to be equestrian. There were also security concerns in the eastern provinces, which had been the base of Niger, one of Severus's rivals for power, in that there was a large concentration of legions under the control of senators.

It is true that in a relatively small number of cases *equites* temporarily replaced a senatorial governor, although in general these were emergencies. Nevertheless, these developments do indicate a significant trend in the increasing use of *equites*, which began before Severus's reign and reached its culmination in the late third century. Furthermore, it is true that instead of emerging from the traditional route of commanding auxiliary units, now more equestrian officials had served as centurions, which might suggest the militarization of government, though it is hard to see a significant upward trend here.

By the late second century AD Roman citizenship was more generously extended and there were more provincial senators. These developments, though significant and ongoing in the time of Severus, were not due to any deliberate policy on his part. In his dealings with the provinces Severus naturally favoured his own birthplace, Africa, while Julia Domna, his Syrian-born wife, had a preference for the east. Otherwise, Severus tended to be generous in extending citizenship and privileges to those communities that had supported him in the civil wars. His actions served his immediate interests, as did the stationing of a legion in Italy for the first time, and the increase in the size of the garrison in Rome. Severus had learned from the ease with which he had captured Rome in 193. Italy was not being deliberately downgraded but slowly the provinces were being brought into line with Italy's status.

Severus did not set out deliberately to change the administrative structure, or change the empire into a military autocracy (in a sense it had always been one), or downgrade the senate and promote military men. Nevertheless, because of the circumstances of his seizure of power he did help to advance significant practices that later in the third century were to undermine the senate's role and status, bring about the advance of equestrians to a greater role in running the government and holding military commands, and confirm the dominant role of the military. From his contemporary senatorial viewpoint, Dio summed up the developments:

> Severus did many things that we did not like and was blamed for making the city rowdy with a huge number of troops, and weighing down the state by vast expenditure, and most of all for placing his main hope of security in the strength of his army rather than in the goodwill of those around him. (75.2.2)

However, in 232 Severus Alexander, the last emperor of the Severan dynasty, could still proclaim:

> Although the law granting imperial power exempts the emperor from the formalities of the law, nothing is so appropriate in the exercise of power as to live according to the laws. (*Codex Justinianus (CJ)* 6.23.3)

CHAPTER SEVEN

Soldiers and Wars

A UGUSTUS HAD EXPRESSED AN AGGRESSIVE DEFINITION OF PEACE 'WON BY victories' throughout the empire of the Roman people (*Res Gestae* 13). The Greek orator and philosopher Dio Chrysostomos ('the Golden Mouth') from Prusa in Bithynia (born *c*.AD 40/50), in a speech about kingship referring to the Roman Empire, took up the same kind of theme: 'Those who are trained to make war most effectively are most able to live in peace.' He went on to compare the emperor and his loyal soldiers to a shepherd and his guard dogs protecting the flocks (*Oration* 1.28). This was certainly an idealistic view of the Roman army from a rich and well-known landowner who was doubtless protected by his eminence from the more unpleasant consequences of a standing army perma- nently based in the provinces. Nevertheless, it is true that the Romans spent huge sums in keeping a large professional army of occupation in a state of disciplined readiness, to maintain and expand Roman territory, to keep the peace, and to ensure loyalty to the emperor.

The Army of the Empire

Augustus's evolutionary changes became part of the permanent structure of the army, which was divided into three sections, the legions, auxiliaries and praeto- rians. The twenty-five legions in service in AD 14 had increased only slowly to thirty-three by the end of the second century. The legions and auxiliaries were permanently billeted either in camps and forts, or, especially in the east, in towns. By 200 the thirty-three legions were located in nineteen provinces. One problem with this arrangement was that large campaigns required the transfer of troops from one province to another, which was both expensive and time-consuming. Therefore, particularly in the second century a practice developed of moving part of a legion (*vexillatio*) instead of the whole legion. A famous inscription

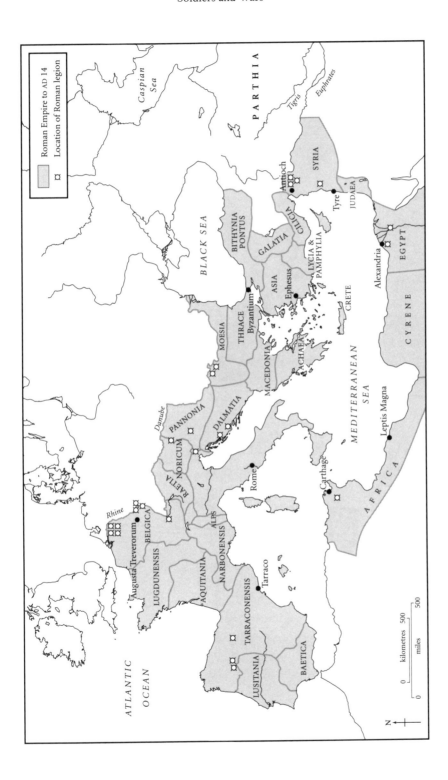

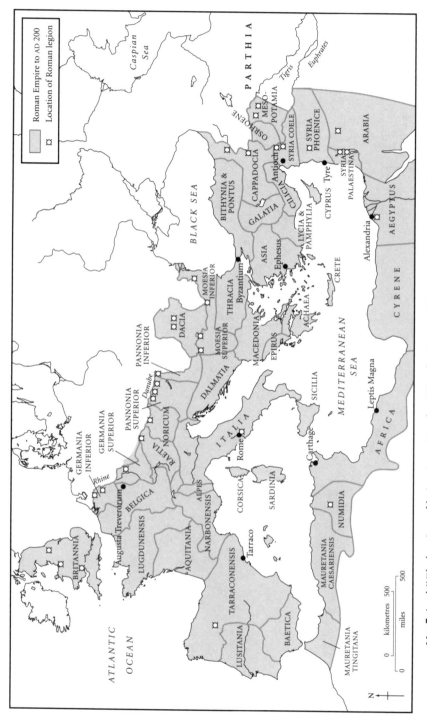

Map 7. *i* and *ii* The locations of legions in AD 14 and AD 200 (after Campbell, *The Roman Army: A Sourcebook* (1994), figures 3–4).

from Rome lists the legions in geographical order from west to east, beginning with Britain. It seems to have been compiled early in the reign of Marcus Aurelius with subsequent legions added at the end of it, and may have served as an official record of army dispositions:

Second, Augusta (Britain)	Second, Adiutrix (Lower Pannonia)	Fourth, Scythica (Syria)
Sixth, Victrix (Britain)	Fourth, Flavia (Upper Moesia)	Sixteenth, Flavia (Syria)
Twentieth, Victrix (Britain)	Seventh, Claudia (Upper Moesia)	Sixth, Ferrata (Judaea)
Eighth, Augusta (Upper Germany)	First, Italica (Lower Moesia)	Tenth, Fretensis (Judaea)
Twenty-second, Primigenia (Upper Germany)	Fifth, Macedonica (Dacia)	Third, Cyrenaica (Arabia)
First, Minervia (Lower Germany)	Eleventh, Claudia (Lower Moesia)	Second, Traiana (Egypt)
Thirtieth, Ulpia (Lower Germany)	Thirteenth, Gemina (Dacia)	Third, Augusta (Africa)
First, Adiutrix (Upper Pannonia)	Twelfth, Fulminata (Cappadocia)	Seventh, Gemina (Spain)
Tenth, Gemina (Upper Pannonia)	Fifteenth, Apollinaris (Cappadocia)	Second, Italica (Noricum)
Fourteenth, Gemina (Upper Pannonia)	Third, Gallica (Syria)	Third, Italica (Raetia)
First, Parthica (Mesopotamia)	Second, Parthica (Italy)	Third, Parthica (Mesopotamia)

(*ILS* 2288 = Campbell, 1994, no. 144)

This is an important historical record showing not only the location of Rome's troops and suggesting the government's strategic thinking, but also confirming willingness to maintain a large army and record it meticulously; Augustus of course had written out in his own hand the numbers of all the troops in the army. Furthermore, the names of the legions reflect the incidents and rhythms of Roman warfare and occasionally political history. Several were named after an emperor: *Augusta* after Augustus; II *Traiana* and XXX *Ulpia* recruited by Trajan *c*.101 for the Dacian wars; *Claudia* was an honorific title for legions VII and XI for loyalty to Claudius in a revolt. Some took their name in honour of a deity favoured by an emperor: XV *Apollinaris* ('Apollo's'); Augustus was devoted to

Apollo; I *Minervia* ('sacred to Minerva'), who was Domitian's favourite goddess. Others were named after fighting qualities: *Victrix* ('Conquering'), *Fulminata* ('Thunderbolt'), *Ferrata* ('Ironclad'), *Fretensis* (from the strait between Sicily and Italy, possibly after a naval battle), *Rapax* ('Predator'). Others took their name from where they served or fought: *Macedonica* and *Scythica*; I, II and III *Parthica* ('Parthian') were raised by Septimius Severus for his Parthian campaign. Other names show the circumstances of the legion's foundation: XV and XXII *Primigenia* ('First-born'), raised probably by Caligula; I and II *Adiutrix* ('Helper'), recruited by Nero in AD 68 and 69 from sailors of the imperial fleet at Misenum and Ravenna; VII *Hispana* ('Spanish'), recruited by Galba in Spain in 68 after his proclamation as emperor; *Gemina* ('Twin'), from an amalgamation of existing legions; I *Italica* ('Italian'), raised by Nero in 66 or 67 for the proposed invasion of the Caspian area, was probably named after its Italian personnel, as was also the case with II and III *Italica* recruited by Marcus Aurelius *c.*165 for the Danube frontier.

The Romans kept up the traditional basis of recruitment, so that legionaries had to be Roman citizens. But there were ways round this, particularly the recruitment of soldiers' sons (normally from unofficial unions with foreign women and therefore not citizens by birth), who got citizenship on joining up. In a crisis normal rules went by the board, as for example during the civil wars of AD 68–69 in the case of the legions I and II Adiutrix (see above). Each year the government needed more than 5,000 recruits, who in the main came from the rural lower classes and were made up of a combination of conscripts and volunteers. At all times the government probably preferred volunteers to both legions and *auxilia* on the grounds that they would make better soldiers. But Tiberius had complained about the quality of recruits in Italy: 'Volunteers were in short supply, and if they appeared, they did not have that same kind of valour and discipline, because those who applied for military service were generally penniless down-and-outs' (Tacitus, *Annals* 4.4).

The young men of Italy were increasingly reluctant to serve for twenty-five years in some distant outpost. Conscription was seemingly used mainly in times of crisis. For example, in the reign of Hadrian (r. AD 117–38) we find that Memmius Macrinus 'was sent to conduct a levy of the young men in the Transpadana region' (*ILS* 1068); this is probably connected with Roman losses during the war in Judaea in 132–35. Limited use of conscription in Italy meant that the largely Italian army of the time of Augustus disappeared, so that by the reign of Hadrian hardly any Italians were serving in the legions. On the other hand, it may have remained the practice that new legions were recruited as far as possible from Italians.

Faced with the increasing disinclination of the youth of Italy to serve in the legions, the government found recruits in the west from Roman citizens in Spain,

Narbonese Gaul and Africa, in the east from Hellenized Syria and Asia Minor. Over a long period localized recruiting came to predominate, beginning with those legions that had Romanized settlements nearby. For example, from the second century AD the legion based at Legio in Spain consisted almost exclusively of men born in Spain. In Africa, where the III Augusta was based, before Trajan about 60 per cent of the troops came from outside Africa, but gradually local men from Roman communities all over Africa made up the bulk of the legion. Conscription certainly occurred in the provinces, but was not employed systematically. For example, the presence of twenty-two legionaries (out of ninety-eight) from Bithynia serving in Africa in the reign of Trajan suggests that conscription had been used. Service far from home would discourage volunteers, but they will have been more plentiful with the development of local recruiting and also improvement in service conditions through the second century.

According to Tacitus, as early as AD 14 the *auxilia* were as numerous as the legions. Now formally part of the army, they consisted of infantry cohorts, part-mounted cohorts (*cohortes equitatae*) and cavalry squadrons (*alae*). All these units had about 500 men, but later 1,000-men units appeared. The *auxilia* were commanded by men of equestrian status. They were also permanently stationed in the provinces along with the legions, or sometimes in separate detachments. For example, at Rapidum in Mauretania Caesariensis, a small fort was occupied by a cohort of Sardians and around this a civilian settlement eventually grew up. The numbers of *auxilia* units probably increased more quickly and they were recruited from most of the peripheral regions of the empire. Spain contributed recruits to most armies, and other important areas were the Alps, Raetia, Pannonia, Thrace (which contributed more than thirty units in the early imperial period) and Syria. In Gaul the Romans used local dignitaries and their organizational structures for recruitment, and there were eight cohorts and one *ala* of Batavians serving in Britain before AD 69. However, it caused resentment that auxiliary units were regularly sent to serve far from their homeland, partly because the government feared that they might join or instigate a native revolt. There was some justification for this since in 69–70 Julius Civilis, a Batavian prince and Roman citizen, led a rebellion on the Rhine with the help of the auxiliary cohorts of his fellow countrymen. Conscription was probably widely employed for the *auxilia* until, in the longer term, units were supplemented by local recruitment from the provinces where they were stationed, and from neighbouring provinces. Consequently, in many cases the ethnic character of a unit was diluted and the army consisted of an extraordinary mixture of peoples. In the case of some specialist fighting units, the ethnic character was maintained for military reasons; the first cohort of Hamesene archers stationed in Pannonia continued to draw recruits from its homeland of Syria. Although the auxiliaries did supply specialist fighters such as archers, slingers, camel riders and cavalry, nevertheless in most cases they fought alongside the legions in a normal infantry deployment.

The praetorians and urban cohorts made up the garrison of Rome. The nine cohorts of the praetorian guard probably numbered 9,000 men, from the time of Tiberius stationed in a camp in Rome. They guarded the emperor and performed ceremonial functions, but part of the guard would accompany the emperor when he left Rome, especially on campaign. A tribune of equestrian rank commanded each cohort and was responsible for bringing the watchword to the emperor. This elite force with superior service conditions continued the arrangements of Augustus; it attracted the young men of Italy who wanted a military life without leaving their native land. Not surprisingly, there was sometimes resentment among other soldiers, as expressed by the mutineers of AD 14, who complained that the praetorians had an easy, pampered life while legionaries could see the enemy from their bases. The Italian recruitment of the guard continued up to Septimius Severus, who disbanded it in 193 and recruited a new force from the legions that had first supported him. But young Italians were not deliberately excluded and they soon appear again.

The urban cohorts were also stationed in Rome, possibly in the same camp, although they came under the command of the Prefect of the City. The three original cohorts were increased to four, and by the time of Septimius Severus the total complement amounted to 6,000 men. Later two further cohorts were created, one for Lugdunum and one for Carthage. The soldiers of the urban cohorts were recruited largely from Italians (up to 88 per cent in the second century AD), like C. Sertorius Justus: 'From Iguvium, solider of the X Urban Cohort, the century of Veturius, served for seventeen years, lived for thirty-three years, ten months and ten days' (*L'Année épigraphique* 1984.57). They had the primary purpose of keeping order in Rome, though their attributes and training and equipment made them more like soldiers than police. They could supplement the praetorians or occasionally be used as a counterweight in moments of political trouble. They did not usually serve in military campaigns.

Another Augustan innovation had been the permanent fleets stationed in Italy at Misenum and Ravenna, which eventually came to be commanded by equestrian prefects. The sailors were recruited on the same basis as the *auxilia*, and in the Ravenna fleet from AD 70 onwards the majority of recruits came from the Balkans, the east, Sardinia and Corsica. Despite the use of Greek terms for the officers, the structure was Roman, with the crew operating as a century under a centurion. Sailors were described legally as soldiers (*milites*). The fleets were not central to Roman military strategy, but an interesting development was the appearance of river fleets, especially on the Rhine and Danube, which transported men and supplies, patrolled the waterways and maintained contact between Roman bases. Rivers remained an important hinge of military operations in frontier zones.

Pay and Service Conditions

As we have seen, Augustus had established the pay and service conditions of his professional standing army. The huge annual cost of the army meant that pay rises were few and far between. Legionaries received 900 *sesterces* a year in three instalments, which was increased to 1,200 by Domitian through the addition of a fourth instalment. There was no further increase for over one hundred years until Septimius Severus increased pay to about 2,000 *sesterces*. This was rapidly followed by another increase ordered by his son Caracalla. This sudden generosity undoubtedly reflects the political problems of a dynasty beset by civil war and internal tensions. What was the value of soldiers' pay? It was not generous, and the mutineers of AD 14 complained about the paltry *stipendium* out of which they had to pay for clothes, weapons, tents and bribes to the centurions to avoid tiresome chores. In the time of Augustus legionaries received $2\frac{1}{2}$ *sesterces* a day; a labourer in Rome could earn 3–4 *sesterces* a day and a farm labourer about half this. Therefore, a soldier was on a par with lowly paid workers. But soldiers had their wages paid regularly, whereas a labourer was paid only for those days when he was working. The soldiers were also housed by the government, never allowed to go hungry, and had medical care. It was in the emperor's interests to keep them reasonably contented. A payroll account from Egypt in AD 81 records the pay and deductions of a legionary cavalryman in Greek drachmas:

Quintus Julius Proculus, from Damascus

Received first salary payment of our lord's first year	248 drachmas
Deductions	
Hay	10
Towards rations	80
Boots, leggings	12
Camp Saturnalia (a festival)	20
Towards clothing	60
Remainder deposited to his account	66
Previous balance	136
Total balance	**202**

(Campbell, 1994, no. 24, extract)

The remaining sections of the account show that deductions were made at standard rates, and despite everything this soldier was able to save some money.

Furthermore, from time to time soldiers received handouts (donatives), which significantly supplemented their regular pay. These might celebrate a victory or some event important to the emperor such as his birthday or the day on which he had been recognized as emperor; it soon became normal practice for an emperor to grant a donative on the day of his accession. Marcus Aurelius paid out 25,000 *sesterces* to the praetorians on this day. Furthermore, soldiers were unique in receiving a pension (*praemium*) on their discharge from the army. For a legionary it was a monetary sum or a grant of land; in the early empire there were complaints about the quality of the land, but veteran colonies continued to be founded until the time of Hadrian. By the later second century AD monetary payments were the norm and under Caracalla legionaries received 20,000 *sesterces*. No other worker received this kind of benefit. The praetorians and urban cohorts received proportionately more in pay, donatives and discharge payments. The *auxilia*, on the other hand, possibly received less, with the infantryman perhaps receiving five-sixths of legionary pay; but there were gradations: for example, a cavalryman would get more since he had to provide for his horse. By the late first century AD all legionaries and *auxilia* served for twenty-five or twenty-six years.

The most striking benefit granted to auxiliary soldiers on discharge was Roman citizenship, and also up to the 140s AD citizenship for any children they had; later only their children born after they left the army received citizenship. These soldiers also received a grant of marriage rights with any one woman, even of non-Roman status. As proof of legitimate discharge and entitlement to privileges, all auxiliaries received a certificate (*diploma* in modern parlance), citing their unit, commander and the province in which it was based. The diploma was a folding tablet made of bronze, and since over two hundred of them have been discovered they are a valuable resource for the history of the Roman army. Praetorians as a mark of respect received similar certificates, also with the privilege of marriage rights. It is likely that legionaries received the same kind of privileges: marriage and citizenship for children, even though certificates were not given to them. Furthermore, soldiers enjoyed some exemptions and special legal rights that, for example, allowed them to make a valid will by a mere expression of intent, and to keep control of their military property even though their father was still alive.

Soldiers discharged from the army because of wounds or ill health were also part of society, and the way in which they were treated comes across in the rather dry legal texts in the Digest of Roman law. These soldiers were given a specific designation (*causarii*) and received their discharge privileges fairly on a sliding scale depending on the number of years of service. We find the emperor Philip (r. 244–49) confirming that *causarii* 'had no stain on their record'. This is an interesting insight into the attitude of the military authorities and the emperor to soldiers who were of no further use to them, in a society not normally renowned for its compassion. But soldiers talk to one another and note what happens to the wounded; the emperor always needed to be popular with his men.

A Soldier's Life

We have unusually detailed evidence for the activities of Roman soldiers in and around the camps through the records kept (often on papyrus) by the military bureaucracy, detailing routine camp duties. Although these records are limited in time and place, they probably give a pretty typical picture. A papyrus describes the daily work of a part-mounted cohort, the First Veteran Mounted Cohort of Spanish (*I Veterana Hispanorum equitata*) based at Stobi in Macedonia in AD 105–6:

FROM THESE ABSENT

in Gaul to obtain clothing
similarly to obtain [grain(?)]
across the river (?) Erar (?) to obtain horses
at Castra in the garrison, including two cavalrymen
in Dardania at the mines

INSIDE THE PROVINCE

Guards of Fabius Justus, the legate . . .
in the office of Latinianus, procurator of the emperor
at Piroboridava in the garrison
at Buridava in the detachment
across the Danube on an expedition . . .
23 cavalrymen, 2 infantrymen on pay and a half
similarly across (the river) to protect the corn supply
similarly on a scouting mission with the centurion . . .
at the grain ships . . .
at headquarters with the clerks
to the Haemus (mountains) to bring in cattle
to guard beasts of burden . . .
similarly on guard duty.

(Campbell, 1994, no. 183)

This gives a snapshot of the range of duties routinely carried out by soldiers and emphasizes how many could be employed outside the camp at any one time. On many occasions soldiers will have spent more time training, exercising and parading than fighting. In his fourth-century handbook on military science Vegetius explained the importance of this: 'We see that the Roman people conquered the world by no other means than training in the military arts, discipline in the camp and practice in warfare' (1.1). Keeping the troops up to the mark was the job of their officers, but sometimes the emperor himself came to supervise. Hadrian had a high-profile policy of visiting the army in its various provincial bases, where: 'He personally investigated absolutely everything, not only the usual camp fixtures . . . but the private business of everyone, both the ordinary soldiers and their commanders, their lifestyle, their quarters and their habits . . .' (Dio 69.9).

Hadrian went to Numidia in 128 to review the training manoeuvres of the legion III Augusta and the auxiliary units. The legion had its own parade ground at its camp in Lambaesis, and the emperor's speech was carved on the corner pillars of the tribunal located in the centre of this parade ground. He commented on the training manoeuvres, showing a sound knowledge and understanding of military exercises, and bestowing praise and sometimes criticism; he did not forget to congratulate the officers:

To the first *ala* of Pannonians

You did everything in order. You filled the plain with your exercises, you threw your javelins with a certain degree of style, although you were using rather short and stiff javelins; several of you hurled your lances with equal skill. Just now you mounted your horses agilely and yesterday you did it swiftly. If anything had been lacking in your performance I should have noted it, if anything had been obviously bad I should have mentioned it, but throughout the entire manoeuvre you satisfied me uniformly. Catullinus, my legate, distinguished man, shows equal concern for all the units of which he is in command. . . . Your prefect apparently looks after you conscientiously. I grant you a donative. . . . (Campbell, 1994, no. 17)

In many ways the army was a self-contained military community in which a strong factor was loyalty to comrades and emperor. Unit loyalty was extremely important, partly inspired by the military standards; the eagle (*aquila*) symbolized the continuity and essence of the legion. Shared experience of military life and death bound soldiers together. Military disasters had a great effect on the psyche, but the military community was satisfied after the defeat of Varus in AD 9 and the loss of 20,000 men with the days of national mourning in Rome, the burial of the fallen on the battlefield by the imperial prince Germanicus in 15, and the persistent search for the three lost eagles. Furthermore, the temple of Mars Ultor ('the Avenger') dedicated in 2 BC was a kind of war memorial, in this case to Roman armies defeated in Parthia. The war memorial (possibly dating from the time of Domitian in the late first century AD) at Adamklissi in southern Romania includes a mausoleum and an altar on which the names of 3,800 legionaries and auxiliaries killed in a battle are recorded in terms that were to be echoed in many modern war memorials: 'In memory of the courageous men who gave their lives for the state' (*ILS* 9107).

Imperial celebrations naturally concentrated on the triumphant progress of Rome's armies, and the great sculptured columns of Trajan and Marcus Aurelius served among other things as monuments to the Roman soldier at war. In memorials of this kind, and on triumphal arches, the emperor figured prominently in the record of war, and it was to him personally that soldiers swore a solemn oath (*sacramentum*) of loyalty and obedience. In military camps the emperor's portrait was kept in the shrine along with the standards and received offerings. The military calendar created by Augustus contained many festivals in honour of emperors, past and present. The surviving example, from Dura-Europos *c.*AD 223–27 in the reign of Severus Alexander, lists the festivals observed by the twentieth cohort of Palmyrenes:

> 6 March. For the imperial power of the [divine Marcus Antoninus and the divine Lucius Verus], to the divine Marcus an ox, [to the divine Lucius] an ox.

> 13 March. Because Emperor [Caesar Marcus Aurelius Severus Alexander] was acclaimed emperor, to Jupiter an ox, [to Juno a cow, to Minerva, a cow], to Mars an ox; and because Alexander our Augustus was [first] acclaimed Imperator by the soldiers [of Emperor Augustus Marcus Aurelius Severus Alexander, a supplication . . .].

> 14 March. Because Alexander our [Augustus] was named [Augustus and father of the fatherland and] chief priest, a supplication; [to the *Genius* of our lord] Alexander [Augustus a bull . . .]. (Campbell, 1994, no. 207)

The calendar expresses the personal association of emperor and army in a military environment, mediated through religious observance.

The army had a fixed code of discipline with theoretically severe punishments, which established the individual soldier's relationship with his comrades, with his officers, and with his military duties. Some commanders had a ferocious reputation for enforcing discipline, but they may have been exceptional and in practice it seems that there was a flexible approach, even in respect of such a serious offence as desertion, which goes right to the emperor himself, as we see in a lawyer's comment: 'When, after a period of desertion, a soldier has been reinstated in the army, he should not receive his pay and donatives for the time when he was a deserter, unless the generosity of the emperor has granted this as a special favour' (*Digesta; Corpus Iuris Civilis* 49.16.10). In the end much responsibility for discipline will have been devolved to local commanders, and it is possible that peer esteem and *esprit de corps* were the most important factors in keeping order at unit level.

The Army in the Provinces

Although the army could manufacture much of the material it required in its own workshops and plant crops in the legionary *territorium* (an area of land in the vicinity of the camp), it was never self-sufficient. In fact, the way in which the Romans organized and stationed the army had profound economic and social effects. By the early third century there were about 450,000 soldiers at large in the empire; feeding and maintaining this huge force brought an increased market for local producers in military provinces. To take two examples, the 80,000 troops stationed along the Rhine would require more than 25,000 tons of wheat a year, while the 55,000 garrison of Britain would have required at least 2,000 calves a year simply for leather replacement, and more than 3,000 replacement horses. Since some materials had to be imported over long distances, for example wine and wheat into Britain, trade routes also benefited. The presence of certain types of parasite in wheat discovered in Britain shows that it came from southern Gaul. Indeed, one of the most important trade routes in the Roman world was that along the Rhône valley to the Rhine armies and Britain.

The military presence also helped the urbanization of the empire as the soldiers built new facilities (admittedly usually for the army's benefit). It was military surveyors who mapped out the route for the construction of new roads, which were often maintained at local expense. In the Republic road building had spread out from Italy, and the via Egnatia linked the Adriatic and the Aegean while the via Domitia ran from the Alps to Spain. In the empire military road building was hugely ambitious in geographical extent and was an imperial prerogative. Augustus had repaired the via Flaminia and Claudius celebrated the completion of his father Drusus's road through the Alps, a route that ran 'from the river Po to the river Danube' (*ILS* 208). Later emperors took up the challenge and a series of roads crisscrossed the empire, linking provinces and regions and giving a highly visible sign of the permanent Roman presence and demonstrating the importance of routes of communication in the control of the empire. The army also developed brand-new towns for veterans, like Timgad in Africa, laid out with regimented regularity like a military camp, but with all the sophisticated amenities of an urban environment. Indeed, the original sites of military camps were chosen not necessarily for their defensive position, but with an eye to communications, both by river transport and the hub of the Roman road network. They therefore often occupied an important location for commerce and trade. Gradually, civilian settlements grew up around the camps, and continuous development has seen many old Roman military camps become major centres and capital cities in modern Europe, such as Bonn, Cologne, Mainz, Budapest, Vienna and Belgrade.

Military camps were a magnet for visitors and settlers of all kinds who had something to offer the soldiers, who had money to spend – traders, shop-keepers, wine-merchants and, of course, women. The largely civilian settlements around legionary camps, the *canabae*, gradually acquired an independent status and some became fully fledged communities to which veteran soldiers were attracted; some provide evidence of local industries like bronze-working and pottery. For example, at Deva (Chester) in Britain the *canabae* were established close to the main camp; the amphitheatre outside the camp could accommodate 7,000 specta-tors and clearly served the legion and most of the civilian population, which also shared the water supply by tapping into the fortress aqueduct. In the first half of the second century there was a noticeable improvement in living conditions in the *canabae* as more elaborate stone houses replaced timber buildings.

The increasing recruitment of non-Italians and the treatment of soldiers' families had significant results. The grants of citizenship to auxiliary soldiers and to soldiers' children encouraged the process of adopting Roman practices and way of life. Soldiers tended to become integrated into the local area where they served because they associated with local women and the legions were based for many years in the same location. Furthermore, with the development of local recruiting many recruits came increasingly from the vicinity of the military camps, often from military families, and this increased the extent to which the army was bound in with the local community.

Our sources occasionally allow us a glimpse of soldiers as normal human beings, not armoured automata, like Hilarianus in 242 to whose petition the emperor Gordian III replied as follows:

If your wife left the province before she could be brought to trial for adultery, you cannot bring an accusation in her absence and your request that she should be brought back to the province where you are serving as a soldier is not just. But you will be able to bring a formal accusation against her when your mili-tary duties permit. For the time that you have given to your military obligations should not deprive you of the retribution, which, with the grief of a betrayed husband, you demand. (*CJ* 9.9.15)

Battle Tactics

No one doubts that the Romans were ruthless and persistent in their military objectives. The extreme brutality of Roman warfare and sieges is legendary, and Polybius gave the Greek view of the appalling aftermath when the Romans stormed New Carthage in Spain in 209 BC:

> Scipio . . . ordered them to kill everyone they met and to spare no one, and not to begin looting until they got the order. The purpose of this practice, I suppose, is to strike terror. So you can often see in cities captured by the Romans not only people who have been butchered, but even dogs hacked in two and the limbs of other animals cut off. (10.15.4–5)

Legionaries over the first three centuries AD were equipped with a throwing spear (*pilum*) and the traditional Spanish stabbing-sword. The normal tactic was to deliver a volley of spears, after which the troops drew swords and moved to close quarters, the object being where possible to engage on a broad front where as many as possible of the trained swordsmen could engage the enemy. A typical formation saw the legionary and auxiliary infantry taking up position in the centre, while cavalry (sometimes with archers) on the flanks protected the deployment and dispersed any opposing cavalry. Although the infantry was normally the crucial factor in battle, cavalry could be deployed to stage ambushes or attack in the rear. Germanicus, fighting the German tribe the Cherusci in AD 16, disrupted their attack by sending the cavalry to attack their flanks and launch a counter-attack in the rear, while his infantry engaged the Germans head-on. There is a suggestion in Tacitus, commenting on the use of auxiliary infantry by his father-in-law Agricola in Britain at the battle of Mons Graupius in AD 83, that the auxiliaries were sometimes used to carry the brunt of the attack and spare the loss of legionaries.

Battlefield tactics were the responsibility of the commander, and it was the legacy of Augustus's policy that most army commanders were senators who continued in the tradition of non-specialist all-round abilities of the upper classes (or so they believed); there was no high command, no military academy and no hierarchy of officers; each post was an 'individuality' and a commander carried out his duties guided by advice, previous experience and whatever he had absorbed from the many books about strategy available; promising men of equestrian rank could be promoted to senatorial status. Over time in periods of crisis there was a certain degree of military specialization, although many senatorial commanders had very limited experience before exercising military leadership. The chain of command was made up of legionary legates, military tribunes, centurions and equestrian officers of auxiliary cavalry and infantry units. Major campaigns were usually conducted in the presence, and sometimes under the direction, of the emperor, who generally had limited or little military experience and would have to seek the guidance of his senior commanders and his companions (*comites*), those officially asked to accompany him and offer advice.

The lack of substantial military experience among army commanders may have inhibited the development of tactics, and in fact the Romans tended to be conservative. Therefore, it may be that military textbooks and collections of past stratagems published in the empire really were intended to guide contemporary generals. Nevertheless, from time to time innovations occurred, most notably in warfare against the Parthians, where the Romans faced mounted archers and formidable cavalry forces, some of which were armoured. At first, Roman commanders resorted to a defensive hollow square with the baggage train in the middle, but this was overwhelmed at the battle of Carrhae in 53 BC. A more successful ploy was to use archers and slingers to keep the cavalry at bay and to deploy the tortoise (*testudo*) in open battle. Here the first rank of legionaries knelt holding their shields in front of them, while succeeding ranks held their shields over the rank in front of them, producing a barrier like a tiled roof. Arrian, defending the province of Cappadocia c.AD 135 against the Alani, who used armoured cavalry, drew up his legionaries in a defensive formation like the Greek phalanx, in which those in the first ranks carried a long thrusting spear. He supported this unusual formation with strong cavalry forces and planned a concentrated barrage of missiles to open the battle. From the second century the Romans developed their own units of heavy cavalry, in some of which both horse and rider wore armour. The intention will have been to intimidate the enemy with their fearsome appearance and steady advance.

Roman Brutality in War

Augustus casually notes in the *Res Gestae*: 'When foreign peoples could safely be pardoned I preferred to spare rather than exterminate them' (3.2). Total destruction was always an option, and Domitian, referring to the defeat of a tribe in Numidia, said: 'I have forbidden the Nasamones to exist' (Dio 67.4.6). As in the Republic, imperial Romans recognized few restraints in dealing with people they felt were obstinate in their resistance, and non-combatants were often targeted. After the mutiny of the German legions in AD 14, Germanicus led the legions across the Rhine to seek redemption for their indiscipline by killing the enemy:

(They) devastated the country with fire and sword for fifty miles around. No pity was shown to age or sex. Religious and well as secular buildings were razed to the ground. . . . (Tacitus, *Annals* 1.51)

Romans were seemingly unconcerned about the peripheral consequences of their military operations. In the aftermath of Trajan's failed invasion of Parthia in 115–17, the Jews of the Diaspora rose in revolt, and in Cyprus 250,000 lives were lost in fighting between Greeks and Jews in AD 117.

After a campaign was over, the Romans often deported men of military age and women and children to a different location. This sometimes involved huge numbers. Plautius Silvanus Aelianus, governor under Nero of Moesia on the Danube, celebrated among his achievements: 'He brought across more than 100,000 of the number of Transdanubians for the payment of taxes, together with their wives and children and leaders or kings' (Braund, 1985, no. 401).

Sheer terror was another tactic, and Julius Frontinus, who served as governor of Britain (AD 73/4–77), and wrote on stratagems as well as the management of the aqueducts, cites the ploy of using severed enemy heads to intimidate the survivors and bring a war to a close after a successful battle. His comments were not merely theoretical. A recently discovered tombstone from Lancaster proudly depicts an auxiliary cavalryman displaying a severed head. Therefore, when Trajan's troops presented him with severed enemy heads, as depicted on his column, they were probably carrying on a well-established Roman practice. In this context it is not surprising to find the second-century historian Florus boasting of the treatment of the Thracians: 'Captives were savagely treated by fire and sword, but the barbarians thought that nothing was more awful than that they should be left alive with their hands cut off and be forced to survive their punishment' (1.39.7). An emperor who was successful in war would enjoy a triumphal procession through the centre of Rome, in which defeated enemy leaders were paraded before the spectators, ritually humiliated and then ceremonially executed.

There was no refuge for the defeated, since the Roman army had powerful artillery and siege engines and could systematically root out all remnants of opposition. This kind of military operation was used sometimes to pacify peoples within Roman provinces and often went on unrecorded by literary sources, but some native revolts developed into full-scale warfare that required substantial military action by Rome. Even after the Jewish rebellion of AD 66 had been crushed and Jerusalem had fallen in 70, the Romans persisted with the war and, for six months, Flavius Silva besieged the Jews holding out in Herod's great fortress of Masada. The Roman siege camp built on sloping ground loomed up threateningly at the defenders and the great siege mound (the remains of which still stand to this day) was raised to a height of more than three hundred feet, and a huge stone platform was constructed on top to provide a secure base for the siege-engines. Water and supplies had to be brought in over long distances by Jewish prisoners, and the besiegers probably required about 26,000 litres of water daily. The operation ended with the storming of the fortress and the suicide of the defenders, 960 men, women and children; there were only seven survivors (Josephus, *Jewish War* 7.275–406). The later revolt in Judaea in AD 132–35 saw more than half a million war casualties on the Jewish side alone. All-out war was one instrument of Roman power even within the confines of the territories they ruled, and the army did not significantly alter its methods and tactics whether dealing with revolts or waging wars of conquest. Tacitus knew very well the psychological impact of Roman violence, as we see from his comments on the massacre of 10,000 people at Uspe in the Crimea: 'The destruction of Uspe instilled terror into the others. Weapons, fortifications, mountains and obstacles, rivers, and cities had all equally been overcome' (*Annals* 12.17).

Strategic Planning

The Roman army was the largest state-sponsored institution in the ancient world. It brought prestige and protection to emperors and also offered the possibility of military adventures. How was this powerful instrument used? In the modern world of nation states, borders and frontiers are of great importance and the study of foreign relations consequently is prominent. But the Roman Empire had no structure for formulating a consistent policy for frontier zones and for managing contact with those peoples on the periphery of the formal provincial structure. There was no foreign office, no foreign minister and no accountable body to monitor decisions. The emperor effectively made decisions that suited him, taking the advice of senior advisers if he wished; each decision would be made individually on an ad hoc basis. In the absence of an army high command, generals might find it hard to tap a fund of experience for dealing with certain hostile peoples. All this militated against the development of a consistent policy.

Another important factor was that the Romans of the imperial period maintained a certain militaristic ethos and never really lost their casual air of superiority going back to Augustus and his programme of conquest. The army by its victories perpetuated and encouraged this ideology. Virgil in the *Aeneid* famously, and pompously, has Jupiter say that he gave the Romans 'power without limit'; he could not have written in this way without believing that it was at least feasible; his words would have seemed ridiculous if his audience had not thought the same way. He also had defined the Romans' role as sparing the downtrodden (i.e. those who recognized Rome's obvious right to rule) and 'warring down' the arrogant (i.e. anyone who resisted). Even the down-to-earth Livy could write that so great was the military glory of the Roman people that it was obvious that their founder was Mars. Before this, the first-century BC satirist Lucilius had claimed that the

Romans had occasionally lost a battle but never a war, and the war meant every-thing. Florus, that bellicose historian, despised foreign peoples and thought that the enemies of Rome were expendable since they did not even know what peace was (2.29). In the Roman way of looking at things there was no concept of a fron-tier as a formal barrier. Therefore, many writers, while assuming Rome's ability to defeat other peoples, argued that if lands were left unconquered it was because they were not worth conquering:

> These emperors added some peoples to the empire and suppressed those that revolted. Being in possession of the best part of the earth and sea, they have prudently aimed to preserve their empire instead of extending their rule endlessly to poverty-stricken and profitless barbarian tribes. . . . They encircle the empire with enormous armies and garrison the entire sweep of land and sea like a stronghold. (Appian, *Roman History*, Preface 7)

Against this kind of intellectual background it is not surprising that the upper classes maintained a strong military ethos, and we cannot doubt the continuing importance for many senators of holding military posts and army commands within the patterns of upper-class office-holding, even though there were other ways to make a name for themselves. There will have been senators who supported an adventurous foreign policy, hoping to benefit from it. This brings us to the top of the social tree and the military ambitions of emperors, who were leading exponents of militaristic ideology, in how they dressed, how they presented themselves in terms of titles, honours and military parades, how they were depicted in art, and most strikingly how they personally took charge of frequent military campaigns. It follows, therefore, that relations with foreign peoples and wars might depend on the personality of the emperor and the rhythms of imperial politics.

Historians face the problem that ancient writers offer only limited analysis of frontier zones and the development of Roman policy. It is true that Tacitus has some useful comments on Roman policy in Germany just after Augustus's death. Apparently quoting a letter from Tiberius to Germanicus, he gives due weight to the advantages of offensive diplomacy over warfare in securing Roman interests on the Rhine. Elsewhere, however, he is critical of the emperor for an indolent foreign policy that saw little Roman initiative or action. But this might be a way of criticizing an unpopular emperor. It is interesting that Cassius Dio, who generally approved of Trajan, can find no motive for his military campaigns in Dacia and Parthia other than a desire for renown; that is, the emperor was proving his *virtus* through military *gloria*. A conflict between militaristic ideology and rational analysis is apparent from the comments made by Dio about

Septimius Severus's policy of invading Parthia and creating the province of Mesopotamia. Severus had claimed that security was his guiding motive – to protect the province of Syria. Dio was scathing; not only was the expedition horrendously expensive, but it had the opposite effect, dragging the Romans into contact with alien peoples and their wars, with no benefit. Severus of course needed a decent war against foreign enemies to take attention away from the recent civil wars. Politics, military ideology and imperialist foreign policy all had their part to play in this acquisition of new territory, which was not to the liking of at least some senators.

In the context of the problems of our sources, archaeology has a crucial role in identifying forts, camps, walls, roads and other military installations, although there are sometimes problems with precise dating and pinpointing the purpose of buildings. In certain areas archaeological investigation is responsible for an eye-catching achievement, as for example in the identification of the site of Varus's defeat at Kalkriese in Germany in AD 9. Another example is the story of the siege and destruction of the Roman outpost at Dura-Europos on the Euphrates by the Persian king Shapur I in 256, which is not mentioned by any literary source. The archaeology of the site vividly shows the battle to control the town, in which the Persians used mines to bring down the fortifications while the Romans responded with a counter-mine. The skeletons of at least nineteen Roman soldiers and one Persian soldier still wearing their armour were found in the mine; the Persians had probably heard them coming and asphyxiated them by introducing fumes into the tunnel. They then dragged the bodies to block the entrance to the Roman mine, before deliberately collapsing it.

However, despite the achievements of archaeology we remain poorly informed on the purpose and development of Roman policy for dealing with foreign peoples, and it is tempting to resort to modern analogies. One striking suggestion is that the Romans had a kind of 'grand strategy', which changed as military circumstances changed. In the first century AD up to the Flavian dynasty, the Romans maintained no formal line of defence but kept large concentrations of troops close to the frontier zones; these were moved around to deal with incursions, and were supported by the forces of friendly rulers. Then, from the late first century up to the end of the second century, a system of linear frontier defence developed, based on carefully arranged or 'scientific' frontiers. This preclusive defence dealt with all threats outside this ideal frontier line, thus protecting the inhabitants of Roman territory. In the critical phase of the third century, up to the military reforms of Diocletian and Constantine, a system of defence-in-depth emerged. The Rhine, the Danube and, to a lesser extent, the Euphrates featured as part of the garrisoned defence lines of the second and third stages. In this system an important feature was the maintenance of control by using the Romans' power

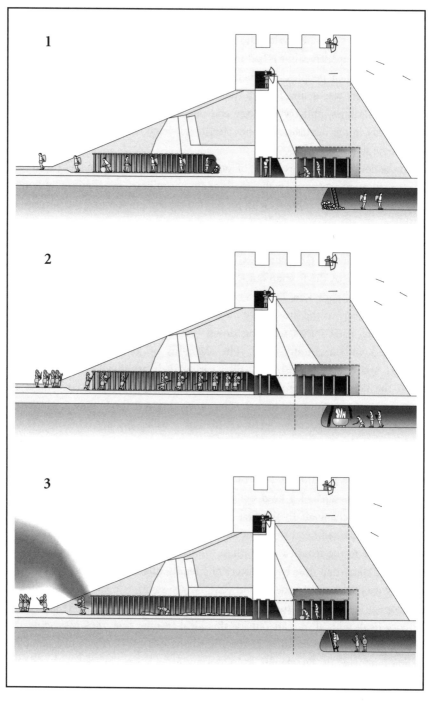

Plan 5. The siege of Dura-Europos, AD 256 (permission of Simon James, *AJA* (2011), figure 20).

and influence over other peoples, and the threat of aggressive action. Force was available through the presence of the legions, but when force was used, then, unlike power, it was expended and reduced.

This analysis is probably too schematic since there were great differences in military deployment in various parts of the empire and it is misleading to talk of an empire-wide strategy. Also it implies an essentially defensive mentality, which does not fit in with Roman thinking. Other explanations are more persuasive; in some areas the Romans may simply have lost their forward impetus because they ran out of troops or resources. Elsewhere in the frontier zones complex social, economic and cultural factors will have contributed to Roman policy. Perhaps the imperial advance faltered when the equation was no longer in their favour, for example in areas of ecological marginality where it was not profitable to occupy land, or feasible in terms of providing supplies. Local conditions around frontier zones will therefore have contributed significantly to the Roman response. Even in the case of Hadrian's Wall in Britain linking Bowness to Wallsend and manned by auxiliaries, a seemingly clear-cut example of a defensive structure to protect Roman territory, the reality was probably more complex; the legions were stationed well in the rear of the wall, which was perhaps partly intended to monitor traffic into and out of the province.

The great offensive adventures, especially those involving major wars when Roman armies invaded Britain, Dacia and Parthia, had much to do with the character of the emperor, the current political situation, and the persistent importance of military ideology. Claudius was an unprepossessing figure with a limp, shaking head and drooling mouth; he was also politically weak because of the way in which he had come to power, pushed forward by the praetorian guard after the murder of Caligula. He tried to assert himself by launching the invasion of Britain in AD 43, which had no clear economic or strategic motives and involved the concentration of a huge fleet, four legions and about 40,000 men. According to Suetonius, Claudius wanted a proper triumph and thought that Britain was the only suitable place for it. He certainly exploited the military glory, turning up in Britain for the climax of the invasion campaign, staging an impressive triumph, extending the sacred boundary of the city of Rome (as having added new territory to the empire), and giving his son the name Britannicus. In a speech to the senate he boasted: 'I am afraid that I may seem somewhat arrogant and to have looked for an excuse for boasting of my own extension of the boundaries of the empire beyond the ocean' (*ILS* 212).

Despite the steady increase in the territory of the empire over two centuries (several areas were annexed without warfare) and the offensive resource of the professional army, the Romans did not ignore the benefits of diplomacy. In the east, from Augustus to Trajan a precarious balance of power had been preserved without serious warfare against the Parthian Empire, which was relatively stable and sophisticated. The essential elements were Rome's nominal control of Armenia by appointing kings, the role of the Euphrates, which effectively served as a frontier (it was unusual for Rome to accept this), and Rome's willingness to keep out of the political affairs of Parthia. After some desultory warfare under Nero conducted by his general, Domitius Corbulo, an intelligent compromise was reached in AD 66; the Parthian nominee for the kingship of Armenia was accepted as long as he came to Rome to be crowned by the emperor. It is unclear whether the subsequent decision by Vespasian in the 70s to convert Cappadocia into an armed province with a garrison of two legions was a response to a perceived weakening of Roman influence in Armenia. In any case, the new arrangement could operate as an alternative to an aggressive policy in Armenia and Parthia. Trajan peremptorily put an end to the détente in 114 by promising to annex Armenia and rejecting all diplomatic overtures from the Parthians. He enjoyed the thrill of commanding men in battle and may have had an eye on the achievement of that great conqueror, Alexander the Great. The subsequent campaign aimed at regime change in Parthia and the acquisition of new provinces was militarily disastrous, and after Trajan's death Hadrian rapidly withdrew the troops in 117. But the damage had been done and Romano-Parthian relations were now to be characterized by suspicion and hostility, culminating in the attack on Parthia by Septimius Severus and the creation of the new province of Mesopotamia.

By AD 200 there were eight provincial governorships along the northern riverine zones of the empire: Lower Germany (two legions), Upper Germany (two legions), Raetia (one legion), Noricum (one legion), Upper Pannonia (three legions), Lower Pannonia (one legion), Upper Moesia (two legions), Lower Moesia (two legions); therefore, fourteen out of thirty-three legions in service were stationed along the banks of the Rhine and Danube, with a further two beyond the Danube in Dacia; in addition, there were more than one hundred units of auxiliary infantry and cavalry. There were also ten legions in the east, most near the Euphrates and Tigris: two in Cappadocia, two in Syria Coele, one in Syria Phoenice, two in Syria Palaestina (Judaea), two in Mesopotamia, and one in Arabia; in addition, in the second century there were at least seven cavalry *alae* and twenty-two auxiliary cohorts in Syria. Although to the Roman way of thinking rivers were not necessarily defensive barriers, but rather a means of communication and a way of transporting men and supplies to their various military bases, nevertheless rivers did act as the hinge of the Roman military structure into the third century. Symbolically, the Romans absorbed rivers into their empire and then presented them as allies. The river, usually personified as a bearded man, then came forward to assist the legions. This is vividly illustrated by a coin minted under Trajan, which depicts the river Danube pressing his knee down on the female figure of a crushed Dacia and grasping her by the throat, emphasizing the Romans' complete control of the country and the environment (*Coins of the Roman Empire in the British Museum* III, p. 168, no. 793).

CHAPTER EIGHT

The World of Imperial Rome

Becoming Roman

'Like a well-swept and enclosed yard . . . the entire world speaks in unison, more clearly than a chorus; and it harmonizes so well under its director-in-chief that it joins in praying that this Empire may last for ever'. The affluent Greek lecturer Aelius Aristides expresses an ideal view of the unifying force of the Roman Empire (Lewis and Reinhold, 1990, vol. II, pp. 23–4). The reality was that the Romans bound their territories together inconsistently and unevenly by granting citizenship to individuals or groups. The next stage was to make these citizens and others as Roman as possible. It is often not clear how far this was deliberate or an accidental product of other activities.

The Romans were always ready to extend their citizenship to those who helped them, especially in war. Under the rule of the emperors, this process continued and new citizens took Roman names, which were combined with their original nomenclature, for example the Athenian orator, the fabulously wealthy Tiberius Claudius Atticus Herodes. The policy of Augustus had been to grant citizenship relatively sparingly and on one occasion he refused to oblige his wife Livia by granting citizenship to a Gaul, instead offering exemption from taxation, declaring that he preferred to lose money than have the honour of the Roman citizenship degraded (Suetonius, *Augustus* 40.3). Indeed, Claudius removed citizenship from one person who could not speak Latin properly. But the trend was steadily towards greater generosity, marked occasionally by sweeping gestures like Vespasian's grant of Latin rights (which were halfway to citizenship) to the whole of Spain. Furthermore, the increase in the numbers of the *auxilia*, who made up half the army by AD 14, was important since they received citizenship on discharge and also citizenship for their children. It was also government practice to confer citizenship on the sons of legionaries if they joined the army.

Gradually, the Romans brought into the citizen body the rich elites of the provinces, where Roman colonies and *municipia* tended to be centres of citizenship. In addition, veteran colonies founded in the provinces enhanced the Roman presence and demonstrated the value of the Roman way of life.

The process of granting citizenship is illustrated by a bronze tablet from Banasa in Mauretania Tingitana (modern Morocco), describing an award of citizenship by Marcus Aurelius and Lucius Verus:

> Copy of the letter of our emperors Antoninus and Verus, Augusti, to Coiiedius Maximus (the governor?):

> We have read the petition of Julianus the Zegrensian attached to your letter, and although it is not usual to give Roman citizenship to men of that tribe except when very great services prompt the emperor to show his kindness, nevertheless since you assert that he is one of the leading men of his people and is very loyal in his readiness to be of help to our affairs, and since we think that there are not many families among the Zegrensians who can make equal boasts about their services, whereas we wish that very many may be impelled to emulate Julianus because of the honour conferred by us upon his house, we do not hesitate to grant Roman citizenship, without impairment of the law of the tribe, to himself, to his wife Ziddina, likewise to his children Julianus, Maximus, Maximinus, Diogenianus. (*Comptes rendus de l'Académie des Inscriptions et Belles-Lettres* 1971, 468)

In Roman ideology the extension of citizenship involved advantages for both sides, had to be earned, and should not cause any loss to the local community. Related evidence shows that a meticulous documentary record was kept of grants of citizenship, including the names and ages of the wife and children.

After years of piecemeal grants of citizenship, Caracalla probably in 212 granted Roman citizenship to the entire population of the empire with only a few exceptions. We have the emperor's own words in the text of his edict:

> Therefore I think that I can on a grand scale and with piety, do that which is commensurate with their divine majesty, if I should bring with me as Romans to the shrines of the gods as many tens of thousands as enter into the number of my people. Accordingly I grant Roman citizenship to all who inhabit the civilized world. . . . (*Die Giessener literarischen Papyri und die Caracalla-Erlasse* 40 col. 1)

Although the precise motivation is unclear (the hostile Cassius Dio thought that it was to raise more money in taxation), it was probably a great act of benevolence in keeping with Caracalla's effusive, unpredictable nature. Obviously the emperor's decision was highly significant, partly in symbolic terms in marking the culmination of a long process of incorporating new citizens. Indeed, even a Roman name was attractive, as is vividly illustrated by Iddibal Caphada Aemilius, son of Himilis, who bestowed a building on Lepcis in Africa. Although not a Roman citizen, he (or his father) has inserted a Roman name into his nomenclature to add to his prestige and standing.

What did being a Roman citizen amount to by the third century? There was no longer any meaningful political activity in passing laws or voting to elect magistrates, even assuming that distant citizens could get to Rome. However, for the better-off there were more opportunities now for marriage with the Roman elite, and there might be certain advantages in business and in law. For instance, Roman citizens had the right of appeal to the emperor on a capital charge. However, in practice this right was being eroded partly because the increase in the number of citizens made it impossible for emperors to cope. By the late second century a distinction between *honestiores* and *humiliores* was becoming more important in judicial practice and punishment. This was a class division, the former being senators, *equites* and members of local councils in Italy and the provinces, the latter being the rest of the population. In fact, those who benefited most from the grant of citizenship were members of the provincial upper classes, who now had an avenue along which they could advance to equestrian or senatorial offices.

Indeed, a striking feature of society in the imperial period was the increase in the number of senators from outside the traditional Italian heartland. In Augustus's time most senators were Italian, but the pool of recruitment was steadily widened by the addition to senatorial rank of well-off provincials. Naturally, provinces with a long-standing Roman presence made greater progress. Asia is foremost here, making up about one-third of senatorial families coming from the eastern provinces. Other provinces like Baetica and Narbonese Gaul also contributed senators relatively quickly, whereas not a single senator from Britain is known in the first three centuries AD. New senators from outside Italy were enormously proud of their achievement, as is demonstrated by numerous honorary inscriptions like that found at Didyma:

> Senator of the Roman people, the fifth man ever to enter the senate from the whole of Asia, and from Miletus and the rest of Ionia the first and only one. (*Didyma* II, 1958, no. 296, lines 6–11)

This feeling of honour extended through a senatorial family and an inscription from Ephesus describes Caninia Severa as: 'Daughter of Tiberius Claudius

Severus, first Ephesian to be consul' (*Jahresheft des Österreichischen Archäologischen Instituts* 45, 1960. Beiblatt 92, no. 19; Talbert, 1984, p. 36). Of course, not everyone could match the pedigree of C. Julius Severus from Ancyra, who became a senator under Hadrian and refers to himself on a memorial inscription as a descendant of king Attalus of Pergamum and of three Galatian dynasts; he was also related to several ex-consuls.

Severus could presumably hold his own in any company, but there was prejudice against provincial senators. A well-known joke was that senators admitted by Julius Caesar could not find their way to the Senate House. Horace notes how snobs might say of a senator: 'Who is that? Who was his father?' (*Satires* 1.6.27–32). It is therefore not surprising that when in AD 48 Claudius addressed the senate on the subject of admitting as new members those representatives of the tribes of northern Gaul who were members of the provincial assembly at Lugdunum, he went out of his way to disarm opposition:

> It was definitely innovative when my great uncle the divine Augustus and my uncle Tiberius Caesar decided to admit to this senate all the flower of the colonies and municipalities everywhere, obviously upstanding and wealthy men. Nevertheless, it might be suggested that an Italian senator is better than a provincial one.... But I think that not even provincials should be excluded provided that they can in any way add distinction to the senate. (*ILS* 212)

In the second century AD some regulations (generally brief and ineffective) were possibly aimed at establishing a closer link between senators and Italy. Trajan laid down that all candidates for office invest one-third of their capital in Italian land, while Marcus Aurelius insisted that senators of non-Italian origin must invest one-quarter of their capital in Italy. In any case there was a large turnover in senatorial membership and a decline of the hereditary element. Most republican families had died out by the end of the Julio-Claudian dynasty, and even new entrants failed to sustain their family at senatorial rank, with the result that new recruits were always required. Membership was always confined to the well-off social elite, so that there was little change in outlook, which remained conservative and deeply concerned with the senate's traditional prerogatives. In the third century Cassius Dio criticized the new emperor Macrinus because he had assumed the imperial titles without waiting for the senate to vote them as was proper.

How Roman were provincial Roman citizens? How successful was Romanization? This refers to the process by which local peoples gradually acquired cultural practices that could be recognized as distinctly Roman and participated in the Roman way of life. This was not imposed by the Roman conquerors, since Rome did not have an overriding cultural ethos but tended to absorb and adapt from others. Therefore, in a two-way exchange indigenous peoples had the opportunity to influence Rome. In some respects, however, the Romans could give a strong direction. First, colonies were centres of the Roman way of life promoting Rome, the emperor and Roman practices. For example, Lugdunum, founded in 43 BC at the confluence of the Rhône and Saône, was at the heart of the road system in Gaul, the capital of the province of Narbonensis, and the centre of the cult of the emperor for the three Gallic provinces. Second, the grants of citizenship not only to the well-off but also to auxiliaries and their families gave expression to the advantages of associating with Rome; they were virtually missionaries of Roman ideology. The rich who were absorbed into the senate were not just a token presence, since the way was open to men of talent who had the emperor's approval to go on to hold high office. For example, Julius Quadratus Bassus, of royal ancestry from Pergamum, had a long and distinguished career during which he was a military commander and companion of Trajan in the Dacian campaign in AD 101–2 and 105–6. When he died during his governorship of Dacia his body was conveyed back to Pergamum for a public funeral on the orders of Hadrian. Third, officials and governors might exploit attractive elements of civilized living to seduce the natives into acceptance of Roman ways, as Agricola is said to have done as governor of Britain; he encouraged the locals to take an interest in typical Roman buildings and facilities and instructed the sons of local chiefs in Latin. Tacitus cynically but not unfairly observed that this looked like civilization but was in fact an aspect of their subjection (*Agricola* 21).

More often Romanization came about indirectly as a result of contact and familiarity with the Roman way of doing things. Therefore, it occurred unevenly depending on many factors – the wealth and receptiveness of the inhabitants, and the length and nature of Roman control. The Latin language was used in administration and in the army and those who wanted to serve here would have to master it. The whole structure of administering the provinces was imposed by the Romans, and with the increase in citizenship came a greater use of Roman law, the principles of which were often adopted in local communities. For example, in the province of Arabia a Jewish woman, Babatha, who was pursuing a legal case concerning the guardianship of her son Jesus, seems voluntarily to have followed Roman juristic rules in making her application (Cotton, *Journal of Roman Studies* 83, 1993, 94). Wherever they went the Romans constructed roads and civic buildings, and these visible signs of the Roman presence and technological achievement became the focal point of many communities in the west and Greek east. Baths, aqueducts, a piped water supply and the excitement of the arena were enthusiastically welcomed. But local traditions were preserved and in particular the Greeks kept their traditional public buildings. As Trajan put it: 'These poor Greeks all love a gymnasium' (Pliny, *Letters*, 10.40).

For many people life was acceptable. In the east Greek was the official second language after Latin, and most Roman officials could communicate in Greek. Hebrew, Aramaic and Greek were spoken in Judaea, Greek in Syria, Syriac further east, and demotic in Egypt though the language of administration here was Greek. Other local languages were also permitted, as is demonstrated by the jurist Ulpian's comment that requests by the maker of a will to his heir could be expressed in any language, whether Latin or Greek, Gallic (= Celtic), Punic or Assyrian (= Syriac), or 'any other language' provided that it was understood by the participants, if necessary through an interpreter. Being in the Roman Empire did not necessarily mean loss of cultural identity. Furthermore, the stable rule of Rome ensured peace in many parts of the empire far from the frontier zones in which wealth and commerce could develop to the advantage of the well-off and also poorer citizens. This encouraged communities to work within the Roman system, and for most people to overthrow this system was beyond comprehension. The Greek communities in Greece and Asia had their own ideas, with emphasis on their common language and paramount loyalty to the city state. Nevertheless, respect for their inherent Greekness could be combined with loyalty to Rome. Indeed, the Roman way of doing things generally benefited the wealthy elites who helped the Romans run the provincial administration. But there was a trickle-down effect as the wealthy, supported and encouraged by the emperors, beautified their cities, undertook the expenses of city government, funded new buildings or repairs, and conferred benefits on their fellow citizens; here rivalry with one another and between city and city was a great incentive.

Status and Social Mobility

The society into which many provincials entered as Roman citizens was dominated by class and status. This will have been familiar and welcome to most of them, as they usually were the wealthiest members of their city, or tribal chieftains. Roman society was a pyramid with a small, elite group at the top consisting of senators and *equites* with their appropriate prerogatives and public symbols of status. The ordinary citizens of Rome owed most of their perks to the emperor, but had little else to celebrate in a crowded, uncomfortable city, which was much subject to the hazards of fire and flooding from the Tiber. The pyramid continued to be based on slavery. There were probably about two million slaves in Italy at the end of the Republic, and numbers remained buoyant in the imperial period. The number of slaves held by individuals was partly a mark of status, and even the less well-off like soldiers and veterans are found owning a few slaves. The master's power of life and death over his slaves was maintained even though emperors sponsored humane legislation. For example, Claudius established that a sick slave abandoned by his master would obtain freedom (Suetonius, *Claudius* 25). The new factor was the emperor as a large slave-owner with a huge household. Although Roman society was status-conscious and hierarchical, there was at times a surprising degree of social mobility and one of the main routes was through the setting free (manumission) of slaves.

Ex-slaves acquired the status of freedmen (*liberti*) and Roman citizenship unless they had committed a serious offence. This practice injected into society a large number of people who had a huge variety of talents. It is not surprising that these individuals are found involved in many occupations and ventures, especially in conurbations like Rome, Ostia and Pompeii. However, to some extent the evidence (mainly from inscriptions) gives an exaggerated view of their role, since successful freedmen tended to set up memorials to establish their status and show that they had made it in a world where free birth still had social cachet. Nevertheless, freedmen were clearly a significant factor in commercial life in the Roman world, and they are found in some of the most important associations of men in the same occupation (*collegia*), and holding jobs such as woodworkers, timber-dealers, shipwrights, corn-measurers, perfume- and incense-manufacturers, potters and traders. They worked in the corn trade (*annona*), where Claudius offered full citizenship to those with Latin rights (that is, those who had not been properly manumitted) in order to encourage investment. Freedmen also served in the Roman fire brigade (*Vigiles*), while the more educated worked as tutors, secretaries and doctors. Freedmen of the emperor tended to have an elevated status because they had the strongest patron. They often held a variety of jobs close to the emperor's person, such as looking after the imperial triumphal clothing, food-tasting, or being an imperial chef. A kind of hierarchy developed: for example, one Theoprepes graduated from being superintendent of the glassware in the palace to become procurator of the imperial dye-works in Achaea. For a time freedmen acted as imperial secretaries, probably the most elevated position to which they could aspire. Augustus from the start had not been blind to the value of keeping freedmen on the side of his regime, and the *Augustales* comprised a college mainly of wealthier freedmen, who officiated in the imperial cult at a local level and organized associated games in small towns; they operated virtually as an order below that of town councillors, acquiring dignity and prestige and using their wealth on behalf of the community.

Roman slaves, unlike Negro slaves in the United Sates, were not usually distinguished by colour; they looked like their masters and so once free they could blend into lower-class society. Furthermore, many freedmen became very wealthy and money brought its own status. Nevertheless they did have to overcome the considerable social stigma of their servile origins. Notably, there was a legal regulation that established the relationship of freedmen with their previous master. The master acted as a kind of patron, and the freedman owed obedience and services of different kinds and was legally subject to severe punishment if he defaulted. Freedmen could not be admitted to the ranks of senators and *equites*, could not marry into the upper classes, were not eligible for the major local magistracies, and could not serve in the legions. More importantly, the upper classes often sneered at freedmen and despised their wealth, though much of this resentment may have been directed at those very prominent imperial freedmen who acted as secretaries and through their proximity to the emperor were able to gain power, influence and benefits well beyond their perceived status. The first-century AD writer Petronius in his novel *The Satyrica* created a magnificent comic character, an ex-slave Trimalchio, who by a lucky inheritance from his master and business acumen had become fabulously wealthy (more so than many senators) but who was still low-born, coarse and vulgar. This perhaps shows a more common critique of the activities of freedmen. The satirist Juvenal was certainly contemptuous of the lively background of social layers in Rome and thought that 'the cosmopolitan mix of immigrants had some very unwholesome qualities: 'For a long time now the Syrian Orontes has been washing its filth into the Tiber' (3.62).

Away from the strictures of the upper classes many freedmen quietly played an important part in local communities. For example, Publius Merula was a freedman doctor who used his wealth to benefit Assisi, where he had settled:

> Publius Decimius Eros Merula, freedman of Publius, clinical doctor, surgeon, oculist, member of the board of six. For his freedom he paid 50,000 sesterces. For his membership of the board of six he contributed to the community 2,000 sesterces. For the erection of statues in the temple of Hercules he gave 30,000 sesterces. For paving streets he contributed to the municipal treasury 37,000 sesterces. On the day before he died he left an estate of . . . sesterces. (*ILS* 7812)

The legal freeing of large numbers of slaves who then became Roman citizens was a distinctive feature of Roman society, opening up an avenue of social mobility and renewal of the citizen body. When in AD 56 the senate debated whether patrons should have the right to re-enslave disrespectful freedmen, a counter-argument was that most *equites* and many senators were descended from former slaves — ex-slaves were everywhere! Relations between former masters and unassuming freedmen were often dutiful and affectionate. In dealing with his own freedmen Pliny the Younger was considerate towards his personal reader, whom he had sent to Egypt in an attempt to cure his consumption (*Letters* 5.19). Many inscriptions also record good relations:

> Marcus Canuleius Zosimus: he lived twenty-eight years; his patron erected this to a well-deserving freedman. In his lifetime he spoke ill of no one. He did nothing without his patron's consent; there was always a great weight of gold and silver in his possession, and he never coveted any of it; in his craft, Clodian engraving, he excelled everybody. (*ILS* 7695; Rome)

Patrons often permitted their freedmen and freed women to be buried in the family tomb, as we see from another inscription from Rome, which also suggests that relations were not always quite so good:

> Marcus Aemilius Artema built this for Marcus Licinius Successus, his well-deserving brother, and for Caecilia Modesta, his wife, and for himself and his freedmen and freedwomen and their descendants, with the exception of the freedman Hermes, to whom, because of his offences I forbid access, approach, or any admittance to this tomb. (*ILS* 8285)

The free-born plebs in Rome worked alongside freedmen, often doing the same kind of work as craftsmen and artisans; they also worked in the building trade and in the ports of Rome and Ostia unloading ships; in rural areas seasonal labour was required in the fields. Among the mass of the population women were widely employed in certain crafts, such as wool-spinning and clothes-mending, and a limited number of professional activities, such as hairdressing, acting as midwives and wet nurses, and even doctors. One Antiochis, who came from Tlos in Lycia, was celebrated for her knowledge of 'doctor's skill'. As in all ages, many women provided relaxation and pleasure in a variety of ways as singers, dancers and waitresses. An inscription from Casinum in Italy reveals how four freedwomen had an agreement to manage the inn at the nearby shrine of Venus:

> Flacceia Lais, freedwoman of Aulus, Orbia Lais, freedwoman of Caia, Cominia Philocaris, freedwoman of Marcus, Venturia Thais, freedwoman of Quintus, established an eating-house for Venus, at their own expense; the franchise can be revoked. (*L'Année épigraphique* 1975.197)

It is likely that these four ladies honoured the goddess of love more directly by also serving as prostitutes. In the Roman world, prostitutes were regarded as socially disreputable and in Rome were required to register with the aediles, who were responsible for public order. This will have allowed the authorities to identify and keep an eye on brothels as a likely source of disturbance. Some grand courtesans could be rich with a string of wealthy clients who were prepared to keep them in the luxury they demanded. Most ordinary prostitutes, who could be spotted by their short, colourful dresses and elaborate coiffure, charged a fee for each client. In Pompeii, while many sexual encounters will have taken place outside in the alleyways of the town or among the tombs, there were at least nine purpose-built brothels in the central area. A business advertisement reads: '(prostitute's sign); I am yours for two *asses* cash'. Some charged sixteen *asses*. The sex business was lucrative, and eventually from the time of Caligula the government imposed a tax, possibly the charge for one sex session per month.

Some of the best evidence for the activities of ordinary people, their concerns and pleasures comes in the record of associations (*collegia*) that were prevalent in Rome, Italy and some provinces. Their membership covered the entire social spectrum of upper classes, freeborn plebs, freedmen and even slaves. A *collegium* was a kind of club of private people with a body of rules enshrined in a constitution, officials, common funds and set meeting times. There were three main types: those honouring individual deities, burial societies, and those associated with people in particular trades or professions. Most *collegia*, however, had some kind of religious association. In general, these clubs performed an important social role, especially for poorer people, satisfying the need to associate and provide a convivial setting; there were frequent dinners, drinks and entertainments, often funded by the wealthier members. One important officer was called 'Master of Dinners'. Furthermore, burial was important for the poor, since there was a real fear that lack of proper burial would mean that a man's spirit wandered ever after. The rules of a society at Lanuvium, for example, provided that if a member died more than twenty miles from town, three men from the society were required to go there to arrange the funeral (*ILS* 7212). The *collegia* also provided an important outlet for personal ambitions of a political kind. At one level rich senatorial patrons who gave money and gifts gained prestige from their role. Less important members had the chance to exercise some power and authority through elections and holding office within the club, which operated on the same model as municipal government. Indeed, *collegia* played a part in municipal politics by publicly endorsing certain candidates. In Pompeii election slogans painted on a wall show this: 'The goldsmiths unanimously urge the election of Gaius Cuspius Pansa as aedile' (*ILS* 6419e).

Although *collegia* did not function like modern trade unions (labour in ancient Rome was organized on a small scale with many casual workers or slaves), the government attitude to them was ambivalent. In the imperial period there was a fear that private clubs outside its direct control might foment public disorder or be a cover for illegal acts. At the same time the government wished to permit association where some public benefit was to be expected. Therefore, from the middle of the first century BC tough legislation was in force to curb freedom of association, and the *Lex Julia* (passed by Julius Caesar or Augustus) banned *collegia*, so that to have a *collegium* was a concession that had to be approved by the emperor or senate. Against this tough background the government made several concessions. At some stage burial clubs were permitted to meet without a licence once a month in order to make their contributions, and assembly for religious purposes was permitted provided that other restrictions were not evaded. But the penalties for convening an illegal club were severe, similar to the case of persons who occupied public places with armed men, that is, treason. And some emperors took a tough line. Trajan refused to allow a fire brigade to be set up in Nicomedia because: 'Societies like these have been responsible for the political disturbances in your province (Bithynia)' (Pliny, *Letters* 10.34).

Elsewhere, clubs continued since ordinary people normally had few other means of help or social support, though an example from Alburnus Maior in Dacia on the edge of the empire shows that not all could prosper, with the rather sad dissolution of a society in AD 167:

> Artemidorus, son of Apollonius, master of the Society of Jupiter Cernenus . . . by deposing this notice publicly attests that of fifty-four members who used to make up the above-mentioned society, there now remain at Alburnus no more than seventeen, and that even Julius . . . his co-master, has not come to Alburnus or to [a meeting of] the society since the day he took office . . . there was not enough for burial expenses and he did not have a single coffin, and over all this time no one has been willing to come to meetings on the days prescribed by the by-laws or to contribute burial money. (*ILS* 7215a = Lewis and Reinhold, 1990, vol. II, pp. 188–9)

Benevolent Patrons

One important thread running through the various levels of society was patronage. Just as in the Republic, upper-class families competed for support and prestige by granting favours to their clients and protégés. Army commanders had a particularly fruitful source of patronage in the junior army posts at their disposal, and their friends sometimes approached them on behalf of others, creating a chain of obligation. The patron would receive gratitude, which might extend to legacies in a will, or public expressions of respect, such as attendance at his morning

salutation and in other business. Important people who had the right contacts could
use their influence to benefit others. An inscription from Rome in the third century
shows the role of a Vestal Virgin in securing a post:

> To Campia Severina, most reverend Vestal Virgin, whose genuine chastity
> confirmed by repeated public praise the senate crowned; Q. Veturius
> Callistratus, eminent man, by her support was appointed procurator of the
> private revenues of the libraries of our Augustus, and his procurator. (*ILS* 4928)

In the provinces the same system operated. Plutarch remarks how provincials
made use of contacts they had with distinguished families in Rome to obtain
governorships and procuratorships (*Moralia* 814D). In his province the governor
exercised enormous patronage since he was responsible for jurisdiction and the
administration of all the local communities. At the personal level a governor could
ensure a swift trial or even protect individuals from prosecution. In the wider
context provincials needed to ensure that they had a point of contact with the
governor, who could interfere in a wide range of activities including offices and
honours, local financial obligations where exemptions were often a bone of
contention, and decisions on public buildings. In particular, when the governor
moved round the province on his judicial rounds (the *conventus*) he would stay at
the houses of important provincials, who by a suitable display of entertainment
and hospitality could establish useful ties that would be exploited in the province
and later in Rome. Again, the important thing was getting close to the governor
or his family and friends and establishing personal bonds. The evidence suggests
that patronage was an upper-class activity, with an emphasis on shared interests
and access to important people. This is partly the result of the nature of the
evidence, and it is likely that there was a patronage relation between landowner
and lower classes; the position of tenant farmers who owned no land but tilled a
plot owned by someone who was better off to some extent approximated to the
position of a client. Municipal patronage could benefit all the members of a
community, including the smallholders who tilled plots perhaps close to the town.

Many rich men and women spent generously on their local community.
Doubtless some were displaying unselfish philanthropy, but others may have
hoped to diffuse social tensions or gain prestige, patronage and political influence
locally. T. Helvius Basila from Atina left money in his will to provide food and a
sum of money for local children until they grew up (*ILS* 977). Similarly, Pliny the
Younger arranged that a permanent charge on a piece of substantial landed property should be set aside to support free-born boys and girls at his home town of
Comum (*Letters* 7.18; *ILS* 2927). The idea of personal generosity is also illustrated by an inscription from Teate Marrucinorum in Italy:

In honour of the imperial house, Dusmia Numisilla, daughter of Marcus, in her own name and that of her husband L. Trebius Secundus, restored at her own expense the water supply, which had been brought through by C. Asinius Gallus and had failed, by tracing it from its source, in addition building a conduit and wells, and augmenting it by new branches. (*ILS* 5761)

In the provinces too the rich competed to offer benefaction to their native city, partly to raise its status with fine buildings and other attributes. For example, an inscription from Castulo in Hispania Tarraconensis records how Annia Victorina in memory of her husband and son celebrated with a formal dedication and banquet her establishment of a water supply and elaborate accessories (*ILS* 5764). At Araegenuae in the province of Lugdunensis a local magistrate, Titus Sennius Sollemnis, who was also well in with Roman officials, was very generous to his community:

> . . . held all offices and performed all public duties [. . .] in his community and at the same time as high priest of Rome and [Augustus at the altar] produced every kind of show; there were contests of gladiators totalling 32 in number, and of these over a period of four days 8 were fought to the death. A bath-house, which Sollemnis [. . .] had left in his will to be an amenity for his fellow-citizens in his colony [. . .], after laying the foundations he brought to completion; likewise he bequeathed [. . .] profit in perpetuity, from which it was to be equipped. (translation in Levick, 2000, no. 178)

The supreme patron was the emperor. He had the greatest range of benefits to confer and was certainly due the greatest deference. At the same time, by encouraging the development of services provided by the state under his auspices, the emperor ensured that there was less need for the role of powerful individuals. As Seneca observed, emperors were in a position to grant many benefits but receive only a few, unequal gifts in return (*De Beneficiis* 5.4.2). In any case the range of personal favours granted by emperors was extensive, including senatorial and equestrian rank, a variety of offices and military posts, grants of money to indigent senators, legal concessions and coveted privileges like those attaching to men who had children. The fact that the emperor was known to be an extender of benefits meant that methods of approaching him were very important. Here, high-ranking senators and *equites* could increase their status if they could get the emperor's ear. There were other routes, for example through influential freedmen or sophists and other men of literary talent who could get an emperor's attention by their intellectual achievements and perhaps win a concession or benefit for their city.

The emperor's distribution of benefits had as its principal backdrop the city of Rome, which was by far the biggest urban settlement in the ancient world and an impressive stage on which many of the great events of Roman history were enacted. It was a considerable achievement to organize and maintain such a large conglomeration getting on for one million, in which the poverty of the private dwellings of the poor, often in tenement blocks of flats, should be contrasted with the monumental grandeur of public architecture. Each emperor tended to add new buildings where it suited him, and so the centre of the city with numerous accretions lacked an overall plan but demonstrated imperial concern by providing the Roman people with a grandiose environment for their daily business and amusement, and of course symbols of their own power.

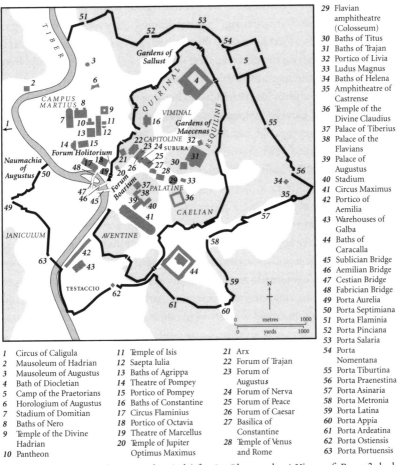

29 Flavian amphitheatre (Colosseum)
30 Baths of Titus
31 Baths of Trajan
32 Portico of Livia
33 Ludus Magnus
34 Baths of Helena
35 Amphitheatre of Castrense
36 Temple of the Divine Claudius
37 Palace of Tiberius
38 Palace of the Flavians
39 Palace of Augustus
40 Stadium
41 Circus Maximus
42 Portico of Aemilia
43 Warehouses of Galba
44 Baths of Caracalla
45 Sublician Bridge
46 Aemilian Bridge
47 Cestian Bridge
48 Fabrician Bridge
49 Porta Aurelia
50 Porta Septimiana
51 Porta Flaminia
52 Porta Pinciana
53 Porta Salaria
54 Porta Nomentana
55 Porta Tiburtina
56 Porta Praenestina
57 Porta Asinaria
58 Porta Metronia
59 Porta Latina
60 Porta Appia
61 Porta Ardeatina
62 Porta Ostiensis
63 Porta Portuensis

1 Circus of Caligula
2 Mausoleum of Hadrian
3 Mausoleum of Augustus
4 Bath of Diocletian
5 Camp of the Praetorians
6 Horologium of Augustus
7 Stadium of Domitian
8 Baths of Nero
9 Temple of the Divine Hadrian
10 Pantheon
11 Temple of Isis
12 Saepta Iulia
13 Baths of Agrippa
14 Theatre of Pompey
15 Portico of Pompey
16 Baths of Constantine
17 Circus Flaminius
18 Portico of Octavia
19 Theatre of Marcellus
20 Temple of Jupiter Optimus Maximus
21 Arx
22 Forum of Trajan
23 Forum of Augustus
24 Forum of Nerva
25 Forum of Peace
26 Forum of Caesar
27 Basilica of Constantine
28 Temple of Venus and Rome

Map 8. The city of Rome in the imperial period (after Le Glay, et. al., *A History of Rome*, 3rd edn (2005), figure 11.1).

The visitor travelling from the north along the left bank of the Tiber would have exciting views of imperial monuments like the mausoleum of Augustus and the Altar of Peace, Augustus's sundial (the *Horologium Augusti*), triumphal arches, temples in honour of various deities (pride of place perhaps going to the Pantheon, originally erected by M. Agrippa in honour of several divinities and then restored by Hadrian, on the edge of the Campus Martius between the Via Flaminia and the river); the theatre of Marcellus (Augustus's nephew who had died in 23 BC) and the stadium of Domitian for chariot-racing (now the Piazza Navona with its characteristic hairpin shape) also stood in this area; further on appeared the great commercial centres, the imperial *fora*, the market of Trajan, other places of entertainment like the Colosseum (capacity 50,000), and the Circus Maximus (capacity 250,000) occupying the valley between the Palatine and Aventine Hills. Of these impressive constructions the Colosseum was the venue for gladiatorial combats and animal hunts, while the Circus Maximus offered four-horse chariot-racing. In these exciting contests the four racing teams (the Blues, Reds, Greens and Whites) had partisan supporters (including emperors) who bet on the outcome, and there was great excitement and frequent violence among the spectators; soldiers were stationed in the crowds at the arena to maintain order. Individual charioteers became famous and set up inscriptions celebrating their careers. For example, Crescens, a Moor, driver for the Green team, twenty-two years old, had 686 starts and 47 victories, 130 second places and 111 third places (*ILS* 5285, Rome).

Numerous public bath buildings were sponsored by emperors; communal bathing was an important part of the urban social experience and baths were constructed, usually close to a forum, on an increasingly elaborate scale and containing special zones: a cold room (*frigidarium*), a warm room (*tepidarium*), and a hot room (*caldarium*), which might contain a hot plunge-pool. In larger establishments there was a swimming pool. The baths of Trajan were on a monumental scale and contained space for many other activities. Most self-respecting towns and cities in Italy and the provinces had bathing establishments. In the second century AD men and women were bathing together and the next stage of luxury leisure provision was the seawater pool, which according to Martial was a potential venue for sexual adventures (*Epigrams* 11.21).

Julius Frontinus, senior curator of aqueducts under Trajan, boasted that aqueducts were enormously useful compared to the pyramids and the famous works of the Greeks. Augustus and Agrippa had set the tone by building three in Rome. They provided clean water for drinking but also had many other uses, including fire-fighting, watering market gardens, supplying the baths and flushing sewers. Aqueducts were built from public funds supplemented with imperial generosity and there was no systematic attempt to charge for water except when it was

22. This is a view looking down from the fortifications of Masada towards the Roman siege mound. Masada is an isolated plateau 1,500 feet high on the western shore of the Dead Sea. Herod had enhanced the fortifications and built a palace. Masada fell to the Romans in AD 73 or 74 at the end of the Jewish rebellion; see p. 159.

XXVII   XXVIII

67   68   69   70

23. Two scenes from the column of Trajan, which stood 38 metres high topped with a three-metre statue of the emperor in military dress. It was voted by senate and people partly to celebrate the extent of Trajan's building work in his new forum. But it was also a monument to the Roman army's victorious campaigns against the Dacians, and Trajan's personal leadership. A continuous frieze 200 metres long carved on the shaft tells the story of the two Dacian wars. Of the scenes illustrated, one depicts Trajan standing on a high tribunal with his officers addressing the troops, who line up with their standards. The other depicts Trajan again with his officers, receiving a deputation of Dacians. See F. Lepper and S. Frere, *Trajan's Column* (1988).

24. Brass sestertius AD 104–111, mint of Rome. Obverse: head of Trajan; legend: IMP CAES NERVAE OPTIMO PRINCIPI TRAIANO AUG GER DAC PM TR P COS V PP (In honour of Imperator Caesar Nerva Trajan Most Excellent Augustus, Germanicus Dacicus, pontifex maximus, holding tribunician power, consul for the fifth time, father of the fatherland). Reverse: the personified figure of the river Danube grabs Dacia (in female form) by the throat and presses down on her with his knee; legend: SPQR OPTIMO PRINCIPI SC (The senate and people of Rome to the most excellent princeps; by decree of the senate). The image vividly portrays how the river Danube itself has been recruited to fight on the Roman side. (*Coins of the Roman Empire in the British Museum* III, p. 168, no. 793).

25. Brass sestertius, AD 116–117, mint of Rome. Obverse: head of Trajan; legend: IMP CAES NER TRAIANO OPTIMO AUG GER DAC PARTHICO PM TR P COS VI PP (In honour of Imperator Caesar Nerva Trajan Most Excellent Augustus, Germanicus Dacicus Parthicus, pontifex maximus, holding tribunician power, consul for the sixth time, father of the fatherland). Reverse: Trajan in military dress holding a spear in his right hand and parazonium in his left. The river gods of the Euphrates and Tigris recline at his feet and between them sits the personified figure of Armenia; legend: Armenia and Mesopotamia brought within the power of the Roman people; by decree of the senate. Despite the positive message of the coinage the invasion of Parthia was ultimately a disaster (*Coins of the Roman Empire in the British Museum* III, p. 221, no. 1033).

26. This sandstone tombstone, C.AD 80, found in Lancaster, honours an auxiliary cavalryman, Insus, son of Vodullus. He is depicted holding the severed head of an enemy who has fallen beneath his horse's hooves.

27. This sepulchral relief, dating from the time of Augustus, probably came from a tomb near Rome and shows L. Vibius and his wife; the figure of the boy between them may represent the funeral mask of their dead child; he bears a striking resemblance to Vibius.

28. This arch was erected in the Roman forum in AD 81–82 by the senate and people in honour of Titus and his victory over the Jewish rebellion in AD 70 and the sack of Jerusalem. This scene depicts Titus's triumphal procession in which he rides in a chariot accompanied by the goddesses Victoria and Roma.

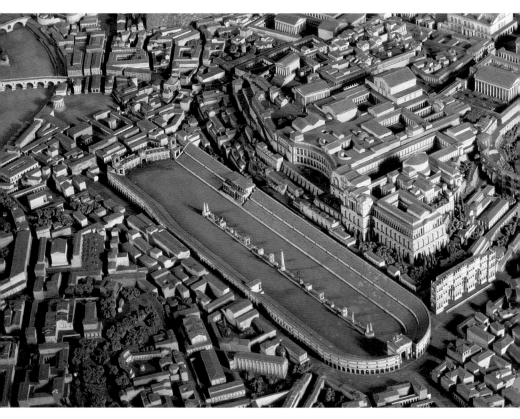

29. The Circus Maximus from the scale model of ancient Rome in the Museo della Civiltà Romana. The Circus was Rome's oldest public space and lay in the valley between the Palatine and Aventine hills. By the end of the first century AD it had a capacity of up to 250,000, with a track 540 metres long by 80 metres wide. It was used for staging various games but principally chariot racing; there were twelve starting gates at the western end, a central barrier (spina) contained ornamented lap counters to mark the seven laps of a race, conical turning posts (metae), and two obelisks originally from Egypt.

30. This sepulchral monument from Foligno in Italy dating from the second or third centuries AD depicts a chariot race in the Circus Maximus.

31. The Pantheon in Rome. This temple was originally planned by Marcus Agrippa but was completed in its present form by Hadrian and dedicated to all the gods. The traditional porch leads to a circular room 43.3 metres in both diameter and height, illuminated by a single central oculus nine metres in diameter. The inscription above the porch refers to Agrippa's original work: Marcus Agrippa, son of Lucius, consul for the third time, made [this].

32. The Ludovisi Sarcophagus, named after its first owner, dates from the mid-third century AD and depicts a battle between Roman troops and barbarians. The Romans are winning though the scene is extremely violent and perhaps reflects something of Rome's struggles with barbarian peoples in the third century. The commander on horseback in the centre of the battle may originally have been buried within the sarcophagus.

33. This bronze equestrian statue of Marcus Aurelius, now stands in the Capitoline Museum in Rome, with a copy outside in the Piazza del Campidoglio.

34. The aqueduct at Segovia in Spain was built from granite blocks during the reign of Claudius; the arcade of arches is 728 metres long with a height of 28 metres; the water was carried in the covered channel on top of the second row of arches. It took its water from the Rio Acebeda about twelve kilometres south of the city.

35. Pompeii was a town and port in southern Campania which was destroyed in the eruption of Vesuvius in AD 79. Along with the neighbouring Herculaneum, which was also destroyed, it is the best known archaeological site in Italy, showing the social, political and economic life of an Italian town. The excavators found the remains of many citizens who had tried to hide or escape. In the human remains there was a void made by decomposition of organic matter after the ash or mud, which had coated the victims, had hardened. Originally concrete or plaster was poured into the void—now a polymer substance is used—which preserved the shape of the bodies while the excavation continued.

36. Statue of Antinous in the form of the god Bacchus. This young man from Bithynia was the favourite and lover of Hadrian, and, while visiting Egypt with the emperor in AD 130, he drowned in the Nile. In his grief Hadrian had Antinous deified and cults were set up in his honour. In this representation, probably from the emperor's villa at Tivoli, Antinous wears a wreath of vines and grapes on his head and in his left hand holds the Bacchic wand (thyrsus).

37. This relief from a rock face in Iran celebrates the victories of King Sapor I over Roman emperors, and in this scene the king holds Valerian, who had been captured, by the arm while another emperor, probably Philip who negotiated his way out of trouble, offers obeisance; the prone figure under the horse's hooves may be Gordian III, who was probably killed in battle against the Persians.

38. This representation of the four rulers of the Tetrarchy (Diocletian, Maximian, Constantius, Galerius) is carved in porphyry and dates to about AD 300. It was originally found in the imperial palace in Constantinople and is designed to submerge the individual identity of the men in the idea of group solidarity, symbolized by the embrace.

39. Billon nummus minted in Ticinum, AD 316. Obverse: heads of Constantine I and Sun god; legend: COMIS CONSTANTINI AUG (comrade of Constantine Augustus). Reverse: the personified figure of Liberality (Liberalitas) wearing a long robe carries the symbol of plenty (cornucopiae) and holds an accounting board in her right hand; legend: Liberality for the eleventh occasion, Imperator for the fourth time, consul, father of the fatherland, proconsul. The coin celebrates the emperor's eleventh distribution of money to the soldiers (*The Roman Imperial Coinage* VII, p. 368, no. 53).

40. Billon minted at Ambianum, Amiens, AD 353. Obverse: head of Magnentius; legend: DN MAGNENTIUS PF AUG (Our lord Magnentius, loyal and true Augustus). Reverse: Chi-Rho symbol with alpha and omega; legend: SALUS DD NN AUG ET CAES (the safety of our lords the Augustus and Caesar) (*The Roman Imperial Coinage* VIII, p. 123, no. 34). Magnentius led a military revolt that overthrew Constans. He made some concessions to pagan religious practices, but on this coin the symbolism is conventionally Christian.

41. Head of Constantine (2.6 metres high) from a colossal statue of the emperor probably placed in the basilica of Maxentius rededicated by Constantine in AD 313. The portrayal of the emperor was intended to exude superhuman strength and awe-inspiring majesty.

42. The Basilica at the imperial capital of Trier was built in the early fourth century AD by Constantine; it was a rectangular building constructed of brick with a projecting apse and probably served as an audience hall.

diverted for private use. There were also watery benefactions in Italy, for example in Campania for a water channel from the Serino spring, and in the provinces. It is a sign of the significance of these public facilities that they were run by the most distinguished men in the state, the senatorial curators. Other senatorial officials were charged with trying to control the tendency of the river Tiber to flood. Fire-fighting was also under imperial responsibility and the *Vigiles*, organized on a paramilitary basis, provided some protection through the first three centuries. Rome was probably marginally safer than in the Republic thanks to the presence in the city of the praetorian guard and urban cohorts (about 13,000–14,000 men), who made a substantial contribution to the preservation of law and order. The emperors tried to administer the city for the benefit of everyone and one aspect of that was to keep order. This was always a matter of concern to the rich, who kept town houses in Rome as well as estates in the country. In this way the urban space of Rome was defined by imperial building and its use controlled by the emperor's officials and soldiers.

From the time of Augustus emperors had intervened to keep the price of corn stable in Rome by importing huge quantities on a regular basis, mainly from Egypt. For some of the plebs there was a free corn distribution on a system by which individuals presented themselves with their tickets at a named location on a particular day to collect their allocation. Later there were distributions of oil and pork. The emperor's concern for the people of Rome especially was not just altruistic. Emperors needed popular support since it was one clear demonstration of stability and control at the heart of the empire. Upper classes, plebs and freedmen could come together (in a segregated way) to join the emperor in a public display. The emperor usually appeared in person at the theatre, or at gladiatorial games, or the chariot races, where he received applause and ritual chants of support and approval. These games and shows were a very important part of the Roman year and a source of release and relaxation for the poorer citizens. For example, after the Dacian wars Trajan gave games lasting a total of 123 days in which 11,000 animals were killed and 10,000 gladiators fought. The importance of keeping the plebs happy is illustrated by the story from the last days of Didius Julianus in AD 193, when the crowds in the arena took up a rhythmic chant against him, which had obviously been organized in advance. It was another sign of the failing authority of an emperor soon to be overthrown. Serious outbreaks of disorder in Rome demonstrated a collapse of political authority. In the reign of Severus Alexander there was a three-day battle between the praetorians and the plebs, who pelted the troops with roof tiles in the narrow streets; the violence ended only when the praetorians set fire to parts of the city.

Outside Rome, the emperor was once again the greatest patron and benefactor. In the early second century AD an official scheme was introduced in Italy

probably by Trajan, by which local landholders received a loan from the government on which they paid annual interest of 5 per cent into a special fund. The
scheme at Veleia shows that a sum of 55,800 *sesterces* was distributed annually to
263 boys, thirty-five girls and two illegitimate children (*ILS* 6675). Presumably
Trajan aimed to maintain the native Italian stock of poorer families, although,
given the disproportion of numbers between boys and girls, he perhaps hoped to
boost manpower for the army. Outside Italy emperors often responded to appropriate diplomatic approaches (here again patronage could be important) to help
provincial communities in need. For example, the city of Smyrna records an
astonishing range of benefactions received from Hadrian and the senate through
the agency of Polemo, a distinguished local orator:

> The things that we obtained from the lord Caesar Hadrian through Antonius
> Polemo: a second decree of the senate by which we obtained a second title of
> temple-Warden, a sacred festival, immunity from taxation, official panegyrists
> of the gods, and hymnodes, 1,500,000 (sesterces?), seventy-two columns of
> Synnadan marble, twenty of Numidian and seven of Porphyrite for the
> anointing-room. (*Inscriptiones Graecae ad Res Romanas Pertinentes* 4.1431)

Family Life

Despite the cosmopolitan colour of Rome, the framework of family life
remained strictly hierarchical and male-dominated through the early empire and
beyond, though our view is conditioned by our sources, which in general
expound the upper-class values of the wealthy. The head of the family, the *pater
familias*, controlled family property and funds. Theoretically and traditionally,
he had the power of life and death within the family. His children were in his
power (*potestas*), could not independently own property, and any they acquired
belonged to the *pater familias*. Even senatorial office-holders might still be in the
power of their father and receive from him only a freely revocable allowance.
Since children in the power of their father had no property they could not
make a will. The overriding concern is the preservation of property within the
family. The law certainly represented the interests of the upper classes and in
early Rome intestate succession was probably the norm, by which family property would go in order of priority to *sui heredes*, that is, all those who had been in
the power of the deceased, and then to agnates, that is people who were
descended from the same male ancestor as the deceased. There was no right of
primogeniture and so all legitimate sons and daughters had the opportunity of
inheriting the family property, which could therefore be subdivided to a
damaging extent.

Gradually, making a will became accepted practice and this established some means of control. The testator named an heir (*heres*), who became responsible for the whole property, including debts as well as assets, and was responsible for paying specific legacies set out in the will. If the testator wished to disinherit one of his family, he had to do so by name. Illegitimate children would have no claim on the property unless they were specifically named. It was possible to refuse to take up the position as *heres*, in which case the responsibility passed on to the second named heir. A number of groups were excluded from inheriting in a Roman will, notably non-citizens.

Marriage obviously could have repercussions for property. A Roman marriage had no moral or religious implications; it simply required certain legal consequences. Therefore, a proper marriage (*iustum matrimonium*) required the agreement of both parties and that both had the legal capacity to contract a valid marriage (*conubium*). In strict legal terms and by social convention a father's consent was required for marriage, if he was able to enforce his right. Soldiers were forbidden to marry, senators could not marry women of inappropriate status, and a citizen could not marry a non-citizen. Normally one could not marry relations nearer than first cousins, and the minimum marriageable age was twelve for girls and fourteen for boys. There was no need for ceremonies or certificates, and consummation was not necessary for a valid marriage. There were essentially two types of marriage. In the older form, the wife passed into the family of the husband in legal terms and any property she owned belonged to her husband. In the second form, which became more common, the wife stayed in her own family in the power of her *pater familias*, or if she was legally independent she owned her own property.

In wealthy marriages the dowry, which consisted of property and assets brought by the bride, was important. This had to be negotiated and shows in a way the inferior position of the woman, but also the determination to ensure that marriage did not compromise the property of the bride's family. The husband got the use of his wife's property but was obliged to preserve the capital. In the case of a divorce the dowry or a proportion of it had to be returned and some could be retained for the children. The dowry could also be controlled by a kind of prenuptial agreement. For example, the writer Apuleius, who had to defend himself against the charge of marrying a rich widow by devious means for her money, pointed out:

In particular the dowry of this very rich woman was only modest, and furthermore was not bestowed but only entrusted on the condition that if she departed her life and no children had been conceived from me, the entire dowry was to remain with her (existing) sons. . . . (*Apologia* 91)

Of course, after the husband had received the dowry he might come under pressure to keep his wife in the style to which she thought she was accustomed. In a comic situation created by the playwright Plautus (second century BC), a wife complains to her husband: 'I brought you a dowry far bigger than the money you had; so it's fair that I should be given purple clothes, gold jewellery and slave-girls, mules, grooms, footmen, pages and a carriage' (*Aulularia* (*Pot of Gold*), 498–502).

In the case of children, if the parents had no right of *conubium* then the child was illegitimate and took the status of the mother; if she was not a citizen then the child was not a citizen. Although there was no formal legal requirement to register the birth of a child, from the time of Augustus there was a process by which not only the father but also the mother or grandfather could declare the birth of a legitimate child who was a Roman citizen. Under Augustan legislation it was beneficial to be able to demonstrate that you had children. A record of these declarations was kept and some survive from the province of Egypt:

> L. Julius Vestinus, prefect of Egypt, has set out the names of those who, in accordance with the *lex Papia Poppaea and Aelia Sentia*, declared to him that children had been born to them. . . . L. Valerius Crispus, son of Lucius, of the tribe Pollia (declared) that a son had been born to him, L. Valerius Crispus, son of Lucius, of the tribe Pollia, from Domitia Paulla, daughter of Lucius, on 29th June just past. He is a Roman citizen. (*Fontes Iuris Romani anteiustiniani* vol. III, no. 2; AD 62)

Many children were unwanted, either because the family was too poor to support them or because they were the result of an illicit liaison. It is not clear to what extent infanticide was practised in Rome; killing children would normally be by exposure or abandonment, which was not formally prohibited until 374. In upper-class families social disapproval was probably an effective deterrent. Poorer families could probably get away with abandoning their children. The children of slaves might also be at risk; it was possible for the owner of a slave woman to sell her children separately from her if he chose. Abortion was not illegal since the foetus was not held legally to be a person until born. Septimius Severus made a ruling against abortion, but he was not protecting the right of the unborn child, rather ensuring that the father's legal rights over any children should not be infringed.

Marriage like all Roman contracts was consensual and when one partner with-drew his or her consent, the contract was overturned. Divorce was a relatively simple matter and required formal notification by the husband, though from the time of Augustus this process required seven witnesses. Easy divorce was a way of ensuring that a man could get a legitimate male heir for the transfer of property, for example in circumstances where his wife proved to be sterile. Divorces were probably very common and in the Republic were related to politics as families manoeuvred for position and support. Some reasons for divorce seem trivial, as when Quintus Antistius Vetus acknowledged no other reason for divorcing his wife than that he had seen her whispering in public to some freedwoman of low repute (Valerius Maximus 6.3.11). A father could intervene to end a marriage of offspring in his *potestas*, but from the time of Marcus Aurelius not if the husband and wife were harmoniously in agreement. Various emperors starting with Augustus attempted to discourage divorce by increasing the (mostly financial) penalties, but they were largely unsuccessful and even under the Christian empire divorce was legally possible for approved reasons, for example, 'Constantine allowed a husband to repudiate a wife who was an adulteress, procuress or poisoner . . .' (*Codex Theodosianus* (*Cod. Theod.*) 3.16.1).

In the male-dominated world of Rome the chastity of women was important, again to ensure that heirs were legitimate. Indeed, laws to prevent improper sexual approaches referred to men who tried to speak to married women or virgins and who lured away their attendant; this assumes that respectable women did not go out without attendants. It is not surprising that under Augustus adultery became a criminal offence, but the law was not applied with equal rigour to both sexes. A married woman was guilty if she had sexual relations with any man other than her husband. On the other hand a man was guilty only if his lover was married, and it was more difficult for the woman to prosecute; the law did not care as long as the unfaithful husband did not interfere with the wives of other men. Therefore, a man who had sexual relations outside marriage with an unmarried upper-class woman committed criminal fornication (*stuprum*), but was not guilty of adultery. The law set out to ensure that a husband could be certain that his wife was faithful to him. Consequently, the penalties for adultery were severe; the husband had sixty days to prosecute an adulterous wife and divorce her, and if he failed to do so he could himself be prosecuted for acting as a pimp. If convicted, a woman lost half of her dowry and one-third of her property, the man half his property; they were then relegated (a kind of exile), specifically to separate islands. A woman condemned in this way was not permitted subsequently to marry a freeborn Roman citizen.

In Roman law bigamy was prohibited; it would obviously have confused inheritance and the status of heirs. The rhetorician Quintilian in one of his training speeches vividly explains the legal situation. He imagines a case where a wife, thinking her husband is dead, marries again. The first husband then returns and murders his wife and her second husband; on trial for murder, he argues that he was taking legitimate revenge on adulterers caught in the act:

A marriage is dissolved in two ways, by divorcing or by death. I have not divorced my wife and I am certainly still alive. . . . Besides, there can be no lawful marriage unless the first marriage has been dissolved. Therefore my marriage remained in existence, and that (other) marriage was not lawful. (*Declamations* 347)

The Romans did, however, accept the position of concubinage, where a concubine, a free woman, lived with a man without being his wife. This was mainly to the advantage of the man, in that he could have a sexual partner (often of a lower social class), but with no other legal responsibilities; the concubine would have no legal claim to his property, and any children would be illegitimate. The freedwoman Caenis was the discreet concubine and virtual wife of the emperor Vespasian.

Most daughters of well-to-do families will have been prepared for marriage from an early age and had little opportunity to engage in any kind of life outside the family. Evidence relating to women who caught the public eye for some reason, often because they were the wife of an emperor, is not likely to be typical. However, a woman who was *sui iuris* could own and administer property and carry out transactions. There were some potential restrictions and a senatorial decree aimed to prevent women from taking on the debts of other people; this would have made it difficult for a woman to act as guarantor for a loan. Wives of upper-class Romans were doubtless able to influence their husbands to assist business operations, and often accompanied them on official duties. Indeed, there was an animated debate in the senate about whether it was appropriate for a provincial governor to be accompanied by his wife (in some cases wives had proved as rapacious as their husbands). At a lower level, Claudia Severa, wife of Aelius Brocchus, an equestrian military officer in northern Britain, was present with her husband and wrote a letter to her friend Sulpicia Lepidina, wife of the commander of the ninth cohort of Batavians, inviting her to her birthday party, 'to make the day more enjoyable for me by your arrival' (Bowman, 1994, no. 21).

Religion and Society

For women, particularly those from the upper classes, a direct route of escape from the constraints of family life lay in the position of priestess. The most high-profile priestesses were the Vestal Virgins, who tended the cult of Vesta, the goddess of the hearth, and kept the sacred fire in her circular shrine in Rome. The priestesses also prepared the grain mixed with salt for public religious observances. Candidates had to be Roman citizens between the ages of six and ten, and had to have both parents living. They normally were expected to serve for thirty years and had to preserve the strictest sexual purity. A Vestal was no longer in her father's power and was held in great respect, though the penalty for breaking their virginity was entombment alive. The role of the Vestals sums up the essence of Roman state religion, with its insistence on strict ritual and proper observation of festivals and taboos in order to promote the well-being and success of the *res publica*. Even the suspicion of improper conduct or impurity in a Vestal could in consequence bring disaster on Rome.

Public ritual and festivals had been the essential framework of Roman religion from the republican period and originally had been closely connected to the agricultural year. But religious observance remained dynamic into the imperial age and there is no reason to discount personal enthusiasm or belief even though private religious feeling is difficult to measure. Rome not only absorbed external religious influences but also exported her own framework of observances through the foundation of colonies outside Rome. In the east conquerors and subjects shared the deities of the Graeco-Roman pantheon, and local cults continued without interference from Rome under the direction of priests from the upper class. These flexible, polytheistic rituals fitted easily into the worship of the emperor, which was to remain a unifying factor in the Roman world as long as it was sensitively managed. It was a sign of the overbearing arrogance of Domitian that he sent round a circular letter to his procurators with the heading: 'Our lord god orders this to be done' (Suetonius, *Domitian* 13.2).

In the west, the Romans encountered distinctly different religious practices. For example, in Britain many non-Roman deities continued to receive worship, often in a local area, like Coventina at Carrawburgh. In time Celtic deities came to be identified with Roman gods and the locals began to adopt Roman methods of depicting their divinities, which even though they appeared in animal form might have other attributes such as Jupiter's thunderbolt. The most famous example of assimilation with Roman practice is Sulis, a Celtic water-goddess who was closely identified with Minerva, and had a temple in the classical form that presided over the bath complex at the hot springs in Aquae Sulis (Bath).

Throughout the Republic the Romans had proved to be responsive to new forms of worship on a selective basis. This continued and the Egyptian Isis, for example, became popular in Rome, as goddess of life and birth, protector of women and the family, and a great healer. From the second century AD onwards an Indo-Iranian God, Mithras, appeared in the Roman world as a sun-god ('the invincible sun-god Mithras'), worshipped by small exclusive groups of men who believed that they were the elect and had been promised eternal life. In the mythology of this mystery cult Mithras had killed the sacred bull, which in some way brought salvation to the believers. The initiates, with many concentrated in Rome and Ostia and the frontier provinces, were generally ordinary people and included many soldiers who were perhaps taken by the idea of close comradeship and the exclusivity of the cult. Furthermore, the Romans had long been familiar with the monotheistic worship of the Jews, for whom Augustus had confirmed freedom of worship, accepting that their rites were ancient and legitimate. The Romans, however, did not understand how closely intertwined was Jewish religious belief with national sentiment and did not fully appreciate the importance of keeping images of the emperor out of the Temple. A series of crass and insensitive actions by Roman governors, and the threat of the emperor Caligula to have his statue placed and worshipped in the Temple, alienated many in Jerusalem. Furthermore, the Jews in Alexandria were attacked by the Greeks in the city with the collusion of the governor. Despite these setbacks to good relations, the Romans perceived the great Jewish War of 66–70 not in religious terms but as an act of political rebellion.

Christians were definitely regarded as outsiders, with their monotheistic belief in a saviour who had died and been resurrected, and the practice by exclusive groups of worshippers of rituals that seemed odd to many pagans, including the Eucharistic ceremony of eating the flesh and drinking the blood of Christ. Christians also incurred suspicion of incestuous relations by addressing each other as 'brother' or 'sister', and of fomenting sedition by referring to Christ as 'Lord'. The Roman government in the first two centuries of the imperial period had little understanding of or interest in Christianity, since its adherents were relatively few in number and were not a threat; furthermore, monotheistic beliefs and an expectation of immortality were not out of place in the Roman Empire. Tacitus is the only pagan Roman writer to mention Christ's execution by Pontius Pilate, and he contemptuously dismisses Christianity as a deadly and depraved superstition (*Annals* 15.44). There was no law banning Christianity, but after the great fire of Rome in AD 64 Nero chose the Christians as scapegoats to deflect hostile attention from himself, and thereafter they were in the Romans' sight as potential troublemakers. Since Roman criminal law did not define Christianity as an offence and there was no public prosecutor, it was up to provincial governors and magistrates to use their discretion in receiving or rejecting accusations from private individuals. The response of these officials would often be conditioned by the situation in their province; resentment and violence against Christians could well provoke the governor into a vigorous prosecution of people who were held vaguely to be up to no good. Local people were stirred up by the scandalous rumours about what went on in Christian worship and by their obvious difference, aloofness from community activities, and tendency to insult local deities by describing them as demons. The spread of Christianity brought tensions as it encountered many people who had strong personal belief in private rituals and traditional cults. But there was no organized persecution of Christians and in some provinces they were left unmolested for generations. Once Christians had been brought to court, their truculent behaviour and willingness to incur martyrdom might well infuriate a governor who saw them as defying his authority. Trajan, writing to Pliny the Younger, his governor in Bithynia in the early second century, sums up a government attitude that was measured but perplexed, enlightened but cruel:

> You have followed the right course of action, my dear Pliny, in your examina-
> tion of the cases of people charged with being Christians, for it is impossible to
> lay down a general rule to a fixed formula. These people must not be hunted
> out; if they are brought before you and the charge against them is proved, they
> must be punished, but in the case of anyone who denies that he is a Christian,
> and confirms that he is not by offering prayers to our gods, he is to be pardoned
> as a result of his repentance however suspect his past conduct may be. But
> pamphlets circulated anonymously must play no part in any accusation. They
> create the worst sort of precedent and are quite out of keeping with the spirit
> of our age. (Pliny, *Letters* 10.97)

Writers and Scholars

For the upper classes it was part of their role in society to take an interest in cultural pursuits, particularly poetry and rhetoric. Pliny the Younger praised his young wife for her interest in his writings, both poetry and prose, and she even discreetly turned up at his recitals: 'If I am giving a reading she sits behind a curtain nearby and greedily drinks in every word of appreciation. She even sets my verses to music and sings them . . .' (Pliny, *Letters*, 4.19). This shows not only Pliny's aspiration to literary elegance but also the importance of public presenta-tion. A significant aspect of the cultural world of Rome was patronage; this tradi-tional obligation on the wealthy was taken up by Augustus and his entourage. The great man or patron could enjoy the reputation of supporting artistic ventures and perhaps a work celebrating his name, while the talented client often received financial benefits and helpful publicity. Having an emperor as patron involved certain sensitivities and a willingness to extend praise where necessary and not offend against government policy. The literature of the imperial period after Augustus is often described as the 'silver age', but that should not detract from a vibrant and innovative period of artistic activity, which also involved emperors. Both Augustus and Tiberius wrote autobiographies; Claudius was a notable antiquarian and historian; Nero was a versifier who liked to sing to the lyre; Hadrian also tried his hand at poetry; and Marcus Aurelius expounded philosophy. All these emperors were reflecting traditional upper-class interests.

The cultivation of writing skills was essential for those who aspired to write history, biography or commentaries of any kind, and also for budding orators. The works of ancient historians are not merely a source of data for modern historians of the Roman world. They were often important literary creations in their own right, in which style was important as well as content, and rhetoric had its place, and not just in the invented speeches that were a common feature of historical writing. It is important to remember that literary works were also read out in public gatherings. In this context Tacitus (*c.*AD 56–*c.*118) of course stands out as one of the greatest historians of the ancient world. Claiming to write without rancour or partisanship ('*sine ira et studio*'), he explains what it was like as a senator to live in an autocracy and what it was also like for the emperor, at the mercy of his own personality and the corruption of power. The historical works of Tacitus offer moral edification by contrasting virtue and depravity, and a kind of commentary for those living under autocratic rule. His epigrammatic and ironic style perfectly suits this approach, in which he also describes the nature of Roman government and analyses the position of the ruled, which can be contrasted with the tumultuous and perilous freedom of those outside the empire.

Suetonius's (*c.*AD 70–*c.*130) scholarly work included studies of distinguished grammarians and rhetoricians, although he is best known for his collection of biographies of Julius Caesar and the emperors up to Domitian, which, though not as stylistically accomplished as Tacitus, offer an entertaining supplement to the usual historical narrative. Suetonius tends to concentrate on the moral character of the subject, his personality and his relationships with others; in this way the subject's private life is a kind of mirror of the direction and failings of public policy. Plutarch of Chaeronea in Greece (*c.*AD 50–*c.*120), who spent some time teaching in Rome and also served as a priest at Delphi, embodied the fruitful combination of Greek culture and the imperial power of Rome. His voluminous writings included philosophical works, antiquarian researches and the series of *Bioi Paralleloi* (*Parallel Lives*), in which he set out side by side the careers of prominent Greek and Roman figures. In this way Plutarch establishes an ethical context against which a man can be judged based on the record of his actions.

Published letters were a literary product in their own right, and the collections of the Younger Pliny (*c.*AD 61–*c.*112) and Cornelius Fronto (*c.*AD 95–*c.*166) in the second century AD are models of carefully modulated prose, designed to set the author in the best possible light as a figure of literary accomplishment and distinguished public service. Of course, incidentally they are an invaluable resource for the historian, because of their comments on government and contemporary personalities. The enormously varied ambitions of prose writers is exemplified by the Elder Pliny (AD 23/4–79; uncle of Pliny the Younger), who brings a completely different style and subject matter in his astonishing thirty-seven-volume *Natural*

History, encompassing most aspects of human, animal and plant life. In this he fulfilled the ambition of many Romans in the systematic collection of information. Others, like the younger Seneca (*c*.4 BC–AD 65), who was prominent under Nero, wrote philosophical essays in the form of letters addressed to friends, while the Greek writer Lucian of Samosata (born *c*.AD 120) produced essays and dialogues that were part satirical and part social commentary; his principal and entirely laudable purpose was to entertain his audience. Aelius Aristides (*c*.AD 117–*c*.181) as well as being an outstanding orator was a great exponent of the classical tradition in his prose works; among his extensive output the *Sacred Tales* stands out with its fascinating description of Aelius's long battle against various illnesses, his water cures at various hot springs and rivers, his supplication of Aesculapius, the god of healing, and the psychology of ill-health. What all these writers have in common is a confidence in the value of linguistic virtuosity, and despite widely different personal approaches they demonstrate the general receptiveness of the upper classes educated in the classical texts.

However, one innovative type of literature that was regarded as unworthy by ancient literary critics was prose fiction. For the modern reader this provides a fresh view of the ancient world partly because it is not constrained by the traditions of classical models. Petronius (probably first century AD; he may also have fallen at the hands of Nero) in the *Satyrica* gives us a narrative told by his anti-hero Encolpius, a thief and smart operator, and through his eyes we see a comic world in which Roman society is examined. Part of the work has been lost and a large part of the rest is taken up by a single incident, the dinner of Trimalchio, the vulgar and grotesquely rich freedman. The humour is scathing, with Trimalchio urinating at table into a silver pot and then wiping his fingers on the head of a slave. Equally amusing is the work of Lucius Appuleius from Africa (mid-second century AD); in the *Golden Ass* his hero Lucius is changed into a donkey and has a series of adventures in a splendidly imaginative fantasy world, which again does much to illuminate life in the empire; the love story of Cupid and Psyche has a central position in the narrative. The work ends when Isis intervenes to restore Lucius to his former shape.

The type of oratory practised by Aelius Aristides was one of the ways in which a man could still speak out on a public platform without fear. He and other wealthy Greek intellectuals (sophists) travelled the empire giving formal public lectures in which they displayed linguistic dexterity on their chosen theme. Aelius's most famous speech was 'In praise of Rome' (p. 42), in which he gives a thoughtful appreciation of the value of settled Roman rule for the rich provincial elite. Dio Chrysostom (*c*.AD 40–*c*.110) from Prusa, another Greek from a rich background, gave numerous speeches on a wide range of topics, many of them delivered to the assembly in Prusa (see p. 142). He illustrates intellectual life in the Greek east, showing belief in his Greek heritage but also respect for Rome, and providing invaluable details about local politics. Other formal speeches were delivered in court, or to the emperor in person as a mark of respect. The Younger Pliny delivered such a speech to Trajan (his *Panegyric*), offering thanks for his election to the consulship in AD 100. Here, the speaker's erudition could be displayed in a way that honoured the emperor. Works about oratorical training by the elder Seneca and Quintilian show the importance of this activity even though genuine political oratory was dead.

Poetry too was for an elite audience and was based on a classical Greek framework, often infused with original themes and a strong personal element. Lucan (AD 39–65), who was forced to commit suicide at the age of twenty-six by Nero (perhaps from jealousy of his literary talent), reinvented the epic genre with the *Pharsalia* on the civil war fought by Caesar and Pompey; this is an epic without a heroic figure, in which the poet interjects his own voice, satirical and critical of the moral and physical destruction of civil war. Other epic poems by Statius (*c*.AD 45–*c*.96), who had the patronage of the Flavians, and Silius Italicus (*c*.AD 26–*c*.102) lack Lucan's originality and rhetorical impact. Valerius Martialis (Martial) (*c*.AD 38–*c*.104) from Spain knew many of the famous writers in the Flavian period; from a poor background he lived by his wits, the sale of his books, and the support of his patrons. His books of epigrams are his most famous work, short poems depicting characters in contemporary Rome and vignettes of local life, often erotic. Pliny the Younger described his poems as combining pungency and wit (*Letters* 3.21). Juvenal (*c*.AD 55–*c*.130) was a powerful and original voice, an acute and well-informed observer of imperial society; his vivid satire criticizes the vulgar and the hypocritical, with examples from Roman life and history. He followed various themes, including the behaviour of women, freedmen who got above themselves, and the privileges of life in the army. As he reviewed the foibles of the upper classes and the upstart freedmen, Juvenal said: 'It is difficult not to write satire; for who can endure this awful city and who is so unfeeling that he can control his anger' (1.30–31).

Intellectual life among the upper classes in the first two centuries AD also embraced science and philosophy. Galen of Pergamum (*c*.129–*c*.199) is one of the outstanding figures. From a wealthy background he first served as a doctor looking after gladiators and rose to be a doctor serving the court of Marcus Aurelius. He had wide intellectual interests ranging from philosophy to medicine and his voluminous writings included work on surgery, pathology and pharmacology. One of the great thinkers of the imperial period, he was very influential into the Middle Ages. Claudius Ptolemaeus (writing in mid-second century AD) was another outstanding Greek writer; working in Alexandria in the mid-second century, he wrote on mathematics, astronomy and geography. In the *Geography* he tried to map the known world, using latitude and longitude with comments on important topography; this work remained extremely influential until the sixteenth century.

Technological developments continued in building techniques, in the science of land measurement, in sophisticated methods for raising water and moving it by mechanical pump, and in building ever better war engines and artillery. The famous mills at Barbegal in France contained sixteen parallel waterwheels geared to horizontal millstones powered by water channelled from an aqueduct, and were sufficient to provide flour for up to 80,000 people, probably in nearby Arles. The meticulous and detailed achievement of Roman technical literature is exemplified by the writings of the land surveyors, who expounded methods of measuring and dividing up land and marking out boundaries for the settlement of colonists and the resolution of land disputes. Lucian's comments on a bath building show pride in the results of technological, engineering and architectural skill:

> For I think that it is a sign of no small intelligence to conceive of new patterns of beauty for common things. Such is the accomplishment the marvellous Hippias provided for us. It has all the virtues of a bath: utility, convenience, good illumination, proportion, harmony with the site, provision for safe enjoyment; and furthermore it is adorned with the other marks of careful planning: two lavatories, numerous exits, and two devices for telling time, one a water-clock with a chime like a bellowing bull, the other a sundial. (*The Bath* 4–8)

Roman interest in philosophical speculation had been strong in the Republic and was still based on principles going back to classical Greece, in particular Platonic doctrine. The main development was that the teaching of the various schools of philosophy tended to come closer together. Philo of Alexandria, a Jewish writer in the early first century AD, wrote commentaries on the Old Testament, which he interpreted in an allegorical manner, claiming that it was the source for some of the doctrines of Plato and Aristotle. He discusses the methods of mediation by which the supreme and perfect god (the ONE) could act in an imperfect universe (the ALL). Plotinus (AD 204/5–270), who was born in Egypt, was the founder of Neoplatonism and became the leading figure in a group of intellectuals in Rome. His biographer Porphyry said of him that he seemed ashamed to be in a body, and that he emphasized the importance of the intellect and the spiritual over the material, and developed the idea of an ascent from the basic matter via soul and reason to god. Individuals should seek the divine by self-discipline and purification. Plotinus was also interested in psychology, especially questions relating to the ability to perceive, awareness and memory. In developing his philosophy he tried to bring together elements of other philosophical systems.

Of course, all intellectual debate took place in an autocracy, and under the Flavian emperors some astrologers and philosophers were expelled from Italy, although not because of any philosophical principle, but because they had annoyed the emperor politically. Stoicism certainly was another important source of intellectual stimulation in Rome and its exponents believed that the materialist world was directed by providence, although humans remained responsible for their actions; virtue is the basis of ethics and the route to correct behaviour in the world; in this the use of reason was paramount. In the imperial period, stoicism was notably expounded by the younger Seneca and by Epictetus (mid-first to mid-second century AD), who was unusual in that he was an ex-slave; he developed the idea of the cultivation of inner peace and to some extent aimed outside the traditional upper-class audience. He was followed by Marcus Aurelius in his collections of reflections, which presented philosophy as a guide to a proper way of life. The emperor's subjects would have been encouraged by his advice to himself: 'Every hour decide stoutly to act as a Roman and a man to carry out the task you have in hand scrupulously with natural dignity, goodwill, independence and justice; and give yourself peace from all other fantasies' (2.5).

CHAPTER NINE

Crisis and Recovery

Emperors, Usurpers and Wars, 235–84

The period after the murder of Severus Alexander in 235 to 284 is characterized by the large number of emperors and pretenders, the brevity of their reigns, and the fact that only Claudius Gothicus avoided a violent end (and he died of plague). Maximinus demonstrates the changed emphasis; he had risen through the ranks of the army as a soldier's man, and when he raised revolt against Severus Alexander in 235 chose to stay with his army on the Rhine, where he actually fought in the battle-line. However, he failed to win over the senatorial class who resented his lowly background, and trouble developed in Africa over high taxes where the governor Gordian (I) and his son (Gordian II) unintentionally found themselves leading a revolt in 238. Although this rebellion was soon put down, in Rome the senate elected two new emperors from a panel of distinguished senators – Pupienus and Balbinus, both elderly men of consular rank. Elements loyal to the Gordians organized a popular demonstration in favour of the grandson of Gordian I, who became a colleague of Pupienus and Balbinus as Gordian III. Instead of marching on Rome, Maximinus directly became embroiled in northern Italy in a lengthy siege of Aquileia in 238, which had declared against him. Increasing military disaffection against the hardship of the campaign and his harsh discipline brought about his murder in 238. But Pupienus and Balbinus could not establish a stable regime and they were soon murdered by the praetorian guard in Rome, who declared in favour of Gordian III.

Gordian III and his advisers consolidated his position, for example disbanding legion III Augusta, which had put down the rebellion of Gordian I. As a foretaste of what was to come, the Persians threatened in the east and the Goths across the Danube. In 244 when Gordian III was defeated by the Persian king Sapor I and probably killed in the battle, his praetorian prefect, M. Julius Philippus (Philip), was proclaimed emperor in 244. Philip bought off Sapor with a huge indemnity and conceded Armenia to Persian control; he needed to get back to Rome as quickly as possible. Having proclaimed his seven-year-old son as Caesar, Philip set out for the Danube and won some military success. Back in Rome, he celebrated the one thousandth anniversary of the founding of the city and proclaimed his son Augustus. But trouble continued on the Danube and in 249 Philip's successful commander C. Messius Quintus Decius was proclaimed emperor by his troops, possibly against his will. Philip was defeated and killed at Verona in 249 and his son was subsequently murdered. Decius initiated a violent persecution of Christians, apparently believing that a revival of official state cults was crucial to the well-being of the empire. He faced the Gothic threat under their warlord Cniva, and after an inconclusive battle the city of Philippopolis in Thrace was surrendered to the Goths. The deteriorating situation led to mutiny and disaffection, showing how much now depended on an emperor's military capacity. Determined to show that he was up to it, Decius took the field in 251 and intercepted Cniva at Abrittus, where he was disastrously defeated and killed.

In this crisis C. Vibius Trebonianus Gallus, governor of Moesia, was chosen as emperor by the troops in 251 and embarrassingly made an agreement with the Goths allowing them to leave the empire with their plunder and captives, and undertaking to pay them an annual indemnity. Meanwhile in the east Sapor I ravaged Roman territory, while on the Danube the governor of Moesia, M. Aemilius Aemilianus, on his own initiative attacked the Goths, was immediately hailed as emperor by his own troops, and set out at once for Rome, leaving the area to the mercy of Cniva whose raids got as far as Macedonia. Gallus confronted Aemilianus (Aemilian) at Interamna in Italy but was killed by his own army in 253. Aemilian had little time to enjoy his success since P. Licinius Valerianus (Valerian), who had been ordered by Gallus to bring up reinforcements, was approaching fast and Aemilian was murdered by his own troops before any conflict.

As the new emperor, Valerian was a senior senator of great renown and he appointed his son Gallienus as his colleague. Their main concern was the military situation and they divided responsibility, with Gallienus heading to the northern zone and Valerian to the east. Here, the first major danger came from Goths, comprising a disparate group of peoples who had made their way from the western side of the Black Sea into Bithynia. While Valerian was dealing with this challenge the Persians under Sapor I advanced threateningly, causing the emperor to return to the Euphrates in 254 and to cooperate with Odenathus, ruler of Palmyra. In 260 Sapor attacked Carrhae and Edessa, and when Valerian entered into negotiations he was tricked and captured along with most of his officers. He ended his life in captivity, allegedly as Sapor's footstool. Meanwhile Gallienus had secured the northern frontier zone in Illyricum before moving to the Rhine in 254; he nominated his son Valerianus as successor (Valerian II). However, when Valerian II died in 258 Gallienus was distracted by a revolt, and attacks by the Alamanni on Gaul and by the Iuthungi into Italy caused serious devastation. It was 260 before Gallienus returned to Italy and defeated the Alamanni at Milan.

By now Gallienus will have been aware of the serious setback in the east, where the Persians had penetrated westwards capturing Roman cities. Fortunately, Odenathus came down on the Roman side and in 261 was rewarded with special recognition and titles – 'Leader, and Director of the entire East' (*Dux, Corrector Totius Orientis*). This was a pragmatic move by Gallienus, and Odenathus proceeded to carry the war into Persian territory. In the west Gallienus, under great pressure, similarly went with events after Postumus, governor of Lower Germany, had revolted and murdered the emperor's young son Saloninus in 260. Postumus controlled as his personal fiefdom a Gallic Empire, comprising Gaul, Britain and Spain; he strongly resisted foreign invaders while declining to cross the Alps into Italy. Therefore Gallienus accepted the situation and concentrated his efforts in the rest of the empire. He remained in Rome, was a vigorous patron of the arts but was condemned for his laziness by our Latin sources. By 267 he faced more trouble from the Goths who invaded Greece, while others attacked Thrace. Gallienus managed to defeat them but soon faced a revolt by Aureolus, who commanded his cavalry. Even though Aureolus was defeated and besieged in Milan in 268, events were undermining Gallienus. After the murder of Odenathus in a family feud, his widow Zenobia ruled in Palmyra on behalf of her son Vaballathus and adopted an increasingly independent stance. Many of Gallienus's senior generals, who came from the Danubian area, conspired against him and murdered him in 268 on campaign.

Their choice for emperor then fell on M. Aurelius Claudius, who had previously served as commander of the cavalry. Claudius was lucky in that the troublesome Aureolus was murdered by his own troops, allowing him to journey to Rome and later back to the Danube to continue the war against the Goths, defeating them decisively at Naïssus in 269 and forcing them to make peace, which lasted a generation. He was rewarded with the honorary name Gothicus Maximus ('the Greatest Conqueror of the Goths'). He may have intended to re-establish Roman control over Dacia, but other problems were looming – first Victorinus, who had replaced Postumus as master of the Gallic Empire, and second in the east where Zenobia was now openly displaying her ambition to control Syria and even Egypt. In any case, Claudius died of plague at Sirmium in 270 and was deified by an appreciative senate. His brother Quintillus briefly succeeded him, but was rapidly challenged by the senior military commander, L. Domitius Aurelianus (Aurelian), and deserted by his troops. Aurelian first secured his position in Rome and then set about a vigorous and successful campaign against the Alamanni and Iuthungi in 270, driving them back across the Danube. Facing various financial difficulties he followed the usual route to political control by displaying military prowess, especially against Zenobia, who now seems to have been in virtual control of Syria and Egypt. In 272 he defeated Palmyrene forces near Antioch in Syria and drove Zenobia (now proclaiming herself Augusta) back to Palmyra, which fell to Roman forces. The situation was restored, Egypt came back under Roman control, and Zenobia was made a prisoner. In 273 after a further rebellion, Palmyra was destroyed. Returning to the west Aurelian defeated Tetricus, the new leader of the Gallic Empire, and, ruling over a united empire, earned his title 'Restorer of the World' (*Restitutor Orbis*). It was at this high point of success that Aurelian had the confidence to abandon formally the old province of Dacia in 274 before celebrating a great triumph. He cleverly camouflaged the withdrawal by using the name 'Dacia' for an area south of the Danube. In 275 he set out eastwards again but was murdered by obscure conspirators who seem to have had no clear plan. In the ensuing confusion, M. Claudius Tacitus, a retired military commander, was brought from Italy to assume the purple. He campaigned briefly against the Goths in Asia Minor before being murdered by his own men in 276 as a result of a local feud. He was briefly succeeded by his praetorian prefect, Florianus, who similarly was killed by his own troops in 276 before he could join battle with Probus, commander of Roman forces in Syria and Egypt, who also claimed the purple.

Probus, of Danubian origins, ruled from 276 to 282 and immediately shifted his focus to the west, first fighting on the Danube and then ensuring the security of Gaul by vigorous campaigns against the Franks and Alamanni, who had caused devastation during Aurelian's absence in the east. He also campaigned in Raetia against Burgundians and Vandals, presenting himself directly as the protector of Italy. Probus then spent some time in the east, but whatever he was planning did not come to pass as he had to return to the west to deal with a serious revolt on the Rhine; when this had been suppressed and he had secured full control of Britain, he celebrated a triumph in 281. Then in 282, despite a military victory in the vicinity of Sirmium, he was killed by his soldiers apparently acting on their own initiative because he was a tough disciplinarian; however, it is possible that he no longer had the full confidence of his generals. Significantly, when M. Aurelius Numerius Carus, praetorian prefect and commander of a large army, declared against the emperor in 282, he assumed the purple without serious resistance. He proclaimed his sons Carinus and Numerianus as Caesars and immediately had to deal with frontier incursions, dividing up responsibility so that Carinus was left to deal with the west. Carus and Numerianus (Numerian) undertook an expedition against Persia and won a splendid victory, capturing Ctesiphon in 283. Carus then allegedly fell victim to a lightning strike, or perhaps was murdered. Carinus was now nominally in control of the whole empire. In the east Aper, the praetorian prefect and father-in-law of Numerian, probably murdered Numerian in 284 on the way back to the west, concealing his body in a litter until the smell of decomposition gave the game away. Even in the turbulent world of military politics this was unacceptable to the senior commanders and C. Valerius Diocles from Dalmatia was chosen, being declared emperor in Nicomedia in 284 with the name C. Valerius Diocletianus (Diocletian). He personally killed Aper, who presumably knew too much. Diocletian then marched west and on the Danube met Carinus in 285, who had already seen off one challenger. In a hard-fought battle Carinus was eventually betrayed and killed by his own troops, apparently because of his sexual exploits with the soldiers' women.

Inevitably this comes across as a confusing and rather depressing period of history; part of the difficulty lies in our entirely inadequate source material, since we lack writers who were contemporary or close in time to the events. We are therefore too reliant on the fourth-century writers Aurelius Victor and Eutropius, and an anonymous work, the *Epitome de Caesaribus*, which are all linked to one another in using similar sources. Little reliable information comes from the spuriously biographical *Historia Augusta*, which purports to be a collection of imperial biographies written by a number of authors but was probably the work of a single author in the fourth century and is inherently unreliable unless it can be confirmed by another source; for this period it contains even more inventions than usual. It is from later Greek writers that more reliable material comes – Zosimus, who wrote his *New History* in the fifth century, and Zonaras, writing the *Annals* in the twelfth century, but both using good earlier sources. For a different view of things and the development of Christianity, Eusebius's *History of the Church* is very important. Some of the gaps are filled by other kinds of literature, such as formal panegyrics to emperors, collections of letters and various tracts. For example, Lactantius (a Christian from Africa born *c*.240) in his work *On the Deaths of the Prosecutors* adopted a strongly pro-Christian stance and tried to demonstrate that the enemies of Christianity always came to a bad end. Given the poverty of the literary sources, inscriptions usefully illuminate important aspects of the administrative structure and military history of the empire, and also some of the main personalities; coins struck by the various emperors or pretenders are a particularly fruitful source of information on the chronology of the period and even the direction of public policy.

Problems, Solutions and Personalities

The period from 235 to 284 was an age of violence; one emperor died in battle, another was captured by the Persians, another died of plague, and most were murdered by their soldiers or their generals. Between 31 BC and AD 235 there were only twenty-seven emperors, but in the next fifty years, about fifty-one men received the title of emperor, at least twenty-two legitimately. This lack of continuity and consistency in government was one of the empire's biggest problems, and it is reasonable to speak of an empire in crisis. The Romans brought a great deal of trouble on themselves through the ambition of leading men. Frequent civil wars destroyed valuable manpower, devoured resources and brought great hardship for the local population where the wars were fought. To make matters worse, Rome's commanding presence in the Mediterranean world was beginning to show cracks, and during this period she should have been concentrating on dealing with dangerous foreign enemies who invaded Roman territory, often taking their cue from the army's distraction by civil conflict. Most seriously, the northern frontier zones along the Rhine and the Danube rivers were threatened, particularly by the Alamanni and the emergence of the Gothic peoples. In the east the kingdom of Persia under the Sasanids was to be a genuine, long-term threat not only to Roman interests in Mesopotamia and on the Euphrates but also from time to time her control of parts of Syria. These foreign incursions happened simultaneously, meaning that the emperor often had to move between the western and eastern frontier zones.

Secessionist movements, which for a time established virtually independent regimes in Gaul and Palmyra, are a clear indication of the military pressure on the empire. However, these events, while potentially embarrassing, did bring certain benefits. The Gallic Empire of Postumus at least managed to guard the Rhine and to some extent protect Gaul from incursions. At Palmyra, Odenathus was a valuable counterweight to the Persians in conducting military campaigns against Sapor. Only when his family overreached itself with ambitions to control part of Syria and Egypt did the Romans take action to restore the status quo.

In this militarily challenging situation the position and role of the emperor were crucial. He was expected to be a competent military leader who could organize an army and take command of a campaign or battle in person. It would help if he had a charismatic relationship with his troops, whose loyalty he also needed. There was, therefore, an increasing militarization of the imperial role in the mid- to late third century and the ability to command an army became equated with capacity to rule. It followed that a man who proved incompetent in military command or who simply lost a battle could lose the confidence of his men and be a target for revolt and assassination. It did not help that the empire failed to find a reliable or benign method of transferring power on the death of an emperor. Furthermore, because many parts of the empire found themselves under threat from invasion, raiders or bandits, and appreciated the need for a competent leader on the spot, there was the danger that soldiers and leaders might create a rival emperor as a focus of loyalty in the area. Obviously the emperor could no longer reside in Rome for long periods; he must be mobile, and if necessary establish major headquarters away from the capital or even outside Italy. On a wider strategic level, emperors had to balance the psychological and emotional importance of keeping the empire's traditional territories intact against rational consideration of whether it was possible to keep a military presence in every frontier zone. In this context the whole structure, organization and deployment of the army came into question.

Any intended solution to these serious problems would be circumscribed by the declining economic condition of the provinces. Civil war and foreign invasion had disrupted agricultural production in certain areas, and the loss or movement of populations had reduced the tax base. The notorious Bacaudae bandits roamed openly through Gaul and from this period many coin hoards have been discovered, suggesting that their owners had been killed or abducted. Along some main roads, for example from Cologne to Trier, there is evidence of fire damage to farm buildings. The surrender of territory, particularly the *Agri Decumates* and Dacia, where there were important gold mines, was damaging. Furthermore, intermittent outbreaks of plague inspired terror, and around AD 250 Dionysius, bishop of Alexandria, exclaimed: 'The human race on earth is constantly being diminished and consumed' (Eusebius, *History of the Church* 7.21.10). The fact that the silver coinage was steadily debased, seemingly as the main way of dealing with a lack of cash, is a sure sign of the government's difficulties.

The problems faced by the empire in this period do reveal several fundamental flaws and weaknesses in the government and economy, notably that the subsistence agricultural economy produced inadequate surplus wealth. Of course, this had always been true, and it is important not to exaggerate the extent of the crisis. Much of our literary evidence is either coloured by a Christian view of the end of the world and divine retribution, or reflects the panic of the upper classes in a world that was less settled than they would have liked. In any case, the effects of battles and even raids and invasions were often short-term and not permanent, and did not necessarily mean the total abandonment of farming land. In some parts of the empire encouraging developments took place: for example, in Africa more land was brought under cultivation, leading to a substantial increase in the production of olive oil, and the manufacture of fine pottery also increased.

Indeed, the empire was remarkably resilient, and its leaders when they had respite from civil war were capable of making constructive changes. Therefore, the framework of stable government was re-established partly because the manpower and resources of the provinces could still sustain a large army and the essential military structure, and the army was still capable of winning substantial victories. This was the difference from the fifth century, when the empire in the west collapsed though its inability to recruit and support soldiers in sufficient numbers.

The crucial factor in the third century was the reorganization of the army and also its command structure to deal with the new range of problems. It was Gallienus who seems to have taken the initiative by intelligently extending some established practices. The second-century army had increasingly used detachments (*vexilla-tiones*) taken from larger units for campaigns; this avoided the need to move entire legions around the empire. The army was also making more use of ethnic groups from peoples within the empire; these retained their separate identity outside the normal organization of the *auxilia*. For example, Moorish horsemen were a very effective component of armies in the third century. In these practices we may find the basis for the subsequent creation of the field army, consisting of independent units not tied to any territorial base. Furthermore, cavalry was now playing a more substantial role in warfare. Gallienus set up at Milan a special cavalry unit that could operate virtually independently under its commander Aureolus, who was consequently very important in imperial councils. A series of coins minted in Milan proclaimed 'the loyalty of the cavalry'. The emperor also fortified several crucial locations, such as Milan, Verona and Aquileia, important in the defence of northern Italy, and stationed there detachments of legions.

These measures were probably temporary but still show the emergence of a strategy of using detachments and strong cavalry forces operating from fortified positions. This fits in with the normal Roman practice of employing a wide variety of methods for controlling the natives in frontier zones, including stone walls in parts of Germany and Britain, and elsewhere river and road patrols and watch-posts. The Romans tended to react to threats when they found out about them; yet they often lacked clear intelligence information, and a structure to discuss military policy in the long term. Therefore, they tried to limit damage and counter-attack when forces had been assembled. One problem was respect for the long-standing role of senators as provincial governors and army commanders. In the first and second centuries the non-specialist approach to generalship and even the incompetence of some commanders had been an acceptable price for the main-tenance of traditional practice. However, in the mid-third century the military position was precarious and the natural superiority of the professional Roman army much less pronounced. Arguably, there was a higher premium on competent officers and generals. By the time of Gallienus a climate had been created in which imaginative solutions were feasible and he used men of equestrian rank to command legions. The pro-senatorial Aurelius Victor was very critical and alleged that Gallienus issued an edict removing senators from army command. This is unlikely since this was probably a gradual process; it does, however, seem that after AD 260 senators no longer commanded legions, being replaced by eques-trian prefects; *equites* now also supplied all six military tribunes in the legion. These men will normally have had more military experience than the average senator. An informal practice of using *equites* gradually became the norm. They also came to command independent bodies of troops, and in this case they had the title 'leader' (*dux*). Now that senators had even less military experience, there was good reason not to appoint them to govern provinces involving the command of large numbers of soldiers, and the last clear evidence of a senator in command of a campaign relates to C. Macrinius Decianus, governor of Numidia in 260. He made the most of it, celebrating the defeat of the Bavares tribe, 'who were routed and slaughtered and their notorious leader captured' (*ILS* 1194).

Claudius II and Aurelian continued the general drift of Gallienus's policies, and Aurelian's cavalry force of Dalmatians and Moors played a major part in the defeat of Zenobia. In this period we also find the breaking down of the old idea that the central part of Rome's forces would be legions made up of Roman citizens. Emperors seeking to build up their forces were prepared to use peoples from outside the empire. Vandals and Alamanni for a price were brought into Rome's service, and this was one controversial way in which Rome tried to avoid manpower problems. It was a pointer to the future.

Diocletian's Achievement, 284–305

Diocletian has a reputation as an enthusiastic innovator, and his achievement is impressive, not least because he had one of the longest reigns of any emperor and managed to die in his bed. Yet the evidence for the details of what he did is patchy and he was able to build on the achievements of some of his predecessors in military and administrative matters. The *Notitia Dignitatum* (List of Offices) was an official survey of civil and military offices for the western and eastern parts of the empire, listing high offices of state; in the case of military officers the units under their command are given. The document refers to the situation in 395 with later revisions, but gives us a good idea of Diocletian's provincial arrangements and military deployments a century earlier. He set out first to reform the imperial structure. On his first visit to Italy he proclaimed another military officer, Maximian, as Caesar and sent him to Gaul to deal with the Bacaudae bandits; in 286 Maximian was made Augustus and on 1 March 293 Diocletian initiated the Tetrarchy ('rule of four'), in which he and Maximian took the role of Augusti, each with a Caesar, Galerius and Constantius respectively. The deal was sealed with marriages – Galerius to Diocletian's daughter Valeria, and Constantius to Theodora, the daughter of Maximian. Provided that the four men stayed loyal to the arrangement each could have his own staff and assume responsibility for a part of the empire, ensuring that there was always someone in the vicinity to take command of military operations. The panel of emperors provided greater stability by making successful revolts less likely, and in time each Caesar could be promoted to take the place of the senior Augustus. There was a hint of the future in that the empire was effectively divided into two, with Diocletian and Galerius taking charge of the east and Maximian and Constantius ruling the west. Nevertheless, the Augusti did not formally divide administrative responsibilities, and edicts were issued in the names of all four and were valid throughout the empire.

A number of imperial centres emerged that the emperors made their base, such as Sirmium, Trier and Nicomedia. The events of previous years had made Rome less important and that reduced status was now confirmed. The institution of the Tetrarchy helped to reinforce the power and prestige of the emperor given its debasement through the usurpations of previous years, and Diocletian raised the status of the imperial position by taking the name Iovius, while Maximian took Herculius, in order to highlight their semi-divine authority (with Diocletian being the senior). Court ceremonial assumed a formal, more grandiose setting in which the Augusti remained aloof and secluded from their courtiers and retinue; Rome's rulers now wore purple and gold robes studded with jewels. The removal of the emperor and imperial business from Rome freed him from the last vestiges of the ideology of the Republic with the ruler as leading man (*princeps*). A votive offering from Dyrrhachium understood the message: 'To our Lords Diocletian and Maximian, the unconquered Augusti, born from gods and creators of gods' (*ILS* 629).

Apart from military security, Diocletian had three crucial areas of concern: the reorganization of the provincial structure, the reform of the tax system and public finance, and the organization of the army. Provincial government had not changed much from the early empire, but Diocletian made dramatic alterations by dividing the provinces into smaller administrative units. By about 314 there were almost one hundred provinces, each with its own governor and administration. One result was a kind of micro-management of the empire with detailed supervision especially of finance and legal matters as well as the systematic enforcement of government regulations. The governor of a province was now called a *praeses*, except in the case of Africa and Asia, which retained senatorial proconsuls. Italy did not escape and was divided into areas, each under the supervision of a *corrector*. Diocletian then created a higher level of administration by grouping together the provinces into twelve dioceses each of which was controlled by an equestrian official known as the *vicarius*, who was effectively the deputy of the praetorian prefects. The *vicarii* were of equestrian status, men of some ability who had worked their way up in the imperial service. It was perhaps a natural sequel to these changes that the provincial bureaucrats in the frontier zones should devote their energies to the civil administration, leaving military duties to specially appointed officers (see below). Bureaucracy became increasingly elaborate with a formal hierarchy supported by titles associated with people of particular rank: *Eminentissimus* ('Your Eminence'), *Perfectissimus* ('Your

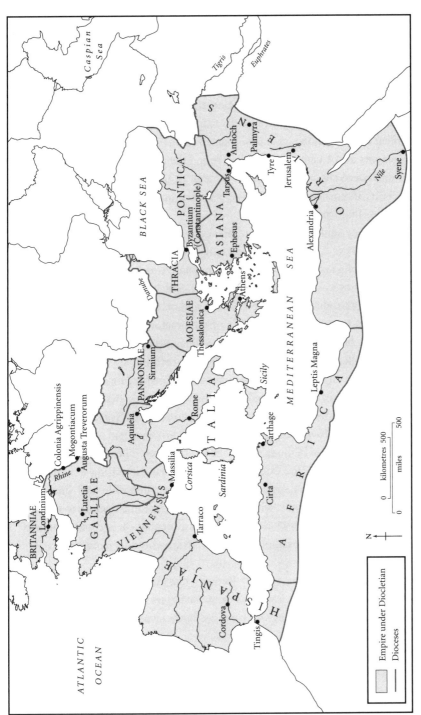

Map 9. The provinces and dioceses under Diocletian (after Williams, *Diocletian and the Roman Recovery* (1985), map 4).

Perfection'), *Egregius* ('Your Egregiousness'). Service in the administration, which came to be called *militia*, as opposed to military service, *militia armata*, conferred a kind of social rank. Lactantius, who rarely misses an opportunity to criticize Diocletian, nevertheless makes an important point about the increase in government officials: 'they were more than the number of taxpayers'. The council of the emperor's advisers now came to be called the Consistory (so-called because they stood in the presence of the emperor) and separate departments of government existed, known as *scrinia* (named from the boxes used to carry official documents as the emperors travelled round the empire). The heads of these departments were the *magistri*, and in charge of all this were the praetorian prefects in an important administrative, financial and judicial role; their duties were now less important militarily.

A bigger army and this elaborate bureaucracy put pressure on the empire's financial resources. A fundamental part of Diocletian's programme was the modification of the taxation system and an innovative reshaping of the economy. Collection of taxes was now based on the *iugum*, which was a piece of land measured by its likely productivity as well as area, and on the 'head' (*caput*), the individual taxpayer. It was the responsibility of the praetorian prefects on an annual basis to publish on 1 September the *indictio*, which was an assessment of the tax (now usually collected in kind, for example oil or cereals) due from each unit of taxation, based on an official census, which was originally to be carried out every five years. This effectively created the Roman Empire's first annual budget (virtually in the modern sense of the word), and after the *indictio* it was then down to the officials to work out how much each province had to pay, since the *iugum* was not calculated in the same way in all provinces. This secured resources for the treasury and to some extent attempted to deal with rising inflation and unfairness in the previous system, which had been inflexible and unable to respond to changing situations, with the high cost of war, the damage to the land and social dislocation. The whole process was probably carried out gradually province by province. For example, in Egypt the governor declared in 297:

> Our provident emperors . . . have learned that the assessment of tax burdens takes place in such a way that some taxpayers are under-charged and some burdened too much. They have decided in the interests of the inhabitants of the provinces to eradicate this disgraceful and pernicious practice, and to publish a beneficial edict, in line with which taxes are to be fixed. (Boak and Youtie, 1960, no. 1)

Diocletian also issued the famous edict on prices in 301, which targeted inflation by setting maximum prices for goods on sale and also wage levels, backed up by severe penalties, including execution. The edict expresses the genuine anger and frustration of the emperors:

> For who is so insensitive and so devoid of human feeling that he can be unaware or has not perceived that uncontrolled prices are widespread in the sales taking place in the markets and in the daily life of the cities? Nor is the uncurbed passion for profiteering lessened either by abundant supplies or by fruitful years ... it is our pleasure therefore that the prices listed in the subjoined schedule be held in observance in the whole of our Empire ... It is our pleasure that anyone who resists the measures of this statute shall be subject to capital penalty for daring to do so. (translation in Lewis and Reinhold, vol. II, 1990, p. 422–6)

The detail of the edict is astonishing and it lists about one thousand items. This is an extract on prices and wages:

Prices

For meat:

Pork –	one Italian pound –	12 denarii
Beef –	one Italian pound –	8 denarii
Leg of pork, Menapic or Cerritane, best –	one Italian pound –	20 denarii
Pheasant, fattened –		250 denarii
Pheasant, wild –		125 denarii

Wages

Barber –	per man –	2 denarii
Sewer cleaner, working full day, with maintenance –	daily –	25 denarii
Scribe, for the best writing –	100 lines –	25 denarii
Scribe, for second-quality writing –	100 lines –	20 denarii

According to Lactantius, who as noted was hostile to Diocletian because of his persecution of Christians, the edict failed completely since goods simply disappeared from the open market (*On the Deaths of Persecutors* 7.6–7). So this aspect of the command economy apparently did not work. But Diocletian also issued an edict on currency in 301, attempting to revalue the coinage on a sound basis and establish a unified currency; it was henceforth based on the *nummus*, a large bronze coin with a mixture of silver, worth 25 *denarii*, to be used in public payments and also private transactions; at the upper end of the three-metal monetary scale he struck a gold coin (*solidus*) at 60 to the pound, and the silver (*argenteus*) at 96 to the pound. Diocletian's policy ultimately failed in the face of lack of public confidence, and consequently he was unable to stabilize prices. He did not have enough gold and silver. Nevertheless, he had made a start to dealing with the persistent decline of the currency's value, and the edict is an important symbol of the extent of government attempts to direct the economy.

The most expensive part of Roman government had always been the army and there is no doubt that Diocletian significantly increased the number of legions to at least sixty-seven, and probably also increased the auxiliary units. The ancient sources give a variety of figures; some are vague, some more precise – for example, John Lydus gives 389,704 for the number of men serving in the army of Diocletian and 45,562 for the fleets. These numbers may have come from official records, but these may themselves have been inaccurate because of fraud or incompetence. If the legions on paper had the same complement as previously (over 5,000), the army will have been at least doubled in size. Commenting on the disposition of military forces under Diocletian, Zosimus is full of praise, noting that (in contrast to Constantine) he defended the empire's frontiers on all sides with cities, garrisons and fortifications, so that enemies could not force their way in (2.34.1–2). Diocletian certainly preserved the traditional structure in which crucial provinces had a permanent complement of soldiers and provided a kind of outer protective ring. Pride of place went to the legions and the cavalry detachments (*vexillationes*), backed up by infantry cohorts and cavalry squadrons (*alae*). For example, in the eastern provinces there were approximately twenty-eight legions, seventy *vexillationes*, fifty-four cohorts and fifty-four *alae*. Furthermore, at least seventeen legions were stationed along the Danube, up to ten in Germany, and two or three in Britain. These arrangements suggest the fundamental strategic concerns of Roman commanders, to protect the tax-rich eastern provinces against the Persians and to guard Gaul and the approaches to Italy from the incursions of marauding tribes. In addition, Africa with its eight legions, eighteen *vexillationes*, seven cohorts and one *ala* is no longer a military backwater; the province's wealth and agricultural products were worth protecting.

Despite this essentially conservative approach, Diocletian did not neglect previous moves towards using a force that was relatively mobile and not tied down permanently to a provincial location. Evidence is limited, but a papyrus from Egypt referring to preparations for the imperial campaign in 295 mentions an officer of the *comites* of the emperor in a composite force, including detachments from several legions and an auxiliary *ala*. Taken along with other evidence this suggests a permanent force in attendance on the emperor's person (*comitatus*). Yet it is unlikely that this was a formal or necessarily permanent arrangement. In his grant of privileges to his veterans, Diocletian particularly favoured legionaries and members of cavalry *vexillationes*, with no special treatment for the *comitatus* (*CJ* 7.64.9; 10.55.3). Doubtless troops were added to or removed from it as circumstances required, although it seems to have had at least three consistent elements: high-quality legions, the *Ioviani* and *Herculiani*, named after the Augusti; *equites promoti*, who perhaps were the remnant of Gallienus's cavalry force; and the *protectores* (literally 'protectors'), whom Diocletian had commanded before assuming the purple and who originally constituted a corps of junior officers serving with the emperor and later took on the role of a permanent bodyguard.

To keep the expanded army up to strength proved difficult, and Diocletian probably had to resort to conscription and also insist that the sons of veterans joined up. Furthermore, local city governments were held accountable for producing an appropriate number of recruits from their territory, and pressure was also put on individual landholders, some of whom grouped together to meet the obligation. It is possible that the *aurum tironicum* (literally, 'recuiting gold') dates from the late third century; by this arrangement the requirement to provide recruits was commuted to a money payment. With the ready cash the government could try to hire suitable foreign peoples to fight for Rome. Apparently the practice of settling non-Romans inside the empire in specific locations and then requiring military service from them and their descendants began during the Tetrarchy. An anonymous orator making a speech in 297 in honour of Constantius said: 'Now the barbarian farmer produces corn . . . and indeed if he is summoned for the levy he presents himself speedily, reduced to complete compliance and totally under our control, and is pleased that he is a mere slave under the name of military service' (*XII Panegyrici Latini* viii (v), 9.3–4).

It is not clear how many men were persuaded to join the army by the prospect of pay and benefits. In the mid-century turmoil there was obviously a much greater chance of being killed. The rate of pay in the late third century cannot accurately be recovered, and in any case will have been seriously undermined by inflation, even though soldiers' income was boosted by regular donatives celebrating the birthday and accession of the emperor (so in a sense the more emperors the better). To an increasing degree soldiers were paid in kind, by distributions of meat, salt, corn and wine, which could be requisitioned from the provinces as part of the tax payment. Diocletian, like all emperors, needed the enthusiastic support of his troops, and his dismay at the financial pressures on them comes across in the admittedly exaggerated complaint in the preamble to his edict on prices that they were spending most of their salary and donatives on a single purchase.

Under the Tetrarchy, with respite from civil war and serious incursions and with shared military responsibility between the four men, it was possible to reassert Roman power and influence. Diocletian aimed to hold the established limits of Roman-controlled territory in the frontier zones and attack where necessary in strategically sensitive areas. In the east the large number of cavalry units shows that deployment was not conceived of in defensive terms; and units of the field army could be moved up in support. To achieve stable frontier zones and opportunities for aggrandizement, Diocletian and Galerius were frequently on the move, though Diocletian spent much of his time in the Danube area and in the east. In 286 he fought the Sarmatians, while in 287 he installed Tiridates as king of Armenia; he may through negotiation with the Persian king have obtained the restoration of Mesopotamia. An inscription from Augsburg in 290 celebrates him as 'Greatest Conqueror of the Persians' (*Persicus Maximus*) (*ILS* 618). By 288 he was back campaigning in Raetia, and in December 290 Diocletian and Maximian staged a grand, formal meeting at Milan.

The story of military success was continued by Constantius, who invaded Britain in 296 and ended the secession of Carausius, who by this time had been killed and replaced by Allectus. Carausius had at one stage served as a helmsman and was then appointed to deal with the Saxon raiders in the English Channel; from this position he usurped control of Britain. Allectus had been his finance minister. A gold victory medallion celebrates Constantius as 'Restorer of the Eternal Light' (of Rome). In 298 Maximian himself was in Africa dealing successfully with a revolt of Moorish tribesmen. Meanwhile Diocletian conducted further campaigns on the Danube against the Sarmatians in 294 and the Carpi in 296. But in 297 in Egypt a serious revolt broke out, which Diocletian stamped out after an eight-month siege of Alexandria. This defiance infuriated the emperor, who vowed that the people of Alexandria would pay in blood until the streets filled up as far as the knees of his horse; but his horse stumbled when entering the city and perhaps out of religious scruple Diocletian spared them the massacre; in gratitude they vowed with their usual feisty spirit to set up a statue in honour of the horse. But Egypt was reorganized, losing its right to a separate coinage, and was divided up with the creation of a new province in the south, the Thebaid. Diocletian travelled up the Nile to expel the troublesome Blemmyes from Upper Egypt.

The most striking success of the Tetrarchy was to come in the east. In 297 Galerius had suffered a defeat at the hands of Narses, the Persian king, who had expelled the Roman nominee Tiridates from Armenia. Leading a Roman counter-attack through Armenia, Galerius confronted Narses and in 298 inflicted a comprehensive defeat, capturing the royal harem and treasury. Subsequently Galerius captured Ctesiphon, and the next year a peace treaty was concluded with the Persians who lost some territory and agreed that the river Tigris should be the frontier. Armenia was now definitely within the Roman orbit and Tiridates was restored as king. In a possibly fictitious account of the peace negotiations, the Byzantine historian Peter the Patrician has one Persian envoy praise humility in success and emphasize the rapid changes of fortune in human affairs. Galerius replied that the Romans were invariably magnanimous to the conquered and did not need guidance from the Persians in this. The peace deal, for which Diocletian is probably largely responsible, lasted forty years. The Tetrarchy had consolidated its position with conspicuous military achievement: Britain had been recovered, Persia defeated and humiliated, Egypt subdued and the Danube pacified, while in the west Constantius kept the Rhine frontier quiet.

Diocletian was both ambitious and successful in military campaigns, but he was also concerned about maintaining the territorial integrity of the empire in the long term, and he exploited developments in the design and building of forts equipped with thick walls, towers and fighting platforms, allowing the positioning of artillery that could hold off the enemy for a long time provided that the defenders had supplies. A series of forts and fortified towns and granaries protected communications along roads and rivers and assisted the movement of troops. A fine example of a network of strongholds is the *Strata Diocletiana* running from northeast Arabia to Palmyra and the Euphrates (a section has been identified by archaeological investigation between Palmyra and Damascus); the forts permanently garrisoned by infantry cohorts were placed at intervals of twenty miles and linked by a military road with a range of mountains in the rear. However, two legions in the vicinity at Palmyra and Danaba reinforced the military presence. Further north, other legions held the line of the frontier. This arrangement of troops and fortifications would be able to deal with raids and also more serious incursions by the Persians, but the motivation was complex and does not indicate a purely defensive attitude. The Tetrarchs established in frontier zones large permanent forces that could move directly along military roads to deal with incursions; the fortified places would allow Romans to contain enemy attacks within a relatively narrow area and prevent extensive damage to provincial territory. Roman forces would still expect to engage in set battles and were still in position to launch offensive operations. Armaments and other military supplies were now manufactured in special factories in centres such as Edessa and Antioch.

The emperors were justly proud of their military success and the achievement of stable rule and relatively peaceful conditions, as they celebrated in the preamble to the edict on prices of 301:

> As we recall the wars that we have successfully fought, we must be grateful to the fortune of our state, second only to the immortal gods, for a tranquil world that reclines in the embrace of the most profound calm, and for the blessings of a peace that was won by great effort. . . . Therefore we, who by the gracious

favour of the gods previously stemmed the tide of the ravages of barbarian nations by destroying them, must surround the peace which we established for eternity with the necessary defences of justice. (translation in Lewis and Reinhold, vol. II, 1990, p. 422)

Under the Tetrarchy the declining role of senators in government service continued; military commands at all levels were now exercised by *equites*, and increasingly by men of military experience, while of provincial governors only Africa and Asia had senatorial proconsuls. The position of *dux* had continued to develop and was now a senior commander of equestrian rank who exercised a military role over a territorial zone covering more than one province. The first clear example we have appears in an inscription dated between 293 and 305, referring to Firminianus who was *dux* of the frontier zone in Scythia.

Diocletian and the Christians

Diocletian always stood by the authority of the law rather than arbitrary decisions (there are one thousand surviving rescripts from his reign), and in social policy had a conservative view of the value of traditional Roman practices and sound discipline, just as Augustus attempted to maintain the moral high ground. In 295 he issued an edict banning incestuous marriages, which were not acceptable in Roman law or religion, and those affected were given until the end of the year to comply with the regulation. We see the same kind of attitude in a rescript of 285: 'It is common knowledge that nobody living under the authority and name of Rome is permitted to have two wives. A praetor's edict has singled out such men as meriting public disgrace, and in no case will the appropriate magistrate allow this to go unpunished' (*CJ* 5.5.2).

Diocletian valued the unity of the empire and he ordered that the Manichees should be suppressed as a damaging foreign cult; this sect believed in redemption based on an ascetic lifestyle pursued in a world that was the battleground for forces of light and darkness, or good and evil. It had developed from Gnosticism and did recognize Jesus as Son of God. Its founder, Mani, was a Parthian aristocrat who had died in 276, and his followers were in Roman eyes associated with Persia.

It is in this context that the Christians attracted Diocletian's unfavourable attention; he took no action against them for eighteen years, although there were sporadic efforts to enforce sacrifice to the gods in the emperor's entourage. Lactantius, with his strongly pro-Christian views, claims that the main motivation for the Great Persecution (starting in 303) came from Galerius. This is unlikely since Diocletian's authority was paramount and he presumably believed that as he strove to revitalize the state the Christians were an impediment, by refusing to fit in and worship the state's gods, for which Diocletian had traditional respect. He pursued the long-established practice of consulting the oracle of Apollo at Didyma, where the god claimed that the 'righteous ones' (i.e. Christians) were preventing a response. The enforcement of the persecution was enthusiastically pursued by Diocletian and Galerius in the eastern provinces. An edict was issued at Nicomedia in 303 aimed at the operation of the Christian Church and it ordered that churches should be destroyed, scriptures surrendered and all religious meetings banned. Those who persisted in worship were deprived of their rank and therefore were subject to torture and summary execution. Things got worse for the Christians after a fire in the imperial palace at Nicomedia; Diocletian himself watched the destruction of a Christian church in Nicomedia opposite the palace. A second edict insisted that all clergy be imprisoned, although a third provided for their release if they sacrificed to the pagan gods. A final edict ordered everyone (including the laity) to sacrifice. Lactantius vividly and emotionally describes the treatment of Christians:

> When this day dawned . . . suddenly while it was still twilight, the prefect came to the church (in Nicomedia) with military leaders, tribunes and accountants; they forced open the doors and searched for the image of God; they found the scriptures and burnt them; all were granted booty; the scene was one of plunder, panic and confusion. . . . Then the praetorians came in formation, bringing axes and other iron tools, and after being ordered in from every direction they levelled the lofty edifice to the ground within a few hours. (*On the Deaths of the Persecutors* 12.2–5; translation in Creed, 1984)

Although acts of great cruelty were undoubtedly perpetrated, the effects of the persecution were uneven. In the west Constantius seems not to have enforced the fourth edict, while in Egypt the governor, Sossianus Hierocles, was enthusiastic in confiscating Church property and forcing Christians to sacrifice to the pagan gods. Events in Egypt and the imperial officials involved are illustrated by a papyrus recounting a statement made by a Christian, a lector in a local church:

> Whereas you gave me orders in accordance with what was written by Aurelius Athanasius, *procurator privatae*, in virtue of a command of the most illustrious *magister privatae* (controlling imperial property) Neratius Apollonides, concerning the surrender of all the goods in the said former church, and whereas I reported that the said church had neither gold nor silver nor money nor clothes nor beasts nor slaves nor lands nor property either from grants or bequests, excepting only the unworked bronze which was found

and delivered to the *logistes* to be carried down to the most glorious Alexandria in accordance with what was written by our most illustrious Prefect Clodius Culcianus. I also swear by the genius of our lords the emperors Diocletian and Maximian, the Augusti, and Constantius and Galerius, the most noble Caesars, that these things are so and that I have falsified nothing, or may I be liable for the divine oath. (*The Oxyrhynchus Papyri* 2,673; translation by J. Rea)

In one sense the Great Persecution illustrates the power of the government in its willingness to attempt micro-management of the affairs of the empire by precisely targeted legislation. However, as a government exercise it also illustrates the limits of intervention, since its ambition was matched by its ineffectiveness and most Christians survived. By 306 most of the impetus for the persecution had ended. Nevertheless, the Great Persecution is an important step in the conflict between paganism and Christianity, and indirectly it had a significant impact, for example in the Donatist conflict between those Christians who had stood firm and those who had complied with government demands.

At the end of 303 Diocletian made his only visit to Rome and with Maximian celebrated the twentieth anniversary of his accession. But his health was failing, and in 305 he returned to Nicomedia where he abdicated, persuading Maximian against his wishes also to abdicate and allowing the two Caesars Galerius and Constantius to become Augusti. New Caesars were appointed: Maximinus Daia, a nephew of Galerius, and Severus, a competent military officer. Diocletian went to his luxurious palace at Split on the coast of Dalmatia, where he amused himself by growing cabbages, and resisted attempts in 308 to persuade him out of retirement; he died *c*.312.

The Tetrarchy was novel and certainly caught the attention of ancient commentators. It is doubtful whether Diocletian had worked out a detailed policy from the start; on one level it can be seen as a response to external events in a typically pragmatic Roman way. Diocletian needed someone to deal with a particular situation – the Bacaudae in Gaul – and so brought in his old friend Maximian, and since this was a success further building blocks could be put on this foundation. The Tetrarchy was stable as long as Diocletian was in charge, but when he became ill and retired it fell apart, and as a method of securing orderly succession and stability it failed in the face of hereditary claims and ambition. There was insufficient preparation for the next stage and the delicate moment of transition of power, and this was a serious flaw in the system. However, the twelve years of the Tetrarchy saw genuine achievements and in modern terms Diocletian would have been a superb manager. He demonstrates the value to Rome of intelligent and competent men from the provinces, especially the Danube area, who were to control the empire's

future. Under his guidance the civil administration was reformed, and at the very
least he recognized the serious financial problems confronting the empire and tried
a remedy. The army was increased in size and revitalized, and the important move
to equestrian domination of military command was completed. The army was put
to good use and the threat of incursions by hostile peoples had receded, while in
the east the Persians had been chastised, allowing a breathing space for the reorganization of the entire frontier zone. In short, Diocletian managed to affirm Roman
belief in stable government and the operation of the law and due process. This was
achieved in a context in which the rulers now occupied an elevated position, but not
in an entirely un-Roman way, and certainly the Tetrarchy does not mark the
appearance of an oriental despotism. Diocletian's last years were soured by the
persecution of the Christians and the accompanying social disruption, violence and
bloodshed. He failed to resolve the issue of the place of Christianity in the empire,
and continuing sporadic persecution was certainly not the answer. The impact of
the two *Augusti* and two *Caesares* is well summed up by Aurelius Victor:

> All these men were natives of Illyria. But although they were comparatively
> uncultured, they were of the greatest value to the state, being brought up to all
> the hardships of rural life and war. . . . Their native abilities and their military
> skills, which they had acquired under the command of Aurelian and Probus,
> almost made up for the lack of a noble character, as is proved by the harmony
> that prevailed between them. And they looked up to Diocletian as to a father,
> or as one would to a mighty god. (*Lives of the Emperors* 39.26–9)

CHAPTER TEN

The Christian Empire

Constantine: From Caesar to Augustus

Events were soon to show that the arrangements for passing on power were deeply flawed. In the aftermath of Diocletian's retirement in 305, Constantine, the love child of Constantius and the ex-barmaid Helena, joined his father, the new Augustus in the west, and when Constantius died at York in 306, the army declared Constantine Augustus. However, after negotiations Galerius the senior Augustus accepted him as Caesar with Severus as Augustus in the west. Further disruption followed when Maxentius, the son of Maximian, made a bid for power and asked his father to resume the role of Augustus. In this violently unstable situation Constantine did a deal with Maximian, offering military neutrality in return for the rank of Augustus; the agreement was sealed by the marriage of Constantine to Fausta, daughter of Maximian; this important public demonstration of the status of Constantine took place at Trier in 307. A conference at Carnuntum in 308 was attended by Diocletian (persuaded by Galerius), who used his prestige to effect an agreement by which Constantine was again confirmed as Caesar, while the new Augustus in the west was to be Licinius. Maximian, deprived of power, came to live with Constantine, his son-in-law and previous ally. This arrangement tried to prop up the principle that the Augusti should appoint the Caesars and organize the structure of government. The various leaders tried to establish their military credentials by conducting campaigns, Constantine crushing the Franks in 310 and building a bridge across the Rhine.

The Diocletian-sponsored rearrangement was fatally undermined when Maximian tried to seize power again; he was rapidly defeated by Constantine in 310 and forced to commit suicide. With Maximian's death Constantine lost his claim to legitimacy and now needed to create a hereditary claim to the purple; therefore, it was alleged that his father Constantius had been related to Claudius

II. In the following months further wrangling saw both Constantine and Maximinus Daia (who was Galerius's Caesar) claiming the title of Augustus along with Licinius. Diocletian's system was collapsing and in 310 Galerius became seriously ill and died the next year, removing the last link to the old system. In 312 Constantine crossed the Alps and invaded Italy; after a rapid advance in which he outmanoeuvred and outfought his opponents in northern Italy, he marched on Rome, defeating Maxentius at the battle of the Milvian Bridge outside the city; his rival was drowned in the Tiber as he fled. Constantine's entry into Rome was subsequently celebrated as the delivery of the city from the grip of a tyrant, and on the arch erected on Constantine's tenth anniversary in 315, which still stands near the Colosseum, the dramatic events are recalled in formal language: 'By the inspiration of the divinity and through the nobility of his own mind, with his army he avenged the *res publica* by a just war all at once against both the tyrant and all his faction' (*ILS* 694). This recalls Augustus, who claimed to liberate the state 'from the tyranny of a faction'.

Constantine then met Licinius at Milan and they agreed to work together, confirming this by the marriage in 313 of Constantine's half-sister Constantia to Licinius, who went on to issue an edict on the restoration of confiscated Christian property (see p. 224). Meanwhile in the east, Maximinus Daia had been subtly moving against Christians by granting the requests of individual communities to organize a persecution. This produced spasmodic violence against Christians, though in late 312 Maximinus issued an edict of toleration. This did not prevent the drift towards war with Licinius, whose troops at the battle of Adrianople in 313 recited a prayer dictated by their emperor to the supreme god; Licinius won the battle and Maximinus fled to Nicomedia where he committed suicide. Licinius was ruthless in eliminating members of his rival's family. The empire was now effectively under the control of Constantine and Licinius, and it was Constantine who became the aggressor and invaded the Balkans in 316. There is no sign that Licinius had begun to persecute Christians (that is a trumped-up charge of pro-Constantine writers), and the main reason for the conflict probably lay in the ambition of both men for supreme power and hereditary succession. After suffering several defeats Licinius manoeuvred Constantine into a stalemate, and a negotiated settlement confined Licinius to the east and Thrace; furthermore, in 317 Crispus and Constantine II, sons of Constantine, were each made a Caesar, as was Licinius II, son of Licinius. From 317 to 323 Constantine campaigned in the Balkans, and after defeating a Gothic invasion turned his attention to the east, discovering or inventing a dispute with Licinius over their imperial responsibilities. After inflicting two defeats on his rival, he forced his abdication at Nicomedia in 324. Licinius's wife Constantia interceded for him and he was initially exiled, but was executed later on the charge of plotting, and his son

Licinius II was executed in 326. Constantine was entirely ruthless in disposing of perceived threats. It was in 324 that he made his third son, Constantius II, Caesar, indicating his strong policy of hereditary succession. Indeed, in 333 his youngest son Constans also received the title of Caesar.

The problem of getting a clear appreciation of Constantine's reign lies in the nature of the sources. The pagan Eunapius, writing in the late fourth century, was hostile because of the emperor's Christian leanings and thought that he had undermined the empire. Zosimus, another pagan writer, was certainly influenced by Eunapius and was scathing about Constantine's military policy. On the other hand Eusebius, bishop of Caesarea, wrote from the Christian perspective and presents Constantine as a hero of the Church. In his *History of the Church* and *Life of Constantine* the champion of Christianity is glorified and can do no wrong. Lactantius, another Christian writer, also gives the emperor a favourable press, although it is true that he wrote before the final confrontation with Licinius. Constantine is one of the most significant figures in the history of the Christian Church and modern commentators (all writing in the context of Christianity's central place within Western culture) have carried on the partisan debate from the ancient world, arguing over the sincerity of the emperor's beliefs and his grasp of the tenets of Christian theology.

Constantine, the Army and the Frontiers

Zosimus complained that Constantine withdrew many troops from the frontiers (presumably to supplement the field army), but merely succeeded in destroying their discipline by an easy life in the cities. But any changes from the policies of Diocletian are likely to have been gradual. Constantine did increase the size and significance of the field army (the *comitatenses*), which attended the person of the emperor and was ready to move with him to any part of the empire, and distinguished it from the frontier troops (*ripenses* or *limitanei*), who were permanently based at one location in the provinces and who had fewer emoluments and privileges. The conditions of service were set out in a law of 325 but were probably organized earlier. The *comitatenses* certainly emerged from Diocletian's embryonic field army and consisted of infantry legions, *auxilia* (newly recruited units), cavalry *vexillationes* and other troops, including detachments from various provinces. In line with the increase in the numbers of the *comitatenses*, military command was reorganized with two senior officers responsible directly to the emperor: the *magister equitum* (senior cavalry commander) and the *magister peditum* (senior infantry commander). As before, the emperor usually took command of major campaigns in person. Constantine did not dismantle Diocletian's arrangements for manning the frontier zones, though he may have reduced the number of troops and some were transferred to the field army on a temporary basis. It should be emphasized that the territorial troops retained their previous organization and indeed shared most of the privileges of the field-army troops. In some areas Constantine reinforced the troops with new cavalry regiments, though overall his army was probably no bigger than before. Sections of the frontier troops were under the command of a *dux*, who in turn was responsible to the supreme cavalry and infantry commanders. Constantine did recruit more foreign soldiers, which had long been a Roman practice and did not amount to the barbarization of the army. In his war against Licinius he was assisted by the Frankish commander Bonitus, and Constantine was prepared to use men of talent in his cause whatever their origin.

Constantine dramatically changed the emperor's personal protection by abolishing the traditional praetorian guard in 312 after his defeat of Maxentius outside Rome. He could hardly do otherwise since it had supported his rival, and he replaced it with a reorganized force, the *scholae palatinae*, along with a unit of foreign troops (*gentiles*) used by Diocletian. A further group known as the *protectores divi lateris* (guards of the revered person) attended the emperor personally, with the *protectores domestici* having a superior rank. The *protectores* were a heterogeneous group, including promoted soldiers and the sons of officers, and in a sense made up a kind of preparation for senior officers of the future.

Zosimus's insistence that Constantine's policy contributed directly to the break-up of the western part of the empire has read too much into the emperor's changes. Constantine in fact sensibly developed the methods and practices of Diocletian but accepted that the empire's resources could not support a military establishment capable of sustaining a defensive line. The larger field army could move with the emperor, who eventually ruled the empire single-handedly, to the zones under threat; this army was an expression of high status, and was intended to intimidate the enemy and impress the provincials. Constantine was in direct command of operations and this army naturally was the first bulwark of his political power. But it was principally a source of strength to Rome and a way of preserving the status of the empire and keeping its territory intact.

Constantine's military arrangements worked in practice, as we see from the history of warfare in the frontier zones. After 325 the emperor campaigned on the Rhine in 328/9 and then moved to the Danube to engage with the Goths whom he defeated in battle in 332. In 334 he campaigned against the Sarmatians and later accommodated many of them into the empire at their request. His expedition north of the Danube in 336 brought about the partial recovery of Dacia and the adoption of the title *Dacicus*. His reign ended on a note of grandiose military ambition with plans for a major campaign against Persia (337). He intervened provocatively by writing to Sapor II advising him to treat his Christian subjects well, and then crowned his own nephew, Hannibalianus, as king of Armenia, an insult that Sapor could never accept. But Constantine died in 337 before he had to deal with the consequences.

Administration

In 324 Constantine famously founded the new city of Constantinople on the site of ancient Byzantium, which had an important strategic position. However, it was not just another headquarters like those of the Tetrarchy, and he endowed it richly with buildings and imported statues; it came to be known as the 'new Rome', which was primarily a mark of respect for the young city, and its governing structure was significantly enhanced, so that ultimately it had its own senate. The emperor also provided sumptuous housing for leading men who came to reside here. The city became a magnet for the elites of the eastern provinces who took government jobs partly because this helped them to escape onerous local obligations in their home communities. Food began to be shipped here for the populace as well as to Rome, an innovation that may have affected trading patterns. But initially Constantinople was not an entirely Christian city (there were pagan and Christian dedication services) and was not intended to outdo Rome, which had already seen other cities like Milan and Trier and Nicomedia replace it as the favoured residences of emperors. Nevertheless, Constantine was to spend most of his free time there after its dedication in 330.

In his financial arrangements Constantine struck a new gold coin (*solidus* at 72) to the pound. He was a 'spend and tax' emperor – his new taxes were onerous and unpopular, especially with people like Eunapius and others in the eastern elite. The *follis* tax was imposed on senators and the *chrysargyron* ('gold and silver') on merchants, to be paid in gold and silver coins. A senior treasury official, 'Count of the Sacred Largesses' (*comes sacrarum largitionum*), was appointed to deal with financial matters including mints, the collection of taxes in coin, arms factories and donatives to the army, while the *comes rei privatae* handled revenues and expenditures not controlled by the praetorian prefects. Zosimus strongly criticized the emperor's taxation policy, thinking that there were too many taxes:

> He did not even allow poor prostitutes to escape. The result was that as each fourth year came round when this tax had to be paid, weeping and wailing were heard throughout the city, because beatings and tortures were in store for those who could not pay owing to extreme poverty. Indeed mothers sold their children and fathers prostituted their daughters under compulsion to pay the exactors of the *chrysargyron*. (2.38)

The government resorted to compulsion and forbade tenant farmers to leave their estates, to ensure that sufficient numbers of people were available to carry out duties and obligations in local communities and to till the fields. The issue was complicated by the fact that Christian clergy were exempted from the expensive task of serving on town councils; so many had the idea of seeking holy orders in order to avoid this onerous obligation that Constantine had to limit the ordination of new clergy to cases where there was a genuine vacancy, for example through death. Despite the criticisms of Constantine, in many ways he seemed to be carrying on the policies of Diocletian, and like many emperors he did try to stop corruption, though this was often frustrated by dishonest officials.

The administrative structure was now increasingly elaborate – the *magister officiorum* was in charge of the secretariats, of which there were three major sections under the direction of the *magister libellorum* (petitions) and the *magister epistularum* (letters), which shows the emperor in his traditional role as a centre for advice and redress in direct dialogue with his subjects; in the third section the *magister memoriae* seems to have been a legal official also perhaps responsible for imperial dealings with foreign peoples. Constantine's rule confirmed the removal of senators from military command, and now provincial governors dealt only with civil administration. But Constantine treated the senate and its members with respect and in the first place created many new senators without any obligation to live in Rome. He was prepared to use senators in important posts, including governorships and the prefecture of Rome. An inscription from Rome set up by a slave, for example, honours his senatorial master: 'In honour of Fabius Titianus, most distinguished man, governor of Flaminia and Picenum (regions of Italy), consular governor of Sicily, proconsul of the province of Asia, judge of the imperial court, companion (*comes*) of the first rank, ordinary consul (AD 337), prefect of the city' (AD 339–41) (*ILS* 1227).

Of the two important groups in society who potentially had a role to play in the administration, senators remained as a distinct group who would have claimed an aristocratic pedigree by birth. But there were also those who, often from a more lowly or equestrian background, held imperial office and were part of the court closely based around the emperor. Constantine made use of both if he thought that they were of value in carrying out his wishes and policies, and also promoted deserving men to the senatorial order. The importance of attendance on the emperor is shown by the role of the *comites*, who were directly descended from the *amici principis* ('friends of the emperor') of the early empire, and who literally accompanied the emperor wherever he went as part of the court, whether holding formal office or not. Constantine gradually made this into a more regimented structure by dividing the *comites* into first, second and third rank, the first rank being reserved for senior officials. A *comes* could be sent on a special task, for example, to govern a diocese. Men of equestrian rank were digni-fied by titles; the praetorian prefect was exclusively 'most eminent' (*vir eminen-tissimus*), lesser officials in the provinces were 'most perfect' (*vir perfectissimus*).

Constantine followed the usual imperial policy of protecting and enhancing the status of cities (though pagan writers thought that he had failed in this), which still formed the essential framework of Roman administration, and the elite groups who ran them:

> Imperator Caesar Flavius Constantinus Augustus. . . . Everything that serves to protect human society we take care of with sleepless concern; but the greatest task for our providence is to ensure that all the cities distinguished by beauty and appearance in the eyes of all the provinces and regions, should not only preserve their previous honour but be moved to an even higher status through the gift of our munificence. (*ILS* 705; Lewis and Reinhold, vol. II (1990), p. 579, from Hispellum in Umbria)

Constantine and Christianity

During his final illness Galerius had issued an edict in April 311 admitting that previous actions against Christians had been unsuccessful; he therefore decided to allow Christians to worship in their traditional way and to pray to their own God for the emperor's well-being. This suggested that the government had accepted that the Christian God had real power and was worth supplicating. This is the context in which we have to assess the conversion of Constantine. He was later to say to Eusebius (*Life of Constantine* 28) that some weeks before the battle of the Milvian bridge in 312 he had seen a vision of a Cross outlined against the sun and the words 'conquer by this'. Later he had a dream in which Christ appeared to him and instructed him to make a standard in the form of a Cross. Yet there was no agreement on this among Christian writers, and Lactantius says that Constantine had a dream immediately before the battle in which he was ordered to place on his soldiers' shields the symbol chi-rho (standing for the first two letters of Christ's name in Greek – Christos), though it is possible that the letters stood for 'good luck' (Greek *chrestos*). The soldiers did perhaps have such a symbol (as well presumably as many others) on their shields, but the dream may be a later Christian invention. There were also earlier claims that Constantine had seen a vision of the sun god accompanied by Victory with the figure XXX to indicate the years of his rule.

These events are controversial, but it would be unwise to say that the whole episode of Constantine's conversion owes more to cynical political considerations than to genuine belief of some kind, since it was no great advantage to him to declare for Christianity as only a small proportion of the empire's population was Christian and they tended to be from the lower social classes. Most of the senate and the officers of the army were pagan, as were the rank-and-file soldiers. There is some evidence of Christianity in the family of Constantius I. Constantine had a sister named Anastasia ('Resurrection'), and he had already expressed toleration of Christianity. Of course, he may have shared the general religious feeling of the age, perhaps thinking that in the civil war he could not afford to leave out any divine assistance; the Christian God was one of his supporters among several in the defeat of Maxentius against superior numbers. Constantine may genuinely have believed in the power of this God without necessarily understanding all the consequences of being a believer, such as putting aside all other deities. Did he fully grasp or apply its ethical teaching? That is doubtful, even allowing for the spirit of the times. Eusebius discreetly avoids mentioning the embarrassing fact that the emperor apparently executed his own son Crispus and also put to death his wife Fausta (boiled to death in her bath), though the whole episode remains mysterious. Hostile pagan writers claimed that he became a Christian in remorse in order to find forgiveness for his crimes.

Subsequently, Constantine tolerated the worship of other gods, and indeed he placed emphasis on the unconquered sun god and issued coins celebrating him until 320–21. The gold medallions specially struck to celebrate the summit meeting of Constantine and Licinius at Milan in 313 depict the heads of Constantine and the sun side by side. In 321 he laid down that on 'the revered day of the Sun' lawcourts and workshops should be closed and the population should rest. Here, Sunday as a day of rest is not associated specifically with Christianity but with the unconquered sun. Other symbols of traditional pagan gods such as Mars and Jupiter continued on the coinage and the emperor could have intervened to prevent this had he wished. Towards the end of his reign, between 333 and 337, Constantine accepted a temple in Italy at Hispellum to his Flavian family:

> At its heart (of Hispellum), as is your wish, we desire that a temple of the Flavian, that is, our family, be erected in magnificent style, on this one condition, that a temple dedicated to our name should not be polluted by the deceptions of contagious superstition. (*ILS* 705; Lewis and Reinhold, vol. II, 1990, p. 580)

He presumably meant that there should be no blood sacrifices. Furthermore, he continued to consult soothsayers, for example in cases where part of the imperial palace had been struck by lightning. There is some ambivalence here, also detectable in the phraseology used in the dedication by the senate of the arch in his honour (in 315), which vaguely ascribes his divine support to 'the inspiration of the divinity' ('instinctu divinitatis'; above, p. 217). It is also true that Constantine did not receive baptism until shortly before his death on 22 May 337, though this was not an unusual practice at the time, in order to avoid the taint of sin.

Constantine naturally espoused the traditional attributes and standing of previous emperors (he was after all Augustus), but sought to present the imperial position in a Christian context. Certainly from 312 onwards he consistently supported Christianity. In the winter of 312–13 he wrote several letters to the bishop of Carthage and to Anullinus, governor of Africa. To the bishop he expressed his decision to subsidize the Church by using public funds to pay the clergy of the 'lawful and most holy Catholic Church'. To the governor he emphasized the importance of restoring Church property, but then went further:

> Whereas from many considerations it appears that the annulment of the worship in which the highest reverence of the most holy heavenly power is maintained has brought the greatest dangers upon the state, and the lawful revival and protection of this same worship has caused the greatest good fortune of the Roman name and exceptional prosperity to all the affairs of men … (Eusebius, *History of the Church* 10.7)

The emperor has clearly moved to associate the worship of the Christian God with the success of the Roman Empire, implying that the God is all-powerful.

Also in 313, after a meeting in Milan and during the campaign against Maximinus in the east, Licinius issued an important edict in his name and that of Constantine, permitting freedom of worship to everyone in the empire: 'No person should be denied the opportunity of devoting himself either to the cult of the Christians or to whatever religion he felt most suitable for himself.' This went some way towards establishing the legal status of the Church and of paganism, and bishops were to acquire new political and legal functions. Constantine continued to issue legislation in support of Christians, such as legalizing bequests to the Church in 321; branding of convicts in the face was banned in 316 since: 'the face, which is formed in the likeness of the heavenly beauty, may not be disfigured'.

He ended certain penalties and restrictions that had first been placed on the celibate and childless by Augustus. He may simply have been attempting to redefine familial social practice, though Eusebius claimed that it was intended to foster celibacy and virginity in a Christian context. One result, whether intended or not, was to open the way for the ascetic lifestyle favoured by some Christians, who could withdraw from the world. Furthermore, rich individuals with no family might tend to leave their wealth to the Church.

Constantine lavished subsidies, gifts and grants of immunity on the Church. He also built churches emphasizing his devotion to Christianity; between 312 and

325 many churches were built in Rome, notably the Lateran Basilica (now St John Lateran) built on the site of the barracks of the old praetorian mounted guard. St Peter's was built on the Vatican Hill on the site of an ancient tomb allegedly holding the bones of St Peter. These churches were adorned with gifts, and estates were set aside to provide income for their upkeep. For the adornment of the Constantine Basilica:

> Presented to the holy Font:
> the estate of Festus [chief of the imperial bedchamber, given by the emperor Constantine], territory of Praeneste, revenue 300 *solidi*
> the estate Gaba, territory of Gabii, revenue 202 *solidi*
> the estate Pictas, same territory, revenue 205 *solidi* (nine more estates in Italy and nine in the provinces). (*Book of Pontiffs* 34, translated by Davis, 1989)

Churches were constructed in Jerusalem and the Holy Land, notably the Church of the Holy Sepulchre, dedicated in 335 and richly decorated. Constantine's mother Helena also went on a pilgrimage to the east and founded churches, beginning a long Christian tradition of Holy Land pilgrimage that has persisted to the present day; later tradition had it that she found a piece of the True Cross. The design of churches was often in the shape of the traditional assembly building (basilica) in use in Rome, with a long rectangular building sometimes with side aisles, terminating in a semicircular apse.

Constantine came to immerse himself in Christian doctrine too, which was to have enormous significance for the future since it linked Church and State together, even if the emperor did not intend this. He intervened in disputes within Christianity and took it upon himself to find a means of solving them so that the bishops looked to him, had ready access to him, and came in a way to depend upon him. This was the origin of the long and undistinguished history of government interference in what people believe. Previous emperors had in the main dealt only with what people did. Constantine encountered the difficulties right away in Africa where a dispute was raging between the Donatists – a group that followed one Donatus who took a tough stance on allowing back clergy who had handed over the Holy Scriptures in the Great Persecution – and the Orthodox, or 'Catholics'. Constantine supported the Orthodox clergy (hence the language of the letters quoted above), persecuted the Donatists, and unsuccessfully tried to resolve the issue by calling a Church council at Arles. In fact, the Donatists in one form or another survived as a rural resistance until the Arab conquest. A more serious doctrinal issue arose over the question of the correct date for Easter, and the view of Arius, a priest from Alexandria, who questioned the relation of God the Son to God the Father, holding that the Son must be secondary to the Father. Once again, in a search for Church unity Constantine summoned the council of Nicaea in 325 and allegedly himself proposed the famous definition (*homoousios* – 'of one substance') that permitted a compromise to be reached, which Eusebius himself signed despite his sympathy for Arius. This provided the essential basis for the Nicene Creed, crucial in the development of Christian worship. Those who declined to sign were exiled. The matter did not end there. Within a few years Arius was allowed back and his chief opponent, Athanasius, bishop of Alexandria, was exiled and the furious controversy was to continue beyond the life of Constantine. According to Eusebius, at the council Constantine gave a patient audience to all the dissenting voices, and:

> The result was that they were not only united in respect of the faith, but also that the time for the celebration of the proper feast of Easter was agreed on by everyone. Furthermore, those points that were agreed by the resolution of the entire body were put in writing, and received the signature of each individual member. Then the emperor, believing that he had in this way obtained a second victory over the enemy of the Church, proceeded to hold a triumphal festival in honour of God. (*Life of Constantine* 3.14)

He also took to preaching to his court, reminding them of the power of God in life. However, Eusebius says that his audience was little disposed to learn and while shouting loud approval ignored the emperor's homily.

Constantine's Legacy

Constantine's activities confirmed the essential framework for the operation of the state and dictated the agenda for many future developments, raising issues that remained important throughout the fourth century. Foremost among these was the question of 'Church and State', in particular the legal position of the 'Church within the State', the role of the bishops and the Church hierarchy, and the emperor's place in all this; the shifting tides of orthodoxy, heresy and Church politics added another level of complication to the social and political history of the fourth century. Nevertheless, the Nicene Creed (325) is still the fundamental statement of Christianity and is Constantine's most enduring legacy. Second, the detailed administrative structure continued to develop, with senior officials grouped round the emperor at court and layers of administration spreading out to the provinces; this emperor-centred system had less local initiative and ever-encroaching central control. Constantinople was destined for a leading place in history as the New Rome after the fall of the western empire, and then as the centre of the Byzantine Empire. But in 337, although a source of strength as a formidable stronghold and communications and administrative centre, the city was also a source of possible tension between the eastern and western parts of the empire. Third, Constantine left a strong and successful army, but there were two crucial problems, principally the role of a sole emperor with his field army, though perhaps supported by his sons as Caesars, and local forces of lesser quality permanently stationed in the provinces; this would not work in the long run without strong dynastic unity. There was also the constant pressure of manpower and the need for recruits; this is related to the admission of foreign peoples into the empire in ever-increasing numbers with the intention of settling them as potential soldiers. Ultimately this was to raise the question: What was a Roman soldier? These issues also underpin ongoing themes of social and economic history and culture. Everything in the fourth century took place against a background of virtually endless war, with the threat of the Persians in the east and the movement of peoples beyond the Rhine and the Danube. The context was one of uncertainty and change, most of it unwelcome, and the role of individual emperors was still important, since the whim of an autocrat remained all-powerful, often inspiring change even if there is no clear explanation of the reason.

The dynastic rivalry between Constantine's three surviving sons was also part of his legacy. The rivalry undermined some of his work of reconstruction and led to civil war, in which Arianism and Athanasius, the frequently exiled bishop of Alexandria, played a subsidiary role. All three sons of Constantine took the title Augustus on his death, with Constantine II, his second son, becoming senior Augustus and ruling in Gaul, Britain and Spain. But after a dispute with Constans, the youngest son, he invaded Italy and was killed at Aquileia in 340; Constans, who had control of Italy, Africa and Illyricum, now moved into the other western provinces. In 341–42 he fought the Franks but in 350 was overthrown and perished at the hands of the usurper Magnentius, a senior general. Constantius II, third son of Constantine, had remained in the east in 337 to deal with the Persian threat, which he achieved by means of a limited war fought round city fortresses. But in 351 he marched to the west and defeated Magnentius at Mursa. Intending to concentrate his efforts in the east, he first installed his cousin Gallus as Caesar in Antioch, but later executed him on suspicion of treachery and replaced him in 355 with Julian, Gallus's brother (they were the children of the half-brother of Constantine). Constantius was a devotee of the Arian version of Christianity and made genuine efforts to achieve Church unity. His formal entry into Rome in 357 is brilliantly described by Ammianus, and most of all in his depiction of the impressively aloof and self-controlled demeanour of the emperor:

Therefore on being saluted Augustus with favourable shouts ... he showed himself just as steady and imperturbable as he normally appeared in the provinces. . . . Like an effigy he kept the gaze of his eyes straight ahead as if his neck were in a vice, did not move his face to the right or left, did not nod his head when a wheel jolted, and was not seen to spit or cover or wipe his mouth or nose or to move his hands. (16.10.10)

Faced with a rebellion by Julian, he died in 361 before he could confront him in battle. This depressing series of events shows not only the destructive impact of individual ambition, but also the weakness of dynastic succession, especially against a background where one man was attempting to rule the entire empire alone in an unstable military situation.

Julian the Apostate

We are particularly well informed about the reign of Julian (r. 361–63) and the sequel, especially since the important history of Ammianus Marcellinus covers the period from 353 to 378 in great detail; he served as an officer in Julian's army in the invasion of Persia and was an eyewitness of many events during these years. Greek pagan writers, notably Eunapius and Zosimus, give a pro-Julian view, and Libanius of Antioch (a wealthy pagan scholar and orator who effectively expressed the conservative values of the eastern Greek city elites) was a great admirer and delivered a funeral oration for the emperor. Much information also comes from Christian writers, but Julian aroused strong feeling on both sides and it is sometimes difficult to get a clear picture. However, we have more written by Julian than by any other emperor, including letters, essays, hymns, orations and satirical pieces; it is a sign of his intelligence, learning and energy that he wrote so much in a short life. It is indeed remarkable that his brief reign has left in some ways a greater mark than that of Theodosius the Great.

Julian had had a traumatic upbringing and after the murder of his father in 337 he was put under the tutelage of an Arian bishop by Constantius II, and for six years was kept secluded on an imperial estate in Cappadocia. Well thought of as an intelligent pupil by his religious mentors, he also read the classical authors, coming to appreciate Neoplatonic philosophy, and eventually convinced himself of the validity of the traditional pagan gods, either sincerely or because he believed that this was the best way to preserve the classical tradition. Plotinus in the mid-third century had developed Plato's philosophy, and in the works of Iamblichus of Chalcis in Syria (died c.325) metaphysical speculation had been integrated with pagan theology. This perhaps offered a kind of intellectual basis for Julian's subsequent treatment of Christianity and other religious cults. Julian

may also have turned towards theurgy, which expressed a quasi-mystical relationship between the material and spirit worlds, so advancing the symbiosis of
the human with the divine soul. For the moment he seems to have concealed his
religious views, and when in 355 he was elevated to the position of Caesar by
Constantius II he had responsibility for Gaul and Britain; he was also to be
married to the emperor's sister Helena. Constantius appointed his senior staff
and gave him a kind of handwritten rule book, 'just as if he was sending a stepson
away to school' (Ammianus 16.5.3). However, this may simply reflect the fact
that Julian, as deputy of Constantius, was inexperienced.

Between 356 and 359 Julian conducted a series of successful campaigns along
the Rhine, winning the battle of Strasbourg in 357 against the Alamanni, demonstrating his military capability and also building up a strong relationship with the
army. In 361 his army mutinied against an order from Constantius for the transfer
of units to the east and declared Julian Augustus; in the traditional German way
the soldiers raised him up on a shield. There is no clear indication that this revolt
was planned by Julian several years in advance. Constantius's timely death
avoided a civil war and Julian was able to take possession of Constantinople
unopposed. He was now free to reveal his pagan sympathies and this had an
impact on Church and State. He demonstrated the intellectual basis for his policies in his many literary works, and in his satires poked fun at Constantine, who
he said could find only Jesus in heaven prepared to forgive him for, among other
things, murdering his firstborn Crispus and his wife Fausta.

In his short but eventful reign Julian proclaimed full religious toleration and
then took steps to promote pagan cults by restoring temples and ensuring that
pagan priesthoods were filled in the cities. He did not endorse any persecution of
Christians (since he did espouse toleration and did not want another parade of
Christian martyrs), but he was probably apt to discriminate against them in
promoting people in his service, and in any case he pruned the imperial
entourage. He then deprived Christian churches of the financial assistance and
privileges that Constantine had granted and ended imperial-sponsored church
building. Believing that Hellenic culture and Hellenic religion were a unity,
Julian banned the teaching of classical literature and philosophy by Christian
scholars, ordering them instead to teach the Gospels of Matthew and Luke.

Julian was keen to maintain the traditional social and administrative structure
represented by the cities, which he tried to revive; he reorganized their finances,
he converted to a voluntary gift the golden wreath usually given by cities on the
accession of an emperor, which had become virtually a regular tax, and removed
restrictions on membership of local councils. These eminently practical measures
can be contrasted with his strange idea of rebuilding the great Jewish Temple at
Jerusalem. He seemingly had no particular interest in the Jews, and Ammianus

comments merely that he wanted to leave a great monument to his reign, but it is possible that he was planning to undermine Constantine's promotion of Jerusalem as a Christian centre and strike a blow against the Christians' culture and social eminence. It would of course disprove Christ's prophecy that not one stone would be left upon another. In any case the idea was abandoned because of unfavourable portents.

Julian's overall policy had intelligence and subtlety; he seems to have been attempting to create, on the model of Christianity that he had had ample opportunity to observe in his education, an organized structure for pagan worship based on a framework of priesthoods extending across the empire, a move to prevent the Christianization of education and to ensure that senior officials were appointed who could carry out his ideas. The problem was that his highly intellectual version of pagan practice was at variance with the simple observances of lower-class people, who made up the majority of pagans. At Antioch, for example, his austere way of life was fundamentally different from the pleasure-seeking Antiochenes. Furthermore, part of Julian's policy for reviving the cities was to compel local councillors to do their duty. To make matters worse, during Julian's visit to Antioch there was a famine and it is perhaps not surprising that he fell out with the local pagan elite who should have been his natural supporters. Although it seems unlikely that his plans could have achieved a mass reinvigoration of pagan worship, contemporary experienced observers like Ammianus and Libanius recognized him as a substantial figure in his own right, not just the wielder of absolute power.

Despite his energy and intelligence, Julian will always be remembered for his disastrous invasion of Persia in 363 and war against Sapor II, who had indeed been a long-term problem for Rome. The idea of inflicting a decisive defeat on the Persians and crippling their offensive capacity was not necessarily wrong but the campaign ran into serious difficulties and the emperor's decision to burn his river fleet and conduct a difficult march was probably a strategic blunder. Then in June 363 Julian was wounded, apparently by a mysterious stray shot, and died soon after. Since he left no heir, the empire was again left in the position of finding the strongest or the most cunning general to succeed him.

From Jovian to the Sack of Rome: The Pattern of Events

The immediate consequences of Julian's death were a weakened army and loss of some territory in the east, and the end of the officially sponsored pagan revival, as with the devout Jovian the Christians were back in an influential position. Jovian had been a senior officer on Julian's military staff, but he had little option in agreeing to an unfavourable deal with the Persians in 363. This included the surrender of the important border fortresses of Nisibis and Sinagara, which particularly distressed Ammianus, to extricate his army from a precarious situation. Jovian had little chance to improve on matters since in 364 he succumbed to fumes from a charcoal stove.

The rule of Valentinian I and Valens marks an important development in imperial politics, namely the de facto split between the empires of the east and of the west. In February 364 Valentinian, a senior military officer, was declared emperor by his colleagues and in the next month he proclaimed his younger brother Valens as his fellow Augustus. Valentinian took primary responsibility for the western areas and immediately restored the situation in Gaul, crushing the Alamanni in 364; he also reinstated defensive lines along both the Rhine and the Danube. A forceful and aggressive character, Valentinian mainly concerned himself with military affairs, and when Pannonia suffered a barbarian incursion he went in person and was so infuriated at the insolence of an embassy from the culprits that he suffered apoplexy and died in 375. In 367, after a serious illness he had taken the unusual step of proclaiming his eight-year-old son Gratian as his co-ruler. In a world dominated by charismatic military commanders, boy emperors were unlikely to have a long lifespan, and after Valentinian's death another younger son was proclaimed emperor as Valentinian II without Gratian's consent.

Meanwhile Valens had in 365 survived a revolt by Procopius, a relative of Julian, and initially defeated the Goths in 369 and protected Roman interests in the east through the work of his generals. Following a version of Arian Christianity, he hounded orthodox Catholics in the east, demonstrating first the reappearance of imperial interest in Church matters and second the elusive nature of Church unity. He is notorious, however, for the disastrous outcome of his dealings with the Goths, against whom he had fought a number of inconclusive wars. When this people fled from the Huns in 376, Valens allowed them to cross the Danube into Roman territory and then settle as separate ethnic groups, which were not properly absorbed into Roman society. In the long term this contributed to the undermining and eventual destruction of the empire in the west. When the Goths rebelled, Valens without waiting for reinforcements from Gratian marched against them and suffered a serious defeat at Adrianople on 9 August 378; he perished on the battlefield (his body was never recovered) and about two-thirds of his army were wiped out (perhaps 30,000–40,000 men). The defeat was not a complete catastrophe but it did serious long-term damage in loss of manpower and damage to Rome's military reputation. When Theodosius came to reassert Roman power in the area in the following year he did not have the resources to destroy the Goths completely, which would have been normal Roman policy.

Gratian made his headquarters at Milan; he rewarded his old tutor, Ausonius, with the position of praetorian prefect and firmly defended Christian interests. Perhaps persuaded by St Ambrose, bishop of Milan, he omitted the traditional

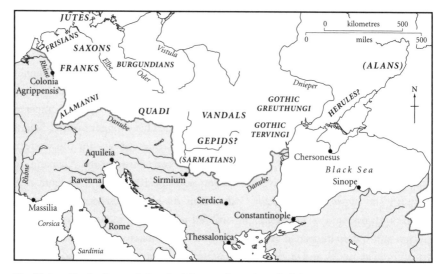

Map 10. Late Empire Germanic Peoples (after Heather, *The Fall of the Roman Empire* (2006), p. 81).

pontifex maximus from his imperial titles and removed the statue of Victory from the senate house in Rome. In an undistinguished reign his most important act was the appointment in 379 of Theodosius I as emperor in the east. Gratian was overthrown by Magnus Maximus, a successful military commander in Britain, who took over responsibility for Gaul and Spain as well. Maximus's position was initially recognized by Theodosius, but when he invaded Italy in 387 and expelled Valentinian II, Theodosius reacted by marching to Italy and defeating him twice in battle; Maximus was executed in 388.

Theodosius was the son of count Theodosius, who had been Valentinian's senior cavalry commander but was then executed in 376. His son had already embarked on a military career and after discreetly lying low was appointed in 378 by Gratian as *magister militum* (senior military commander) to sort things out after Adrianople, before next year being proclaimed Augustus for the eastern part of the empire, including the Danube. After a long and inconclusive struggle, Theodosius made an agreement with the Goths in 382 in which they were recognized as Roman allies and placed on lands in Thrace and Lower Moesia along the Danube. Negotiations with the Persians brought another treaty in 386, which provided for the partition of Armenia between the two empires. In the tradition of Augustus, he presented these diplomatic arrangements as grand military achievements. Theodosius then spent some time in the west after his successful campaign against Maximus and formally entered Rome as emperor in 389. Valentinian II was reinstated with responsibility for Gaul and the emperor's son Arcadius (declared Augustus in 383) was left temporarily in charge of the east.

Theodosius visited the east in 391 but returned to the western empire to put down the usurper Eugenius, who had taken over the role of Valentinian II after he had died in mysterious circumstances in 392. Arcadius remained in the east while the emperor's younger son Honorius was proclaimed Augustus in 393 and followed his father to the west. Theodosius won a great victory over Eugenius at the river Frigidus in 394 but died in January of 395. The dynastic idea prevailed and his sons Arcadius (eastern empire) and Honorius (western empire) succeeded him.

There was no formal split in the empire, however, and Stilicho (a Vandal), who effectively acted as regent for Honorius (the emperor successively married Stilicho's two daughters) and was the principal minister in west, tried to keep the empire together. He faced serious problems from marauding Visigoths led by Alaric, who had succeeded in uniting the Gothic peoples, had commanded the Gothic levy for Theodosius, and used threats, diplomacy and outright force to achieve a permanent settlement with Rome. When Alaric moved from the Balkans to Italy, Stilicho was able to block him in 402 in the hope of using him in the east. But Stilicho was beset with problems, particularly the usurper Constantine III, proclaimed by the soldiers in Britain, who tried to invade Italy in 409 and was recognized as emperor by Honorius before being defeated and executed. Stilicho tried to buy off Alaric, but the plan backfired when he was not paid and between 408 and 410 the Gothic leader besieged Rome three times, finally taking and sacking the city on 24 August 410. Honorius's half-sister Galla Placidia was captured by a Gothic chief, Athaulf, while the emperor resided undisturbed at Ravenna. Luckily for him, Alaric died soon after. In the east meanwhile, Arcadius (r. 395–408) did not give a strong coherent direction to policy, relying heavily on his court entourage and senior officials, particularly Rufinus and the eunuch Eutropius, who were mainly concerned in the early years in blocking the schemes of Stilicho.

Emperors, Generals and Armies

Throughout this period the empire faced a number of serious challenges; its survival in a recognizable form was a considerable achievement, but there were worrying indications for its long-term future. After the Tetrarchy many generals probably recognized that more than one emperor was needed to control the vast Roman territories against so many potential threats. But there was no clear pattern of succession and tension had emerged between dynastic succession within a family and the deliberate choice of the best, most respected soldier. Dynastic loyalty might contribute to stability but could produce child emperors, who fell under the influence of over-powerful and unpredictable mentors. In the west, imperial advisers often had a military character and were drawn from a coterie of generals, who tended to fight among themselves and encourage more usurpations. In the east, guidance more often came from high civil officials, which perhaps encouraged a more consistent, stable approach to government and helped the eastern empire to survive. This highlights the lingering threat that eastern and western parts of the empire might permanently split.

The empire had no respite from military problems, and occasional victories did not permanently solve the deteriorating strategic situation. Serious defeats like that at Adrianople in 378 not only had an immediate impact in the loss of manpower that was difficult to replace, but in the longer run undermined Rome's prestige and ability to influence other peoples without fighting battles. Not blessed with hindsight, the Roman government was unlikely to appreciate the serious changes taking place beyond the Danube, which they now regarded as their frontier. It was not unreasonable for them to think that they were dealing with a series of individual incursions that could be turned back piecemeal. In fact, large-scale economic shifts north of the Danube and a changing relationship between settled farmers and nomadic peoples were creating permanent instability. The Huns were a particular concern; they were Mongolian nomads and superb horsemen who had attacked the Gothic communities on the Black Sea in the 370s with the result that refugees started making their way across the Danube into Roman territory. The Romans characterized the Huns as dangerous savages, and even the experienced Ammianus was alarmed and vividly describes the barbaric lifestyle of men who did not live in houses: 'They are so ferocious that they do not need fire or tasty food, but eat wild roots and any kind of raw meat, which they warm by placing it between their thighs and the flanks of their horses' (31.2).

In the east the Sasanid Persians were persistently dangerous, and under aggressive kings like Sapor I and II and Narses were a direct threat to Roman interests and even important fortified Roman cities. Antioch, relatively distant from the action, had been captured in AD 260. Roman interest in the area was sustained by a variety of factors – a long tradition of warfare in the region, the cultural assumption of the inferiority of orientals going back to Alexander the Great, the established concept of a frontier along the Euphrates or Tigris, and important Roman concerns in Syria and Egypt. However, two relatively sophisticated empires meant that diplomacy was possible and in this way a certain balance could be maintained. Both sides sought allies from lesser peoples in the region. Another element was religion; although the Sasanids generally practised religious toleration, from time to time it was expedient for the Romans to stand up for the Christian population in Persia, as Constantine did in his letter to Sapor II. As late as the seventh century the emperor Heraclius was still fighting in Persia, keeping up this remarkable record of warfare. But at the opposite end of the empire, in Britain, the position deteriorated rapidly and after the usurper Constantine III had marched from Britain, even though he was defeated, Roman forces were seemingly withdrawn by Honorius and the cities were told to look out for themselves. Furthermore, the picture in the west grew bleaker with the undermining of Roman control in Spain and Africa. By 439 the Vandals had taken over the very rich area of northern Africa, which among other things was an important source of grain. The Romans were also losing control of Spain.

This survey raises fundamental questions about the quality and efficiency of the late Roman army and the major issue of the role of barbarian peoples in the army and the empire. Unfortunately, deficiencies in our sources make a clear answer impossible, and even the size of the army in the mid-fourth century is unclear. The increased use of barbarian allies (*foederati* – federates) presumably reflects the difficulty of keeping up army numbers, and it is unlikely that the figure of 645,000 given by Agathias can be accurate. Nevertheless, the army was still able to win important battles and the Romans were still capable of keeping large armies in the field; after all, Julian had 65,000 for the invasion of Persia in 363.

There is no reason to suppose that military generalship was defective; if anything, commanders were more experienced and better trained in war than in the high empire, when armies were in the hands of non-specialist senators and emperors did not necessarily have any military experience. The military framework remained intact in the west into the fifth century and of course much longer in the east. In fact, the military structure, which had been developed by Constantine, continued to work well with its strong field army (*comitatenses*), though increasingly composed of non-Romans, and troops assigned to frontier zones (*limitanei*), who had an important role and should not be dismissed as part-time soldiers. However, as explained above, the range of problems was more extensive and more persistent, and in particular the Romans could not rely on superiority in weaponry and the materials of war; their fabled *disciplina* and training might not be enough. Furthermore, relations with the local communities within the empire were not always clear-cut since the benefits of Roman rule were no longer quite so obvious, and in driving out barbarians the Romans did not always receive a welcome from the locals. The balance of power had shifted to the extent that dealing with incursions and hostile forces was not just a matter of direct military response in the old Roman way, but sometimes involved negotiation and concessions. At times the empire simply paid large sums of gold to barbarians to go away. This was potentially destructive but perhaps not as damaging as admitting barbarians to settle in the empire.

This practice was often connected to the army's constant need for manpower, and there was no doubt that many barbarians were good fighters. The Romans had always used non-Romans, originally for their specialist fighting techniques, and from the time of Augustus had recruited large numbers of non-citizens from the less Romanized parts of the empire as auxiliary troops. These troops received citizenship on discharge and were brought into the Roman way of life. To recruit soldiers from outside the empire or to settle barbarians in the expectation that they would provide soldiers can be seen as an extension of this, but was potentially dangerous. The Romans of course despised barbarian peoples as inherently uncivilized and outside their traditional culture. For example, Sidonius Apollinaris, who distinguished himself in literary and political life in the fifth century and became bishop of Clermont in 470, replied to Arbogastes, the Frankish count of Trier, who had written an eloquent Latin letter to him asking for a theological work. Sidonius noted rather patronizingly that although Arbogastes lived among barbarians he really was quite civilized, which he expressed as follows: 'Though you now drink the waters of the Moselle, the words you utter are those of the Tiber' (*Letters* 4.17.1).

He draws a vivid contrast between the civilized world of Italy represented by the Tiber and outsiders. Doubtless some foreign peoples were more acceptable than others. The Goths at least had been converted to Christianity. Bishop Ulfila, who followed the Arian teaching, had with the approval of Constantius II gone as a missionary among the Goths and translated the Bible into Gothic.

In 376 the Visigoths, threatened by the looming Huns, petitioned the emperor Valens for permission to settle in the empire in return for military service. He accepted their request, probably with an eye on large numbers of new soldiers and the opportunity of collecting revenue from Roman communities by commuting their requirement to supply recruits. The Visigoths were to be settled in the diocese of Thrace, but the whole process was bungled and the final outcome was the disastrous battle of Adrianople in 378. Then in 382 Theodosius concluded a peace treaty with the Goths, which apparently provided for their settlement as a group in Roman lands along the Danube; they were exempt from taxation, received a yearly payment, and served under their own chiefs, fighting as allies (federates) of the Romans. The Goths provided a large contingent for the army of Theodosius, perhaps as many as 20,000 men. This policy had disastrous consequences for the future, though Theodosius had limited options after Adrianople. The Goths lived as separate groups with no mingling or marriage with Roman communities and were not brought into the practices and customs of the empire. Furthermore, arguably a vital frontier was in the hands of people who had often penetrated it and made war on Rome. Unassimilated groups promoting their own culture within Roman society and with quasi-independent military resources were potentially damaging to the ideology of imperial unity and Roman identity, and the ability to sustain and defend the empire.

The tensions produced by the recruitment of barbarians appeared at all levels, and even holders of high office could incur suspicion and hostility because of their barbarian origins. Ammianus, commenting on the revolt in the reign of Constantius of the Frankish general Silvanus, who had been trying to restore order in Gaul subjected to the depredations of his own countrymen among others, noted that he could point to the distinguished career of his father Bonitus, *even though* he was a Frank (15.5.33). Even Stilicho, who was the senior adviser of Theodosius I, was subject to suspicion because of his Vandal background. And his dubious deals with Alaric, leader of the Visigoths, reveal the split loyalties and the ambiguity of the relationship; the government needed foreign military help, yet often feared and loathed the people who brought it. From 401 Stilicho had to fight several campaigns to drive Alaric's Visigoths out of northern Italy, but then made an agreement in which Alaric was appointed *magister militum* and subsequently offered a huge bribe to keep him in Roman service. But palace intrigue saw the murder of Stilicho in 408, after which regular Roman troops in north Italy seized the opportunity and massacred the families of the federates recruited by Stilicho, with the result that over 30,000 of these troops defected to Alaric and helped him in his attack on the city of Rome. In the east, meanwhile, the Gothic leader Gainas had become very influential with Arcadius and began to threaten Constantinople with his troops in 399, but there was strong opposition from the inhabitants and in 400 they massacred 7,000 Goths by setting fire to the church in which they had taken refuge. The outcome of this appalling violence was that the government in Constantinople was wary of using large numbers of foreign recruits and managed to keep control of the military more effectively than in the west. However, on the whole, more damage was done to the military efficiency of Roman forces by civil war and disruption brought about by the rivalry and ambition of generals than by the disloyalty of federates, who fought reasonably well and in general did not desert in significant numbers even when fighting other barbarians.

Government and Revenues

At the top presided the emperor, the centre of authority, who had to control the workings of the administration and the behaviour of officials, yet also take command of the army, be militarily competent, and satisfy the soldiers and commanders. He was increasingly an object of adulation, and might offer his purple robe for favoured courtiers to kiss. His presence or his actions were greeted with fulsome chants and acclamations. When the Theodosian Code (all laws issued from AD 312 had been collected by order of Theodosius) was presented to the senate in Rome in 438, it was received with 352 acclamations of the emperors such as:

'The Augusti of the Augusti, greatest of the Augusti!' (repeated eight times)
'God gave you to us, may God preserve you for us!' (repeated twenty-seven times)
'Hope in you, safety in you!' (repeated twenty-six times)
'Dearer than our children, dearer than our parents!' (repeated sixteen times)
'Destroyers of informers, destroyers of false charges!' (repeated twenty-eight times)

Below the emperor was a hierarchical system in which rank depended on the office held. Those at the top were the *illustres*, next came the *spectabiles*, and then the *clarissimi*; the last term had been the designation of a senator, previously the most prestigious position in society, but it was no longer enough just to be a senator.

The apparatus of government and tax collection became increasingly complex. By the early fifth century the civil service employed about 35,000 personnel and was itself a financial burden as members of local councils sought government jobs, thus removing themselves from their duties and financial responsibilities in local communities, and in a vicious circle endangering the collection of taxes. Imperial legislation from 389 attempted to ensure that local obligations were fulfilled by stopping people holding higher office (*Cod. Theod.* 12.1.120). The administrators seem to have interfered more and more to keep the system moving.

The sheer quantity of late Roman legislation from Constantine onwards is impressive and reflects the initiating role of the emperor. Some of it strikes us as restrictive, if not increasingly totalitarian, for example in dealing with the tenant farmers (*coloni*) who were forbidden to move off the land and to some extent were equated with slaves. In a decision relating to the diocese of Thrace, Theodosius ruled that:

Even though *coloni* may appear to be freeborn, they shall still be considered to be slaves of the soil where they were born and they shall not have the power to go where they choose or to change their residence, but the owners of the land shall exercise over them the rights and care of patrons and the authority of masters. (*CJ* 11.52(51).1)

Men in other occupations were also constrained: for example, a law of 369 forbade members of the association of rag-pickers to go away surreptitiously to a municipal council, and threatened a penalty on the association unless it lodged a complaint about the withdrawal (*Cod. Theod.* 14.8.2). It is likely, however, that there was a contrast between legislative ambition and the reality of successful execution, and we know that in the early empire imperial orders often had to be repeated. Despite the census of the empire's resources, the government was often ill-informed about its poorer citizens and its responsibility was limited to hand-outs in big cities like Rome and Constantinople. Rich landholders could some-times seem to offer more immediate and valuable support as patrons, and they might also want to recruit workers for their estates.

The military and civil administration continued to become more elaborate; the military command of field-army units was shared between six regional *magistri equitum* and *magistri peditum* reporting directly to the emperor. *Magister equitum praesentalis* and *magister peditum praesentalis* were senior positions commanding the cavalry and infantry of the field army and actually attending the emperor's person. Some very powerful individuals like Stilicho combined these positions as *magister utrius militiae* ('commander of both military arms'). Important civilian positions in addition to those already mentioned (p. 221) were the *cubicularius* (usually a eunuch in charge of the emperor's bedchamber and to some extent of access to him); the praetorian prefect (with judicial responsibilities and supervi-sion of provincial governors); the *quaestor* (drafting new laws); the *magister scrin-iorum* (answering legal questions); the *primicerius notariorum* (directing the palace secretaries); and the *magister officiorum* (collecting information relating to domestic and foreign business).

The maintenance of the military structure and payments to barbarians required a constant stream of revenue, particularly gold. A large part of the administrative structure was designed to ensure that taxes were collected, though of course that structure was itself very expensive to maintain. Imperial govern-ment took place in the context of an economic outlook that, although uncertain, was not entirely gloomy, despite continuing inflation and special problems in some areas. There were, of course, enormous discrepancies in wealth in this period, and the grand style in which some senators lived cannot be taken as indicative of the empire's economic performance. But it is significant that Symmachus had nineteen residences and estates in Italy, Sicily and north Africa. Rich and powerful men might become more effective than the state and facilitate the emergence of warlords who could support private armies. Many large estates in troubled times were concentrated in single hands and reached a size where they were almost self-sufficient and traded with one another, which may have reduced the need for open markets. This was more the case in the west where the vast senatorial estates tended to act as a constraint on the imperial government, while in the east the government could control and command more of the resources.

Many slaves still existed and became available through the frequent battles with invading tribes; they probably worked in the fields alongside free labour, where, as noted above, the *coloni* were increasingly restricted in their movements. Local trading conditions will have been affected by the need for distributions to the people in Rome and Constantinople, for which corn from Egypt and Africa was levied as part of their taxes; at Constantinople distributions were made by tickets to 80,000 people on the list, and the tickets were hereditary and saleable. Oil and pork were also distributed at Rome as well as wine at a reduced price, all of which were collected from Italy. All this meant a stagnant market in some respects, but not all; for example, there is evidence of a population increase in Africa and in the Near East, and some cities flourished. Antioch, the home town of Libanius, who writes as if it was the centre of the Roman world, was indeed a vibrant and wealthy place where extensive trading and numerous skilled crafts were carried on.

Church and Society

Amid the major economic problems, inflation and the inequalities of wealth, the place of the Christian Church in government and society continued to be very challenging for contemporaries at a number of levels. At the top of society there was the question of the structure of the Church, the role of bishops and their relationship with the emperor, and the empire he represented in respect of Church affairs, doctrine and the emperor's behaviour and policy. The relationship between Ambrose, bishop of Milan, and Theodosius I certainly catches the eye. Ambrose accepted the separation of Church and State when it suited him, appearing on one occasion in the imperial Consistory, or council, to plead against the surrender of a church to the Arians, but on another occasion declining to attend on the grounds that theological matters were beyond the remit of the Consistory. But he maintained a close relationship with the emperor and bullied him on a number of religious issues. For example, in 388 he succeeded in having the emperor reverse his instruction to rebuild a synagogue at Callinicum torn down in a Christian riot, and in 390 famously refused the emperor communion until he did penance because he had ordered the massacre of thousands of people at Thessalonica to avenge the death of one of his generals. Ambrose may also have influenced Theodosius in his anti-pagan stance, which in 391 saw the passing of a law closing temples and forbidding pagan cult practices. Ambrose supported this stance, opposing Symmachus's proposal for the restoration of the Altar of Victory to the senate house in Rome in 384. The Christian Church was now clearly part of the rhythms of imperial government and power. The emperor also took rigorous action against Christian heretics. As a strong supporter of the Nicene Creed (325), he was at one with Ambrose in his opposition to Arianism, and in 380 issued a constitution declaring the true Catholic faith as the official religion of the state.

The battle of wills between Theodosius and Ambrose offers a new outlook on government and raises again the issue of Caesaropapism, namely the imperial control of the Church and the implication of counter-influence from the clergy. But this has been exaggerated, and much depended on the status and inclinations of individual emperors and the mindset of the prominent Church leaders. Theodosius was a naturally pious man who had been baptized early and was probably susceptible to persuasive theological arguments put by Ambrose, who was a powerful character, highly educated and experienced in administration. Although Theodosius's reign does mark a step forward in the association of Church and State, which is reflected in the reaction of historians (the emperor was admired by the Christians Socrates and Sozomen, but hated by the pagan Eunapius), it did not necessarily establish a blueprint guiding future relations.

One factor in the increasing power of the Church was its accumulated property and wealth, acquired through imperial benefaction, bequests and profitable ventures (which is not surprising since most bishops came from the wealthy upper classes and knew about finance). The Church was then able to take on the role of a charitable institution, and the interest it took in the lowly people of the empire, not to speak of women, gradually brought about a change in the outlook of late Roman society. This concern for the poor and downtrodden with gifts of money and clothes (and also the ransoming of prisoners) was a noble aspect of Christian teaching, and differentiated Christian charity from the earlier civic euergetism so common among the upper classes. In third-century Rome the Church was responsible for 1,800 widows, orphans and poor. Porphyry, bishop of Gaza in the late fourth century, arranged regular distributions of money to the needy and in his will ensured that this continued after his death. Other wealthy people sold up part of their estates for the benefit of the Church. On the other hand, Christianity showed no interest in criticizing the institution of slavery or moving from the injunction: 'Slaves, be obedient to those that are your masters according to the flesh, with fear and trembling . . .' (*Ephesians* 6.5).

Upper-class women were prominent in the role of benefactors, and to some extent could seek a kind of liberation in the Church, by rejecting the conventions of marriage and subservience to a husband, by going on pilgrimage, and by following the ascetic lifestyle and cultivating virginity. Jerome (scholar, ascetic and priest who began translating the scriptures that formed the Latin version of the Bible, the Vulgate) famously celebrated Marcella, a high-born Roman who had become an ascetic and delighted in the divine Scriptures, and who, during the sack of Rome by the Visigoths in 410, calmly defied the soldiers who burst into her house demanding gold, and protected her female companion (*Letter* 127). However, in terms of marriage and family life, women probably found the traditions of the early empire continuing, although emperors did try to prevent the ancient custom of exposing unwanted children. Negative feeling against women remained in the writings of Christian theologians, who regarded sex as dangerous and potentially destructive of the holy life and saw women as a seductive distraction, however valuable their financial donations might be. Against this background should be seen the vigorous debate at the end of the fourth century over the nature of the virginity of the Virgin Mary, who was destined to be a great solace for women in a Church dominated by men. It is interesting that in the fifth-century basilica of Santa Maria Maggiore the Virgin is depicted with the dress and accoutrements of a Roman Augusta. The Council of Ephesus in 431 was to debate the nature of the Virgin's virginity, which had important implications for the question of the Incarnation.

The influence of the Christian Church affected society in other ways. Holy men and ascetics became increasingly common and had influence; they were not regarded merely as deluded zealots. Hermits often lived individually in the desert and some became known as the Desert Fathers; many were semi-literate, but others like Evagrius Ponticus were highly educated. Egypt saw the first organization of the novel institution of monasteries and eventually in some communities monastic rule was established, which was to become very influential. Monasticism spread to Syria and Judaea, and well-off women competed to set up monasteries in the Holy Land based on the running of the traditional household. Furthermore, holy pilgrimage assumed greater importance in the lives of those who could afford to travel. Constantine's mother Helena had set the pattern in 326 by her visit to Jerusalem, and many followed. The Spanish nun Egeria set out in 384 on a journey to the Holy Land, helped by bishops and monks, and also by the state with military escorts where necessary. The number of visitors may have had a considerable economic impact since they will have required accommodation and supplies, and the usual apparatus of tourism in all ages – souvenirs.

Although Christianity brought many unusual features to the Roman world, it was linked directly to pagan society in many respects, not least in education and the classical tradition. The combination and sometimes clash of ideas contributed to the vibrant cultural life of the late empire, which shows the upper classes involved with their traditional pursuits and not obsessed with invasions or economic decline. Education makes an enormous contribution to the cultural identity of a people, and throughout the first three centuries of the imperial period it was the traditional Graeco-Roman education that had produced stability and continuity. This ideology was less static in the late empire, but for the rich an education based on rhetoric and the reading of the classical authors was fundamental. Rhetoric, with perhaps also instruction in law and philosophy, was essential not only in politics and administration, but also in Church affairs, as we can see from the huge number of sermons and very learned commentaries written about biblical texts and their interpretation. In fact, there was no clear dividing line between pagan and Christian culture and no specifically Christian education, although some Christians did have problems with the context of classical literature in pagan culture. Many

Christian theologians were well schooled in classical authors and had common ground with the pagan aristocracy who had no religious axe to grind but merely sought to continue living in security. The more thoughtful might dabble in the intellectual paganism represented by Neoplatonism. At the highest level Christian and pagan debate would not be accessible to the masses. Similarly in art, Christian ideas could be presented in a classical style, and the respect for the artistic and literary traditions associated with Greece and Rome set both Roman pagans and Christians apart from barbarian immigrants. Civilized intercourse between pagans and Christians was disturbed from time to time by pagan-inspired persecution, as under Julian, or Christian aggression and occasional heavy-handed government interference, such as trials for participation in magic and divination under Constantius II (Ammianus 19.12), and Theodosius's measures to close temples and prevent cult practices.

For the mass of the population recreation centred on the cities, which apart from the obvious benefits of government handouts and the charitable efforts of churches, provided the games and shows that had been popular in the high empire. In fact, in 342 Constans established in a letter to the Prefect of Rome that the abolition of pagan superstition did not involve the destruction of temples outside the walls: 'Since the origin of many of the games, chariot races, and contests arose from many of these, it is not right that those places be destroyed, from which the celebration of ancient pleasures is provided to the Roman people' (*Cod. Theod.* 16.10.3). The Circus Maximus in Rome, the Hippodrome in Constantinople and smaller stadia in other cities offered chariot-racing where the four teams – the greens, the blues, the reds and the whites – still inspired partisan loyalty and enthusiastic betting. Gladiators continued to fight for the enjoyment of spectators despite the disapproval of churchmen and the efforts of emperors to curtail them; beast-hunts were also popular as well as theatrical shows and all this entertainment was now supplemented by Christian religious festivals. Popular emotion was no less inhibited in the later empire, and groups could quickly stir up feeling as can be seen in the notorious riot at Antioch in 387 over food shortages and the rate of tax. Government reaction was swift, troops were brought in, many rioters were executed, and Theodosius demoted Antioch in status. Some local councillors were put on trial, but amid widespread resentment and appeals to the emperor they were eventually released. It was at public spectacles that ordinary people could still express opinions, and the Church was now another diplomatic channel to the emperor to protect local interests. In this, bishops and clergy were supplementing the role of the rich local elites as the later empire developed and adapted to changing circumstances, with a greater element of cultural diversity. It does not seem that this society or government ever lost the confidence, flexibility or inventiveness that had characterized the best of Roman government.

The Fall of the Western Empire, 410 to 476

The sack of Rome in 410 is one of the famous landmark dates in ancient history. In a cool historical evaluation it was less catastrophic than it seems at first sight, but nevertheless it had an enormous impact on the thinking classes. It certainly influenced Augustine of Hippo in writing his *City of God*, composed between 413 and 426 (he died in 430), in which he discussed the relationship of the secular to the religious and in particular the position of the Church within the state. He gives a Christian view of historical development and on a personal level explains the significance of man's sinful nature, which requires God's grace for forgiveness, and also denigrates the idea of free will. This was to have great influence on Christian thinking. In some respects the work has an air of foreboding; even the glorious past of Rome had seen many disasters, and the Christian state would also endure a time of trial; Augustine needed to explain to believers why God had permitted the sack of Rome. The trial was not long in coming. In the west traditional Roman authority declined rapidly. Although Honorius made an effort to restore authority by sending Constantius to deal with the usurper Constantine III in 410 the Burgundians got their own kingdom *c.*412 in Upper Germany on Roman territory, demonstrating the virtual breakdown of Roman control in parts of Gaul. Meanwhile the Gothic chief Athaulf married Honorius's half-sister Galla Placidia and seized southern Gaul in 412; in a way this symbolized the increasing mingling of Germans with local inhabitants. After the murder of Athaulf in 415 his successor Wallia returned Placidia to Honorius and operated in Spain generally in Rome's interests, the reward for which was a grant of land in south-west Gaul. Placidia then agreed to marry the general Constantius and in 419 produced a son, Valentinian. When Constantius died soon after, there was a family quarrel and the unfortunate Placidia fled to Theodosius II in the east.

Theodosius II had become emperor in 408 at the age of seven and was generally under the influence of his sister, wife and various ministers. Apart from his generally unsuccessful military operations he fulfilled the emperor's traditional role in jurisdiction by arranging for the collection and codification of about 2,500 laws issued since 312 (the Theodosian Code). This massive undertaking succeeded in arranging the laws in chronological order under headings by subject, and tried to deal with inconsistency between laws. On the death of Honorius in 423, the eastern government hatched a plan to install Valentinian as emperor instead of John, an uncharismatic official who had been proclaimed emperor in Ravenna. The six-year-old Valentinian III was at first under the influence of his mother Placidia and his military commanders, Boniface and Aëtius, who attempted to maintain control in Italy and Gaul. But Boniface revolted while on campaign in Africa, and to bolster his position persuaded the Vandals to leave

Spain and come to Africa; in 429 Gaiseric arrived with 80,000 of his people. Gaiseric turned out to be a courageous and astute leader and turned on Boniface, who now had the support of the Roman government, and besieged him in Hippo (where Augustine was bishop). After diplomatic deals, Gaeseric remained in control of the richest province, proconsular Africa; Roman central authority had been progressively undermined in Africa despite the relative economic prosperity, and the army was ineffective. The Vandals were Arian Christians, hostile to the local orthodox Catholics, and remained as a separate, dominant social group until the province was reconquered by Justinian over one hundred years later.

By the 440s Britain too had been overrun while Romans still concentrated on fighting one another. In Italy, Boniface defeated Aëtius but died soon afterwards leaving Aëtius still in control. At this point a new threat emerged in the person of Atilla, who had succeeded in uniting the various groups of Huns into a ferociously successful force. After Honoria, Valentinian's sister, had curiously made contact with him, Atilla claimed that she was his betrothed and demanded to marry her. This was rejected and when the Huns invaded Gaul they were defeated by a Roman army that included many Goths under their king Theodoric, who was killed in the fighting. But in 452 the Huns returned and invaded Italy, destroying Aquileia, but did not press their attack after an outbreak of plague. Atilla died in 453 and Hunnic power declined. During this respite Valentinian, who had become suspicious of the influence of Aëtius, murdered him with his own hands in 454. In turn Valentinian was murdered in 455 after a plot by Petronius Maximus, who had encouraged his resentment against Aëtius and who married his widow. Maximus was soon killed in the chaos as the Vandals invaded Italy and spent two weeks sacking Rome in 455. Amid the increasing dislocation in Italy, Avitus was briefly recognized as emperor but soon deposed (and unusually was allowed to survive and become bishop of Placentia) by the general Ricimer, who then came to exercise military power in the west. When eventually Majorian was recognized as the western emperor by Leo, the eastern emperor, Ricimer was also formally made supreme commander, and in 461 he had Majorian murdered, seeking to install a puppet emperor. As the threats to the Italian homeland from Visigoths, Burgundians and Vandals multiplied, Leo made another attempt to sort things out and set up Anthemius as emperor in the west in 467. This was followed by a joint expedition of east and west against the Vandals in Africa. It cost a huge amount and was a disastrous failure, finally undermining the prestige of the western empire and ending all pretensions of its ruler to control lands outside Italy. Gaul and Spain fell entirely into the hands of the Visigoths and when Ricimer died in 472, having attacked and killed Anthemius in Rome, the empire in the west ended; generals and warlords fought for control of a shrinking territory and set up puppet emperors to provide some legitimacy. The finale came when Orestes, a one-time secretary of Atilla, became commander in

Italy and in 475 declared his son child-emperor; he was sarcastically called Romulus Augustulus ('little Augustus'), but in 476 Orestes was killed by the Germanic soldiers in Italy and the last Roman emperor was deposed. Italy disappeared under the rule of a Germanic officer, Odoacer, until in 489 Theodoric established the Ostrogothic kingdom.

Epilogue

From the early Republic the Romans had shown themselves to be innovative, flexible and adaptable. They created an extraordinary arrangement by which, instead of annexing defeated communities in Italy, they made alliances and exploited their military strength. Aggressive war combined with imaginative diplomacy saw the gradual creation of an overseas empire. In politics a complex system of assemblies and magistrates sustained the collective government of the oligarchic elite, though that was always in competition with the role and ambition of individuals in great magistracies. Eventually the individuals won out through the consulship and the command of the provincial armies, with an ever-increasing pattern of war, conquest and exploitation. The rural peasantry of Italy who served in the armies that overthrew the Republic were to get little out of the revolution except a measure of peace and order and the eventual disappearance of conscription.

As the most successful of the military dynasts, Augustus transformed the Roman state. He was a pivotal figure, absorbing the traditions, slogans and methodologies of the Republic and transforming them into personal rule apparently within a constitutional framework in which he based his position on legal powers duly voted. His blueprint for autocracy and the management of the empire cast a long shadow even into the later empire, and in a way contributed to the difficulties of imperial government: the expensive need to indulge the plebs in Rome with corn and amenities; the lack of a clear policy of dynastic succession; the vast territorial extent of the empire with few clear boundaries and a military arrangement based on an assumption of Roman superiority (this took a long time to wear off); a large professional army, which was paid for in a hand-to-mouth fashion by taxes; the personal bond of loyalty between soldiers and emperor, and the emperor's role as commander-in-chief who was expected to go in person to battle zones.

In a period of rapid change during the third century, a social system based on the senate and the equestrian order provided a strong basis for continuity and stability. In a typically Roman way this social system was continually refreshed from beneath through upwardly mobile freedmen and through army service, and by local town councillors and the wealthy elites of the provinces. There was a pragmatic community of interest in preserving settled government even if the emperor was incompetent or an imbecile. It was best 'to hope for a good emperor and put up with a bad'. The fabric of government was strong enough to withstand the increasing impotence of senate and people, and the last and most striking example of social change and the flexibility of the ruling structure was the acceptance of effective soldiers and administrators especially from Danubian lands far from the Italian heartland, who in many cases in the fourth century came from a poor background and were acclaimed as emperors. Diocletian and Constantine are the most important examples and also had a transforming role.

The civil war between the future Augustus and Marcus Antonius could be seen as a kind of forerunner of the split into a western and eastern empire, and it was a notable achievement to preserve imperial unity for over four hundred years. But we are left with the obvious question: how did the western empire, which seemed reasonably solid in 395 (and was even more solid in 375 on the death of Valentinian I), fall apart so quickly, never to rise again, whereas the eastern empire survived in some form or other until the fall of Constantinople in 1453? The basis of any attempt to answer this question must of course lie in long-term developments, not in the depressing tale of the last few years of western decline. There are several relevant factors, none of which on its own can account for the final collapse, but which collectively can explain the context. The Romans were religiously tolerant and paradoxically the one group who were persecuted, the Christians, came to be an integral part of the state and imperial government and entered the circles of power in a way that no other religious group had. Many resented this and Orosius, a Christian from Spain, wrote his *Histories against the Pagans* from the Creation down to 417 in order to defend against the pagan view that Christianity had been disastrous for the Roman world. However, it is unlikely that the Christianization of the empire played an important role in the fall of the west by undermining its unity, although it is true that imperial leaders were sometimes distracted by religious controversies. Christianity after all was rather more embedded in the east where imperial government on the Roman model survived. Furthermore, traditional polytheism had given no central unifying cultural force to the empire; it was disparate with the frequent accretion of new gods, and the same deity was often worshipped in different ways in different parts of the empire.

The western empire was militarily weaker since in its frontier zones more areas were vulnerable to attack, especially from the movement of northern peoples; as lands were progressively lost, the west became economically weaker with fewer tax resources; to make matters worse, the landholders of the traditionally powerful western aristocracy became remote from the government, since most of the important officers of state and army no longer came from this class; the rich landholders could work with the leaders of the invaders as long as a good proportion of their lands was guaranteed; consequently, western emperors had less control over resources than the eastern government. In common with most ancient governments, the later Roman emperors were unable directly to change economic and social trends across the empire. The west rather more than the east suffered from revolts, usurpation and civil wars, which brought about weak and unstable rule, sometimes with the elevation of boy-emperors, who were mere figureheads. This highlighted the importance of generals who could win the loyalty of the troops and act as mentors and guardians of young emperors. Formulation of a coherent policy for government was often superseded by the struggles of various groups to push forward their own sectional interests.

Western emperors increasingly struggled to find sufficient numbers of recruits, and powerful warlords commanded virtual private armies that were deployed as suited them. It is symptomatic of the problems in the west that just when the empire was coming under more external pressure, the battle of the river Frigidus where Theodosius defeated the usurper Eugenius in 394 was very costly in soldiers. The main reason for the decline of the western empire was the government's inability to find and maintain reliable soldiers. Because of this, greater reliance was placed on barbarian troops (sometimes commanded by non-Roman officers) in the west than in the east; connected with this was the settlement on Roman territory of barbarians who could not be assimilated into the social structure and in many areas eventually took over control. Barbarian soldiers were not necessarily less efficient militarily, but the links between the army and the Roman people and provincial society were broken and the ideological ethos of the government was significantly changed. The whole imperial structure in a way relied on conservative local elites who, imbued with classical culture and never questioning the imperial ethos, regarded themselves as effortlessly superior to outsiders and supported the government as long as it was able to express that ideal and guarantee their wealth and status. By the fifth century in the west that was no longer the case. Therefore, the inability of the central government to ensure social cohesion and the economic success of its territories undermined its authority. North Africa with its wealth and natural resources was one of the most important provinces, but when the Vandals arrived with their families the Roman army and local resistance simply melted away and in 439 the Vandals took over the established framework of government, pointing the way to the end of the Roman Empire in the west.

Suggested Reading

General Collections of Translated Ancient Sources

Braund, D.C. *Augustus to Nero: A Sourcebook on Roman History 31 BC–AD 68* (London and Sydney, 1985)

Campbell, J.B. *The Roman Army 31 BC–AD 337: A Sourcebook* (London and New York, 1994)

Campbell, J.B. *Greek and Roman Military Writers: Selected Readings* (London and New York, 2004)

Champion, C.B. *Roman Imperialism: Readings and Sources* (Blackwell, 2004). This includes ancient sources and articles on aspects of imperial history.

Chisholm, K. and Ferguson, J. *Rome: The Augustan Age* (Oxford, 1981)

Ireland, S. *Roman Britain: A Sourcebook* (London and Sydney, 1986)

Jones, A.H.M. *A History of Rome through the Fifth Century II: The Empire* (London, 1970)

Lacey, W.K. and Wilson, B.W.J.G. *Res Publica: Roman Politics and Society according to Cicero* (Oxford, 1970)

Levick, B. *The Government of the Roman Empire: A Sourcebook*, 2nd edn (London and New York, 2000)

Lewis, N. and Reinhold, M. *Roman Civilization*, 2nd edn, 2 vols (New York and Oxford, 1990)

Sabben-Clare, J. *Caesar and Roman Politics 60–50 BC* (Oxford, 1971)

Sage, M. *The Republican Roman Army: A Sourcebook* (New York and London, 2008)

Sherk, R.K. *Rome and the Greek East to the Death of Augustus* (Cambridge, 1984)

Sherk, R.K. *The Roman Empire: Augustus to Hadrian* (Cambridge, 1988)

Translations of Ancient Sources

Ammianus Marcellinus: Rolfe, J.C. *Ammianus Marcellinus*, 3 vols (Loeb Classical Library, Cambridge, Mass., 1935)

Appian: White, H. *Appian's Roman History*, 4 vols (Loeb Classical Library, Cambridge, Mass., 1912–13)

Apuleius: Butler, H.E. *Apuleius, Apologia (The Defense)* Internet Classics Archive (http://classics.mit.edu/Apuleius/apol.html)

Augustus: Brunt, P.A. and Moore, J.M. *Res Gestae Divi Augusti* (Oxford, 1967). Online translation: penelope.uchicago.edu/Thayer/E/Roman/Texts/Augustus/Res_Gestae/home.html

Cassius Dio: Scott-Kilvert, I. and Carter, J. *Cassius Dio, The Roman History: The Reign of Augustus* (Harmondsworth, 1987). Online translation: penelope.uchicago.edu/Thayer/E/Roman/Texts/Cassius_Dio/home.html

Catullus: Whigham, P. *The Poems of Catullus* (Harmondsworth, 1966)

Cicero: Cicero's works are best consulted in the Loeb Classical Library translations.

Dio Chrysostomos: Cohoon, J.W. and Lamar Crosby, H. *Dio Chrysostom, Discourses*, 5 vols (Loeb Classical Library; Cambridge, Mass., 1932–51)

Eusebius: Williamson, G.A. *Eusebius: The History of the Church* (Harmondsworth, 1965); Cameron, Averil and Hall, S.G. *Life of Constantine/Eusebius: Introduction, Translation and Commentary* (Oxford, 1999)

Florus: Forster, E.S. and Rolfe, J.C. *Florus. Cornelius Nepos* (Loeb Classical Library; Cambridge, Mass., 1929)

Frontinus: Bennett, C.E. *Frontinus: Stratagems and Aqueducts* (Loeb Classical Library; Cambridge, Mass., 1925)

Horace: Michie, J. *The Odes of Horace* (Harmondsworth, 1967); Bovie, S.P. *Satires and Epistles of Horace* (Chicago, 1959)

Josephus: Williamson, G.A. (revised with an introduction by E.M. Smallwood) *Josephus, The Jewish War* (Harmondsworth, 1981)

Lactantius: Creed, J.L. (ed.) *De Mortibus Persecutorum* (Oxford, 1984)

Livy: Foster, B.O. *Livy*, 14 vols (Loeb Classical Library, Cambridge, Mass., 1919)

Lucian: Harmon, A.M. *Lucian* (vol. I, including *The Bath*, Loeb Classical Library, Cambridge, Mass., 1913)

Marcus Aurelius: Haines, C.R. *Marcus Aurelius* (Loeb Classical Library, Cambridge, Mass., 1916)

Martial: Shackleton Bailey, D.R. *Martial, Epigrams*, 3 vols (Loeb Classical Library, Cambridge, Mass., 1993)

Panegyrics: Nixon, C.E.V and Rogers, B.S. (eds, with translation) *In Praise of Later Roman Emperors: The Panegyrici Latini* (Berkeley, 1994)

Papyri from Oxyrhynchus: *The Oxyrhynchus Papyri* (London, 1898–)

Petronius: Sullivan, J. *Petronius: The Satyricon and the Fragments* (Harmondsworth, 1965)

Plautus: Nixon, P. *Plautus* (vol. I, Loeb Classical Library, Cambridge, Mass., 1916)

Pliny the Elder: Rackham, H. *Pliny: Natural History*, 10 vols (Loeb Classical Library; Cambridge, Mass., 1949). Online translation: penelope.uchicago.edu/Thayer/E/Roman/Texts/Pliny_the_Elder/home.hmtl

Pliny the Younger: Radice, B. *The Letters of the Younger Pliny* (Harmondsworth, 1963)

Plutarch: Perrin, B. *Plutarch's Lives*, 11 vols (Loeb Classical Library, Cambridge, Mass., 1914)

Polybius: Paton, R. *Polybius, The Histories*, 6 vols (Loeb Classical Library, Cambridge, Mass., 1922–27)

Quintilian: Shackleton Bailey, D.R. *Quintilian, The Lesser Declamations*, 2 vols (Loeb Classical Library, Cambridge, Mass., 2006)

Sallust: Handford, S.A. *Sallust: Jugurthine War; Conspiracy of Catiline* (Harmondsworth, 1963)

Seneca the Younger: Basore, J.W. *Seneca, Moral Essays: De Beneficiis* (vol. III, Loeb Classical Library, Cambridge, Mass., 1935)

Sidonius Apollinaris: Anderson, W.B. *Sidonius, Letters* (vol. II, Loeb Classical Library, Cambridge, Mass., 1965)

Strabo: Jones, H.L. *Strabo: Geography*, 8 vols (Loeb Classical Library, Cambridge, Mass., 1917–1932)

Suetonius: Graves, R. *Suetonius: The Twelve Caesars* (Harmondsworth, 1962). Online translation: penelope.uchicago.edu/Thayer/E/Roman/Texts/Suetonius/12Caesars/home.html

Tacitus: Grant, M. *Tacitus: The Annals of Imperial Rome* (Harmondsworth, revised edn 1977); Wellesley, K. *Tacitus: The Histories* (Harmondsworth, 1964); Mattingly, H. *Tacitus: On Britain and Germany* (*Agricola* and *Germania*) (Harmondsworth, 1948). Online translation: http://classics.mit.edu/Tacitus/annals.html

Terence: Radice, B. *Terence: The Brothers and Other Plays* (Harmondsworth, 1965)

Vegetius: Milner, N.P. *Vegetius: Epitome of Military Science* (Liverpool, 1993)

Velleius Paterculus: Shipley, F.W. *Velleius Paterculus* (Loeb Classical Library; Cambridge, Mass., 1924). Online translation: penelope.uchicago.edu/Thayer/E/Roman/Texts/Velleius-Paterculus/home.html

Virgil: Jackson Knight, W.F. *Virgil: The Aeneid* (Harmondsworth, 1956)

Vitruvius: Rowland, I.D. and Howe, T.N. *Vitruvius: Ten Books on Architecture* (Cambridge, 1999). Online translation: penelope.uchicago.edu/Thayer/E/Roman/Texts/Vitruvius/home.html

Zosimus: Buchanan, J.J. and Davis, H.T. *Zosimus: Historia Nova: The Decline of Rome* (San Antonio, 1967)

Studies in the Use of Historical Evidence

Bagnall, R.S. *Reading Papyri, Writing Ancient History* (London and New York, 1995)

Bodel, J. *Epigraphic Evidence: Ancient History from Inscriptions* (London and New York, 2001)

Crawford, M.H. (ed.) *Sources for Ancient History* (Cambridge, 1983)

Howgego, C. *Ancient History from Coins* (London and New York, 1995)

Keppie, L. *Understanding Roman Inscriptions* (London, 1991)

Potter, D.S. *Literary Texts and the Roman Historian* (London and New York, 1999)

Robinson, O.F. *The Sources of Roman Law: Problems and Methods for Ancient Historians* (London and New York, 1997)

Some General Histories of the Period, Reference Works, and Collections of Coins, Inscriptions and Papyri

L'Année épigraphique (Paris, 1893–)

Codex Justinianus (CJ), ed. P. Krüger (Berlin, 1877)

Codex Theodosianus (Cod. Theod.), ed. Th. Mommsen and P.M. Meyer (Berlin, 1905)

Coins of the Roman Empire in the British Museum, ed. E.H. Mattingly, et al. (vols 1–6, London, 1923–66)

Cornell, T.J. and Matthews J.F. *Atlas of the Roman World* (Oxford, 1982)

Corpus Inscriptionum Latinarum, ed. Th. Mommsen, et al., (Berlin, 1863–)

Didyma, ed. R. Harder, vol. II (Inscriptions) (Berlin, 1958)

Digesta; Corpus Iuris Civilis, ed. Th. Mommsen, vol. I (Berlin, 1872)

Erdkamp, P. (ed.) *A Companion to the Roman Army* (Oxford, Blackwell, 2007)

Fontes iuris Romani anteiustiniani, ed. S. Riccobono, et al., 3 vols (2nd edn of vol. 1, Florence, 1940–3)

Die Giessener literarischen Papyri und die Caracalla-Erlasse, P.A. Kuhlmann (Giessen, 1994)

Hornblower, S. and Spawforth, A. *The Oxford Classical Dictionary*, 3rd revised edn (Oxford, 2003)

Inscriptiones Graecae (Berlin, 1873–)

Inscriptiones Graecae ad Res Romanas Pertinentes, ed. R. Cagnat, et al. (Paris, 1906–27)

Inscriptiones Latinae Selectae (ILS), ed. H. Dessau, (Berlin, 1892–1916)

Jones, B. and Mattingly, D. *An Atlas of Roman Britain* (Oxford, 1990)

Kam, A. *The Romans: An Introduction* (London and New York, 2008)

Le Glay, M., Voisin, J.-L. and Le Bohec, Y. *A History of Rome*, 3rd edn (Oxford, 2005)

McKay, C.S. *Ancient Rome: A Military and Political History* (Cambridge, 2004)

The Oxyrhynchus Papyri, B.P. Grenfell, et al. (London, 1898–)

Potter, D.S. (ed.) *A Companion to the Roman Empire* (Oxford, 2006)

Potter, D.S. *Rome in the Ancient World: From Romulus to Justinian* (London, 2009)

Reynolds, J., *Aphrodisias and Rome (Journal of Roman Studies Monograph* no. 1, London, 1982)

Rosenstein, N. and Morstein-Marx, R. (eds) *A Companion to the Roman Republic* (Oxford, 2007)

Talbert, R. (ed.) *The Barrington Atlas of the Greek and Roman World* (Princeton, N.J., 2000). The best atlas of the ancient world.

XII Panegyrici Latini, ed. R.A.B. Mynors (Oxford, 1964)

Chapters 1 and 2

Adcock, F.E. and Mosley, D.M. *Diplomacy in Ancient Greece* (London, 1975). A survey of diplomatic method and contact between communities.

Alföldi, A. *Early Rome and the Latins* (Ann Arbor, Mich., 1965). A useful study of Rome's developing relationships in Italy.

Badian, E. *Roman Imperialism in the Late Republic* (Ithaca, N.Y., 1968). Examines context of and motives for Roman expansion.

Barker, G. *Landscape and Society: Prehistoric Central Italy* (London, 1981). A valuable general survey.

Bremner, J.N. and Horsfall, N.M. *Roman Myth and Mythography* (London, 1987). Considers the creation of a mythological background for early Rome.

Cornell, T.J. 'The Annals of Quintus Ennius', *JRS* 76 (1986), 244–50. A review article dealing with the importance of Ennius for educating later Romans on their early history.

Cornell, T.J. *The Beginnings of Rome: Italy and Rome from the Bronze Age to the Punic Wars (c. 1000–264 BC)* (London and New York, 1995). A fundamental study of early Rome.

Crawford, M.H. *Coinage and Money under the Roman Republic: Italy and the Mediterranean Economy* (London, 1985). Deals with the economic results of Rome's victorious wars in the Mediterranean.

Crawford, M.H. *The Roman Republic*, 2nd edn (London, 1992). A stimulating, concise history of the development of Roman power and political thought.

Crawford, M.H. (ed.) *Roman Statutes*, 2 vols (London, 1996). Assembles Roman laws with text, translation and detailed commentary.

Degrassi, A. *Fasti Capitolini* (Turin, 1954). Sets out the list of consuls and winners of a triumph.

Derow, P.S. 'Polybius, Rome and the East', *JRS* 69 (1979), 1–15. Analyses Polybius's view of the nature of Roman leadership in the east.

Dorey, T.A. (ed.) *Livy* (London, 1971). Useful material on Livy's history.

Eckstein, A.M. *Mediterranean Anarchy, Interstate War, and the Rise of Rome* (Berkeley and Los Angeles, 2006). On Rome's contacts with the Greek east.

Eckstein, A.M. *Rome Enters the Greek East: From Anarchy to Hierarchy in the Hellenistic Mediterranean, 230–175 BC* (Oxford, 2008). An analysis of the nature of Roman contact with Greek states; argues for pact between Philip IV of Macedon and the Seleucid king Antiochus III.

Errington, R.M. *A History of the Mediterranean World, 323–30 BC* (Oxford, 2008). An excellent general survey of Greek communities and the looming power of Rome.

Erskine, A. (ed.) *Troy between Greece and Rome: Local Tradition and Imperial Power* (Oxford, 2003). Considers Troy as a symbol of the changing relationship between Greeks and Romans.

Gabba, E. *Dionysius and the History of Archaic Rome* (Berkeley, 1991). Examines the importance of Dionysius's history.

Grant, M. *The Etruscans* (London, 1980). A good general study.

Gruen, E.S. *The Hellenistic World and the Coming of Rome*, 2 vols (Berkeley, Los Angeles and London, 1984). Deals with Rome's emergence into the Greek world.

Harris, W.V. *Rome in Etruria and Umbria* (Oxford, 1971). Examines aspects of Rome's expansion in Italy.

Harris, W.V. *War and Imperialism in Republican Rome, 327–70 BC* (Oxford, 1979). Considers the reasons for Roman warfare and expansion.

Harris, W.V. (ed.) *The Imperialism of Mid-Republican Rome* (Rome, 1984). Presents a range of scholarly views on Roman imperialism.

Hoyos, B.D. *Unplanned Wars: The Origins of the First and Second Punic Wars* (Berlin, 1998). A detailed survey of Rome's wars with Carthage.

Hoyos, B.D. *Hannibal's Dynasty: Power and Politics in the Western Mediterranean, 247–183 BC* (London, 2003). An excellent account of Hannibal.

Lazenby, J.F. *Hannibal's War* (London, 1978). A useful account of the second war with Carthage.

Momigliano, A. *Studies in Historiography* (London, 1966). Includes several studies of historians of the early Republic.

Morrison, J.S. *Greek and Roman Oared Warships* (Oxford, 1996). Deals with the emergence of a Roman navy.

North, J.A. 'The Development of Roman Imperialism', *JRS* 71 (1981), 1–9. A valuable reappraisal of the work of William Harris and the question of Roman imperialism.

Oakley, S.P. 'The Roman Conquest of Italy', in Rich and Shipley (1993), 9–37. Examines the dynamics of the conquest of Italy before the first war with Carthage.

Ogilvie, R.M. *Early Rome and the Etruscans* (London, 1976). A valuable short guide.

Pallottino, M. *A History of Earliest Italy* (London, 1991). A good general history of early Italian society.

Potter, T.W. *Roman Italy* (London, 1987). Uses archaeological and epigraphical evidence to trace the development of Italy from early times.

Raaflaub, K.A. (ed.) *Social Struggles in Archaic Rome: New Perspectives on the Conflict of the Orders* (Berkeley, 1986). Offers a range of views on social conflict in the early Republic.

Rich, J.W. and Shipley, G. *War and Society in the Roman World* (London, 1993). Several studies on the nature of warfare and its impact on society in the Republic and Empire.

Salmon, E.T. *Samnium and the Samnites* (Cambridge, 1967). An account of this Italic people and their relations with Rome.

Salmon, E.T. *The Making of Roman Italy* (London, 1982). Offers a basic narrative to explain the Romanization and political unification of Italy.

Schullard, H.H. *The Etruscan Cities and Rome* (London, 1967). Covers Rome's developing relations with the Etruscans.

Shipley, G. *The Greek World after Alexander 323–30 BC* (London and New York, 2000). A comprehensive study of the Hellenistic world; chapter 10 deals with Rome.

Sprenger, M. and Bartoloni, G. *The Etruscans: Their History, Art and Architecture* (New York, 1983). An important work of reference for Etruscan civilization.

Staveley, E.S. *Greek and Roman Voting and Elections* (London, 1972). Part II describes the process in Rome to permit expressions of the public will.

Taylor, L.R. *Roman Voting Assemblies* (Ann Arbor, Mich., 1966). Explains how Romans cast their votes in the Republic.

Walbank, F.W. *Polybius* (Berkeley and Los Angeles, 1972). An indispensable guide to the work of Polybius.

Walbank, F.W. (ed.) *Polybius, Rome and the Hellenistic World: Essays and Reflections* (Cambridge, 2002). Contributions to Polybius's analysis of Rome's relations with the Greeks.

Walbank, F.W., Astin, A.E., Frederiksen, M.W., Ogilvie R.M. and Drummond A. (eds) *The Cambridge Ancient History*, vol. VII part 2: *The Rise of Rome to 220 BC*, 2nd edn (Cambridge, 1989). A standard reference book covering many aspects of the period.

Walsh, P.G. *Livy, his Historical Aims and Methods* (Cambridge, 1961). A still very valuable analysis of Livy's historical writing.

Williams, G. *The Third Book of Horace's Odes* (Oxford, 1969). Text, translation and commentary.

Wiseman, T.P. *The Myths of Rome* (University of Exeter, 2008). Vividly describes Roman mythology and its development from the sixth century BC to the imperial period.

Chapters 3 and 4

Astin, A.E. *Scipio Aemilianus* (Oxford, 1967). Examines social, political and cultural aspects of the Republic.

Astin, A.E. *Cato the Censor* (Oxford, 1978). As above.

Astin, A.E., Walbank, F.W., Frederiksen M.W. and Ogilvie R.M. (eds) *Cambridge Ancient History*, vol. 8: *Rome and the Mediterranean to 133 BC*, 2nd edn (Cambridge, 1989). A detailed survey of the period.

Badian, E. *Roman Imperialism in the Late Republic* (Oxford, 1968). A penetrating study of the exploitation of the provinces.

Badian, E. *Lucius Sulla, the Deadly Reformer* (Sydney, 1970). An interesting and lively interpretation of Sulla's career.

Bradley, K.R. *Slavery and Rebellion in the Roman World* (Bloomington, Ind., 1989). This mainly concerns the slave wars in Sicily.

Brunt, P.A. 'The Army and the Land in the Roman Revolution', *JRS* 52 (1962), 69 = *Fall of Roman Republic* (1988), 240–80. Fundamental for understanding the late Republic.

Brunt, P.A. 'The Roman Mob', *Past and Present*, 35 (1966), 3–27. Examines the conditions and role of plebs in Rome.

Brunt, P.A. *Italian Manpower* (Oxford, 1971). Has an enormous quarry of information on a wide range of social, economic and political topics.

Brunt, P.A. *Social Conflicts in the Roman Republic* (London, 1971). An absolutely outstanding and readable analysis of the social and political conflicts between classes and groups in Rome.

Brunt, P.A. *The Fall of the Roman Republic* (Oxford, 1988). An exceptionally important collection of essays on political and social themes.

Crawford, M.H. (ed.) *Roman Statutes*, 2 vols (London, 1992). Assembles Roman laws with text, translation and detailed commentary.

Gabba, E. *Republican Rome. The Army and the Allies* (Oxford, 1977). Deals with a wide range of social and economic issues beyond what is suggested by the title.

Gelzer, M. *Caesar: Politician and Statesman* (Oxford, 1969). A classic biography offering a favourable view of Caesar.

Lintott, A. *Violence in Republican Rome* (Oxford, 1968). An excellent survey of political violence and its consequences.

Malcovati, H. *Oratorum Romanorum Fragmenta Liberae Rei Publicae* (Turin, 1953). Collects what can be recovered of political oratory in the Republic; Latin text.

Millar, F. 'Politics, Persuasion and the People before the Social War (150–90 BC)', *JRS* 76 (1986), 1–11. Considers how Roman politics worked in respect of addressing and persuading the people.

Momigliano, A.D. *Alien Wisdom* (Cambridge, 1975). Examines how the Greeks viewed the Romans.

Richardson, J.S. *Hispaniae: Spain and the Development of Roman Imperialism, 218–82 BC* (Cambridge, 1986). Fundamental for understanding Roman policy in Spain.

Rosenstein, N. *Imperatores Victi: Military Defeat and Aristocratic Competition in the Middle and Late Republic* (Berkeley and Los Angeles, 1990). Examines the relationship between military defeat and aristocratic competition.

Rosenstein, N. *Rome at War: Farms, Families and Death in the Middle Republic* (Chapel Hill, N.J., and London, 2004). A fresh analysis of the relationship between military service and work on the land.

Salmon, E.T. *Roman Colonization* (London, 1969). Examines the foundation, organization and status of colonies in Italy.

Schullard, H.H. *Scipio Africanus: Soldier and Politician* (London, 1970). A traditional biography.

Seager, R. *Pompey: A Political Biography* (Oxford, 1979). A useful political biography.

Sherwin-White, A.N. *The Roman Citizenship*, 2nd edn (Oxford, 1973). Analyses the meaning, development and legal consequences of Roman citizenship.

Sherwin-White, A.N. *Roman Foreign Policy in the East, 168 BC to AD 1* (London, 1984). Examines Roman military and diplomatic operations in the east.

Stockton, D. *Cicero: A Political Biography* (Oxford, 1971). A clear and concise biography.

Stockton, D. *The Gracchi* (Oxford, 1979). A useful general account.

Syme, R. *The Roman Revolution* (Oxford, 1939). Fundamental to understanding the factors and personalities in the fall of the Republic.

Syme, R. *Sallust* (Berkeley, Los Angeles and London, 1964). Places Sallust in his political and literary context.

Taylor, L.R. *Party Politics in the Age of Caesar* (Berkeley and Los Angeles, 1968). An excellent evocation of political life in the Republic.

Treggiari, S. *Roman Freedmen during the Late Republic* (Oxford, 1969). A fundamental work of reference.

Wiseman, T.P. *New Men in the Roman Senate* (Oxford, 1971). Examines the careers of men outside traditional families.

Wiseman, T.P. *The World of Catullus* (Cambridge, 1985). Explains society in the late Republic.

Chapter 5

Barrett, A.A. *Livia: First Lady of Imperial Rome* (New Haven, Conn. and London, 2002). Explores the life and influence of Augustus's wife.

Bowersock, G.W. *Augustus and the Greek World* (Oxford, 1965). Shows how a Graeco-Roman elite emerged.

Bowman, A.K., Champlin, E. and Lintott, A. (eds) *Cambridge Ancient History*, vol. X: *The Augustan Empire*, 2nd edn (Cambridge, 1996). A wide-ranging survey of early empire.

Earl, D.C. *The Age of Augustus* (London, 1968). Useful discussion and illustrations.

Eck, W. *The Age of Augustus* (Oxford, 2003). A brief outline of Augustus's rule.

Favaro, S.D. *The Urban Image of Augustus* (Cambridge, 1996). Explains Augustus's building work in Rome.

Galinsky, K. *Augustan Culture* (Princeton, N.J., 1996). Covers aspects of the culture and society of Rome under Augustus.

Galinsky K. (ed.) *The Cambridge Companion to the Age of Augustus* (Cambridge, 2005). Good coverage of numerous aspects of life under Augustus.

Jones, A.H.M. *Augustus* (London, 1970). A useful, brief biography.

Levick, B. *Tiberius the Politician* (London, 1976). Offers an interesting analysis of imperial politics in the early empire.

MacMullen, R. *Romanization in the Time of Augustus* (New Haven, Conn. and London, 2000). Documents the spread of Roman civilization.

Millar, F. and Segal, E. (eds) *Caesar Augustus: Seven Aspects* (Oxford, 1984). Wide-ranging contributions, including the succession, the impact of monarchy, and the *Res Gestae*.

Raaflaub, K. and Toher, M. (eds) *Between Republic and Empire* (Berkeley, Los Angeles and London, 1990). A substantial contribution to a range of topics covering historiography, poetry, art, religion and politics.

Rickman, G.E. *The Corn Supply of Ancient Rome* (Oxford, 1980). Surveys the importance and mechanism of the corn supply.

Saeger, R. *Tiberius* (London, 1972). A routine though clear biography.

Southern, P. *Augustus* (London and New York, 1998). A useful biography though limited in analysis.

Syme, R. *The Roman Revolution* (Oxford, 1939). A vivid portrait of the basis of Augustus's power and the nature of his rule.

Zanker, P. *The Power of Images in the Age of Augustus* (Ann Arbor, Mich., 1988). Discusses the dissemination of the Augustan view through artistic presentation.

Chapters 6–8

Barnes, T.D. 'Legislation against the Christians', *JRS* 58 (1968), 32–50. On the legal position of Christians in the early empire.

Barrett, A.A. *Caligula: The Corruption of Power* (London, 1989). A clearly argued biography.

Beard, M., North, J. and Price, S. *Religions of Rome*, 2 vols (Cambridge 1998). Examines Roman religious experience, with original documents.

Birley, A.R. *Marcus Aurelius* (London, 1966). A routine biography.

Birley, A.R. *Septimius Severus, the African Emperor* (London, 1971). A straightforward biography that lacks analysis of the political context.

Birley, A.R. *Hadrian, the Restless Emperor* (London and New York, 1997). A wide-ranging survey of the Hadrianic age with good maps and illustrations.

Blake, M.E. and Bishop, D.T. *Roman Construction in Italy from Nerva through the Antonines* (Philadelphia, 1973). Useful for Roman building techniques.

Bowman, A.K. *Egypt after the Pharaohs 332 BC–AD 642* (London, 1986). A valuable account of Roman rule in the province.

Bowman, A.K. *Life and Letters on the Roman Frontier* (London, 1994). A vivid account of the lifestyle of soldiers and their families in Britain.

Bradley, K.R. *Slaves and Masters in the Roman Empire: A Study in Social Control* (Oxford, 1987). Covers the main aspects of slavery.

Braund, D.C. *Rome and the Friendly King* (London and Canberra, 1984). A useful examination of Rome's employment of local rulers.

Brunt, P.A. 'The Revenues of Rome', *JRS* 71 (1981), 161–72 = *Roman Imperial Themes* (1990). Chapter 15 examines what we know of Roman taxation.

Brunt, P.A. *Roman Imperial Themes* (Oxford, 1990). A collection of fundamental articles on the Roman Empire.

Brunt, P.A. 'The Romanization of the Local Ruling Classes in the Roman Empire' in Brunt, *Roman Imperial Themes* (1990). Chapter 12 discusses the idea that the empire depended on consent not on force, and the importance in this of local men of property.

Campbell, J.B. *The Emperor and the Roman Army 31 BC–AD 235* (Oxford, 1984). Analyses the emperor's political relationship with soldiers.

Campbell, J.B. *War and Society in Imperial Rome 31 BC–AD 284* (London and New York, 2002). Examines the place of war and soldiers in Roman society.

Chadwick, H. *The Early Church* (Pelican History of the Church, 1967). The standard work on early Christianity.

Champlin, E. *Fronto and Antonine Rome* (Cambridge, Mass., 1980). Usefully examines second-century society.

Champlin, E. *Nero* (Cambridge, Mass., 2003). Interesting description of the Neronian age.

Cheesman, G.L. *The Auxilia of the Roman Imperial Army* (Oxford 1914; reprint Chicago, 1975). Still the best general account of auxiliary troops.

Claridge, A. *Rome: An Oxford Archaeological Guide* (Oxford, 1998). Excellent on the city of Rome and its monuments.

Connolly, P. *Greece and Rome at War* (London, 1981). A well-illustrated guide to all things military.

Cotton, H. 'The Guardianship of Jesus Son of Babatha: Roman Law and Local Law in the Province of Arabia', *JRS* 83 (1993), 94–108. Discusses the archive of a Jewish woman who lived on the southern shore of the Dead Sea, from AD 106 part of the province of Arabia.

Crook, J.A. *Law and Life of Rome* (London, 1967). A clear account of life as revealed by legal texts.

Curchin, L.A. *Roman Spain: Conquest and Assimilation* (London, 1991). Describes Spain's adaptation to Roman ways.

Dalby, A. *Empire of Pleasures: Luxury and Indulgence in the Roman World* (London and New York, 2000). A vivid social history of food and entertainment.

De Lange, N.R.M. 'Jewish Attitudes to the Roman Empire', in P. Garnsey and C.R. Whittaker, *Imperialism in the Ancient World* (Cambridge, 1978), 255–81. Helps to explain the second Jewish revolt in 132–35.

Dixon, K.R. and Southern, P. *The Roman Cavalry* (London, 1992). Studies the organization of cavalry forces.

Dixon, S. *The Roman Mother* (London and Sydney, 1988). On the position and duties of mothers in the family.

Dodge, H. 'The Architectural Impact of Rome in the East', in M. Henig (ed.) *Architectural Sculpture in the Roman Empire* (Oxford, 1990), 108–20. Discusses the Roman building style in the east.

Duncan-Jones, R. *The Economy of the Roman Empire: Quantitative Studies*, 2nd edn (Cambridge, 1982). Examines wealth, price levels and demography.

Finley, M.I. *Ancient Slavery and Modern Ideology* (London, 1980). Emphasizes the importance of slavery in the ancient world.

Finley, M.I. *The Ancient Economy* (London, 1985). Argues the classic 'primitive' view of ancient economic history.

Frend, W.H.C. *Martyrdom and Persecution in the Early Church: A Study of Conflict from the Maccabees to Donatus* (Oxford, 1965). Excellent on the persecution of early Christians.

Frere, S. *Britannia: A History of Roman Britain*, 3rd edn (London, 1987). The standard history of Roman Britain.

Frere, S. and Lepper, F. *Trajan's Column* (Gloucester, 1988). Detailed discussion of the column, with good illustrations.

Gardner, J.F. *Women in Roman Law and Society* (London and Sydney, 1986). Excellent evocation of the role and place of women.

Garnsey, P. *Famine and Food Supply in the Graeco-Roman World: Responses to Risk and Crisis* (Cambridge, 1988). Comprehensively deals with potential sources of shortage and the consequences.

Garnsey, P. and Saller, R.P. *The Roman Empire: Economy, Society and Culture* (Berkeley and Los Angeles, 1987). Wide-ranging on social and economic issues.

Goldsworthy, A.K. *The Roman Army at War 100 BC–AD 200* (Oxford, 1996). A vivid account of fighting techniques and military organization.

Grant, M. *Cities of Vesuvius: Pompeii and Herculaneum* (London, 1971). A good general guide to the cities destroyed in AD 79.

Harris, W.V. *Ancient Literacy* (Cambridge, Mass., 1985). Plays down the extent of literacy.

Henig, M. (ed.) *A Handbook of Roman Art: A Survey of the Visual Arts of the Roman World* (London, 1983). One of the best general introductions.

Hodges, A.T. *Roman Aqueducts and Water Supply* (London, 2002). The best introduction to the Roman provision of water.

Hopkins, K. *Conquerors and Slaves* (Cambridge, 1978). A stimulating and challenging analysis of social, economic and cultural issues.

Hopkins, K. 'Taxes and Trade in the Roman empire (200 BC–AD 400)', *JRS* 70 (1980), 101–25. Explains the importance of taxation in the Roman economy.

Hopkins, K. *Death and Renewal* (Cambridge, 1983). Includes particularly useful discussions of gladiators and the survival of senatorial families.

Hyland, A. *Equus: The Horse in the Roman World* (London, 1990). Covers all aspects of horses and horse training.

Isaac, B. *The Limits of Empire*, revised edn (Oxford, 1992). Explains policy in Roman frontier zones especially in the east, and the role of the Roman army.

James, S.T. 'Stratagems, Combat, and "Chemical Warfare" in the Siege Mines of Dura-Europos', *American Journal of Archaeology* 115 (2011), 69–101. Vividly describes the siege of Dura-Europos and the discovery of soldiers' bodies in a siege tunnel.

Jones, A.H.M. *The Roman Economy*, ed. P.A. Brunt (London, 1974). A general survey of economic history.

Jones, C.P. *Plutarch and Rome* (Oxford, reprt 1971). Covers Greek intellectual history and the place of Plutarch.

Keppie, L. *The Making of the Roman Army: From Republic to Empire* (London, 1984). The best study of the emergence of the imperial army from the legions of the Republic.

Lendon, J.E. *Empire of Honour: The Art of Government in the Roman World* (Oxford, 1997). Argues that Roman government worked partly through an aristocratic culture of honour that was shared by the Romans and their better-off subjects.

Lendon, J.E. *Soldiers and Ghosts: A History of Battle in Classical Antiquity* (New Haven, Conn. and London, 2005). Vividly examines Greek and Roman warfare and the functioning of armies partly based on past traditions.

Levick, B. *Claudius* (London, 1990). A thoughtful biography.

Levick, B. *Vespasian* (London and New York, 1999). Offers a wide-ranging analysis of imperial policy in the Flavian age.

Liebeschuetz, J.H.W.G. *Continuity and Change in Roman Religion* (Oxford, 1979). Covers religious issues and society.

Ling, R. *Roman Painting* (Cambridge, 1991). An excellent introduction to the subject.

Lintott, A. *Imperium Romanum: Politics and Administration* (London and New York, 1993) A clear guide to the workings of Roman government.

Luttwak, E. *The Grand Strategy of the Roman Empire* (Baltimore, Md. and London, 1976). A challenging study that attempts to demonstrate an empire-wide strategy for frontier zones.

MacMullen, R. *Soldier and Civilian in the Later Roman Empire* (Cambridge, Mass., 1963). Describes how soldiers became entrenched in civilian life in the empire; ranges more widely than the title suggests.

MacMullen, R. *Enemies of the Roman Order* (Cambridge, Mass., 1967). Discusses social and political conditions in the empire with a wide collection of evidence, and opposition to the established order.

MacMullen, R. *Roman Social Relations 50 BC–AD 284* (New Haven, Conn. and London, 1974). Aims to explain what life was like for ordinary people such as freedmen, artisans and agricultural workers.

MacMullen, R. *Paganism in the Roman Empire* (New Haven, Conn. and London, 1981). Covers a wide range of evidence in a very useful introduction to the subject.

MacMullen, R. *Christianizing the Roman Empire* (New Haven, Conn. and London, 1984). On early Christians and the Roman government.

Magie, D. *Roman Rule in Asia Minor*, 2 vols (Princeton, N.J., 1950). The standard history of this important province.

Mattern, S. *Rome and the Enemy: Imperial Strategy in the Principate* (Berkeley, Los Angeles and London, 1999). Analyses various approaches to Roman policy in frontier zones.

Mattingly, D.J. *Dialogues in Roman Imperialism* (*Journal of Roman Archaeology*, Supplementary Series, no. 23, Portsmouth, Rhode Island, 1997). Discusses the reception of Rome and Roman practices in various parts of the empire.

Mellor, R. *Tacitus* (London and New York, 1993). Offers a brief account of the historian's ideas, methods and influence.

Millar, F. *A Study of Cassius Dio* (Oxford, 1964). A comprehensive survey of Dio and especially important for the Severan period.

Millar, F. *The Emperor in the Roman World* (London, 1977). One of the most important accounts of the personal though passive role of the emperor in administration.

Millar, F. *The Roman Empire and its Neighbours*, 2nd edn (London, 1981). An extremely useful account of the workings of the empire and its relations with outside peoples.

Millar, F. *The Roman Near East 31 BC–AD 337* (Cambridge, Mass., 1993). An outstanding exploration of the nature of Roman rule in Syria, Judaea, Arabia and Mesopotamia in the context of society and culture, and questions of religious and ethnic identity.

North, J.A. 'Religion and Politics, from Republic to Principate', *JRS* 76 (1986), 251–8. A judicious assessment of the role of religion in Rome.

Oliver, J.H. *The Ruling Power: A Study of the Roman Empire in the Second Century after Christ through the Roman Oration of Aelius Aristides* (Philadelphia, 1980). Examines various Greek attitudes to Rome.

Price, S. *Rituals and Power: The Roman Imperial Cult in Asia Minor* (Oxford, 1984). A splendid account of the origins and development of worship of the emperor.

Raven, S. *Rome in Africa* (London and New York, 1984). Offers an excellent introduction.

Richardson, jr. L. *A New Topographical Dictionary of Ancient Rome* (Baltimore, Md., and London, 1992). Standard one-volume reference work on the city of Rome.

Robinson, O.F. *Ancient Rome: City Planning and Administration* (London and New York, 1992). Looks at the running of Rome in the context of the laws.

Rostovtzeff, M. *Social and Economic History of the Roman Empire* (revised edition, P. Fraser, Oxford, 1957). A classic study, massive in scope and documentation, though some conclusions are disputed.

Saller, R.P. *Personal Patronage under the Early Empire* (Cambridge, 1981). Discusses the patron–client relationship in Roman society.

Shaw, B. *Environment and Society in North Africa: Studies in History and Archaeology* (Aldershot, 1995). A collection of articles analysing in depth the workings of a Roman province and the life of locals.

Starr, C.G. *The Roman Imperial Navy 31 BC–AD 324* (London, 1960). Still important as a basic textbook of Roman naval organization.

Ste. Croix, G. de *The Class Struggle in the Ancient Greek World* (London, 1981). A Marxist view of history with many important observations on Rome's impact on the Greek world; appendix 3 deals with barbarian settlement in the empire.

Syme, R. *Tacitus* 2 vols (Oxford, 1958). Fundamental treatment of the life and writings of Tacitus.

Talbert, R.J.A. *The Senate of Imperial Rome* (Princeton, N.J., 1984). The only detailed study of the senate's role in the empire, with analysis of senatorial decrees.

Wacher, J. (ed.) *The Roman World* (London, 1987). A useful general survey.

Watson, G. *The Roman Soldier* (London, 1969). Concentrates on soldiers, their duties, pay and conditions.

Webster, G. *The Roman Imperial Army*, 3rd edn (London, 1985). Standard reference book on all aspects of the army.

Wellesley, K. *The Long Year AD 69* (London, 1975). On the civil wars and the year of four emperors.

Wells, C. *The Roman Empire* (London, 1992). One of the best short surveys of the Roman empire, with quotations from many ancient sources.

White, K.D. *Roman Farming* (London, 1970). Wide-ranging on farms, crops, livestock and farming methods.

Whittaker, C.R. *Frontiers of the Roman Empire: A Social and Economic Study* (Baltimore, Md., and London, 1984). Tries to explain the emergence of frontier zones and reasons behind Roman policy.

Wilkes, J.J. *Dalmatia* (London, 1969). A detailed survey of a province and the impact of Rome.

Woolf, G. *Becoming Roman: The Origins of Provincial Civilization in Gaul* (Cambridge, 1998). Deals with the question of Romanization.

Chapters 9 and 10

Barnes, T.D. *Constantine and Eusebius* (Cambridge, Mass., 1981). A detailed examination of the policies of Constantine.

Barnes, T.D. *The New Empire of Diocletian and Constantine* (Cambridge, Mass., 1982). A fundamental collection of evidence on the personnel of government in this era.

Barnes, T.D. 'Christians and Pagans in the Reign of Constantius', in A. Dihle (ed.) *L'Église et l'empire au iv siècle. Sept exposés suivis de discussions* (Geneva, 1989), 301–43. Examines the social and political development of Christianity.

Barnes, T.D. *Athanasius and Constantius: Theology and Politics in the Constantinian Empire* (Cambridge, Mass., 1993). Examines Church and State and religious debate.

Boak, A.E.R. and Youtie, H.C. *The Archive of Aurelius Isidorus* (Ann Arbor, Mich., 1960).

Bowersock, G.W. *Julian the Apostate* (Cambridge, Mass., 1978). Classic biography of the emperor.

Bowman, A.K., Garnsey, P. and Cameron, Averil (eds) *Cambridge Ancient History*, vol. XII: *The Crisis of Empire*, AD *193–337* (Cambridge, 2005). A wide-ranging review up to the death of Constantine.

Brown, P. *The World of Late Antiquity* (London, 1966). A splendid evocation of life and thought in the late empire.

Brown, P. *Augustine of Hippo* (London, 1967). Explains the complex influences on St Augustine, and his attitude to Donatism.

Brown, P. *Religion and Society in the Age of St Augustine* (London, 1972). Splendid account of the difference between the classical world and later empire, and the nature of Donatism.

Browning, R. *The Emperor Julian* (Berkeley and Los Angeles, 1976). Excellent survey of the emperor and his times.

Cameron, Alan *Circus Factions: Blues and Greens at Rome and Byzantium* (Oxford, 1976). Highlights the importance of the arena and circus demonstrations in late Roman politics.

Cameron, Averil *Christianity and the Rhetoric of Empire* (Berkeley and Los Angeles, 1991). Examines the writings of Christians and the significance of their use of language.

Cameron, Averil *The Later Roman Empire* (London, 1993). A masterly short survey.

Cameron, Averil *The Mediterranean World in Late Antiquity* AD *395–600* (London and New York, 1993). An excellent survey of the period.

Cameron, Averil and Garnsey, P. (eds) *Cambridge Ancient History*, vol XIII: *The Late Empire*, AD *334–425*, 2nd edn (Cambridge, 1998). A wide-ranging view of the late empire.

Chitty, D. *The Desert a City* (Oxford, 1966). Deals with Egyptian monasticism.

Clark, E.A. *Ascetic Piety and Women's Faith* (Lewiston, 1986). Examines women and ascetism in the late empire.

Clark, G. *Women in Late Antiquity* (Oxford, 1993). Looks at the role of women in society.

Crawford, M.H. 'Finance, Coinage and Money from the Severans to Constantine', *Aufstieg und Niedergang der Antiken Welt* II, 2 (Berlin, 1975), 560–93. A very useful guide to coins and money in the late empire.

Creed, J.L. (ed., trans.) *De Mortibus Persecutorum* (Oxford, 1984). Examines the work of Lactantius on the persecution of Christians.

Curran, J. *Pagan City and Christian Capital: Rome in the Fourth Century* (Oxford, 2000). A splendid survey of how the building activities of Constantine and his successors altered the landscape of Rome, emphasizing the political considerations.

Davis, R.P. *The Book of Pontiffs (Liber Pontificalis)*, translated with an introduction (Liverpool, 1989). Important for imperial benefactions to the Church.

Dodgeon, M.H. and Lieu, S.C.N. *The Roman Frontier and the Persian Wars AD 226–363: A Documentary History* (London, 1991). Detailed examination of the ancient evidence of Rome's relations with the Persians.

Downey, *A History of Antioch in Syria* (Princeton, N.J., 1961). A splendidly detailed survey of life in Antioch.

Drinkwater, J. *The Gallic Empire: Separatism and Continuity in the North-Western Provinces of the Roman Empire* (Stuttgart, 1987). Of fundamental importance for the Gallic Empire.

Edwards, M. *Constantine and Christendom* (*Translated Texts for Historians* 39, Liverpool 2003). A collection of source material for Constantine's rule.

Elton, H. *Frontiers of the Roman Empire* (London, 1996). Deals with Rome's management of relations with foreign peoples.

Faulkner, N. *The Decline and Fall of Roman Britain* (Stroud, 2000). Useful discussion of the circumstances leading to the end of Roman Britain.

Hanson, R.P.C. *The Search for the Christian Doctrine of God: The Arian Controversy, 318–381* (Edinburgh, 1988). Deals with theological debate over Arianism.

Heather, P. *Goths and Romans, 332–489* (Oxford, 1991). Deals with the Goths and their relations with the empire.

Heather, P. *The Fall of the Roman Empire: A New History of Rome and the Barbarians* (Oxford, 2006). Examines the impact of Roman imperialism on neighbouring peoples and its role in the complex picture of the overthrow of the empire.

Heather, P. and Matthews, J.F. *The Goths in the Fourth Century* (Liverpool, 1991). Examines the customs and role of the Goths.

Herrin, J. 'Ideals of Charity, Realities in Welfare: The Philanthropic Activity of the Byzantine Church', in R. Morris (ed.) *Church and People in Byzantium* (Manchester, 1991), 151–64. On the development of charity by Christians.

Hopkins, K. 'Social Mobility in the Late Roman Empire: The case of Ausonius', *Classical Quarterly* 11 (1961), 239–300. On rhetoric as an avenue to social advancement.

Humphrey, J. *Roman Circuses* (London, 1986). Exploits the archaeological evidence for circuses in late-empire cities.

Hunt, E.D. *Holy Land Pilgrimage in the Later Roman Empire* (Oxford, 1982). Carefully expounds this important topic.

Isaac B. *The Limits of Empire* (Oxford, 1992). Chapters 4–5 deal with the wars with Persia and more generally the Roman army.

James, E. *The Franks* (Oxford, 1988). A detailed study of the Franks.

Johnson, S. *Later Roman Britain* (London, 1980). Examines the position and government of Britain in the late empire.

Jones, A.H.M. *Constantine and the Conversion of Europe* (London, 1948; reprt 1978). An excellent effort to explain Constantine's religious feelings and the impact of Christianity on the empire.

Jones, A.H.M. *The Later Roman Empire 284–602: A Social, Administrative and Economic Survey*, 2 vols (Oxford, 1964). The classic history of the late empire with massive documentation.

Kennedy, D. and Riley, D. *Rome's Desert Frontier from the Air* (London, 1990). Brilliant aerial photos of Roman installations in the east, with commentary.

King, C.E. (ed.) *Imperial Revenue, Expenditure and Monetary Policy in the Fourth-Century AD* (Oxford, 1980). Explains income and expenditure and the general economy.

Krautheimer, R. *Three Christian Capitals* (Berkeley and Los Angeles, 1983). Deals with Rome, Constantinople and Milan.

Lane Fox, R. *Pagans and Christians* (Harmondsworth, 1986). Informative on relations between pagans and Christians.

Lee, D. *War in Late Antiquity: A Social History* (Oxford, 2007). Considers the impact of warfare and the Roman army on society and political and economic life.

Lenski, N. *The Cambridge Companion to the Age of Constantine* (Cambridge, 2006). An excellent guide to the period.

Liebeschuetz, J.H.W.G. *Antioch: City and Imperial Administration in the Later Roman Empire* (Oxford, 1972). Examines the city and its relations with its hinterland and the Roman government.

Liebeschuetz, J.H.W.G. *Barbarians and Bishops: Army, Church and State in the Age of Arcadius and Chrysostom* (Oxford, 1990). Chapters 1–2 deal with the Roman army and the battle of Adrianople.

Lieu, J., North, J. and Rajak, T. (eds) *The Jews among Pagans and Christians in the Roman Empire* (London, 1992). Deals with religious identities in the empire.

Lieu, S.N.C. *The Emperor Julian: Panegyric and Polemic* (*Translated Texts for Historians*, 2nd edn, Liverpool, 1989). An excellent collection of material on Julian.

Lieu, S.N.C. and Montserrat, D. (ed.) *Constantine: History, Historiography and Legend* (London, 1998). Collected papers on the emergence of the historical tradition on Constantine.

McLynn, N. *Ambrose of Milan* (Berkeley, 1994). A good biography.

MacMullen, R. *Constantine* (New York, 1969). A short, easy-to-read and informative biography.

MacMullen, R. *Roman Government's Response to Crisis, AD 235–337* (New Haven, Conn. and London, 1976). Very valuable on emperors' attempts at reform.

MacMullen, R. 'How Big Was the Roman Army?', *Klio*, 62 (1980), 451–60. On the size of Diocletian's army.

MacMullen, R. *Christianizing the Roman Empire, AD 100–400* (New Haven, Conn., and London, 1984). A useful account of the spread of Christianity.

MacMullen, R. 'Late Roman Slavery', *Historia* 36 (1987), 359–82. On the continuation of slavery in the late empire.

MacMullen, R. *Corruption and Decline of Rome* (New Haven, Conn. and London, 1988). Exposes the extent of corruption that undermined the administrative system.

Maenchen-Helfen, O. *The World of the Huns* (Berkeley and Los Angeles, 1973). A basic reference work on Hunnish society.

Markus, R. 'Paganism, Christianity and the Latin Classics in the Fourth Century', in J.W. Binns (ed.) *Latin Literature of the Fourth Century* (London, 1974), 1–21. Includes the response of pagans to Christian culture.

Matthews, J.F. *Western Aristocracies and the Imperial Court AD 364–425* (Oxford, 1975; revised edition, 1991). Considers the relations between the late Roman upper class and emperors.

Matthews, J.F. *The Roman Empire of Ammianus* (London, 1989). A fundamental study of the history of Ammianus in its social and political context.

Millar, F. *The Roman Empire and its Neighbours*, 2nd edn (London, 1981). Chapter 13 offers an excellent survey of the third century.

Momigliano, A. *The Conflict between Paganism and Christianity in the Fourth Century* (Oxford, 1963). Deals with the late Roman aristocracy and religion.

Odahl, C.M. *Constantine and the Christian Empire* (London, 2004). Examines secular and religious policies, covering the full range of evidence.

Rousseau, P. *Pachomius* (Berkeley and Los Angeles, 1975). On the development of monasticism.

Sirks, B. *Food for Rome* (Amsterdam, 1991). Discusses late empire corn doles.

Southern, P. and Dixon, K.R. *The Late Roman Army* (New Haven, Conn. and London, 1996). A good general survey of all aspects of the army.

Stevenson, J. *A New Eusebius*, revised edn (London, 1987). Very valuable for Constantine's religious policies and the Church.

Stevenson, J. *Creeds, Councils and Controversies* (revised edition, London, 1989). Deals with doctrinal debate after Constantine.

Swain, S. and Edwards, M. (eds) *Approaching Late Antiquity: The Transformation from Early to Late Empire* (Oxford, 2004). Several scholars analyse trends in the changing social and political conditions of the empire.

Van Dam, T. *The Roman Revolution of Constantine* (Cambridge, 2007). Sets Constantine in the context of fundamental changes in the Roman world, with emphasis on ideological and cultural aspects.

Wallis, R.T. *Neoplatonism* (London, 1972). On the importance of this philosophy.

Ward-Perkins, B. *From Classical Antiquity to the Middle Ages: Urban and Public*

Building in Northern and Central Italy AD 300–850 (Oxford, 1984). Covers all aspects of Christian buildings.

Ward-Perkins, B. *The Fall of Rome and the End of Civiliẓation* (Oxford, 2005). Emphasizes that the empire fell to a violent barbarian invasion and that the end of the Roman world brought a disastrous collapse in living standards.

Williams, S. *Diocletian and the Roman Recovery* (London, 1985). Excellent account of Diocletian's changes.

Wimbush, V. (ed.) *Ascetic Behaviour in Greco-Roman Antiquity* (Minneapolis, 1990). Valuable on the ascetic in relation to Christianity.

Index